NOLO *Your Legal Companion*

"In Nolo you can trust." —**THE NEW YORK TIMES**

Whether you have a simple question or a complex problem, turn to us at:

NOLO.COM

Your all-in-one legal resource

Need quick information about wills, patents, adoptions, starting a business—or anything else that's affected by the law? **Nolo.com** is packed with free articles, legal updates, resources and a complete catalog of our books and software.

NOLO NOW

Make your legal documents online

Creating a legal document has never been easier or more cost-effective! Featuring Nolo's Online Will, as well as online forms for LLC formation, incorporation, divorce, name change—and many more! Check it out at **http://nolonow.nolo.com**.

NOLO'S LAWYER DIRECTORY

Meet your new attorney

If you want advice from a qualified attorney, turn to Nolo's Lawyer Directory—the only directory that lets you see hundreds of in-depth attorney profiles so you can pick the one that's right for you. Find it at **http://lawyers.nolo.com**.

ALWAYS UP TO DATE

Sign up for NOLO'S LEGAL UPDATER

Old law is bad law. We'll email you when we publish an updated edition of this book—sign up for this free service at nolo.com/legalupdater.

Find the latest updates at NOLO.COM

Recognizing that the law can change even before you use this book, we post legal updates during the life of this edition at **nolo.com/updates**.

Is this edition the newest? ASK US!

To make sure that this is the most recent available, just give us a call at **800-728-3555**.

(Please note that we cannot offer legal advice.)

Please note

We believe accurate, plain-English legal information should help you solve many of your own legal problems. But this text is not a substitute for personalized advice from a knowledgeable lawyer. If you want the help of a trained professional—and we'll always point out situations in which we think that's a good idea— consult an attorney licensed to practice in your state.

4th edition

Every Landlord's Tax Deduction Guide

By Attorney Stephen Fishman

NOLO

FOURTH EDITION	NOVEMBER 2007
Editors	DIANA FITZPATRICK
	JANET PORTMAN
Cover Design	JALEH DOANE
Book Design	TERRI HEARSH
Production	MARGARET LIVINGSTON
Proofreading	ROBERT WELLS
Index	JEAN MANN
Printing	DELTA PRINTING SOLUTIONS, INC.

Fishman, Stephen.
  Every landlord's tax deduction guide / by Stephen Fishman. -- 4th ed.
     p. cm.
  Includes index.
  ISBN-13: 978-1-4133-0721-4 (pbk.)
  ISBN-10: 1-4133-0721-3 (pbk.)
     1. Rental housing--Taxation--Law and legislation--United States--Popular
works. 2. Income tax deductions--United States--Popular works. 3.
Landlords--Taxation--Law and legislation--United States--Popular works. I.
Title.
  KF6377.Z9F57 2007
  343.7305'23--dc22

                                   2007021458

Quantity sales: For information on bulk purchases or corporate premium sales, please contact the
Special Sales Department. For academic sales or textbook adoptions, ask for Academic Sales. Call
800-955-4775 or write to Nolo, 950 Parker Street, Berkeley, CA 94710.

Acknowledgments

Many thanks to:

Diana Fitzpatrick and Janet Portman for their superb editing

Terri Hearsh for her outstanding book design, and

Jean Mann for the useful index.

Table of Contents

Your Tax Deduction Companion for Landlords

12 Hiring Help

13 Casualty and Theft Losses

14 Additional Deductions

15 Vacation Homes

16 Deducting Rental Losses

17 Record Keeping and Accounting

18 All About Schedule E

19 Claiming Tax Deductions for Prior Years

20 Help Beyond This Book

Index

Introduction

Your Tax Deduction Companion for Landlords

This is a book about income tax deductions for landlords—that is, people who own residential rental property. If you are one of the millions of Americans who owns a small number of residential rental units (one to ten), this book is for you. And even landlords who own dozens of residential rental properties will find lots of useful information in this book that can help them save money.

No landlord would pay more than necessary for utilities or other operating expenses for a rental property. But, every year millions of landlords pay more taxes on their rental income than they have to. Why? Because they fail to take advantage of all the tax deductions available to owners of residential rental property.

Rental real estate provides more tax benefits than almost any other investment. Often, these benefits make the difference between losing money and earning a profit on a rental property. But tax deductions are worthless if you don't take advantage of them. That's where this book comes in. It gives you all the information you need to maximize your deductions—and avoid common deduction mistakes. You can (and should) use this book all year long, to make April 15th as painless as possible.

To take advantage of the benefits tax deductions offer, you'll have to figure out which deductions you are entitled to take—and keep proper records documenting your expenses. You will also learn how to make the most of the deductions available to you as a landlord. For example, did you know that:

- Landlords can greatly increase the depreciation deductions they receive the first few years they own rental property by using segmented depreciation (Chapter 6).
- Careful planning can permit you to deduct in a single year the cost of improvements to rental property that you would otherwise have to deduct over 27.5 years (Chapter 5).
- You can rent out a vacation home tax free in some cases (Chapter 15).
- Although the IRS doesn't publicize it, landlords can qualify for the home office deduction (Chapter 9).
- Most small landlords can deduct up to $25,000 in rental property losses each year (Chapter 16).
- A special tax rule permits some landlords to deduct 100% of their rental property losses every year, no matter how great those losses are (Chapter 16).
- People who rent property to their family or friends could lose virtually all of their tax deductions (Chapter 15).

If you didn't know one or more of these facts, you could be paying far more in taxes than you need to.

Even if you work with an accountant or another tax professional, you need to learn about rental property tax deductions. No tax professional will ever know as much about your rental business as you do, and you can't expect a hired professional to search high and low for every deduction you might be able to take, especially during the busy tax preparation season. The information in this book will help you provide your tax professional with better records, ask better questions, obtain better advice, and, just as importantly, evaluate the advice you get from tax professionals, websites, and other sources.

If you do your taxes yourself (as more and more landlords are doing, especially with the help of tax preparation software), your need for knowledge is even greater. Not even the most sophisticated tax preparation program can decide which tax deductions you should take or tell you whether you've overlooked a valuable deduction. That's where this book comes in. We provide you with the practical advice and information you need so you can rest assured you are taking full advantage of the many deductions available to landlords.

Icons Used in This Book

   This icon alerts you to a practical tip or good idea.

   This is a caution to slow down and consider potential problems.

   This icon tells you where you can read more about a particular topic.

   This icon means that you may be able to skip some material that doesn't apply to your situation.

Chapter 1

Tax Deduction Basics for Landlords

T he tax code is full of deductions for landlords. Before you can start taking advantage of these deductions, however, you need a basic understanding of how landlords pay taxes and how tax deductions work. This chapter gives you all the information you need to get started, including:

- how the IRS taxes landlords
- how tax deductions work
- how forms of property ownership affect landlord taxes, and
- IRS audits—how they work and how to avoid them.

How Landlords Are Taxed

When you own residential rental property, you are required to pay the following taxes:

- income taxes on rental income and profits from property sales
- property taxes, and
- Social Security and Medicare taxes (for some landlords).

Let's look at each type of tax.

Income Taxes on Rental Income

You must pay federal income taxes on the income (rent and other money) you receive from your rental property each year. When you file your yearly tax return, you add your rental income to your other income for the year, such as salary income from a job, interest on savings, and investment income.

This book covers rental property deductions for federal income taxes. However, 43 states also have income taxes. State income tax laws generally track federal tax law, but there are some exceptions. The states without income taxes are Alaska, Florida, Nevada, South Dakota, Texas, Washington, and Wyoming. For details on your state's income tax law, visit your state tax agency's website, or contact your local state tax office. You can find links to all 50 state tax agency websites at www.taxsites.com/state.html.

Income Taxes on Profits When You Sell Your Property

When you sell your property, any profit you earn is added to your income for the year and is subject to taxation. Profits from the sale of rental property owned for more than one year are taxed at capital gains rates. These rates are generally lower than income tax rates—usually 20% lower, except for taxpayers in the lowest tax brackets. (See Chapter 5 for an example of the tax effects of a rental property sale.)

However, you may be able to defer tax on your profits—perhaps indefinitely—by selling your property through a like-kind exchange (also called a Section 1031 exchange or tax-free exchange). This kind of exchange involves swapping your property for similar property owned by someone else. These property swaps are subject to complex tax rules that are beyond the scope of this book, since they have nothing to do with income tax deductions. For more information, see IRS Publication 544, *Sales and Other Disposition of Assets.*

Social Security and Medicare Taxes

Everyone who works as an employee or who owns his or her own business must pay Social Security and Medicare taxes. These are two separate taxes:

- a 12.4% Social Security tax, up to an annual income ceiling or cap—in 2007 the cap was $97,500 per year, and
- a 2.9% Medicare tax on all employee wages or self-employment profits.

Together, these amount to a 15.3% tax, up to the annual Social Security tax ceiling. Employees pay half of these taxes themselves and their employers pay the other half. Self-employed people must pay it all themselves.

You may have to pay (and withhold) Social Security and Medicare taxes if you hire employees to work in your rental activity—for example, if you hire a resident manager. The employer's share of such taxes is a deductible expense. (See Chapter 12.)

Fortunately, the income you earn from your rental property is not subject to Social Security and Medicare taxes. (IRC Sec. 1402(a)(1).) This is so even if your rental activities constitute a business for tax purposes. (See Chapter 2.) This is one of the great tax benefits of owning rental property. A person who owns a hot dog stand must pay the 15.3% self-employment tax on his or her annual profits, whereas a person who owns a rental house or other real estate need pay no self-employment taxes on his or her rental income.

There is one exception to this rule, which will not apply to many readers of this book: You must pay Social Security and Medicare taxes on rental income if you provide "substantial services" along with the rental. This exception would apply, for example, if you owned a boardinghouse, hotel, or motel and provided maid service, room service, or concierge services. The exception does not apply to services commonly provided for residential rentals, such as repairs, cleaning, maintenance, trash removal, elevators, security, or cable television.

In addition, if you qualify as a real estate dealer, you'll have to pay Social Security and Medicare taxes on your annual profits. (See Chapter 2.)

Property Taxes

Property owners in all states pay property taxes imposed by cities, counties, and other local governments. They are a tax on the value of your rental property. Property taxes are not covered in this book.

How Income Tax Deductions Work

The tax law recognizes that you must spend money on your rental properties for such things as mortgage interest, repairs, maintenance, and many other expenses. The law allows you to subtract these expenses, plus an amount for the depreciation of your property, from your effective gross rental income (all the money actually earned from the property) to determine your "taxable income." You pay income tax only on your taxable income, if any. Expenses you can deduct from your income are called tax deductions or tax write-offs. These deductions are what this book is about.

Although some tax deduction calculations can get a bit complicated, the basic math is simple: The entire tax regimen for rental real estate can be reduced to the following simple equation:

Effective Gross Rental Income

minus Operating Expenses (including mortgage interest)

minus Depreciation and Amortization Expenses

= Taxable Income

(People who analyze real estate investments don't include mortgage interest as a real estate operating expense, but it is an operating expense for tax purposes.)

EXAMPLE: Karen owns a rental house. This year, her effective gross rental income (all the income she actually earned from the property) was $10,000. She doesn't pay tax on the entire $10,000 because she had the following expenses—$5,000 in mortgage interest, $1,000 for other operating expenses, and $2,000 for depreciation. She gets to deduct these as outlined in the above equation:

Effective Gross Rental Income	$10,000
– Operating Expenses	6,000
– Depreciation and Amortization	2,000
Taxable Income	$ 2,000

Karen only pays income tax on her $2,000 taxable income.

Many landlords have so many deductions that they end up with a net loss when they subtract all their deductions from their effective gross rental income. In that situation, they owe no tax at all on their rental income. This is especially common in the early years of owning rental property, when you haven't had time to raise the rents much. Indeed, it is common for landlords to have a loss for tax purposes even if they take in more in rental income than they pay in expenses each month.

Having a tax loss on your rental property is not necessarily a bad thing. You may be able to deduct it from other income you earn during the year, such as salary income from a job or income from other investments. However, there are significant restrictions on a landlord's ability to deduct rental losses from nonrental income. Many small landlords can avoid them, but not all. These restrictions—known as the passive loss rules and at-risk rules—are covered in detail in Chapter 16.

What Is Rental Income?

Your rental income consists primarily of the rent your tenants pay you each month. But it also includes:

- laundry income from coin-operated washers and dryers provided for tenants' use
- fees you charge tenants for paying rent late
- garage or other parking charges
- fees you charge tenants for use of storage facilities
- interest you earn on tenant security deposits (however, many states and cities require landlords to credit interest on security deposits to the tenants)
- security deposits you retain to pay for repairs, unpaid rent, or other expenses
- the value of services tenants provide in lieu of rent, or
- payments tenants make to you for repairs or other expenses.

Of course, real property ordinarily increases in value each year, often substantially. Your rental property appreciation is not rental income until you sell or otherwise dispose of your property. Any profit you earn on the sale or other disposition is taxable income.

What Can You Deduct?

All tax deductions are a matter of legislative grace, which means that you can take a deduction only if it is specifically allowed by one or more provisions of the tax law. You usually do not have to indicate on your tax return which tax law provision gives you the right to take a particular deduction. If you are audited by the IRS, however, you'll have to provide a legal basis for every deduction you take. If the IRS concludes that your deduction wasn't justified, it will deny the deduction and charge you back taxes and penalties.

Landlords can deduct three broad categories of rental expenses:

- start-up expenses
- operating expenses, and
- capital expenses.

This section provides an introduction to each of these categories (they are covered in greater detail in later chapters).

Keep track of your rental expenses. You can deduct only those expenses that you actually incur. You need to keep records of these expenses to know for sure how much you actually spent and prove to the IRS that you really spent the money you deducted on your tax return, in case you are audited. Accounting and bookkeeping are discussed in detail in Chapter 17.

Start-Up Expenses

The first money you will have to shell out will be for your rental activity's start-up expenses. These include most of the costs of getting your rental business up and running, like license fees, advertising costs, attorney and accounting fees, travel expenses, market research, and office supplies expenses. Start-up expenses do not include the cost of buying rental property. Up to $5,000 of start-up expenses may be deducted for the year in which they're incurred. The remainder, if any, must be deducted in equal installments over the first 180 months you're in business—a process called amortization. (See Chapter 8 for a detailed discussion of deducting start-up expenses.)

Operating Expenses

Operating expenses are the ongoing, day-to-day costs a landlord incurs to operate a rental property. They include such things as mortgage interest, utilities, salaries, supplies, travel expenses, car expenses, and repairs and maintenance. These expenses (unlike start-up expenses) are currently deductible—that is, you can deduct them all in the same year when you pay them. (See Chapter 3.)

Capital Expenses

Capital assets are things you buy for your rental activity that have a useful life of more than one year. A landlord's main capital asset is the building or buildings he or she rents out. However, capital assets also include such things as equipment, vehicles, furniture, and appliances. These costs, called capital expenses, are considered to be part of your investment in your rental activity, not day-to-day operating expenses.

The cost of your capital assets must be deducted a little at a time over several years—a process called depreciation. Residential rental buildings are depreciated over 27.5 years. Capital assets other than real estate are depreciated over a much shorter period—for example, vehicles and furniture are depreciated over five years. The cost of land is not deductible—you must wait until land is sold to recover the cost. (See Chapter 5 for more on this topic.)

Tax Credits for Landlords

Tax credits are not the same as tax deductions—they are even better. A tax credit is subtracted from your tax liability after you calculate your taxes. For example, a $1,000 tax credit will reduce your taxes for the year by $1,000. There are many different types of federal income tax credits, but only two can be used by owners of residential rental property:

- the rehabilitation tax credit, available to owners of historic property, and
- the low-income housing tax credit.

There are no federal income tax credits for the cost of eliminating lead paint, asbestos, or mold contamination. However, your state may offer tax credits or other tax incentives for such environmental remediation.

Historic property. The rehabilitation tax credit can be used only by owners of residential rental property that is listed on the National Register of Historic Places or located in a Registered Historical District and determined to be "significant" to that district. Moreover, the Secretary of the Interior must certify to the Secretary of the Treasury that the project meets their standards and is a "Certified Rehabilitation." The property owner obtains this certification by filing an application with the National Park Service.

Obviously, not many rental properties are registered historic sites. But, if you own a property that qualifies, you can receive a tax credit equal to 20% of the amount you spend to rehabilitate your historic building, up to certain limits. You can nominate your building for historic status, if you think it qualifies, by contacting your state historical officer. The following websites provide detailed information on the rehabilitation tax credit:

National Trust for Historic Preservation: www.nationaltrust.org

National Park Service Heritage Preservation: www.nps.gov/history.

Low-income housing. Congress enacted the low-income housing tax credit to encourage new construction and rehabilitation of existing rental housing for low-income households. The IRS and state tax credit allocation agencies jointly administer the low-income housing tax credit, which is used mostly by large real estate developers to build new low-income housing projects. For more information, contact your state tax credit allocation agency. You can find a list at www.novoco.com/stcaa.shtml. Useful information can also be obtained from the National Housing & Rehabilitation Association website at www.housingonline.com.

How Your Tax Status Affects Your Deductions

Owning rental property can be a business for tax purposes, an investment, or, in some cases, a not-for-profit activity. Landlords whose rental activities qualify as a business are entitled to all the tax deductions discussed in this book. However, those whose rentals are an investment lose certain useful deductions, such as the home office deduction. Tax deductions are extremely limited for landlords who, in the eyes of the IRS, are operating a not-for-profit activity.

Your tax status is determined by how much time and effort you put into your rental activity, and whether you earn profits each year or act like you want to. Most landlords who manage their property themselves qualify as for-profit businesses. (See Chapter 2 for more on determining your tax status.)

The Value of a Tax Deduction

Most taxpayers, even sophisticated businesspeople, don't fully appreciate just how they save with tax deductions. Only part of any deduction will end up back in your pocket as money saved. Because a deduction represents income on which you don't have to pay tax, the value of any deduction is the amount of tax you would have had to pay on that income had you not deducted it. So a deduction of $1,000 won't save you $1,000—it will save you whatever you would otherwise have had to pay as tax on that $1,000 of income.

To determine how much income tax a deduction will save you, you must first figure out your income tax bracket. The United States has a progressive income tax system for individual taxpayers with six different tax rates (called tax brackets), ranging from 10% of taxable income to 35% (see the chart below). The higher your income, the higher your tax rate will be.

You move from one bracket to the next only when your taxable income exceeds the bracket amount. For example, if you are a single taxpayer, you pay 10% income tax on all your taxable income up to $7,550. If your taxable income exceeds $7,550, the next tax rate (15%) applies to all your income over $7,550— but the 10% rate still applies to the first $7,550. If your income exceeds the 15% bracket amount, the next tax rate (25%) applies to the excess amount, and so on until the top bracket of 35% is reached.

The tax bracket in which the last dollar you earn for the year falls is called your "marginal tax bracket." For example, if you have $60,000 in taxable income, your marginal tax bracket is 25%. To determine how much federal income tax a deduction will save you, multiply the amount of the deduction by your marginal tax bracket. For example, if your marginal tax bracket is 25%, you will save 25¢ in federal income taxes for every dollar you are able to claim as a deductible business expense (25% x $1 = 25¢). This calculation is only approximate because an additional deduction may move you from one tax bracket to another and thus lower your marginal tax rate. For example, if you're single and your taxable income is $75,000, an additional $1,000 deduction will lower your marginal tax rate from 28% to 25%. The first $800 of the deduction will save you $224 in tax (28% x $800 = $224); the remaining $200 will save you $50 (25% x $200 = $50). So your total tax saving is $274, instead of the $280 you would get if, say, your taxable income had been $76,000.

The following table lists the 2007 federal income tax brackets for single and married individual taxpayers and shows the tax savings for each dollar of deductions.

2007 Federal Personal Income Tax Brackets		
Tax Bracket	Income If Single	Income If Married Filing Jointly
10%	Up to $7,825	Up to $15,560
15%	From $7,826 to $31,850	$15,561 to $63,700
25%	$31,851 to $77,100	$63,701 to $128,500
28%	$77,101 to $160,850	$128,501 to $195,850
33%	$160,851 to $349,700	$195,851 to $349,700
35%	All over $349,700	All over $349,700

Each year, the federal government adjusts income tax brackets for inflation. For current brackets, see IRS Publication 505, *Tax Withholding and Estimated Tax*.

You can also deduct your rental activity expenses from any state income tax you must pay. The average state income tax rate is about 6%, although seven states (Alaska, Florida, Nevada, South Dakota, Texas, Washington, and Wyoming) don't have an income tax. You can find a list of all state income tax rates at www.taxadmin.org/FTA/rate/ind_inc.html.

When you add up your savings in federal and state income taxes, you can see the true value of a tax deduction. For example, if you're in the 25% federal income tax bracket, a deduction can be worth 25% (in federal income taxes) plus 6% (in state income taxes). That adds up to a whopping 31% savings. (If you itemize your personal deductions, your actual tax savings from a business deduction is a bit less because it reduces your state income tax and therefore reduces the federal income tax savings from this itemized deduction.) If you buy a $1,000 computer for your rental activity and you deduct the expense, you save about $310 in income taxes. In effect, the government is paying for almost one-third of your rental expenses. This is why it's so important to know all the deductions you are entitled to take and to take advantage of every one.

You should get into the habit of thinking about your rental expenses in terms of after-tax dollars—what the item really costs you after you deduct the cost from your income taxes.

> ⚠️ **Don't buy things just to get a tax deduction.** Although tax deductions can be worth a lot, it doesn't make sense to buy something you don't need just to get a deduction. After all, you still have to pay for the item, and the tax deduction you get in return will cover only a portion of the cost. If you buy a $500 lawn mower to use for your rental properties, you'll be able to deduct less than half the cost. That means you're still out over $300—money you've spent for something you may not have needed. On the other hand, if you really do need a new lawn mower, the deduction you're entitled to is like found money—and it may help you buy a better lawn mower than you could otherwise afford.

How Property Ownership Affects Taxes

How you own your residential rental property affects the tax returns you must file each year. The main ownership options for a small landlord are:

- sole proprietorship
- general partnership
- limited partnership
- limited liability company (LLC)
- corporation
- tenancy in common, or
- joint tenancy.

These can be sorted into two broad categories: individual ownership and ownership through a business entity. If you don't know how you hold title to the rental property you already own, look at your property deed.

Individual Ownership

Most small landlords (owners of from one to ten residential rental units) own their property as individuals—either alone, or with one or more co-owners.

One Property Owner

If you own the property by yourself, you can take title to the property in your own name and be a sole proprietor for tax purposes. This is by far the simplest and easiest way to own residential rental property. Any rental income you earn is added to your other income, such as salary from a job, interest income, or investment income. Losses you incur can be deducted from your other income, subject to the restrictions discussed in Chapter 16. You report your rental income and losses on IRS Schedule E and attach it to your individual tax return. (See Chapter 18 for a detailed discussion of Schedule E.)

Two or More Co-Owners

If you own the property with one or more co-owners, you can take title in your own name as a tenant in common along with your co-owners. Each co-owner owns an undivided interest in the entire property. The interests can be equal or divided in unequal amounts, however the owners agree. The ownership interest of each owner should be listed on the property deed.

> **EXAMPLE:** Al and Alice, brother and sister, buy a rental house together, taking title as tenants in common. They decide that because Al put more money down on the property, he should own a 60% interest and Alice 40%. This means that Al is legally entitled to 60% of the income the property generates and is supposed to pay 60% of the expenses. Alice gets the remaining 40%.

Each cotenant reports his or her share of the income and deductions from the rental property on his or her own tax return, filing Schedule E. Each owner's share is based on his or her ownership interest—for example, Alice in the example above lists her 40% share of the income and deductions from the co-owned rental house on her Schedule E and pays tax on that amount. Al lists the other 60% on his own Schedule E.

If one cotenant pays more than his or her proportionate share of the expenses, the overpayment is treated as a loan to the other cotenants and may not be deducted. The cotenant who overpays is legally entitled to be reimbursed by the other cotenants. (IRS Reg. 301.7701-3(a).)

> **EXAMPLE:** Alice from the example above pays 80% of the annual expenses for the rental house this year, instead of the 40% she should pay based on her ownership interest. She may not deduct her overpayment, which amounts to $10,000. Instead, it is treated as a loan to her cotenant Al. Alice is entitled to be repaid the $10,000 by Al. If he doesn't pay, she can sue him to collect. If he does pay, he can deduct the amount as a rental expense.

Co-Ownership by Spouses

Spouses who own rental property together typically take title as joint tenants—rather than tenants in common. Joint tenants are treated exactly the same as tenants in common for tax purposes, but there are significant nontax differences. Joint tenants must own the property 50-50. In addition, joint tenancy always includes "the right of survivorship." When one joint tenant dies, his or her share automatically goes to the survivor. This is not the case with tenants in common, who can leave their share of the co-owned property to anyone they want. Unmarried people can also be joint tenants, but this isn't commonly done.

If a married couple who jointly own rental property file a joint income tax return, as most do, their joint ownership produces the same tax result as individual ownership by one of the spouses. This is because the spouses' shares of the income and deductions from the rental property are combined on the joint tax return.

> **EXAMPLE:** Sam and Samantha are a married couple who jointly own an apartment building. They file a single joint tax return, so all their income and deductions from the apartment building are listed on a single Schedule E they file with their joint return.

If You Live in a Community Property State

Nine states have community property laws governing ownership of property acquired during marriage: Arizona, California, Idaho, Louisiana, Nevada, New Mexico, Texas, Washington, and Wisconsin. If you live in one of these states, you and your spouse will automatically be co-owners of any rental property you acquire while you're married, unless you agree otherwise.

Like married people in non-community property states, spouses in community property states ordinarily take title to their real property as joint tenants. However, they may take title as tenants in common instead, if they wish.

There are no special concerns for spouses in community property states who file joint returns, as most do. However, if a married couple in a community property state files separate returns for each spouse, the income or loss from their rental properties must be allocated among them. Unless they agree otherwise, each spouse gets a 50% share of the income or loss. For more information, refer to IRS Publication 555, *Federal Tax Information on Community Property*.

Ownership Through a Business Entity

Instead of owning your rental property in your own name, you can form a business entity to own it, and own all or part of the entity.

> **EXAMPLE:** Vicki and Victor, a married couple, own a small apartment building. Instead of taking title in their own names as joint tenants, they form a limited liability company (LLC). The LLC owns the building and they, in turn, own the LLC.

The tax deductions available from rental property are the same whether you own it in your own name or through a business entity.

 This section provides only the briefest possible introduction to business entities. To learn more, refer to *LLC or Corporation? How to Choose the Right Form for Your Business,* by Anthony Mancuso (Nolo).

Types of Entities

There are several different business entities that can own rental property:

Partnerships. A partnership is a form of shared ownership and management of a business. The partners contribute money, property, or services to the partnership; in return, they receive a share of the profits it earns, if any. The partners jointly manage the partnership business. Although many partners enter into written partnership agreements, no agreement is required to form a partnership. A partnership can hold title to real estate and other property.

Limited partnerships. A limited partnership is a special type of partnership that can only be created by filing limited partnership documents with your state government. It consists of one or more general partners who manage the partnership and any number of limited partners who are passive investors—they contribute money and share in the partnership's income (or losses) but do not actively manage the partnership business. Limited partnerships are especially popular for real estate projects that are owned by multiple investors.

Corporations. A corporation can only be created by filing incorporation documents with your state government. A corporation is a legal entity distinct from its owners, who are called shareholders. It can hold title to property, sue and be sued, have bank accounts, borrow money, hire employees, and perform other business functions. For tax purposes, there are two types of corporations: S corporations (also called small business corporations) and C corporations (also called regular corporations). The most important difference between the two types of corporations is how they are taxed. An S corporation pays no taxes itself—instead, its income or loss is passed on to its owners, who must pay personal income taxes on their share of the corporation's profits. A C corporation is a separate taxpaying entity that pays taxes on its profits. C corporations are rarely used to own rental property.

Limited liability companies. The limited liability company (LLC) is like a sole proprietorship or partnership in that its owners (called members) jointly own and manage the business and share in the profits. However, an LLC is also like a corporation because its owners must file papers with the state to create the LLC and it exists as a separate legal entity.

Tenants in Common Are Not Partnerships

A partnership automatically comes into existence whenever two or more people enter into business together to earn a profit and don't incorporate or form a limited liability company. Does this mean that whenever two or more people own a rental property together they automatically become partners in partnership and have to file a partnership tax return? No. IRS regulations provide that tenants in common or joint tenants do not become partners in a partnership when they own rental property together and merely maintain, repair, and rent it. However, the IRS may decide that co-owners are partners if they actively carry on a business venture or financial operation—for example, a partnership exists if co-owners of an apartment building lease space and also provide services to their tenants beyond those normally provided in residential rental properties, such as maid service or concierge services. (IRS Reg. 301.7701-3(a).)

Tax Treatment of Business Entities

Partnerships, limited partnerships, LLCs, and S corporations are all pass-through entities. A pass-through entity does not pay any taxes itself. Instead, the business's profits or losses are passed through to its owners, who include them on their own personal tax returns (IRS Form 1040). When a profit is passed through to the owner, the owner must add that money to any income from other sources, and pay tax on the total amount. If a loss is passed through to the owner, he or she can deduct it from other income, subject to the restrictions on deducting rental losses discussed in Chapter 16. Because pass-through taxation permits property owners to deduct losses from their personal taxes, it is considered the best form of taxation for real estate ownership.

Although pass-through entities don't pay taxes, their income and expenses must still be reported to the IRS as follows:

Partnerships and limited partnerships. These must file an annual tax form with the IRS (Form 1065, U.S. Return of Partnership Income). Form 1065 is used to report partnership revenues, expenses, gains, and losses. The partnership must also provide each partner with an IRS Schedule K-1, Partner's Share of Income, Credits, Deductions, etc., listing the partner's share of partnership income and expenses (copies of these schedules must also be attached to IRS Form 1065).

The partners must then file IRS Schedule E, Supplemental Income and Loss, with their individual income tax returns, showing the income or losses from all the partnerships in which they own an interest. Partners complete the second page of Schedule E, not the first page, which individuals use to report their income and deductions from rental property. (See Chapter 18.)

S corporations. These entities must file information returns with the IRS on Form 1120S, U.S. Income Tax Return for an S Corporation, showing how much the business earned or lost and each shareholder's portion of the corporate income or loss. (An information return is a return filed by an entity that doesn't pay any taxes itself. Its purpose is to show the IRS how much tax the entity's owners owe.) Like partners in a partnership, the shareholders must complete the second page of Schedule E, showing their shares of the corporation's income or losses, and file it with their individual tax returns.

LLCs. LLCs with only one member are treated like a sole proprietorship for tax purposes. The member reports profits, losses, and deductions on Schedule C, Profit or Loss from a Business. An LLC with two or more members is treated like a partnership for tax purposes, except in the unusual situation where the owners choose to have it treated like a C or S corporation.

Landlords who own their properties through business entities don't use individual Schedule Es to report their rental income or losses. Instead, the partnership, limited partnership, LLC, or S corporation files IRS Form 8825, Rental Real Estate Income and Expenses of a Partnership or an S Corporation to report the income and deductions from the property owned by the entity. This form is very similar to Schedule E.

Why Form a Business Entity?

The primary reason small landlords form business entities to own their property has nothing to with taxes. Rather, they use business entities to attempt to avoid personal liability for debts and lawsuits arising from rental property ownership.

When you own rental property in your own name, alone or with co-owners, you are personally liable for all the debts arising from the property. This means that a creditor—a person or company to whom you owe money for items you use in your rental activity—can go after all your assets, both business and personal. This may include, for example, your personal bank accounts, your car, and even your house. Similarly, a personal creditor—a person or company to whom you owe money for personal items—can go after your rental property. The main creditor that rental property owners worry about is the bank or some other financial institution from which they have borrowed money to purchase their property. If they default on their loan, they could be personally liable for the debt. (However, this isn't always the case. It depends on the nature of your loan and how your state law deals with real estate foreclosures.)

If you own property in your own name, you'll also be personally liable for rental-related lawsuits—for example, if someone slips and falls at your rental property and sues for damages.

In theory, limited partnerships, LLCs, and corporations provide their owners with limited liability from debts and lawsuits. (Only the limited partners in a limited partnership have limited liability. General partners are personally liable for partnership debts and lawsuits.) Limited liability means that you are not personally liable for the debts incurred by your business entity, or for lawsuits arising from its ownership of rental property. Thus, your personal assets are not at risk; at most, you'll lose your investment in the business entity (which, of course, is often substantial).

In real life, however, limited liability is often hard to come by, even when you form a business entity. Lenders may require small landlords who form business entities to personally guarantee any loans their entities obtain to purchase property. This means the landlord will be personally liable if there is a default on the loan. In addition, you'll always be personally liable if someone is injured on property due to your personal negligence. For example, if someone slips and falls on your property, they can sue you personally by claiming your own negligence caused or contributed to the accident. This is so even though your property is owned by a business entity, not you personally. You can far more effectively protect yourself from such lawsuits by obtaining liability insurance for your rental property. The cost is a deductible rental expense. (See Chapter 14.)

However, if you're dead set on owning your rental property through a business entity, the entity of choice is the LLC. It provides the same degree of limited liability as a corporation, while also giving its owners pass-through taxation—the most advantageous tax treatment for real property. As a result, LLCs have become very popular among real property owners in recent years.

 For detailed guidance about LLCs, refer to *Form Your Own Limited Liability Company,* by Anthony Mancuso (Nolo).

The Mini-Landlord: Renting Out a Room in Your Home

If you rent out a room in your home, the tax deductions and other tax rules discussed in this book apply to you in the same way as they do for landlords who rent out entire properties. There is one big difference however: You must divide certain expenses between the part of the property you rent out and the part you live in, just as though you actually had two separate pieces of property.

You can fully deduct (or, where applicable, depreciate) any expenses *just for the room you rent*—for example, repairing a window in the room, installing carpet or drapes, painting the room, or providing your tenant with furniture (such as a bed). In addition, if you pay extra homeowner's insurance premiums because you're renting out a room, the full cost is a deductible operating expense. If you install a second phone line just for your tenant's use, the full cost is deductible as a rental expense. However, you cannot deduct any part of the cost of the first phone line even if your tenant has unlimited use of it.

Expenses for your entire home must be divided between the part you rent and the part you live in. This includes your payments for:

- mortgage interest
- repairs for your entire home—for example, repairing the roof or furnace, or painting the entire home
- improvements for your entire home—for example, replacing the roof
- homeowners' insurance
- utilities such as electricity, gas and heating, oil
- housecleaning or gardening services for your whole home
- trash removal
- snow removal costs
- security system costs, and
- condominium association fees.

You can also deduct depreciation on the part of your home you rent.

You can use any reasonable method for dividing these expenses. It may be reasonable to divide the cost of some items (for example, water) based on the number of people using them. However, the two most common methods for dividing an expense are either based on the number of rooms in your home or based on the square footage of your home.

EXAMPLE 1: Jane rents a room in her house to a college student. The room is 10 × 20 feet, or 200 square feet. Her entire house has 1,200 square feet of floor space. Thus, one-sixth, or 16.67% of her home is rented out. She can deduct as a rental expense one-sixth of any expense that must be divided between rental use and personal use.

EXAMPLE 2: Instead of using the square footage of her house, Jane figures that her home has five rooms of about equal size, and she is renting out one of them. She determines that one-fifth, or 20%, of her home is being rented. She deducts 20% of her expenses that must be divided between rental and personal use.

As the examples show, you can often get a larger deduction by using the room method instead of the square footage of your home. This is discussed in greater detail in the chapter on home office deduction (Chapter 9).

Let's see how much Jane can deduct for her bedroom rental.

Expense	Deduction Percentage	Deductible Amount
Mortgage Interest—$12,000	20%	$2,400
Painting entire home exterior—$2,000	20%	$400
Utilities—$1,200	20%	$240
Trash removal—$500	20%	$100
Painting rental bedroom—$400	100%	$400
Total		$3,540

Jane also gets to depreciate 20% of the cost of her home over 27.5 years. Her home cost $200,000 so she depreciates $40,000. The first year she deducts 3.485% of this amount for a $1,394 deduction.

The IRS and the Landlord

I-R-S. For generations, these three letters have struck fear into the hearts of Americans. Some landlords don't take deductions to which they are legally entitled because they are afraid of being audited. Others believe that the IRS has become a toothless tiger—and take questionable tax deductions hoping that the IRS won't catch on. Which group is right? Is the IRS a clear and present danger or a phantom menace? Here are the facts.

For a detailed discussion of IRS audits, see *Stand Up to the IRS,* by Frederick Daily (Nolo).

Anatomy of an Audit

You can claim any deductions you want to take on your tax return—after all, you (or your tax preparer) fill it out, not the government. However, all the deductions you claim are subject to review by the IRS. This review is called a tax audit. There are three types of audits: correspondence audits, office audits, and field audits.

Correspondence audits. As the name indicates, correspondence audits are handled entirely by mail. These are the simplest and shortest type of IRS audit, usually involving a single issue. The IRS sends you written questions about your tax return and may request additional information and/or documentation. If you don't provide satisfactory answers or information, you'll be assessed additional taxes.

Office audits. Office audits take place face-to-face with an IRS auditor at one of the 33 IRS district offices. These are more complex than correspondence audits, often involving more than one issue or more than one tax year. If you make less than $100,000 per year, this is the type of in-person audit you're likely to face.

Field audits. The field audit is the most comprehensive IRS audit, conducted by an experienced revenue officer. In a field audit, the officer examines your finances, your landlord and other business activities, your tax returns, and the records you used to create the returns. As the name implies, a field audit is normally conducted at the taxpayer's place of business, which allows the auditor to learn as much about you as possible. Field audits are ordinarily reserved for taxpayers who earn a lot of money. You probably won't be subjected to one unless you earn more than $100,000 per year.

How Landlords Get in Trouble With the IRS

When auditing small landlords, the IRS is most concerned about whether you have:

- underreported your rental income
- claimed tax deductions to which you were not entitled
- properly documented the amount of your deductions, and
- complied with the passive loss rules and other restrictions on deducting rental losses.

Records Available to Auditors

An IRS auditor is entitled to examine the records you used to prepare your tax returns, including your books, check registers, canceled checks, and receipts. The auditor can also ask to see records supporting your tax deductions, such as a mileage record (if you took a deduction for business use of your car). The auditor can also get copies of your bank records, either from you or your bank, and will check them to see whether your deposits match the income you reported on your tax return. If you deposited a lot more money than you reported earning, the auditor will assume that you didn't report all of your income, unless you can show that the deposits you didn't include in your tax return weren't income. For example, you might be able to show that they were loans, inheritances, or transfers from other accounts. This is why you need to keep good financial records.

The IRS: Clear and Present Danger or Phantom Menace?

In 1963, an incredible 5.6% of all Americans had their tax returns audited. However, by 2006, an IRS audit had become a relatively rare event and only .80% of all Americans were audited. There are several reasons for the change:

- The IRS workforce declined—between 1997 and 2006, the IRS workforce declined by 16%; the number of revenue agents dropped by 14%.
- The IRS workload increased—at the same time the IRS workforce was declining, its workload was increasing. Between 1995 and 2004, the number of tax returns filed increased 12%, reaching 174 million.
- Starting in the mid-1990s, the IRS began to emphasize taxpayer service, rather than enforcement. Staff work shifted from audits to service functions, such as answering taxpayer questions.
- Congress enacted new laws in 1998 that were intended to prevent perceived abuses by IRS agents and auditors. These new protections also made it more difficult for the IRS to go after tax cheats.

Both the IRS and the Congress are aware of the IRS's enforcement problems and have taken some steps to ameliorate them. The IRS has received moderate budget increases in the past few years and has placed a renewed emphasis on enforcement. The precipitous decline in audit rates that began in the mid-1990s has stopped, but audit rates remain at very low levels. However, the IRS commissioner promises that audit rates will go up in the next few years. With huge federal budget deficits yawning as far as the eye can see, it seems likely that this is one government promise that will be kept.

Aggressive or Dishonest?

Given the relatively low audit rates in recent years, many tax experts say that this is a good time to be aggressive about taking tax deductions. In this context, "aggressive" means taking every deduction to which you might arguably be entitled. If a deduction falls into a gray area of law, you would decide the question in your favor. This is *tax avoidance*, which is perfectly legal.

However, being aggressive does not mean being dishonest—that is, taking phony deductions that you are clearly not entitled to take or falsely increasing the amount of the deductions to which you are entitled. This is *tax evasion*, which is a crime.

Audit Rates for Landlords

Are small landlords a target for the IRS? No one knows for sure, but the answer appears to be no. An analysis of over 1,200 tax returns conducted by a professor of statistics in the mid-1990s could find no correlation between filing Schedule E (the tax form used to report rental income and losses) and an increased risk of an audit. (See *How to Beat the IRS At Its Own Game*, by Amir D. Aczel (Four Walls Eight Windows, 1995).)

The IRS does not release any statistics on how many Schedule E filers are audited. However, it does release detailed audit statistics for individuals who are not in business and for business filers—sole proprietors who file Schedule C, partnerships, and corporations. Given the fact that landlords don't appear to be an IRS audit target, it's not likely that small landlords are audited any more often than sole proprietors filing Schedule C—they are probably audited less often.

Six Tips for Avoiding an Audit

Here are six things you can do to minimize your chances of getting audited.

Tip #1: Be Neat, Thorough, and Exact

If you file by mail (as you should) and submit a tax return that looks professional, this will help you avoid unwanted attention from the IRS. Your return shouldn't contain erasures or be difficult to read. Your math should be correct. Avoid round numbers on your return (like $100 or $5,000). This looks like you're making up the numbers instead of taking them from accurate records. You should include, and completely fill out, all necessary forms and schedules. Moreover, your state tax return should be consistent with your federal return. If you do your own taxes, using a tax preparation computer program will help you produce an accurate return that looks professional.

Tip #2: Mail Your Return by Registered Mail

Mail your tax return by registered or certified mail, return receipt requested. In case the IRS loses or misplaces your return, your receipt will prove that you submitted it. The IRS also accepts returns from four private delivery services: Airborne Express, DHL Worldwide Express, Federal Express, and United Parcel Service. Contact these companies for details on which of their service options qualify and how to get proof of timely filing.

Tip #3: Don't File Early

Unless you're owed a substantial refund, you shouldn't file your taxes early. The IRS generally has three years after April 15 to decide whether to audit your return. Filing early just gives the IRS more time to think about whether you should be audited. You can reduce your audit chances even more by getting an extension to file until October 15. Note, however, that filing an extension does not extend the date by which you have to pay any taxes due for the prior year—these must be paid by April 15.

Tip #4: Don't File Electronically

The IRS would like all taxpayers to file their returns electronically—that is, by email. There is a good reason for this: It saves the agency substantial time and money. Every year, the IRS must hire thousands of temp workers to enter the numbers from millions of paper returns into its computer system. This is expensive, so the IRS only has about 40% of the data on paper returns transcribed. The paper returns are then sent to a warehouse where they are kept for six years and then destroyed. The IRS makes its audit decisions based on this transcribed data. By filing electronically, you give the IRS easy electronic access to 100% of the data on your return instead of just 40%. Moreover, if you file electronically, you cannot add written explanations of any deductions the IRS might question (see Tip #5). No one can say for sure whether filing a paper return lessens your chance of an audit, but why make life easier for the IRS if you don't have to?

Tip #5: Explain Items the IRS Will Question

If your return contains an item that the IRS may question or that could increase the likelihood of an audit, include an explanation and documentation to prove everything is on the up and up. For example, if your return contains a substantial casualty loss deduction, explain the circumstances. This won't necessarily avoid an audit, but it may reduce your chances. Here's why: If the IRS computer determines that your return is a good candidate for an audit, an IRS classifier screens it to see whether it really warrants an audit. If your explanation looks reasonable, the screener may decide you shouldn't be audited after all.

Tip #6: Report All Your Rental Income

You should always report all the income you receive. The IRS has a pretty good idea how much money rental properties ordinarily bring in. If the income you list on your Schedule E looks disproportionately low for the size, location, or value of your rental property, your return may be tagged for an audit.

Chapter 2

Landlord Tax Classifications

This chapter explains how to determine your tax status—that is, how to classify your rental activities for tax purposes. This is not a topic that most residential landlords give much thought to. However, your tax status is extremely important because it will determine whether (and to what extent) you can deduct your rental expenses. Your tax status also significantly affects your taxes when you sell your property.

The Landlord Tax Categories

A landlord can fall into any one of the following four tax categories:

- a business owner
- a real estate investor
- a dealer in real estate, or
- a person who owns rental property as a not-for-profit activity.

The vast majority of residential landlords are either business owners or investors—although this doesn't necessarily mean that you'll fall into one of these two categories. Ultimately, your behavior and motive for owning rental property will determine your tax status.

Initially, it's up to you to decide which category your rental activities fall into for tax purposes. However, if the IRS audits you, it can review your tax classification. If the IRS decides that you misclassified your rental activities, you could have to pay back taxes, interest, and penalties.

You can determine your status by answering the following questions:

- Do you work regularly and continuously at your rental activity?
- Is earning a profit the primary reason you own rental property?
- Do you make your money primarily by buying and selling real estate?

Let's take a look at each of these questions—this will help you figure out which category you fall into. The tax consequences of the different classifications are also explained.

Business Owner Versus Investor

The crucial tax question for most landlords is whether they qualify as business owners or investors. This distinction has important tax consequences. If, like most landlords, you are a business owner, you get certain valuable tax deductions that investors can't use (including the home office and start-up expenses deductions, and Section 179 expensing). It is important, therefore, to understand the difference between these two categories and know where you belong.

⚠ **Do you continually lose money on your rentals?** If you do, the IRS may claim you're engaged in a not-for-profit activity, with disastrous tax consequences. See "Are You Profit Motivated?", below, for detailed guidance on how to show the IRS that you want to earn a profit from your rental property.

Are You a Business Owner or an Investor?

What's the difference between an investor and a business owner? It's not their motivation—they both want to earn a profit. The difference is that business owners earn their profits by actively running a business, either themselves or with the help of others they hire, such as managers. Investors are passive—they put their money in someone else's business and hope their investment will increase in value due to the other person's efforts. Or, they buy an item like land or gold, and then sit and wait for it to increase in value.

Owning rental property qualifies as a business if you do it to earn a profit and work at it regularly, systematically, and continuously. (*Alvary v. United States,* 302 F.2d 790 (2nd Cir. 1962).)

> **EXAMPLE:** Edwin Curphey, a dermatologist, owned six rental properties in Hawaii. He converted a bedroom in his home into an office for his real estate activities. Curphey personally managed his rentals, which included seeking new tenants, supplying furnishings, and cleaning and otherwise preparing the units for new tenants. The court held that these activities were sufficiently systematic and continuous to place him in the business of real estate rental. (*Curphey v. Comm'r.,* 73 T.C. 766 (1980).)

However, you don't have to do all the work yourself: You can hire a manager to help you and still qualify as a business.

> **EXAMPLE:** Gilford, her two sisters, and other relatives jointly owned eight apartment buildings in Manhattan. They hired a real estate agent to manage the properties and pay each family member their share of the net income. Gilford was found to be in business even though she spent little or no time managing the buildings. The court reasoned that the ownership and management of the buildings was a business because it required considerable

time and effort by the real estate agent over several years. Because the agent acted for Gilford and was ultimately under her control, Gilford was in business through her agent. (*Gilford v. Comm'r.*, 201 F.2d 735 (2nd Cir. 1953).)

Rental ownership, on the other hand, is an investment, not a business, if you do it to earn a profit, but don't work at it regularly, systematically, and continuously—either by yourself or with the help of a manager, agent, or others.

> **EXAMPLE:** Byron Anderson rented a farm to a tenant farmer. Both the IRS and tax court found that he was an investor, not a business owner, because all he did was pay bills relating to the farm, deposit rent checks, keep records and files for the farm, and talk occasionally with his tenant on the telephone about operating the farm. They found these activities were not sufficiently continuous, systematic, or regular to be a business. (*Anderson v. Comm'r.*, T.C. Memo 1982-576.)

In theory, a landlord who owns only a single residential rental unit can qualify as a business. As a practical matter, however, you could have trouble showing that your management activities (or those of an agent) are sufficiently continuous, systematic, and regular if you own only one or a few units. Ironically, this is more likely where you have good stable tenants who cause few problems and make little demand on your time.

> **EXAMPLE:** Edgar Grier inherited a house from his mother that she had rented out for many years to the same tenant. This same tenant continued to occupy the property until Grier sold it 14 years later. Over the years, Grier managed the property himself or with the help of an agent. Little management work was required, but Grier did take care of such details as replacing the furnace. The IRS and court found that the house was an investment, not a business for Grier. The court noted that this was the only rental property Grier had ever owned and concluded that his landlord activities were too minimal to rise to the level of a business. (*Grier v. United States*, 120 F. Supp. 395 (D.CT 1954).)

Other cases where landlords have been found to be investors are those involving net leases of commercial properties where the tenant is required to manage the property and pay all taxes, insurance, and other expenses. The landlord does nothing but deposit the rent checks. (*Neill v. Comm'r.*, 46 B.T.A. 197.) Net leases are not usually used for residential rental properties. However, if you have an arrangement with a tenant that requires the tenant, not you, to take care of the property the IRS could conclude you're not in business.

Also, if your rental property is vacant all or most of the time, the IRS could decide that you are an investor, because you wouldn't need to spend much time dealing with the property. The IRS might also take the position that vacant properties involve a not-for-profit activity.

Finally, people who purchase interests in business entities that own real estate, but aren't actively involved in management of the entities, are also investors for tax purposes. These include the limited partners in limited partnerships that own real estate, and people who own shares in corporations and REITs (real estate investment trusts).

The Importance of Good Records

If you want to make sure you qualify as a business owner, it is important that you keep track of the landlord tasks you perform and the time you spend performing these tasks. Your records don't have to be fancy—notes on a calendar will do. (See Chapter 17.) But keep track of the dates and time you spend on tasks such as taking care of repairs, dealing with tenant complaints, showing the property, negotiating leases, and so forth. This will show that you were actively engaged in the business of being a landlord. Good record keeping will not only help establish you are in business, but can also help you avoid restrictive rules on deducting losses from real estate. (See Chapter 16.)

Tax Consequences

At first glance, there may not seem to be much difference, taxwise, between landlords who are business owners and those who are investors. They both file the same tax form to report their income and expenses—Schedule E. And, they don't need to indicate on their tax returns whether their rental activities are businesses or investments. In addition, neither one has to pay self-employment taxes on any rental income. (See Chapter 12.)

Investors and business owners are also entitled to many of the same deductions. People who own businesses are entitled to deduct their ordinary and necessary expenses. (I.R.C. § 162.) Investors are entitled to deduct any ordinary and necessary expenses they incur in connection with producing or collecting income, or managing, conserving, or maintaining property they hold to produce income—for example, a real estate rental. (I.R.C. § 212.)

Thus, both business owners and investors may deduct:

- repair costs (see Chapter 4)
- depreciation (see Chapter 5)
- interest (see Chapter 7)
- taxes (see Chapter 14)
- car and local travel expenses (see Chapter 10)
- long distance travel expenses (see Chapter 11)
- meal and entertainment expenses (see Chapter 14)
- the costs of hiring workers (see Chapter 12)
- casualty losses (see Chapter 13)
- payments for professional services (see Chapter 3), and
- other operating expenses, such as advertising and insurance (see Chapter 3).

And the requirements to qualify for these deductions are the same for business owners and investors.

The similarities end there, however. Taxwise, business owners are much better off than investors because they are entitled to take certain valuable deductions that investors can't take. These business-only deductions include:

- **Home office deduction.** Investors can't take a home office deduction. This important deduction is available only for businesses conducted from home. (See Chapter 9.)
- **Section 179 expensing.** Investors cannot take advantage of Section 179, the tax code provision that allows businesspeople to deduct up to $125,000 in purchases of long-term personal property in a single year (see Chapter 5).
- **Seminar or convention deductions.** Investors cannot deduct their expenses for attending conventions, seminars, or similar events. Thus, for example, the cost of attending a real estate investment seminar is not deductible for investors. Businesspeople can qualify for such deductions. (See Chapter 11.)
- **Start-up expense deduction.** Up to $5,000 of the costs you incur to start your rental business may be deducted in the first year your business is in operation. Any amount over $5,000 must be deducted in equal installments over the first 180 months you're in business. (See Chapter 8 for more on deducting start-up costs.) You get no deduction at all for expenses incurred in starting up an investment activity.

- **Real estate losses.** If an investor loses money when he or she sells real estate, the loss is a capital loss. Investors can deduct only $3,000 in capital losses each year from their ordinary income—that is, income not derived from capital assets like real estate, stocks, bonds, and other investments. Business owners get much better tax treatment when it comes to losses. Any gains they earn when they sell real estate used in their business and held for more than one year are taxed at capital gains rates—usually lower than the normal income tax rates. But, if a business owner sells business real property at a loss, the loss is deductible in full from all of the owner's income, not just income from capital assets. (I.R.C. § 1231.) Thus, when it comes to buying and selling real estate, business owners have the best of both worlds—their gains are taxed as capital gains, but their losses are treated as ordinary losses. (See Chapter 16 for more on real estate losses.)

Because of these valuable deductions, it is better to qualify as a business owner than an investor. Be careful, however, when you decide which deductions you are entitled to take. If you decide you are a business and take some business-only deductions, the IRS could audit your return and conclude that you are an investor instead. Not only would you be denied the business-only deductions in the future, you would also have to pay back taxes and interest on any business-only deductions you took.

> **EXAMPLE:** Byron Anderson, a nurse-anesthetist, owned an 80-acre farm that he rented to a tenant farmer. He used a room in his home as a home office from which he conducted his landlord activities. He claimed a home office deduction for the room. The IRS audited Anderson and denied the deduction because it claimed his rental activities were an investment, not a business. The tax court agreed with the IRS, and Anderson lost the deduction. (*Anderson v. Comm'r,* T.C. Memo 19820576.)

Are You Profit Motivated?

It goes without saying that the primary reason most people own residential rental property is to earn a profit—that is, to make more money than they spend on the activity. But this isn't always the case. If your primary motivation for owning a rental is something other than earning a profit, your rental activity must be classified as a not-for-profit activity. This is a classification to be avoided whenever possible—it is a tax disaster.

→ **If you earn a profit from your rental activities every year (or at least most years), you can skip this section.** If you're earning a profit, you'll have no trouble showing the IRS that you are profit motivated. Indeed, under those circumstances, it's highly unlikely that the profit issue would even be brought up in an audit.

What Is a Not-for-Profit Activity?

A not-for-profit activity is something you do primarily for a reason other than earning money—for example, for recreational or charitable purposes. Activities like artwork, coin and stamp collecting, and writing typically qualify as not-for-profit activities for tax purposes. Horse and dog breeding are also frequently found to be not-for-profit activities by the IRS.

Owning rental real estate, on the other hand, is not usually a not-for-profit activity. However, there are three common situations where owning rental property could be a not-for-profit activity:

- you rent out a vacation home you or your family also use
- you rent property to others at below-market rates, or
- you allow your rental property to sit vacant for a substantial time.

Vacation Homes

If you consistently lose money on a vacation home or second home that you rent out part of the year and also live in part of the time, there's a good chance the IRS will view your home ownership as a not-for-profit activity. To overcome this, you would have to be able to show that you made real efforts to earn a profit.

EXAMPLE: Mr. and Mrs. Hilliard, both full-time physicians, purchased a rental condominium for $106,000 in beautiful Lake Tahoe. Unfortunately, their investment didn't turn out to be so beautiful—they consistently spent more on mortgage payments, maintenance, interest, taxes, and depreciation than they took in in rental income. They averaged only $711 in rental income per year over a five-year period, while their expenses averaged over $19,000. Both the IRS and tax court found that the Hilliard's vacation rental was a not-for-profit activity. (*Hilliard v. Comm'r*, 70 TCM 898.)

Renting to Relatives

Renting out property at below-market rates (or for nothing) to relatives, friends, or others can be a red flag for the IRS and courts, indicating that you lack a profit motive.

> **EXAMPLE:** Eugene Walet, a successful businessman, purchased a house in New Orleans and allowed his ex-wife and their son to live in it rent free for seven years. Walet's ex-wife had health problems and didn't work, so Walet never expected to be able to collect rent from her. Both the IRS and tax court found that Walet had purchased and maintained the house for the personal motive of helping his ex-wife and son and not to earn a profit, either from rent or appreciation. Therefore, the activity had to be classified as a not-for-profit activity for tax purposes. As a result, Walet could not deduct depreciation and repair expenses for the house. (*Walet v. Comm'r.,* 31 T.C. 461.)

! Vacation homes used as residences and below-market rentals are subject to special tax rules. Even if you have a profit motive, you could be subject to special tax rules if you or your family uses the property more than 15 days a year, or an amount equal to more than 10% of the time it's rented out. The same goes for the time you rent the property at below-market rates. These rules have much the same effect as the not-for-profit rules—you'll only be able to deduct your rental expenses against your rental income. (See Chapter 15.)

Vacant Rental Property

Allowing your rental property to stand vacant for a substantial time can also lead the IRS to conclude you lack a profit motive unless there is a good reason you've been unable to find a tenant.

> **EXAMPLE:** Gertrude Gorod lived in the upper unit of a duplex near Boston and attempted to rent out the lower unit. Although she continually advertised the unit for rent in newspapers and at supermarkets, she was unable to find a suitable renter and the unit remained vacant for ten years. The IRS audited her and found that her rental was a not-for-profit activity. Gorod objected, claiming that she wanted to rent out the unit and earn money from it, but was unable to do so because her duplex was located in a high-crime, run-

down area. The tax court agreed and found that Gorod had a profit motive in keeping the vacant rental. (*Gorod v. Comm'r.,* 42 TCM 1569.)

However, Gorod was audited by the IRS again three years later. Her rental unit was still vacant, and the IRS again found that she lacked a profit motive. Gorod appealed again, but this time she lost. The tax court noted that by this time, the unit had been vacant for over 13 years and Gorod had allowed the space to become uninhabitable and had it boarded up. Thus, the court concluded that Gorod no longer had a profit motive. (*Gorod v. Comm'r.,* 49 TCM 526.)

Tax Consequences of Not-for-Profit Rentals

If your rental activity is deemed a not-for-profit activity by the IRS, your deductions will be severely limited. Namely, you will be able to deduct only your expenses from whatever income your rental activity generates. If you have no income, you get no deductions. And you can't carry over any deductions to use in future years when you earn income—you lose them forever.

EXAMPLE: Charles, a Chicago resident, inherits a small house in Ann Arbor, Michigan. The house is old and vacant, and Charles doesn't want to go to the time and trouble of fixing it up and renting it out. Instead, he allows his unemployed brother-in-law to live in the house rent free. He spends $2,000 on taxes for the house each year. If his rental activity is classified as not-for-profit, his $2,000 in expenses may be deducted only from any income he earns from the not-for-profit activity. Because he earned no money from the house during the year, he can't deduct any of his expenses this year and he can't carry over the deduction to any future years.

Even if you have income, if your activity is considered not-for-profit, you must deduct your expenses in a way that is less advantageous (and more complicated) than regular landlord deductions. With a not-for-profit activity, you must deduct your expenses as a miscellaneous itemized deduction on IRS Schedule A (the form that you file with your Form 1040 to claim itemized deductions). This means that you must itemize your deductions instead of taking the standard deduction. You can do this only if your total deductions are greater than the standard deduction. (In 2007, the standard deduction was $5,350 for single people and married people filing separately, and $10,700 for married people filing jointly.)

If you itemize your deductions, your not-for-profit activity expenses can be used to offset your not-for-profit activity income but only to the extent that all of your expenses plus your other miscellaneous itemized deductions exceed 2% of your adjusted gross income (your total income minus business expenses and a few other expenses).

> **EXAMPLE:** In 2008, Charles decides to rent his Ann Arbor house for one weekend to football fans visiting town for the Michigan–Ohio State game (he kicks his brother-in-law out for that weekend). He earns $300 in rent, has no other income from the property for the year, and has a total of $2,000 in expenses from the property for the year. If this rental is a not-for-profit activity, his deductions for 2008 would be limited to a maximum of $300—he could not deduct the remaining $1,700 in expenses he had. Moreover, he would have to deduct the $300 as an itemized deduction. To do this, his total personal deductions for the year would have to exceed $5,350 (the standard deduction amount for single people) and his expenses plus his other miscellaneous itemized deductions would have to exceed 2% of his adjusted gross income (AGI) for the year. In contrast, if the rental was profit motivated, Charles could deduct the entire $2,000 as a rental expense on his Schedule E. The amount could be deducted from any income he earned that year, subject to the passive loss rules covered in Chapter 16.

How to Show Your Profit Motive

It's usually not difficult to show that your primary motive for owning real estate is to earn a profit. You can do this by actually earning a profit from your rental activities or acting like you want to earn a profit.

Three-of-Five Test

If you earn a profit from your rentals in three out of five consecutive years, the IRS must presume that you have a profit motive. Any legitimate profit no matter how small qualifies; you don't have to earn a particular amount or percentage. If you meet the three-of-five test, the IRS can still claim that your activity is a not-for-profit activity, but it will have to prove that you don't have a profit motive. In practice, the IRS usually doesn't attack ventures that pass the profit test unless the numbers have clearly been manipulated to meet the standard.

The presumption that you are engaged in a for-profit activity applies to your third profitable year and extends to all later years within the five-year period beginning with your first profitable year.

> **EXAMPLE:** Tom purchased a fixer-upper duplex in 2004 and rented out both units. Because Tom had to make extensive repairs to the property, the rent he collected was less than his expenses for the first two years. However, he managed to earn a profit in the next three years so he passed the three-of-five profit test.
>
> | Year | Losses | Profits |
> |------|--------|---------|
> | 2004 | $5,000 | |
> | 2005 | $2,000 | |
> | 2006 | | $2,000 |
> | 2007 | | $4,000 |
> | 2008 | | $5,000 |
>
> If the IRS audits Tom's taxes for 2008, it must presume that he was engaged in a for-profit activity during that year. Tom earned a profit during three out of the five consecutive years ending with 2008, so the presumption that Tom is not engaged in a not-for-profit activity extends to 2010, five years after his first profitable year.

The IRS doesn't have to wait for five years after you become a landlord to decide whether it is a for-profit or not-for-profit activity. It can audit you and classify your venture as a business or not-for-profit activity at any time. However, you can give yourself some breathing room by filing IRS Form 5213, which requires the IRS to postpone its determination until you've been engaged in the activity for at least five years. Although this may sound like a good idea, filing the election only alerts the IRS to the fact that you might be a good candidate to audit on the not-for-profit activity issue after five years. It also adds two years to the statute of limitations—the period in which the IRS can audit you and assess a tax deficiency. For this reason, almost no one ever files Form 5213.

Behavior Test

It is not necessary that you actually earn a profit for your rental activities to be viewed as profit motivated. Even if you consistently lose money, your rental activity is profit motivated if you entered into the activity primarily to earn profits—not to get tax deductions, help your relatives, have a place to vacation, or for some other reason not involving profit. Many people who want to earn profits from real estate rentals have negative cash flows—that is, they spend more on their rental property than they get back in rent. Indeed, IRS statistics show that of the 8.6 million tax returns filed by landlords in the year 2003, more than 4.5 million showed a loss. However, these landlords expect to eventually earn a profit either from an appreciation in the value of the real estate, an increase in rent, a decrease in expenses, or some combination of these.

How does the IRS figure out whether you really want to earn a profit? IRS auditors can't read your mind to establish your motives, and they certainly aren't going to take your word for it. Instead, the IRS looks at the following "objective" factors to determine whether you are behaving like a person who wants to earn a profit. You don't have to satisfy all of these factors to pass the test. The first three listed below (acting like a business, expertise, and time and effort expended) are the most important by far. Studies demonstrate that taxpayers who meet these three factors are always found to be profit motivated, regardless of how they do on the rest of the criteria.

- **How the activity is carried on.** Among other things, acting like a business means you keep good books and other records and carry on your rental activities in a professional manner.
- **Your expertise.** People who are trying to make money usually have some knowledge and skill in the field of their endeavor.
- **The time and effort you spend.** People who want to make profits work regularly and continuously. You don't have to work full-time, but you must work regularly.
- **Your track record.** Having a track record of success in other businesses— whether or not they are related to your landlord activities—helps show that you are trying to make money in your most recent venture.
- **Your history of income and losses.** Even if you can't satisfy the profit test described above, earning a profit in at least some years helps show that you have a profit motive.
- **Your profits.** Earning a substantial profit, even after years of losses, can help show that you are trying to make a go of it. On the other hand,

earning only small or occasional yearly profits when you have years of large losses and/or a large investment in the activity tends to show that you aren't in it for the money.

- **Appreciation.** Your profit includes money you make through the appreciation (increase in value) of your business assets. For a landlord, this primarily includes the increase in value of the rental properties that are owned. Even if you don't make any profit from your day-to-day rental operations, you can still show a profit motive if you stand to earn substantial profits when you sell your real estate.

- **Your personal wealth.** The IRS figures that you probably have a profit motive if you don't have substantial income from other sources. After all, you'll need to earn money from your venture to survive. On the other hand, the IRS may be suspicious if you have substantial income from other sources (particularly if the losses from your real estate venture generate substantial tax deductions).

- **Elements of fun or recreation.** You'll have a harder time convincing the IRS that you're profit motivated if your rental activity involves fun or recreation. For example, a person who owns a rental unit at a resort and spends substantial time vacationing there, will have a hard time claiming he is profit motivated (assuming no profits are earned on the rental).

EXAMPLE: Recall Mr. and Mrs. Hilliard, the doctor couple that purchased a rental condominium in Lake Tahoe. They averaged only $711 in rental income per year over a five-year period, while their expenses averaged over $19,000. Naturally, they wanted to deduct their losses from their other income, which was substantial; together, the Hilliards earned more than $250,000 per year from their medical practices. The IRS claimed that the Hilliards were not entitled to deduct their rental losses from their nonrental income because their rental activity was not profit motivated. They appealed to the tax court and lost. The court went through all the factors listed above, and found they lacked a profit motive.

Among other things, the court found that they did not carry on their rental activity in a businesslike manner—their only attempt to advertise their rental's availability was posting flyers at the hospitals where they practiced medicine, they had no business plan, and they didn't maintain separate books and records or bank accounts for the property. The court also found that their use and circumstances indicated that they bought the condo to obtain tax benefits (deductions to offset their income) and have a vacation home, not to earn rental income.

Because the Hilliard's rental was a not-for-profit activity, their annual deduction for their losses was limited to their annual rental income—that is, they could deduct only about $700 per year. (*Hilliard v. Comm'r.,* 70 TCM 898.)

How to Pass the Behavior Test

If you continually lose money on your rentals, particularly if you rent them out at below-market rates or keep them vacant, you should take steps to ensure that the IRS will not claim that you lack a profit motive in the event you're audited.

- **Keep good business records.** Keeping good records of your expenses and income from your activity is the single most important thing you can do to show that you want to earn a profit. Lack of records shows that you don't really care whether you make money or not. You don't need an elaborate set of books; a simple record of your expenses and income will usually suffice. (See Chapter 17 for a detailed discussion of record keeping.)

- **Keep a separate checking account.** Open up a separate checking account for your rental activity. This will help you keep your personal and rental expenses separate—another factor that shows you want to make money.

- **Keep track of the time you spend.** It is not necessary that you work full-time at being a landlord in order to have a profit motive. However, the more time you spend at being a landlord, the more it will look like you want to earn a profit. Keep track of your time. This will also be necessary if you want to avoid application of the restrictive rules on deducting real estate losses (see Chapter 16).

- **Make efforts to rent your property.** Letting a property stand vacant without making any efforts to find a renter tends to show you don't care about earning a profit. If your property is vacant, try to find renters by advertising and listing it with rental services. Keep records of your efforts.

- **Establish your expertise.** If you lack a solid background in owning and managing rental property, make up for it by attending educational seminars and other programs—for example, educational events sponsored by your local apartment owners association.

- **Show you expect your property to appreciate in value.** Real estate appreciation is often the pot of gold at the end of the landlord rainbow.

The fact that you expect your property to substantially increase in value in the future is strong evidence you want to earn a profit, even if you are incurring losses right now. You can show the IRS that you expect your property to appreciate in value because (1) you've owned similar properties that have gone up in value, (2) similar properties in the area have appreciated, and (3) the property has, in fact, gone up in value since you bought it.

- **Prepare a business plan showing how much money you expect to earn or lose over the next several years.** This is a projection of how much money your rental activity will bring in, your expenses, and how much profit you expect to make (or losses you'll incur). The forecast should cover at least the next five or ten years. It should show you earning a profit sometime in the future (although it doesn't have to be within five years). This profit can result from anticipated increases in your rents, decreases in expenses, appreciation in the value of your property, or some combination of all three. You can prepare such projections yourself (special software is available for this purpose), or you can have an accountant or real estate professional create one for you.

What If You Make a Bad Investment?

What if you went into rental property ownership to make money, but your investment turned out badly? Fortunately, the IRS recognizes that owning rental property can end up being a bad investment, but still be profit motivated. IRS regulations provide that a taxpayer may be deemed to be profit motivated, even if his or her property is not currently productive and "there is no likelihood that the property will be sold at a profit or will otherwise be productive of income; and even though the property is held merely to minimize a loss." (IRS Reg. Sec. 1.212-1(b).) Thus, you can be profit motivated even if your rental property doesn't produce any current income. For example, an owner of a vacant rental might want to earn a profit, but be prevented from doing so by a bad rental market or other circumstances beyond his or her control.

Real Estate Dealers

Some people who own rental real estate are not primarily interested in earning money from collecting rents or the long-term appreciation of their property. Instead, they try to earn profits from buying and selling real estate. The IRS calls these people real estate dealers. They have a special tax status, which is usually not advantageous. Indeed, most people who buy real estate try to avoid dealer status like the plague.

What Is a Real Estate Dealer?

A real estate dealer is someone who is in the business of owning property primarily for the purpose of reselling it. A dealer buys property and resells it, usually at a price higher than the purchase price, and normally after only a short holding period.

A real estate dealer resembles a merchant or retailer of goods, except that his or her product is real estate. For example, a merchant in the business of selling computers typically purchases numerous computers each year—not for his own use or to rent out to users—but to resell as quickly as possible to customers at a profit. Likewise, a real estate dealer buys real property to resell at a profit to customers. A real estate dealer's holdings are inventory for sale to customers, the same as any merchant's inventory.

Real estate dealers typically include (but are not limited to):

- real estate speculators who buy and sell many properties each year
- subdividers who buy large tracts of vacant land, divide them into smaller lots, and then resell the lots piecemeal
- real estate developers and home builders who construct new houses and resell them soon after completion, and
- people in the business of converting apartment buildings into condominiums for resale.

Determining If You Are a Dealer

An owner of residential rental property can be classified as a dealer. The IRS and courts look at the following factors to determine if a person holds property as a dealer. The first three factors are the most important.

The Number and Frequency of Sales

Numerous and continuous sales over an extended time period are the hallmark of a real estate dealer. Indeed, this factor alone is often enough to make a person a property dealer. On the other hand, someone who sells property infrequently is less likely to be a dealer, particularly if a sale is due to changed circumstances or results from an unsolicited offer.

There is no set number of sales required to make a person a dealer. As the following chart shows, courts have been inconsistent in deciding how many sales make you a dealer. However, if you only sell one or two properties in a year, it's not likely you'll be classified as a dealer, and it's possible you could sell substantially more and still avoid dealer status.

Dealer Versus Nondealer Status: Number of Sales	
Dealer	**Nondealer**
26 lots sold over 5 years (*Harris v. Comm'r.*, 47 TCM 760 (1983))	10 properties sold in two years (*Jenkins v. Comm'r.*, 29 TC 240 (1970))
39 sales over 7 years (*Norris v. Comm'r.*, T.C. Memo 1986-151)	22 sales over three years (*Byram v. Comm'r.*, 705 F.2d 1418 (9th Cir. 1983))
71 properties sold in 3 years (*Sottong v. Comm'r.*, 25 TCM 1366 (1966))	28 lots sold over 3 years (*Brodnax v. Comm'r.*, 29 TCM 733 (1970))
244 sales over 32 years (*Biedenharn Realty Co. v. United States*, 526 F.2d 409 (5th Cir. 1976))	45 sales over 7 years. (*Williams v. Comm'r.*, 53 AFTR2d 84-844)

Intent for Buying Property

A real estate dealer buys properties with the intent of making money from reselling them. A person who buys property to earn income and/or benefit from long-term appreciation is not a dealer. However, the fact that you buy a rental property with the idea that you will eventually resell it does not automatically make you a real estate dealer. A dealer is a person who is in the business of buying and selling properties. Buying a single, or even a few, properties to resell does not mean you are in the resale business.

Some real estate purchasers attempt to establish their intent to hold the property as an investment by adding a clause to that effect in their purchase agreement. Such a clause is unlikely to be much of help in establishing you are not a dealer; on the other hand, it can't hurt. Keep in mind that your intent can change—for example, you could purchase a rental property for quick resale and then change your mind and decide to hold on to it long-term for the rental income.

Extent of Improvements

Dealers often improve the property they own to increase its value for purposes of resale. Flipping is the practice of buying a run-down property, fixing it up, and then quickly reselling it at a profit. A person who frequently flips property would likely be a dealer.

Other Factors That Point to Dealership

The IRS uses additional factors when deciding whether a person's activities amount to those of a real estate dealer. They include:

Sales efforts. Dealers make extensive efforts to resell their properties—for example, they hire real estate brokers, list their property for sale, engage in advertising, and may have their own sales office and sales staff. A person who engages in extensive marketing efforts is more likely to be considered a dealer than one who takes a passive sales approach.

How the property is acquired. Dealers go out and buy properties themselves. A person who acquires real property through an inheritance or gift is not likely to be viewed as a dealer.

Holding period. Like any merchant, real estate dealers want to sell their inventory as quickly as possible. People who hold on to real property for a long time before selling it are much less likely to be considered dealers than those who hold their properties for a short time.

Income generated by sales. A person is more likely to be viewed as a dealer if the income generated from selling real estate constitutes a substantial amount of the total income he or she earns.

Continuous effort. Dealers work continuously throughout the year to sell their properties and spend substantial time at their business. A person whose sales transactions are only intermittent is not likely to be a dealer.

Facilities. Real estate dealers often have outside offices or other facilities to help them conduct their frequent real estate sales. They are often licensed real estate brokers and associated with real estate sales companies. However, not all licensed brokers are dealers; this is just one factor that is considered.

A landlord who owns rental property primarily to earn income from rents and/or long-term appreciation is not a dealer. This is so even though a landlord ultimately sells his or her property. This includes the great majority of landlords.

EXAMPLE: Randolph Rouse purchased about 40 rental houses in a Washington, D.C., suburb and owned them for over two years, during which time he earned income from the rents. When he first purchased the homes, rentals were in great demand in the area and he had no trouble finding good tenants. However, these conditions began to change and it became more and more difficult to obtain desirable tenants. Some of Rouse's rental houses stood vacant for several months at a time and in some instances the rent had to be reduced. Whenever Rouse was unable to rent a house within a reasonable time, he would offer it for sale. Prospective purchasers were often referred to him by real estate agents who had seen his For Rent sign on vacant houses. He ended up selling all his houses over a four-year period, and didn't purchase any other rental houses. The court held that he was not a real estate dealer because he purchased the houses to earn rental income, not to profit from resales. (*Rouse v. Comm'r.,* 36 T.C. 70.)

Even if you are a real estate dealer, you can still own nondealer property (also called investment property). Whether you are a dealer is determined on a property-by-property basis. You can own some property for sale as a dealer, and other property as a long-term investment.

EXAMPLE: Peter Miller, a real estate broker, purchased an apartment building and sold it two years later for a substantial profit. At the same time, he worked as a dealer in real estate: He was involved in several real estate sales businesses, including subdividing land for resale and home building. Nevertheless, the tax court found that the apartment building was not dealer property. Miller owned the apartment building primarily to earn rental income, not for resale. (*Miller v. Comm'r.,* 20 B.T.A. 230.)

However, the mere fact that you rent a property does not by itself make it investment property. Many dealers rent out property they have up for sale, but earning income from rentals is not the primary reason they own the property. Their rental income is simply icing on the cake—the cake itself consists of the profits they earn from their sales.

If you are a real estate dealer who also owns investment property, be sure to keep the two types of property separate. Keep separate records for your investment property. If possible, establish a separate business entity for your dealer activities and purchase your investment property as an individual in your own name, not through your business.

Tax Consequences of Being a Dealer

Being classified as a dealer is usually not advantageous taxwise, particularly where real property is sold for a substantial gain. Indeed, it can often be disastrous. For this reason, there have been many legal disputes over whether a real estate seller should be classified as a dealer.

Real estate dealer classification has the following important tax consequences:

- **Ordinary income or loss treatment.** Gains and losses from sales of real property by a dealer are subject to ordinary income tax rates. In contrast, gains realized by a nondealer are usually taxed at capital gains rates, which are lower. However, dealers are better off if real estate proves to be a money-losing proposition, because a dealer is typically permitted to deduct the full amount of a loss, while an investor's deductions for losses may be strictly limited.

- **No depreciation.** Real estate dealers may not take a deduction for depreciation of their property.

- **No tax-free exchanges.** Taxpayers who are not real estate dealers may take advantage of a special provision of the tax law that allows them to exchange their property for other similar property without having to pay any income tax. Real estate dealers cannot use tax-free exchanges.

- **No installment sales.** Real estate dealers are also barred from using installment sales. This is where the purchase price for real estate is paid over several years, with the taxes due being paid by the seller over the same period as the payments are made, instead in one lump sum in the year of sale.

- **Self-employment tax due.** Since they sell real estate as a business, real estate dealers must pay self-employment taxes on their profits. Real estate investors and businesspeople who are not dealers do not have to pay such taxes. (See Chapter 12.)

- **Schedule C must be filed.** Real estate dealers who are sole proprietors file IRS Schedule C, Profit or Loss From Business, to report their income and expenses from real estate sales. However, they file Schedule E to report their income and expenses from real estate they own as an investment.

Chapter 3

Deducting Your Operating Expenses

Thishis chapter covers the basic rules for deducting operating expenses you incur from your residential rental activities. These are the bread and butter expenses virtually every landlord has for things like repairs, management fees, and advertising.

Requirements for Deducting Operating Expenses

There are so many different kinds of operating expenses that the tax code couldn't possibly list them all. Instead, the code gives you the definition of an operating expense, and it's up to you to make sure the expenditures you deduct meet the requirements. If they do, they will qualify as deductible operating expenses. To qualify, the expense must be:

- ordinary and necessary
- current
- directly related to your rental activity, and
- reasonable in amount. (I.R.C. § 162.)

Ordinary and Necessary

The first requirement is that the expense must be ordinary and necessary. This means that the expense is common, "helpful and appropriate" for your activity. (*Welch v. Helvering*, 290 U.S.111 (1933).) The expense doesn't have to be indispensable to be necessary; it need only help your rental activity in some way—even if it's minor. A one-time expenditure can be ordinary and necessary.

It's usually fairly easy to figure out whether an expense passes the ordinary and necessary test. Many of the most common types of landlord operating expenses are listed on IRS Schedule E, including:

- advertising your rental units in newspapers or on the Internet
- auto and travel expenses incurred by you or your staff
- cleaning and maintenance
- commissions you pay to rental brokers, if you use them
- insurance, such as property and commercial general liability insurance, and part of your automobile insurance if you use your car for rental activities
- legal and other professional fees, such as accounting fees
- management fees, should you decide to hire a management company to handle day-to-day operations
- mortgage interest paid to banks or other financial institutions

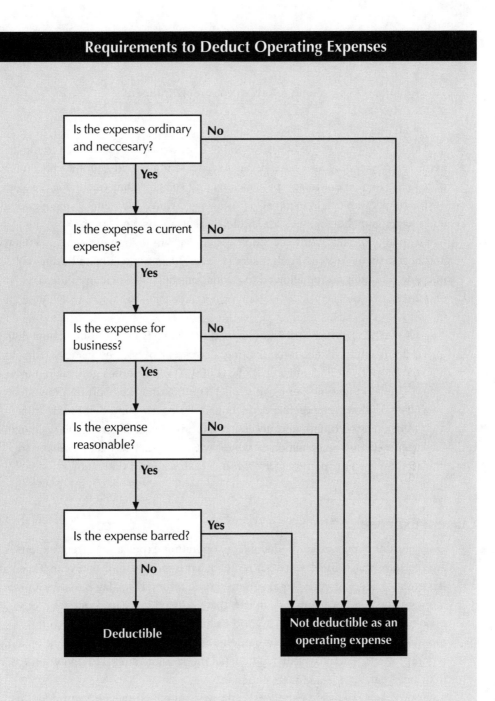

Requirements to Deduct Operating Expenses

- other interest expenses, such as interest on a credit card you use to buy items for your rental activity
- repairs
- supplies to clean and refurbish your rental property
- taxes, and
- utilities.

This list created by the IRS is by no means exhaustive. In addition to the items listed, you may also have deductible operating expenses for such things as office rent, equipment rental, publications and subscriptions (including the cost of this book!), education expenses, postage, software, payments to independent contractors, membership fees for landlord associations, and so on.

Generally, the IRS won't second-guess your claim that an expense is ordinary and necessary, unless the item or service clearly has no legitimate business purpose. You will not be allowed to deduct off-the-wall or clearly ridiculous expenses.

EXAMPLE: Rayford Strickland owned two parcels of real estate about 500 miles from his Texas home. During a two-year period, he made 80 trips to the property at a claimed cost of $11,000. The properties generated a total of $1,653 in income during this time. The IRS and tax court disallowed Strickland's travel expense deductions. The court found that the 80 trips were not an ordinary and necessary expense because Strickland was unable to provide any explanation of why it was necessary to make so many trips to these two properties. (*Strickland v. Comm'r*, 43 T.C.M. 1061.)

Current Expense

Only current expenses are deductible as operating expenses. Current expenses are for items that will benefit your rental activity for less than one year. These are the costs of keeping your rental venture going on a day-to-day basis, including money you spend on items or services that get used up, wear out, or become obsolete in less than one year. A good example of a current expense is the monthly fee a landlord pays to a gardener to perform landscaping work on a rental property. Each monthly fee benefits the landlord's rental activity for less than one year, so it is a current expense.

You deduct operating expenses in the year in which they're incurred—this helps your bottom line. Not everything you buy for your rental activity qualifies as a current expense. Anything you purchase that will benefit your rental activity for more than one year is a capital, not a current, expense. For example, if a landlord purchases a lawn mower to use for his rental properties, the purchase would be a capital expense (not a current expense) because the lawn mower will benefit the rental activity for more than one year. In contrast to current expenses, capital expenses may only be deducted a little at a time over many years. This process is known as depreciation.

Repairs to real property are current expenses that may be deducted in a single year. For example, the cost of buying a replacement part for a water heater in a rental unit is a repair that can be currently deducted. However, improvements to real property that extend the property's useful life or make it more valuable must be depreciated. Thus, the cost of purchasing a brand new water heater for a rental unit would be a capital expense that would have to be depreciated over several years. It is sometimes difficult to tell the difference between a deductible repair and depreciable improvement. This important issue is covered in detail in Chapter 5.

Business-Related

An expenditure must be *directly related to your rental activity* to be deductible as an operating expense. This means that you cannot deduct personal expenses. For example, the cost of a personal computer is a deductible operating expense only if you use the computer for your rental activities; it is not deductible if you use it to pay personal bills or play computer games.

Allocating Business and Personal Use

If you buy something for both personal and landlord use, you can deduct only the business portion of the expense. You must figure out how much of the time you used the item for landlord purposes and how much for personal purposes. You then allocate the total cost between the two purposes, and deduct only the landlord portion of the cost.

> **EXAMPLE:** Sam rents a personal computer for $100 per month. He uses it five hours a week for his rental activities and 15 hours for personal use. Therefore, he uses it 25% of the time for landlord purposes and 75% for personal reasons. He may deduct only 25% of the cost of the computer, or $25 per month, as an operating expense.

The same allocation rule applies when you rent out part of a house that you live in.

> **EXAMPLE:** Sheila owns a three-bedroom house that she uses as her residence. She rents out one of the bedrooms, which represents 15% of the total house. Her tenant pays her $300 per month rent and Sheila pays for the utilities for the whole house. Sheila may deduct 15% of the cost of utilities and maintenance for the whole house as a landlord operating expense. She could deduct 100% of the cost of any expense incurred just for the rented bedroom—for example, the cost of repainting the bedroom.

Special allocation rules apply when you rent out your entire residence, or a vacation or second home. These are discussed in detail in Chapter 15.

Stricter Rules for Certain Expenses

Many expenses have both a personal and a business component, which can make it difficult to tell if an expense is business related. For example, what if a landlord drives to the hardware store and buys one item for his rental property and another for his personal residence? Should he be allowed to deduct all, part, or none of the cost of driving to the hardware store?

The IRS has created rules and regulations for some operating expenses that commonly involve a crossover of personal and business use. Some of these rules lay out guidelines to help you figure out when an expense is and isn't deductible. Others impose record-keeping and other requirements to prevent abuses by dishonest taxpayers. Much of the complexity in determining whether an expense is deductible as a business operating expense involves understanding and applying these special rules and regulations.

The expenses that present the most common problems (and are, therefore, subject to the most comprehensive IRS rules and regulation) include:

- home office expenses (see Chapter 9)
- meals and entertainment (see Chapter 14)
- travel (see Chapter 11)
- car and truck expenses (see Chapter 10)
- business gifts (see Chapter 14)
- bad debts (see Chapter 14)
- employee benefits (see Chapter 12)
- interest payments (see Chapter 7)

- casualty losses (see Chapter 13)
- taxes (see Chapter 14), and
- education expenses (see Chapter 14).

Landlord's Personal Labor Not Deductible

A landlord may never deduct the value of his or her own time and personal labor working on rental activities. For example, a landlord who spends 50 hours repainting an apartment building gets no deduction for the value of his time. He may only deduct the cost of the paint, brushes, and other materials he uses. This rule prevents the kind of abuse the IRS fears would happen if personal labor were deductible.

Landlords may deduct labor costs only when they hire other people to do the work and pay them for it. The labor can be performed by an employee or independent contractor (nonemployee), or even a member of the landlord's family. (See Chapter 12.)

However, this doesn't mean landlords should never do any work on their rental properties themselves. Although your personal labor is not deductible, you'll still save money by doing the work yourself because only a part of the money you deduct for labor costs ends up as a tax savings. (See Chapter 12.)

Reasonable in Amount

Subject to some important exceptions, there is no limit on how much you can deduct, as long as the amount is reasonable and you don't deduct more than you spend. As a rule of thumb, an expense is reasonable unless there are more economical and practical ways to achieve the same result. If the IRS finds that your deductions are unreasonably large, it will disallow them or at least disallow the portion it finds unreasonable.

Certain areas are hot buttons for the IRS—especially entertainment, travel, and meal expenses. The IRS won't allow any lavish expenses here, and you will have to follow strict rules requiring you to fully document these deductions (see Chapters 11 and 14). The reasonableness issue also comes up when a business pays excessive salaries to employees to obtain a large tax deduction. For example, a landlord might hire his 14-year-old son to do yard work for his rental units and pay him $50 an hour—clearly an excessive wage for this type of work.

For a few types of operating expenses, the IRS limits how much you can deduct. These include:

- the home office deduction, which is limited to the profit from your business (although you can carry over and deduct any excess amount in future years) (see Chapter 9)
- business meals and entertainment, which are only 50% deductible (see Chapter 14)
- travel expenses, which are limited depending on the length of your trip and the time you spend on business while away (see Chapter 11), and
- business gifts, which are subject to a $25 maximum deduction per individual per year (see Chapter 14).

Operating Expenses That Are Not Deductible

Even though they might be ordinary and necessary, some types of operating expenses are not deductible under any circumstances. In some cases, this is because Congress has declared that it would be morally wrong or otherwise contrary to sound public policy to allow people to deduct these costs. In other cases, Congress simply doesn't want to allow the deduction. These nondeductible expenses include:

- fines and penalties paid to the government for violation of any law—for example, tax penalties, parking tickets, or fines for violating city housing codes (I.R.C. § 162(f))
- illegal bribes or kickbacks to private parties or government officials (I.R.C. § 162(c))
- lobbying expenses or political contributions; however, a landlord may deduct up to $2,000 per year in expenses to influence local legislation (state, county, or city), not including the expense of hiring a professional lobbyist (such lobbyist expenses are not deductible)
- two-thirds of any damages paid for violation of the federal antitrust laws (I.R.C. § 162(g)) (other court judgments and legal settlements arising from business activities are ordinarily fully deductible operating expenses)
- real estate examination or licensing fees, or other professional examination fees (see Chapter 8)
- charitable donations by any business other than a C corporation (these donations are deductible only as personal expenses; see Chapter 14)
- country club, social club, or athletic club dues
- federal income taxes you pay on your rental income (see Chapter 14), and
- certain interest payments (see Chapter 7).

A Deductible Day in the Life of a Landlord

Gina is a full-time suburban mom who rents out a duplex she owns across town. One day, she drives to the local home improvement store to buy a replacement part for the stove in one of her rental units, which is currently vacant. She then drives to her duplex where she meets Tom, a handyman, who she pays $100 to repair the stove. She returns home and goes to her home office, which she uses exclusively for her rental business. There, she composes an advertisement for her vacant rental and emails it to her local newspaper (she pays for the ad online, too). Later that day, the maid comes to clean the house, including Gina's home office (which takes up 20% of her home). After dinner, she returns to her home office where she pays her monthly bills for her duplex, including mortgage interest, water, electricity for the vacant unit, and garbage pick-up.

Here are Gina's tax deductions for rental operating expenses:

Activity	Type of Business Expense	Amount of Business Expense	
Driving to buy part for stove	Business transportation	5 miles at 48.5 cents per mile	$ 2.43
Buying part for stove	Repair		50.00
Driving to rental unit	Business transportation	7 miles at 48.5 cents per mile	3.40
Paying Tom, the handyman, to repair stove	Repair		100.00
Paying mortgage interest	Interest		1,000.00
Paying water, electricity, and garbage bills	Utilities		100.00
Cleaning home office	Home office	20% of $75 house-cleaning fee	15.00
Total Deductions			$ 1,270.83

As this example shows, you should get into the habit of looking for possible operating expense deductions whenever you spend money on anything related to your rental activities.

Chapter 4

Repairs

Repair expenses are among the most valuable deductions landlords have. However, many landlords are surprised to discover that some of the changes they make to their property are not repairs at all; instead, they are improvements that must be deducted much more slowly than repairs. This chapter shows you how to tell the difference between a repair and an improvement, and how to deduct as quickly as possible the expenses you incur to maintain your property.

Repair Versus Improvement

Provided they are ordinary, necessary, and reasonable in amount, repairs to your rental property are operating expenses that are fully deductible in the year in which they are incurred. However, not all upkeep constitutes a repair for tax purposes. Some changes landlords make to their rental property are capital improvements. Unlike repairs, improvements cannot be deducted in a single year. Instead, their cost must be depreciated over several years. Improvements to residential rental property must be depreciated over an especially long period— 27.5 years.

You don't need to understand depreciation to learn about deducting repairs. All you need to know is that you are usually better off taxwise if you can characterize an expense as a repair instead of an improvement. If it's a repair, you can deduct the whole cost in a single year instead of having to deduct a little at a time over many years. In simple terms, when it comes to taxes, repairs are good and improvements are bad.

How to Tell the Difference

How do you tell the difference between a repair and an improvement? Here's the basic rule from the IRS: A repair keeps your rental property in good operating condition, but it does *not*:

- materially add to the value of your property
- substantially prolong its useful life, or
- make it more useful. (Reg. § 1.162-4.)

In contrast, an improvement adds to the value of your property, prolongs its life, or adapts it to new uses.

The problem with this definition is that virtually all repairs increase both the value and useful life of the property being repaired. The key difference between a repair and an improvement is that *a repair merely returns property to more or less the state it was in before it stopped working properly*. The property is not substantially more valuable, long-lived, or useful than it was before the need for the repair arose. In contrast, an improvement makes property *substantially* more valuable and/or long-lived or useful than it was before the improvement.

To determine whether you're dealing with a repair or an improvement, you need to compare the situation before and after you made the expenditure involved. Have you just returned your rental property to the state it was in before the need for the repair arose? Or, have you made it much better? If the answer to the first question is "yes," you've done a repair. If the answer to the second question is "yes," you've paid for an improvement.

> **EXAMPLE:** Sally discovers a leak in the roof of her small apartment building. She pays a roofing contractor $1,000 to fix the leak. Sally has paid for a repair because she is simply returning the property to the same state it was in before the leak. She's out $1,000, but at least the repair is a currently deductible operating expense that she may deduct in full from her taxes for the year. This may reduce her income tax bill by as much as $300 or $400 depending on her tax bracket.

The cost of fixing a leaky roof is a repair because the roof is in the same condition, more or less, as it was in before it began leaking. As a result of the work, the roof may be stronger than it was and it may last a little longer—and therefore be somewhat more valuable. But this increase in value and life is not substantial enough to make the expense an improvement.

On the other hand, if you install a new roof in an apartment building, you've paid for an improvement. A building with a brand new roof is substantially more valuable and long-lived than one with an old roof.

> **EXAMPLE:** The roofing contractor tells Sally she has two options for fixing the leaky roof of her apartment building: She can have the leaking portion of the roof patched for $1,000, or she can have an entirely new roof installed for $10,000. Sally elects to have a new roof installed. This $10,000 expense is an improvement that she will have to depreciate over 27.5 years. She'll only be able to deduct $364 of the cost each year (but her deductions for the first and last year will be somewhat smaller).

Other examples of repairs include repainting your property, fixing gutters or floors, fixing leaks, plastering, and replacing broken windows. Examples of improvements include adding a deck to a rental unit, installing a new heating system, or installing a new foundation. The chart below lists some examples of repairs versus improvements.

Repairs vs. Improvements		
	Repair	**Improvement**
Roofing	Roof shingles that were blown off a barn during a storm were replaced. (*Pontel Family Estate v. Comm'r.*, T.C. Memo 1981-303.)	Landlord completely recovered wooden shingle roof on rental house with new and better composition shingles. (*Craig v. Comm'r.*, 7 TCM 432.)
Walls	Two exterior brick walls of a bank building were sandblasted to remove dirt, and old mortar was patched where it had decayed. (*City Nat. Bank v. Comm'r.*, 11 TCM 411.)	50-foot-wide brick wall of office building that had cracked was torn out and replaced with new brick wall. (*Stewart Supply Co. v. Comm'r.*, 22 TCM 246.)
Windows	Steel window sash in factory building was straightened and repainted, and old concrete window sills replaced. Court found building was merely restored to its original condition. (*Buckland v. U.S.*, 66 F. Supp. 681(D.CT 1946).)	New, larger, ventilating windows were installed in a garage building. (*Wright v. Comm'r.*, 12 B.T.A. 1149.)
Building Interior	Landlord replaced only worn sections of carpet in rental units. (*Beck v. Comm'r.*, T.C. Memo 1994-122.)	Landlord installed new carpets and drapes in rental unit. (*Otis v. Comm'r.*, 73 T.C. 671.)
Electrical	Temporary electrical wiring was installed in temporary factory building used less than one year. (*Buedingen v. Comm'r.*, 6 B.T.A. 335.)	Electrical system permanently replaced in an office building. (*Harris v. Comm'r.*, 55 T.C.M 769.)

Repairs vs. Improvements (continued)		
	Repair	**Improvement**
Flooring	Small portions of rotted wooden flooring in a dairy building were replaced. The work helped prevent the building from collapsing, but did not improve it or extend its useful life. (*Farmers Creamery Corp. v. Comm'r.*, 14 TC 879.)	Wooden floors of barn were replaced with cement floors. (*Best v. Comm'r.*, 13 TCM 948.)
Foundations	Office building foundation piles that suffered dry rot when water level in Chicago River unexpectedly receded were shored up with concrete supports. (*Illinois Merchants Trust Co. v. Comm'r.*, 4 B.T.A. 103.)	Office building foundation extended 10 feet further below ground to strengthen building for addition of new stories. (*Crocker First Nat'l. Bank v. Comm'r.*, 59 F.2d 37 (9th Cir. 1932).)
Outside	Asphalt parking lot that had subsided was resurfaced with the same material. Parking lot was only restored to its original condition. (*Toledo Home Federal S&L Assoc. v. U.S.*, 203 F.Supp. 491 (ND OH 1962).)	Gravel driveway replaced with concrete driveway. (*Jones v. Comm'r.*, 25 TC 1100.)

As a general rule, repairs cost less than improvements. Nevertheless, repairs can be quite expensive. In one case, a farmer was permitted to deduct as a repair the $50,000 it cost to fix a leaky earthen dam. The court figured the dam was in no better shape after the work was done than it was before it began to leak, so the work was a repair. (*Evans v. Comm'r.*, 557 F.2d 1095 (5th Cir. 1977).)

Maintenance Versus Repairs

Maintenance is not the same thing as repairs. Maintenance is undertaken to prevent something from breaking down. A repair is done after a breakdown has occurred. For example, the cost of oiling the circulator pump in a hot water heater is maintenance; the cost of fixing an unlubricated pump that has failed is a repair. There is no practical tax difference between maintenance and repairs—they are both currently deductible operating expenses. However, because IRS Schedule E requires that you separately list what you spent for each category, you must keep track of these expenditures separately.

Replacing Appliances

Replacing appliances and similar personal property items in a rental unit is considered an improvement. This is true even though providing a rental unit with a new refrigerator, stove, dishwasher, air conditioner, or water heater may not make it substantially more valuable.

Complying With Government Regulations

If you change a rental property to comply with government regulations, such as bringing the building up to building codes or health codes, you have improved the property, as far as the IRS is concerned. This is true even if a government agency forces you to make the change. In one case, for example, the city building commissioner required a landlord to shore up his property by installing steel rods in the walls and new roof beams. The expenses were an improvement, not a repair, even though they were forced on the landlord by a government agency. (*Boland v. Comm'r.*, 19 TCM 1030.)

Tax Break for Disabled and Elderly Accessibility Changes

A special tax law provision allows businesses (including landlords) to currently deduct up to $15,000 of the cost of making their buildings or other facilities— such as roads, walks, and parking lots—accessible to the elderly or disabled. (IRC Sec. 190.) These changes would ordinarily constitute improvements for tax purposes that would have to be depreciated over many years. This tax break is intended to encourage landlords and other business owners to make their facilities more accessible to the disabled and elderly. You may take this deduction whether or not the improvements you make are required by law.

The most you can deduct as a cost of removing barriers to the disabled and the elderly for any tax year is $15,000. However, you can add any costs over this limit to the basis of the property and depreciate them.

To qualify for the deduction, your renovations must comply with applicable accessibility standards. Detailed standards are set forth in the ADA Accessibility Guidelines, which can be found on the Internet at www.access-board.gov/adaag/html/adaag.htm. IRS Publication 535, *Business Expenses*, also contains a summary of these standards.

You may claim the deduction on your income tax return for the tax year you paid for the work, or the year you incurred the expenses. Identify the deduction as a separate item. The choice applies to all of the qualifying costs you have during the year, up to the $15,000 limit. You must maintain adequate records to support your deduction—keep your receipts.

> **EXAMPLE:** Jason owns an 80-year-old apartment building that is not wheelchair accessible. He installs four wheelchair ramps at a cost of $5,000. Ordinarily, this would be an improvement that Jason would have to depreciate. But due to the special rule, he may deduct the entire $5,000 in one year.

Environmental Cleanup Costs

It is depressingly common for landlords to discover that their property contains environmental hazards, such as lead paint, that may endanger the health of their tenants and others who visit the property. Landlords can be held legally liable for such hazards and be subjected to expensive lawsuits by injured tenants. Any decent landlord will seek to clean up ("remediate") such hazards on his or her property. Environmental remediation can be very expensive. Obviously, it would be very helpful if a landlord could currently deduct the expense as a repair. Unfortunately, the IRS often considers such expenses to be improvements that must be depreciated over 27.5 years.

Hazards That Occur After You Acquire the Building

You're in the best position if the environmental hazard occurs after you purchase or otherwise acquire the building. Property owners may currently deduct as a repair the cost of environmental remediation if:

- the property was in clean condition when it was acquired
- it became contaminated during the course of the property owner's ordinary business operations
- the cleanup restores the property to its precontamination state, and
- the cleanup does not allow the owner to put the property to a new or different use. (*United Dairy Farmers, Inc. v. United States*, 267 F.3d 510 (6th Cir. 2001).)

EXAMPLE: A company acquired a large nursing home that was free of mold when they purchased it. However, one wing of the building later developed a severe mold problem due to roof leaks. To eliminate the mold, the property owner replaced 70% of the wall and ceiling drywall in the wing; it also removed and replaced doors, faucets, sinks, and most of the electrical fixtures. All of the old doors and sinks and most of the electrical fixtures were decontaminated and reused. The IRS ruled that the cost was a currently deductible repair, not an improvement, because the project was to restore the building to the same physical condition that existed before the onset of mold. The new materials used were of substantially similar quality as the materials that were replaced. The existing floor plan was not altered, and no structural components were repaired or replaced. The project did not substantially prolong the building's useful life, add to its value, or adapt it to a new use. Instead, it merely kept the building in efficient operating condition. (IRS Private Letter Ruling 200607003 (2006).)

Preexisting Hazards

Environmental hazards can be present before a landlord purchases a building— for example, a landlord purchases a building that was painted with lead paint or contains asbestos. This is particularly common where the building is over 25 years old.

Historically, the IRS had held that remediation of such preexisting environmental hazards is an improvement that must be depreciated. The rationale for this rule was that the remediation does not restore the property to its original

The Foul Four: Lead, Asbestos, Radon, and Mold

The big four environmental hazards in rental properties are lead paint, asbestos, radon, and mold.

Lead paint. Because of the health problems caused by lead poisoning, the Residential Lead-Based Paint Hazard Reduction Act was enacted in 1992. This law is commonly known as Title X (ten). Environmental Protection Agency (EPA) regulations implementing Title X apply to rental property built before 1978. Under Title X, before signing or renewing a lease or rental agreement, both the landlord and tenant must sign an EPA-approved disclosure form to prove that the landlord told the tenants about any known lead-based paint or hazards on the premises. Property owners must keep this disclosure form as part of their records for three years from the date that the tenancy begins. A landlord who fails to comply with EPA regulations faces penalties of up to $10,000 for each violation. And a landlord who is found liable for tenant injuries from lead may have to pay three times what the tenant suffered in damages.

Asbestos. Landlords may also be liable for tenant health problems caused by exposure to asbestos. Regulations issued by the Occupational Safety and Health Administration (OSHA) set strict standards for the testing, maintenance, and disclosure of asbestos in buildings constructed before 1981. For information call the nearest OSHA office or check OSHA's website at www.osha.gov.

Radon. This is a naturally occurring radioactive gas that can cause lung cancer in high concentrations. It can enter and contaminate a house or an apartment building built on soil and rock containing uranium deposits, or enter through water from private wells drilled in uranium-rich soil. It's easy to test for radon and inexpensive to fix. According to the EPA, a typical radon household problem can be solved for $500 to $2,500—money well spent, since a landlord could be held liable if a tenant gets lung cancer from a contaminated rental property.

Mold. Landlords are also getting sued for illnesses such as rashes and chronic fatigue allegedly caused by mold. It is as yet unclear whether, and to what extent, mold poses a health risk, but this doesn't stop lawsuits from being filed.

For a detailed discussion of the risks environmental hazards pose to landlords and how to deal with them, see *Every Landlord's Legal Guide*, by Marcia Stewart, Ralph Warner, and Janet Portman (Nolo).

condition when purchased—rather, it makes the property more valuable and it may also prolong its useful life. For example, the IRS ruled that the cost of removing asbestos insulation in manufacturing equipment and replacing it with new insulation was an improvement. (PLR 9240004 (June 29, 1992).)

In recent years, the IRS has softened its position somewhat, ruling that a manufacturer could currently deduct the cost of removing wastes in underground storage tanks, even though the removal process required the construction of new storage tanks. (Rev. Rul. 98-25.) The IRS also permitted the cost of encapsulating exposed asbestos in a warehouse to be deducted as a repair because encapsulation left the asbestos in place, instead of removing it. (Technical Advice Memo. 94-11-002 (Nov. 19, 1993).) But these rulings have not presaged a wholesale change in the IRS's view as some hoped. The IRS still says that "environmental cleanup (remediation) costs are generally capital expenditures"—that is, they are improvements that must be depreciated. (IRS Publication 535, *Business Expenses.*)

Arguably, environmental remediation of hazardous substances such as lead paint or asbestos should be a repair because it usually does not add value to the property or prolong its useful life—rather, it restores lost property value due to subsequent discoveries about the dangers of exposure to such substances. In other words, the building is restored to its original condition—a building that, according to the latest health standards, is safe to use. However, neither the IRS nor have the courts accepted this argument.

Energy Efficiency Deduction

The Energy Tax Incentives Act, enacted by Congress in 2005, created a brand-new deduction for expenses to make commercial buildings more energy efficient. It's intended to encourage building owners to upgrade their existing buildings and to design more energy-efficient new structures. The deduction may be used for both used and new buildings, but not for any building placed in service after December 31, 2007.

This deduction is not available for single-family homes or multifamily structures of three stories or less. In other words, you must own an apartment building of four or more stories to qualify. For details on how this complex deduction works, see IRS Notice 2006-52 (you can download it from the IRS website at www.irs.gov).

In a nutshell, you may deduct in one year up to $1.80 per building square foot when, as part of a plan to reduce your total energy costs, you upgrade your building's:

- interior lighting system
- heating, cooling, ventilation, and hot water system, or
- building envelope. (IRC Section 179D.)

For example, the owner of a 10,000-square-foot apartment building who qualified for the deduction could deduct $18,000 ($1.80 x 10,000 = $18,000).

To obtain the full deduction, the upgrade must reduce the power costs for the system involved by at least 50% as compared with a hypothetical reference building that meets the minimum requirements of Standard 90.1-2001 of the American Society of Heating, Refrigerating and Air-Conditioning Engineers (ASHRAE) and the Illuminating Engineering Society of North America. Copies of these standards can be obtained from the ASHRAE website (see below). If the reduction is less than 50%, a partial tax deduction of 60 cents per square foot is available if a 16⅔% energy savings target is met. There is no dollar limit on the deduction. The tax basis of your building is reduced by the amount of the deduction allowed.

The energy savings must be calculated using software that satisfies IRS requirements. Moreover, your building must be inspected by a "qualified individual" who certifies to the IRS that you've complied with all the requirements. IRS Notice 2006-52 details how to comply with these rules.

You'll likely need to hire a heating and ventilating engineer, refrigerating engineer, illuminating engineer, or other similar expert to get this deduction. For more information about such professionals visit the following websites:

* American Society of Heating, Refrigerating and Air-Conditioning Engineers: www.ashrae.org, and
* Illuminating Engineering Society of North America: www.iesna.org.

The General Plan of Improvement Rule: A Trap for the Unwary

Savvy landlords often decide to implement repairs as part of an overall plan to improve their property. For example, they may decide to wait until turnover time to take care of needed fixing, and decide that it would be most efficient to take care of other potential problems at the same time. (Indeed, it's often more expensive to deal with repairs when tenants are inconvenienced and likely to ask for rent reductions or, worse, alternate housing.)

When planning improvements to property, beware of a nasty tax trap: the general plan of improvement rule. Under this rule, a repair expense that is incurred as part of an overall plan of improvement, rehabilitation, or modernization must be depreciated—even though the same expense, standing alone, would be a currently deductible operating expense. Landlords can often be tricked by this rule because work, such as patching a roof, that would ordinarily constitute a repair, must be treated as an improvement if it is part of a general plan of improvement.

What Is a General Plan of Improvement?

You have a general plan of improvement when you undertake a number of repairs and/or improvements at about the same time, or consecutively, to achieve an overall goal: remodeling, rehabilitating, or modernizing your rental property. A general plan of improvement can cover an entire building, or just one rental unit within a multiunit building.

The classic example of a general plan of improvement is when a landlord buys a dilapidated apartment building, hires an architect to draw up detailed plans for rehabilitating it, and hires a contractor to do all the work. However, it is not necessary to have a formal, written document outlining your plan of improvement or renovation. And you don't need to hire a building contractor to do the work. The IRS and courts look at all of the surrounding facts and circumstances, including the purpose, nature, extent, and value of the work done—for example, was the work done to suit the needs of an incoming tenant or to adapt the property to a different use, or did it result in any appreciable increase in the property's value? (A "yes" to any of these questions indicates a plan of improvement.)

> **EXAMPLE:** Clair and Ruth Cobleigh purchased a dilapidated four-unit apartment building in Lincoln, Nebraska. They decided to fix up the building and hired a contractor who, over a two-year period:
> - painted part of the building
> - patched the roof where needed
> - replaced broken tiles
> - installed a new outside stairway
> - poured a new cement floor in the basement

- replaced screen doors and gutters
- installed new doors
- laid new floor joists and flooring in the first floor
- placed new counter tops in each apartment kitchen, and
- installed new sinks and lavatories in some of the apartments.

The Cobleighs thought the work done was repair work, so they deducted the entire cost each year as it was paid for. To their astonishment, the IRS claimed the work was an improvement that had to be depreciated over several years. They appealed to the tax court and lost. (*Cobleigh v. Comm'r.*, T.C. Memo 1956-261.)

To determine if an expense is a repair or part of a general plan of improvement, you can't look at it in isolation. You must consider whether the work is being done alone or in conjunction with other items. This is what the court did in the *Cobleigh* case. It didn't buy their claim that they had merely paid for a number of small repairs that were not part of an overall plan to improve their building. Instead, the court concluded that the money for the repair work was spent as part of an "overall plan to recondition a dilapidated building into an efficient business building," and each expense "was an integral part of the overall permanent betterment of the building." The repairs cost a lot of money and greatly improved the building's potential to generate rental income. Moreover, the Cobleighs had entered into an oral agreement with a single building contractor to perform all of the work.

Avoiding the Trap

There are ways to get around the general plan of improvement rule. However, you can't avoid it simply by having a contractor bill you separately for each task the contractor performs, or by labeling some work "repairs" and others "improvements." Instead, you must act in a way that shows you lack a general improvement plan. To do this, you should:

- spread your work out over as much time as possible—preferably, do only one major repair project each year
- hire different contractors and repair people to do the work
- make sure you are billed separately for each repair or improvement
- never allow a contractor or repairperson to label the work performed as an "improvement" in a contract or invoice, and

- not create any written plan showing how you intend to remodel or rehabilitate your building.

EXAMPLE: Lester wants to fix up his one bedroom rental unit by replacing the worn carpet in the bedroom, replastering several walls that have cracks, repainting the entire unit, replacing broken tile over the bathtub, and refinishing the living room and kitchen floors. Separately, each of these tasks is a repair. But if Lester did them all at once, he would likely have to classify them as improvements because they are all part of a general plan of improvement to upgrade the rental unit. To avoid this, Lester spreads the work out over two years.

The fact that you are remodeling or rehabilitating a building does not mean you can't do currently deductible repairs at the same time. You can treat any work you do that is not a part of your general plan of improvement as a currently deductible repair.

EXAMPLE: David owns a duplex that he rents out. He decides to modernize one of the units when the tenant moves out. He hires a contractor to completely redo the kitchen and bathroom. While the contractor is working in this unit, the toilet in David's other rental unit gets stopped up. He hires a plumber to fix the problem. The plumber's repair is not part of David's general plan of improvement for his other rental unit. Therefore, he may currently deduct the cost of fixing the toilet.

⚠ **Don't outsmart yourself.** Don't let your desire to obtain all the tax deductions you can, as soon as you can, blind you to the economic realities of being a landlord. In some cases, you'll be better off going ahead and fixing everything that is wrong in a rental property, or upgrading it, all at once, even though you'll become subject to the general plan of improvement rule. The extra rent you'll be able to charge for a completely fixed-up or upgraded unit could far outweigh the tax consequences of not being able to currently deduct the cost of your improvements. This is particularly likely where you purchase a rental building that is in poor condition, as did the Cobleighs in the above example.

How to Deduct Repairs

Repairs are an operating expense that you deduct on Schedule E. The schedule helpfully includes a line just for repairs.

You need to keep track of what you spend on repairs throughout the year and list the total in Schedule E when you do your taxes for the year. The cost of repairs includes what you spend on materials, parts, and labor. If you do a repair yourself, you don't get a deduction for the value of your own labor.

> **EXAMPLE:** One of Kim's tenants complains that the fan in his bathroom is making a funny noise. Kim hires Andy, a handyman, to repair the fan. Andy finds that the fan just needs to be cleaned. He does so, and charges Kim $50, which she pays. Kim may add the $50 to the repair expenses she lists in her Schedule E for the year.
>
> If instead of hiring Andy, Kim cleans the fan herself, the value of her labor does not count as a deductible repair. Kim spent nothing for materials or parts, so she gets no deduction for repairing the fan herself.

Combining Repairs With Improvements

If you've found a responsible, good contractor or repairperson, chances are you'll want to hire that contractor to do both repairs and improvements. Using the same person for both kinds of work shouldn't affect the tax treatment you choose for each. Ask to be billed separately for repairs and improvements—that is, have the contractor submit separate invoices for each category of work. If both kinds of work are covered in a single bill, you must separate the charges for repairs from those for improvements and deduct them accordingly.

> **EXAMPLE:** Jessica owns a five-unit apartment building. She hires a plumber to install a new toilet in one unit and to fix a leak in the plumbing of another unit. The cost of the toilet is an improvement, whereas fixing the leak is a repair. She should have the contractor submit separate invoices for each.

Making Tenants Pay for Repairs

It's common for landlords to require their tenants to pay for repairs when they cause damage. Typically, this is done after the tenant moves out, and the landlord deducts the cost of the repair from the tenant's security deposit.

Landlords may charge tenants for any repairs necessary to restore a rental unit to its condition at the beginning of the tenancy. This includes the cost of repairing damage to rental property caused by tenants and restoring property that has been subjected to unreasonable wear and tear. Landlords may not, however, use the tenant's security deposit to cover the costs of ordinary wear and tear.

Ordinary Wear and Tear: Landlord's Responsibility	Damage or Excessive Filth: Tenant's Responsibility
Curtains faded by the sun	Cigarette burns in curtains or carpets
Water-stained linoleum by shower	Broken tiles in bathroom
Dents in the wall where a door handle bumped it	Door off its hinges
A few small tack or nail holes in wall	Lots of picture holes or gouges in walls that require patching as well as repainting
Worn gaskets on refrigerator doors	Broken refrigerator shelf
Faded paint on bedroom wall	Water damage on wall from hanging plants
Toilet flushes inadequately because mineral deposits have clogged the jets	Toilet won't flush properly because it's stopped up with a diaper

Courtesy nolo.com website

Moreover, you may not use a tenant's deposit to repair damage the tenant did not cause—for example, you can't deduct the cost of repairing a broken window caused by a windstorm. Nor may you use a deposit to pay for improvements to a rental unit—for example, replacing a wooden kitchen counter with a granite counter.

A security deposit does not constitute taxable income for a landlord. But, where a landlord keeps all or part of a security deposit because the tenant has caused damage to the rental unit, that amount is taxable income. If the landlord fixes the damage, the amount spent on the repair is a deductible expense that will offset the landlord's additional income.

EXAMPLE: Ed owns a three-unit apartment building. After one of his tenants moves out, he discovers a broken window in the unit. He hires a repairman to fix the window at a cost of $100 and deducts the amount from the tenant's $1,000 security deposit. He refunds the remaining $900 to the tenant. The $100 Ed kept is rental income he must report on his Schedule E for the year. But the $100 he spent to fix the window is an expense he can deduct that year. This offsets the $100 he kept, so he ends up paying no tax on the amount.

If you deduct money from a tenant's deposit for damage and don't fix it, you'll have no expense deduction to offset the increased rental income. Of course, no decent landlord would do this. This is one case where the tax law encourages landlords to act honestly.

Repairs Paid for or Performed by Tenants

What happens if a tenant pays for a repair? For example, your tenant hires a handyman to fix a broken bathroom fan and pays him $50. If you reimburse the tenant or allow him to deduct the amount from the next month's rent, the repair is treated like any other repair for tax purposes: You get to currently deduct the full amount.

However, if a tenant takes it upon him- or herself to pay for a repair without your prior knowledge and consent, you have no legal obligation to reimburse him or her. The same goes for improvements the tenant pays for without your approval. If you don't reimburse the tenant, you'll get no tax deduction, but you'll get a free repair or improvement. You'll also own the repaired item or improvement. This is the result of an age-old doctrine of property law called the law of fixtures: Whatever a tenant attaches to a landlord's property, as an alteration or an improvement, becomes the landlord's property unless there is an agreement to the contrary. You need not pay any tax on the value of a repair or improvement the tenant makes without your approval.

The rules are exactly the same if a tenant performs a repair, instead of hiring someone else to do it. You can deduct the amount of any reimbursement you give the tenant, whether in cash or a rent reduction. But you have no legal obligation to pay for any repairs a tenant performs without your prior approval.

Tips for Maximizing Your Repair Deductions

Here are some simple tips that will help you maximize your repair deductions.

Patch, Mend, and Make Do—Don't Replace

There is no law that says that if something in your rental property is broken it has to be replaced. A replacement is almost always an improvement—not a repair—for tax deduction purposes. You'll obtain the best tax results if you patch, mend, or fix things that are broken, instead of replacing them. For example:

- if the roof is leaking or damaged, repair or replace only the damaged shingles; don't replace the whole roof
- if a tenant damages a portion of a carpet, have that part mended or cleaned instead of replacing the entire carpet
- if plaster is peeling on a wall, repair that portion of the wall only; don't replaster the whole wall, and
- if the dryer in your laundry room stops working, have a repairperson fix it; don't buy a new dryer.

You'll be able to deduct the entire cost of such repairs in a single year, rather than depreciating them over as many as 27.5 years. Moreover, repairs are usually much cheaper than replacements.

Of course, sometimes an item is so old or worn out, it makes more economic sense to replace it than repair it. Also, tenants like shiny new things and sometimes it makes more sense to keep your tenants happy. Also, you should factor into the repair or replace equation the fact that you may be able to charge more rent for a unit with new appliances, carpets, or other things than one with old mended appliances or other amenities.

Be careful with upgrades—they are improvements. When you fix something that is broken you should use the same quality materials and parts it contained originally. Your goal is to restore the item to the condition it was in before it stopped working, not to make it better. Upgrades are usually improvements, not repairs. In one case, a landlord who replaced wooden roof shingles with better composition shingles was found to have made an improvement.

Properly Document Repairs

Good documentation is the key to winning any argument with the IRS. Here are some tips for properly documenting your repairs:

- Repairs to rental property usually happen after a tenant complains. Document the complaint by writing a note—this can be on your calendar, appointment book, or on an invoice a repairperson gives you. This will help show that something was broken and you had it fixed—which is what a repair is. (For a sample written request for repair form, see *Every Landlord's Legal Guide*, by Marcia Stewart, Ralph Warner, and Janet Portman (Nolo).)

- Get an invoice for every repair. Make sure it describes the work in a way that is consistent with a repair, not an improvement. Good words to use include repair, fix, patch, mend, redo, recondition, and restore. An invoice should not include any words that indicate an improvement—for example: improvement, replacement, remodel, renovation, addition, construction, rehab, upgrade, or new. Of course, your invoice will not, by itself, establish whether something is a repair or an improvement—the facts must be consistent with what the invoice says.

- Make sure your repairs are classified as such in all your books and accounting records. This problem can easily crop up if you have a bookkeeper or accountant do your books—they may list a repair as a capital improvement. If an IRS auditor sees this, it will be curtains for your repair deduction.

- If you're doing an extensive repair, take before and after photographs to show the extent of the work and that the property has not been made substantially more valuable. Using a digital camera is a good idea because the photos will be automatically dated.

Do Preventive Maintenance

Maintenance means taking steps to prevent your property from breaking down or deteriorating. Preventive maintenance costs are always currently deductible operating expenses. A great way to avoid the repair versus improvement hassle—and to keep your tenants happy—is to keep your rental property well maintained. This will prevent it from breaking or wearing out quickly, thereby avoiding the need for replacements. Examples of preventive maintenance include periodically changing the filters on your heating and air conditioning system, and installing zinc control strips on a wood shake or shingle roof to keep fungus and algae away.

Delay Big Repair Expenses After Purchasing a Building

Improvements are commonly done immediately after a landlord buys a building, particularly if the building is unoccupied. A series of repairs made at this time will likely look like a general plan of improvement to the IRS, as they were in the *Cobleigh* case described in "What Is a General Plan of Improvement?" above. You'll get larger repair deductions if you spend as little money as possible immediately after you buy a building and, instead, spread the work out over as long a period as you can. Of course, you should do whatever work must be done to make the property habitable and rentable. ■

Chapter 5

Depreciation Basics

Of all the chapters in this book, this one should give you the most pleasure to read. Admittedly, depreciation is a rather dry, technical subject. But depreciation means money in a landlord's pocket. So, whenever you hear the word "depreciation," think "money."

This chapter covers the basics of depreciation. It shows you why depreciation is such a great deal for landlords, and how to calculate and take the deduction. It also explains Section 179 expensing, an alternative to depreciation that landlords can use for some personal property.

Depreciation: The Landlord's Best Tax Break

The largest expense landlords have is the purchase price for the rental property they own. However, unlike the interest you pay on a loan to buy the property or other operating expenses related to the property, you can't deduct the cost of the rental property in the year in which you pay for it. Because real estate lasts for more than one year, you must deduct its cost over a much longer time period through a process called depreciation.

The basic idea behind depreciation is simple: Real estate and other long-term property may last longer than a year, but they don't last forever. Little by little, year by year, buildings and other types of long-term property wear out, decay, become unusable or obsolete, or get used up. The annual decline in the value of such property is a cost of doing business or engaging in an investment activity. Depreciation is an annual tax deduction that business owners and investors take to reflect this annual cost.

The reason depreciation is such a valuable deduction for landlords is that you get it year after year (27.5 years for residential real property) without having to pay anything beyond your original investment in the property. Moreover, rental real property owners are entitled to depreciation even if their property goes up in value over time (as it usually does).

> **EXAMPLE:** George buys a rental condominium with a depreciable value of $100,000. He is entitled to an annual depreciation deduction of $3,636 for the next 27.5 years (excluding the first and last years, which will be somewhat less). All George has to do to obtain these annual deductions is continue to own the condo as a rental property, file a tax return every year, and do some simple bookkeeping. He need not spend an additional penny on his property. And he is entitled to depreciation even though his condominium increases in value every year. What a deal!

Depreciation is a complicated subject. The IRS publication describing it is over 100 pages long (IRS Publication 946, *How to Depreciate Property*). Many landlords simply have their accountants handle their depreciation and never bother to learn much about it. However, it's worth your time and trouble to understand it in some detail. This will enable you to:

- make sure your accountant determines your depreciation deductions properly—depreciation is not as cut and dried as you might think, and the way your accountant figures your depreciation may not be the best way
- figure your depreciation deduction yourself if you choose to prepare your own tax returns, and
- make better informed decisions on whether to invest in a particular rental property, since you fully understand the tax benefits you can obtain.

Depreciation is one of the largest deductions a landlord has. It can be the difference between earning an annual profit or losing money each year on a rental property. That's why it's so important that you understand it and take full advantage of it.

> ⚠ **Depreciation is not optional.** Unlike all the other tax deductions discussed in this book, depreciation is not optional. You *must* take a depreciation deduction if you qualify for it. If you fail to take it, the IRS will treat you as if you had taken it. This means that when you sell your property, its basis (value for tax purposes) will be reduced by the amount of depreciation you failed to claim. As a result, you'll have a larger profit from the sale that you'll have to pay taxes on. If you realize later that you failed to take a depreciation deduction that you should have taken, you may file an amended tax return to claim any deductions that you should have taken in prior years. (See Chapter 19.)

Understanding the Basics

The fundamentals of depreciation are not difficult to grasp. Gaining familiarity with these basic concepts will help you understand the later sections in this chapter that describe in detail how to depreciate real and personal property.

What Property Can Be Depreciated?

You may depreciate only property that:

- lasts for more than one year
- wears out or gets used up over time

- you own for more than one year, and
- you use in your rental activity (or some other business or income-producing activity). (IRC Sec. 167.)

Let's look at these requirements in some detail.

Long-Term Property

You can depreciate only property that lasts longer than one year—for example, buildings, tangible personal property like stoves and refrigerators, office or construction equipment, cars, and other vehicles. In tax parlance, such long-term property is called a capital asset because it is part of your capital investment in your rental business or investment activity.

Inventory—property a business holds for sale to others—is not a capital asset and may not be depreciated. Instead, this cost is deducted as it is sold. Inventory includes real property held for sale by real estate dealers. Thus, real estate dealers may not take depreciation deductions for the property they buy and sell—one reason why you should avoid being classed as a dealer whenever possible. (See Chapter 2.)

Items you buy that are for, or related to, your rental activity that are not long-term property (such as the food you eat when traveling for your rental activity, fertilizer you use for your rental property landscaping, and chlorine you buy to clean an apartment complex swimming pool) can usually be fully deducted in the year in which you purchase them as operating expenses. (See Chapter 3.)

Property That Wears Out or Gets Used Up

You can depreciate only property that wears out, decays, gets used up, or becomes obsolete over time. Thus, for example, you can't depreciate stocks, bonds, or other securities. These assets never wear out. And you can't depreciate collectibles that appreciate in value over time—for example, antiques, coins, or artwork.

Land—that is, the ground a building rests on and the surrounding area—cannot be depreciated because, for all practical purposes, it lasts forever. (If the land you own permanently disappears due to flooding, earthquake, or some other catastrophe, you'll have a deductible casualty loss; see Chapter 13.) When you determine your depreciation deduction for a rental building or other structure, you cannot include the value of the land it rests on in its value for tax purposes. Only the cost of the building itself can be depreciated.

Unlike land, buildings and structures on land don't last forever and, therefore, can be depreciated. Indeed, all or most of your depreciation deduction will come from the value of your rental buildings. You can depreciate any type of structure you use for your rental activity—apartment buildings, houses, duplexes, condominiums, mobile homes, swimming pools, parking lots, parking garages, tennis courts, clubhouses, and other facilities for your tenants. You can also depreciate structures that you own and use for your rental activity even though they are not used by your tenants—for example, a building you use as your rental office, or a storage shed where you keep maintenance equipment. The cost of landscaping for rental property can also be depreciated.

You can also depreciate tangible *personal* property that lasts for more than one year. This includes property inside a rental unit, such as stoves, refrigerators, furniture, and carpets. Other personal property that you use in connection with your rental activity can also be depreciated, even if it is not located on your rental property—for example, a computer, fax machine, cell phone, lawn mower, or automobile you use to conduct your rental activity.

You get no annual tax deductions for capital assets that can't be depreciated. This is one reason why depreciable assets like rental properties are better investments, taxwise, than nondepreciable assets like stocks, antiques, or art.

Property You Own for More Than One Year

You can only depreciate property that you own. You can't depreciate property that you lease for your rental activity (such as office space). In addition, you must own the property for at least one year to depreciate it. You get no depreciation for property you buy and sell, or otherwise dispose of, in the same year.

It makes no difference if you own the property free and clear or if you borrow money to buy it. If you hold title to the property, you get the depreciation—even if you have little or no equity in the property. The amount of your depreciation is determined by the cost of the property; how much you borrowed to purchase it is irrelevant.

Property You Use in Your Rental Activity

You may only depreciate property that you use in your rental business or investment activity (or some other business or investment activity you conduct). You may not depreciate property you use solely for personal purposes. This means you get no depreciation for your personal residence. If you convert a rental property to personal use, you must stop taking the depreciation for the property.

If you use property for both rental and personal uses, you may depreciate only a part of its value, based on the percentage of the property used for rental purposes.

> **EXAMPLE:** Jennifer owns a duplex. She lives in one unit and rents the other. Because she uses 50% of the duplex for rental purposes, she may depreciate only 50% of its value.

How Depreciation Works

At its core, depreciation is simple: You figure out how much the property is worth for tax purposes (the property's basis), how long the IRS says it will last (its recovery period), and then you deduct a certain percentage of its basis each year during its recovery period. The devil is in the details:

- When does depreciation begin (and end)? This depends on when rental property is placed in service.
- How do you determine how much your property is worth for depreciation purposes? You'll have to understand the concept of basis and how to calculate it.
- How long do you have to depreciate your property? The answer lies in knowing which recovery period applies.
- How much of your property's value do you get to deduct each year? This depends on which depreciation method you use and which depreciation convention applies.

All of these topics are explained below.

When Depreciation Begins and Ends

You don't necessarily begin to depreciate property when you buy it. Rather, depreciation begins when property is "placed in service." Property is considered placed in service in a rental activity when it is ready and available to rent. This can occur at the same time that you buy the property, or later (see "How to Depreciate Buildings," below).

You stop depreciating property either when you have fully recovered its value or when you retire it from service, whichever occurs first. Property is retired from service when you stop using it for your rental activity, sell it, destroy it, or otherwise dispose of it.

EXAMPLE: Wilma purchased a rental house that she placed in service by advertising it as available for rent in January of 1998. She rented the property to various tenants over the next ten years. She sold it on April 15, 2008. She gets no more depreciation as of the date of the sale—April 15, 2008. Had she not sold the property, she would have continued to depreciate the property over its 27.5 year depreciation period.

Determining Your Property's Basis

Depreciation allows you to deduct your total investment in a long-term asset that you buy for your rental activity. You take this deduction over the property's depreciation period, as determined by the IRS. In tax lingo, your investment is called your basis or tax basis. Basis is a word you'll hear over and over again when the subject of depreciation comes up. Don't let it confuse you; it just means the amount of your total investment in the property for tax purposes.

Usually, your basis is the cost of the property, plus expenses of the sale such as real estate transfer taxes and other fees. Land cannot be depreciated, so it must be deducted from the cost of real property to determine its basis for depreciation.

EXAMPLE: Jean buys a rental house that cost $100,000, not including the value of the land. The $100,000 cost is her basis in the property. She uses this amount to determine her annual depreciation deduction.

Your Recovery Period

The depreciation period (also called the recovery period) is the time over which you must take your depreciation deductions for an asset. The tax code has assigned depreciation periods to all types of business assets. These periods are somewhat arbitrary. However, property that can be expected to last a long time generally has a longer recovery period than property that has a short life. Thus, software has a three-year period, while the period for commercial real property is 39 years.

Landlords must continue to use the rules in effect at the time they placed their property into service. This can make life difficult at times—landlords who placed property into service in the mid-1980s and later may have to use as many as four different depreciation methods to depreciate all of their property each year.

This chapter covers only the depreciation rules that apply to property placed into service after January 1, 1987, because there aren't many landlords still depreciating property placed into service before 1987. For detailed information on how to depreciate property placed into service before 1987, refer to IRS Publication 534, *Depreciating Property Placed In Service Before 1987.*

The Modified Accelerated Cost Recovery System (MACRS)

Real property placed into service after 1986 is depreciated under the Modified Accelerated Cost Recovery System (MACRS). Under this system, the depreciation period for residential real property placed in service after 1986 is 27.5 years. Prior to 1987, different depreciation methods with different depreciation periods were in effect.

When Residential Real Property Placed In Service	Depreciation Method	Depreciation Period
Before 1981	ADR (Asset Depreciation Range)	Economic life of property
1/1/81–3/14/84	ACRS (Accelerated Cost Recovery System)	15 years
3/15/84–5/8/85	ACRS	18 years
5/9/85–12/31/86	ACRS	19 years
1/1/87 to present	MACRS (Modified Accelerated Cost Recovery System)	27.5 years

The periods are the same whether the property being depreciated is old or new. When you buy property, you start a new depreciation period beginning with year one, even if the prior owner previously depreciated the property for several years or fully depreciated it. If you buy an old building that has changed hands many times over the years, it may have been fully depreciated several times. This makes no difference to you—your depreciation period starts when you purchase the property and lasts for 27.5 years.

Calculating Your Deduction Amount

Your depreciation deduction is a set percentage of the basis of your property each year. The amount of the percentage depends on the depreciation method you use. All real property must be depreciated using the straight-line method. Under this method, you deduct an equal amount each year over the depreciation period (see "How to Depreciate Buildings," below, for more on how to calculate your depreciation deduction). Personal property can be deducted using accelerated depreciation, which provides larger depreciation deductions in the early years than the straight-line method (see "Depreciating Personal Property," below, for more on depreciating personal property).

The amount of your first year deduction is prorated depending upon which month you place your property into service. Special depreciation rules called conventions govern how much you can depreciate the first year.

Taking Separate Deductions

Typically, landlords don't have a single depreciation deduction. Instead, they have many separate depreciation deductions over time.

Rental Property Placed in Service

When a rental property is first placed in service, the landlord gets to depreciate its value. This includes the value of:

- the building and building components
- land improvements, such as landscaping and fences, and
- personal property items that are inside the building, but that are not physically part of it—for example, refrigerators, stoves, dishwashers, and carpeting.

These items can all be depreciated together. However, you have the option of separately depreciating personal property inside a rental property and certain land improvements. This is more complicated, but yields a larger total deduction during the first years that you own the property. Such segmented depreciation is described in detail in Chapter 6.

Later Additions and Improvements

Landlords typically make additions and improvements to their rental property after it has been placed into service—that is, after it has been made available for rent. These may consist of:

- improvements to the building itself, or building components—for example, replacing iron pipes with copper,
- land improvements, such as planting new trees or shrubbery, and
- adding new personal property to the rental building—for example, placing a new refrigerator in a rental unit.

You depreciate these additions and improvements separately from the original rental property.

Personal Property Used by the Landlord

Landlords usually have some personal property that they use in connection with their rental activity—computers and office furniture, for example. This property is for the landlord's use, not the tenant's. The landlord separately depreciates this property as it is placed into service each year.

How to Depreciate Buildings

By far, the largest portion of your depreciation deductions will consist of the building or buildings you use in your rental activities. The good news is that the rules for depreciating buildings are relatively simple. The bad news is that they require that buildings be depreciated over a long time using the slowest method possible, which reduces your annual deductions.

What Is a Building?

Buildings are made up of various structural components that are assembled together, including walls, floors, ceilings, windows, doors, plumbing fixtures (such as sinks and bathtubs), pipes, ducts, bathroom fixtures, stairs, fire escapes, electrical wiring, lighting fixtures, chimneys, air conditioning and heating systems, and other parts that form the structure. These structural components are all part of the building for depreciation purposes.

The land on which a building sits is not depreciable—it's not part of the building for depreciation purposes.

Buildings that are rented out for people to live in are called residential real property. Buildings that people do not live in are called nonresidential real property.

When a Building Is Placed in Service

Depreciation begins when property is placed in service, that is, when it's ready and available for use in your rental activity. A building doesn't have to be occupied by tenants to be depreciated. Rather, a building is considered placed in service in a rental activity when it is ready and available to rent. This can occur at the same time that you buy the property, or later.

> **EXAMPLE 1:** On April 6, Jan purchased a house to use as residential rental property. She made extensive repairs to the house during May and June. By July 5, she had it ready to rent and placed an ad in the local paper. She rented it in August with the rental date beginning September 1. The house is considered placed in service in July because it was ready and available for rent on that date. Jan can begin to depreciate the house in July.

> **EXAMPLE 2:** On February 1, Jan buys a house that is already being used as a rental and is currently occupied by a tenant. She continues renting out the unit to the tenant. She can begin to depreciate the house on February 1 because she placed it in service on that date.

> **EXAMPLE 3:** Jan moved from her home in July. During August and September, she made several repairs to the house. On October 1, she listed the property for rent with a real estate company and rented it on December 1. The property is considered placed in service on October 1.

Keep documentation showing the date your property was placed in service. For example, keep copies of any rental ads or other rental listings you place to rent a newly acquired vacant property.

Determining a Building's Basis

How much you can depreciate each year depends, first and foremost, on how much your property is worth for tax purposes—its basis. The larger your basis, the larger your depreciation deductions will be.

Cost Basis

If, like most landlords, you've purchased your rental property, your starting point for determining the property's basis is what you paid for it. Logically enough, this is called its cost basis. Your cost basis is the purchase price, plus certain other expenses, less the cost of your land.

Purchase price. You use the full purchase price as your starting point, regardless of how you pay for the property—with cash or a loan. If you buy property and take over an existing mortgage, you use the amount you pay for the property, plus the amount that still must be paid on the mortgage.

> **EXAMPLE:** Jan buys a building for $60,000 cash and assumes a mortgage of $240,000 on it. The starting point for determining her basis is $300,000.

Other expenses. Certain fees and other expenses you pay when you buy a building are added to your basis in the property. Most of these costs should be listed on the closing statement you receive after escrow on your property closes. However, some may not be listed there, so be sure to check your records to see if you've made any other payments that should be added to your property's basis.

Real estate taxes. If you buy a building and agree to pay real estate taxes on it that were owed by the seller and the seller did not reimburse you, the taxes you pay are treated as part of your basis in the property. You cannot deduct them as taxes paid.

If you reimburse the seller for real estate taxes the seller paid for you, you can usually deduct that amount. Do not include that amount in your basis in the property.

Settlement fees and other costs. Some settlement fees and closing costs you pay for buying the property are part of your basis in property. These include:

- abstract fees
- attorneys' fees
- charges for installing utility services
- escrow fees
- legal fees
- recording fees
- termite inspection fees
- survey costs
- transfer taxes
- title insurance costs, and
- any amounts the seller owes that you agree to pay, such as back taxes or interest, recording or mortgage fees, charges for improvements or repairs, and sales commissions.

However, the following settlement fees and closing costs cannot be included in your basis:

- fire insurance premiums—these are operating expenses deducted as paid (see Chapter 3), and
- charges connected with getting or refinancing a loan, such as points (discount points, loan origination fees), mortgage insurance premiums, loan assumption fees, credit report costs, and fees for an appraisal required by a lender (see Chapter 7 on how to deduct these costs).

Also, do not include amounts placed in escrow for the future payment of items such as taxes and insurance.

The cost of your land. Ordinarily, when you purchase a building with a structure or structures on it, you pay a single lump sum to the seller that includes both the cost of the building (along with its contents) and the land on which it sits. Because you can't depreciate land, you must deduct the value of the land from the purchase price to figure the basis for depreciation of the building.

> **EXAMPLE:** Leslie buys a rental house for $200,000. She determines that the land is worth $50,000. She must deduct the value of the land ($50,000) from the purchase price ($200,000) to determine her basis ($150,000).

There are several ways to determine how much your land is worth. Obviously, the less it's worth, the more depreciation you will have to deduct. Land valuation is the single most important factor within your control affecting the amount of your depreciation deductions. This topic is covered in detail in Chapter 6.

Condos Have Land Too

Some people think that condominium owners own only the airspace inside their condo unit, and don't own any land. This is not true. When you buy a condo, you receive title to the airspace inside your unit, and you also get an undivided part interest in the land the condominium building occupies and other common areas. For example, if a condominium building contains 10 units, each unit owner could own an undivided 1/10 interest in all the land. However, the interests don't have to be equal. The size of your undivided interest in the land should be listed on your deed. You need to calculate the land value to determine a rental condo's basis.

EXAMPLE: Ondine purchases a rental house for $200,000. She figures her starting basis in the property as follows:

Purchase price		$200,000
Other expenses		
Real estate taxes	$1,200	
Transfer taxes	2,000	
Title insurance	250	
Recording fees	50	
Total other		3,500
Cost of land:		(40,000)
Basis ($200,000 + $3,500) − $40,000		$163,500

When Cost Is Not the Basis

You cannot use cost as a basis for property that you received:
- in an exchange for other property
- as a gift, or
- as an inheritance.

The basis of property you inherit is usually the property's fair market value at the time the owner died. Thus, if you hold on to your rental property until death, your heirs will be able to resell it and pay little or no tax—the ultimate tax loophole.

EXAMPLE: Victoria inherits an apartment building from her late Uncle Ralph. The property's fair market value (excluding the land) is $300,000 at the time of her uncle's death. This is Victoria's basis. She sells the property for $310,000. Her total taxable profit on the sale is only $10,000 (her profit is the sales price minus the property's tax basis).

The basis of rental property you receive as a gift is its adjusted basis in the hands of the gift giver when the gift was made. (The adjusted basis is generally the property's original basis, minus depreciation deductions, plus the cost of improvements.)

EXAMPLE: Victoria's Uncle Ralph gave her his apartment building before he died. Ralph purchased the building in 1990 and his adjusted basis in the property at the time he gave it to her was $150,000. This is Victoria's basis.

For more information about determining basis other than cost basis, see IRS Publication 551, *Basis of Assets*.

Property Converted to Rental Use

When you change property you held for personal use to rental use (for example, you rent your former home), your basis is the *lesser* of the following values on the date of the change:

- the property's fair market value, or
- your adjusted basis.

Your adjusted basis is calculated as described in "Cost Basis," above. Fair market value is the price at which the property would change hands between a buyer and a seller, neither under undue pressure to buy or sell, and both having reasonable knowledge of all the relevant facts. Sales of similar property in the area are helpful in figuring out the fair market value of the property.

Ordinarily, your adjusted basis will be lower than the fair market value because residential real estate usually appreciates in value each year (often substantially).

> **EXAMPLE:** Several years ago, John built his home for $140,000 on a lot that cost $14,000. Before changing the property to rental use last year, he added $28,000 of permanent improvements. Because land is not depreciable, John only includes the cost of the house and improvements when figuring his adjusted basis for depreciation—$168,000 ($140,000 + $28,000). The house has a fair market value of $250,000. John must use his adjusted basis of $168,000 as the basis for depreciation on the house because it is less than the fair market value on the date of the conversion to rental use.

Because of this rule, if your personal residence has lost value since you bought it, turning it into a rental home won't allow you to deduct the loss when you eventually sell it. Only the drop in value *after* the conversion is deductible.

Mixed-Use Property

If you use a building for both rental and personal purposes, you must reduce your depreciable basis by the proportion of the property you use personally.

> **EXAMPLE:** Mary owns a triplex whose cost, excluding the cost of the land, was $300,000. She rents two of the units and lives in the other one. All of the units are the same size. She must reduce her depreciable basis by

one-third—that is, her basis is $200,000. If the units were different sizes, she would determine their value by counting the number of rooms or by comparing their square footage (see Chapter 9).

Buildings You Construct Yourself

If you construct a rental building yourself, your basis is the cost of construction. The cost includes the cost of materials, equipment, and labor. However, you may not add the cost of your own labor to the property's basis. Add the interest you pay during the construction period, but deduct interest you pay before and after construction as an operating expense. (See Chapter 3.)

Property Acquired in an Exchange

A like-kind exchange is where you swap your property for similar property owned by someone else. If the two properties have the same value, the basis of your old property becomes the basis of the new property received in the exchange. The new property's basis is called a substitute basis because the basis of the old property is substituted for the basis of the new property. This is one of the most complex areas of real estate taxation and is beyond the scope of this book. For more information, see IRS Publication 544, *Sales and Other Disposition of Assets*, and IRS Form 8824 Instructions "Like-Kind Exchanges."

The Depreciation Period

The depreciation period for residential real property is 27.5 years. The period for nonresidential real property is 39 years. Either way, it takes a long time to collect all of your depreciation deductions. Indeed, the great majority of landlords sell their rental property before they fully depreciate it. The recovery periods for personal property—office furniture and computers, for example—are much shorter, usually five or seven years.

If a building is used for both commercial and residential purposes, the 27.5 year period applies only if 80% or more of the gross rental income for the tax year is from the dwelling units. How much space the dwelling units take up in the building is irrelevant; all that counts is how much money you earn from them. Thus, you could have to use the 39-year period for nonresidential property even if a majority of the space in the building is used for dwelling units.

Residential Rental Property
Mid-Month Convention—Straight-Line 27.5 Years

Year	Month property placed in service					
	1	2	3	4	5	6
1	3.485%	3.182%	2.879%	2.576%	2.273%	1.970%
2–9	3.636	3.636	3.636	3.636	3.636	3.636
10	3.637	3.637	3.637	3.637	3.637	3.637
11	3.636	3.636	3.636	3.636	3.636	3.636
12	3.637	3.637	3.637	3.637	3.637	3.637
13	3.636	3.636	3.636	3.636	3.636	3.636
14	3.637	3.637	3.637	3.637	3.637	3.637
15	3.636	3.636	3.636	3.636	3.636	3.636
16	3.637	3.637	3.637	3.637	3.637	3.637
17	3.636	3.636	3.636	3.636	3.636	3.636
18	3.637	3.637	3.637	3.637	3.637	3.637
19	3.636	3.636	3.636	3.636	3.636	3.636
20	3.637	3.637	3.637	3.637	3.637	3.637
21	3.636	3.636	3.636	3.636	3.636	3.636
22	3.637	3.637	3.637	3.637	3.637	3.637
23	3.636	3.636	3.636	3.636	3.636	3.636
24	3.637	3.637	3.637	3.637	3.637	3.637
25	3.636	3.636	3.636	3.636	3.636	3.636
26	3.637	3.637	3.637	3.637	3.637	3.637
27	3.636	3.636	3.636	3.636	3.636	3.636
28	1.970	2.273	2.576	2.879	3.182	3.485
29						

Residential Rental Property
Mid-Month Convention—Straight-Line 27.5 Years

Year	Month property placed in service					
	7	8	9	10	11	12
1	1.667%	1.364%	1.061%	0.758%	0.455%	0.152%
2–9	3.636	3.636	3.636	3.636	3.636	3.636
10	3.636	3.636	3.636	3.636	3.636	3.636
11	3.637	3.637	3.637	3.637	3.637	3.637
12	3.636	3.636	3.636	3.636	3.636	3.636
13	3.637	3.637	3.637	3.637	3.637	3.637
14	3.636	3.636	3.636	3.636	3.636	3.636
15	3.637	3.637	3.637	3.637	3.637	3.637
16	3.636	3.636	3.636	3.636	3.636	3.636
17	3.637	3.637	3.637	3.637	3.637	3.637
18	3.636	3.636	3.636	3.636	3.636	3.636
19	3.637	3.637	3.637	3.637	3.637	3.637
20	3.636	3.636	3.636	3.636	3.636	3.636
21	3.637	3.637	3.637	3.637	3.637	3.637
22	3.636	3.636	3.636	3.636	3.636	3.636
23	3.637	3.637	3.637	3.637	3.637	3.637
24	3.636	3.636	3.636	3.636	3.636	3.636
25	3.637	3.637	3.637	3.637	3.637	3.637
26	3.636	3.636	3.636	3.636	3.636	3.636
27	3.637	3.637	3.637	3.637	3.637	3.637
28	3.636	3.636	3.636	3.636	3.636	3.636
29	0.152	0.455	0.758	1.061	1.364	1.667

EXAMPLE 1: Bill owns a two-story building that consists of a storefront on the first floor and four apartments on the second floor. He receives $1,000 rent per month from the store and $4,000 per month from the four apartments. He may use the 27.5 year depreciation period because 80% of his total rental income from the property comes from the apartments ($4,000 is 80% of $5,000).

EXAMPLE 2: Bill raises the rent on the store to $1,500 per month, while leaving the rents on the apartments the same. Now, less than 80% of his total rental income comes from the apartments ($4,000 of $5,500 is only 73%). Thus, he must use the 39-year depreciation period, which gives him a much smaller depreciation deduction each year.

If you live in any part of the building, the gross rental income includes the fair rental value of the part you occupy. In a boon to landlords with home offices, the IRS has held that the 27.5-year depreciation period for residential buildings (instead of the 39-year period for commercial buildings) may be used to depreciate such offices so long as the 80% rule is met. (ILM 200526002 (May 9, 2005).)

How Much You Depreciate Each Year

To depreciate buildings, use the straight-line method, which is the simplest—though the slowest—depreciation method. Deduct an equal amount of the property's basis each year, except for the first and last years. Thus, you deduct approximately 1/27th of the basis of residential real property each year.

You do not get a full year's worth of depreciation for the first year your property is placed in service. Instead, your first year deduction depends on what month of the year you placed the property into service—the later in the year, the less depreciation you get. No matter what day of the month you place your residential real property into service, you treat it as being placed in service at the midpoint of that month. You then get an extra one/half month of depreciation the year you sell your property. This rule is called the mid-month convention.

The IRS has a table showing how much deprecation you are entitled to for each year you own residential real property (expressed as a percentage of the property's starting basis). The table takes into account the mid-month convention. Except for the first and last years, you depreciate 3.636% of your property's basis each year (give or take .001%). If you use the IRS tables to figure your depreciation for the first year, you must continue to use them for the remainder of the asset's recovery period unless you deduct a casualty loss, in which case you must stop using them.

Using the IRS tables is not mandatory. You can figure your depreciation yourself—this requires some serious math. If you use tax preparation software, it will calculate your depreciation deduction for you. If you don't use the tables, you'll usually end up with a slightly different amount than when using the tables—but not enough to matter. Even if you don't use the IRS tables, they are still a helpful guide if you ever want to know how much depreciation you'll be able to deduct for a property each year.

> **EXAMPLE:** Jim purchased a single-family rental house and placed it in service in June. His basis in the house is $160,000. Using the table, he finds that the percentage for property placed in service in June of Year 1 is 1.970%. His depreciation deduction for that year is $3,152 ($160,000 x .01970 = $3,152). The following year, the applicable depreciation percentage is 3.636%. Thus, his depreciation deduction for that year is $5,817.60 ($160,000 x .03636 = $5,817.60).

If you sell your property, figure your depreciation for the year of sale by multiplying a full year of depreciation by the number of months you owned the property, and then divide by 12. Treat the month of the sale as one-half of one month, no matter what day of the month you actually sold the property.

> **EXAMPLE:** Jim sells his rental house in the fifth year after he placed it in service. Title passes to the buyer on July 2. A full year of depreciation for Jim's property is worth $3,636. To figure his depreciation for the year of sale, he multiplies this amount by 6.5 (January through June, plus one/half of July = 6.5). He then divides the total by 12. The result is $1,970 in depreciation for the year (($3,636 x 6.5) ÷ 12 = $1,970).

Depreciating Additions and Improvements

Additions and improvements to a building must also be depreciated. However, you'll do this separately from the original building itself.

What Is a Building Improvement?

A building addition or improvement is a change you make to the structures on your land, or to structural components of the building, that substantially adds to your property's value, prolongs its life, or adapts it to new uses. For example, you:

- add a new bathroom or bedroom
- replace the roof
- put in new cabinets
- put up a fence
- install new plumbing or wiring, or
- install new kitchen appliances.

Changes that don't substantially add to your property's value or increase its life are repairs, not improvements. These include:

- painting a bedroom
- patching the roof, or
- mending a hole in a worn carpet.

Unlike improvements, the cost of repairs is a landlord operating expense that can be fully deducted in one year. Obviously, you're much better off tax-wise if you can characterize a change as a repair, rather than an improvement. The differences between repairs and improvements are discussed in detail in Chapter 4.

Special Assessments for Improvements

If your rental is in a condominium complex that is governed by a homeowners association, you may be required to pay special assessments to cover building improvements. Such assessments are depreciated in the same way as any building improvement described above. Special assessments are not the same as the monthly homeowner association fees condo owners must pay to cover the condo's operating expenses. These monthly fees are currently deductible each year as an operating expense.

EXAMPLE: Ida owns a one-bedroom condominium in a 20-story high-rise that she rents out. The condominium homeowners association requires every owner to pay a special $2,000 assessment for a major upgrade of the building's aging plumbing system. This is a building improvement that Ida must depreciate over 27.5 years. Ida also pays $2,400 each year in homeowner association fees. She may deduct that entire amount as an operating expense.

How to Depreciate Building Improvements

Treat depreciable additions or improvements that you make to any property as separate property items for depreciation purposes.

When depreciation begins. Depreciation of an addition or improvement to a building begins when the improvement is placed in service—that is, when it is ready for use in your rental property.

Basis for depreciation. Depreciate the amount that an addition or improvement actually costs you, including any amount you borrowed to make the addition or improvement. This includes all direct costs, such as material and labor, but not your own labor. It also includes all expenses related to the addition or improvement. For example, if you had an architect draw up plans for remodeling your property, the architect's fee is a part of the cost; or, if you had your lot surveyed to put up a fence, the cost of the survey is a part of the cost of the fence.

Depreciation method and recovery period. If the improvement is a building or depreciable landscaping improvement, depreciate it over 27.5 years, using the same method used for the original building as described above.

> **EXAMPLE:** Mona buys a rental house in 2000. In 2008, her old tenant moves out and she hires a contractor to remodel the house, adding a new kitchen and bathroom, and installing new floors. The cost of this building improvement was $10,000. The work was completed on June 1, 2008, and she immediately placed the house into service as a rental unit by offering it for rent. She depreciates the $10,000 over 27.5 years. The beginning date for her first year of depreciation is June 2008. She gets $197 in depreciation for this improvement the first year and $367 each year thereafter. She claims this amount in addition to the depreciation she has already been receiving on the house since she placed it in service in 2000.

You must keep separate accounts for depreciable additions or improvements made after you place your rental property in service.

You add the cost of depreciable additions and improvements to the adjusted basis of your property, which will reduce your tax liability when you sell the property.

Depreciating Land Improvements

As mentioned above, land itself cannot be depreciated because it lasts virtually forever. However, certain improvements you make to your land can be depreciated. There are two types of land improvements:

- changes to the land itself, and
- changes or additions to permanent structures on the land other than buildings and building components.

Changes to Land

Changes to the land include grading, clearing, excavations, and landscaping. The IRS says that such changes are depreciable only if it they are "directly associated" with a building, rather than "inextricably associated" with the land itself. (Rev. Rul. 65-265.) Translated into English, this means that these land improvements are depreciable if they are intended for use with a specific building. Changes that permanently improve the land itself are not depreciable.

The rationale is that work directly associated with a building will cease to be useful when the building is demolished; thus, it has a determinable useful life. But work inextricably associated with land is not depreciable because we don't know whether it will cease to be useful. The cost of such work is added to the basis of the land. Thus, landscaping is depreciable if it will have to be replaced when the building is replaced.

> **EXAMPLE 1:** Milt plants some new bushes and trees right next to his rental triplex. If he replaced the building, he'd have to destroy these bushes and trees. They have a determinable useful life so he may depreciate them.

> **EXAMPLE 2:** Milt also plants trees and bushes around the outer boundary of his lot. These trees and bushes would not have to be replaced if the building was demolished. Thus, they can't be depreciated and Milt must instead add their cost to the basis of his land.

Similarly, preliminary land clearing and grading to get land ready for construction is not depreciable. However, excavating, grading, and dirt removal costs necessary for the proper setting of a specific building can be depreciated because this work will have to be redone when the building is replaced.

Structures Other Than Buildings

Permanent structures other than buildings include fences, outdoor lighting, swimming pools, driveways, paved parking areas and other pavements, walkways, sprinkler systems, and drainage facilities.

In contrast to changes to land, depreciation of permanent structures other than buildings is straightforward—they are depreciated over 15 years as described below. You don't have to worry about the "directly associated" or "inextricably associated" test because man-made structures, unlike changes to land itself, have a determinable useful life—that is, none of them can last forever.

Calculating Your Depreciation Deduction

Depreciate land improvements in the same way as personal property. As explained more fully below, you depreciate them over 15 years, using the 150% declining balance method. This way, you get your depreciation deductions more quickly than you would for a building or building improvement, which you must depreciate over 27.5 years.

The depreciable basis of a land improvement is its cost, including labor and installation charges. If you depreciate a new improvement, you'll have no problem determining the cost—just look at your bills and use the total you paid for it.

If you wish to depreciate an existing improvement—for example, a driveway in a rental property you have purchased—you can determine the cost by using construction cost guides such as the *National Repair & Remodeling Estimator* (Craftsman Book Company, available as a download at www.costbook.com). You can also obtain cost estimates from experts such as garden supply companies, landscape architects, and local builders and contractors. You don't need to obtain a precise formal written cost estimate prepared by the expert—which the expert will probably charge you for. You can simply obtain a ballpark estimate from the expert over the phone—be sure to write it down, date it, and keep it in your records. (See Chapter 6 for a detailed discussion of how to determine the tax basis of land improvements.)

Depreciating Personal Property

Obviously, all landlords own real property—that is, land and buildings and other permanent structures on the land. But they own personal property as well—for example, computers, maintenance equipment, and appliances in rental units. Thus, you need to understand how to depreciate personal property.

What Is Personal Property?

For tax purposes, personal property is any tangible property other than:
- land and land improvements
- buildings and other inherently permanent structures, such as swimming pools and parking lots, and
- structural components of buildings and other permanent structures. (IRS Reg. Sec. 1.48-1(e)(2); *Whiteco Industries, Inc. v. Comm'r, 65 T.C. 664.*)

You must depreciate personal property used in a rental activity if it lasts more than one year and wears out or gets used up over time. Personal property that lasts less than one year is an operating expense that you fully deduct in the year in which you buy it. For example, you can currently deduct the cost of cleaning supplies for your rental activity, but you must depreciate a stove you buy for a rental unit.

Personal property is depreciated over a much shorter time period than real property—usually just five or seven years. This means you'll obtain your full depreciation deduction much more quickly. For this reason, it is to a landlord's advantage to be able to classify as much rental property as possible as personal property, rather than real property.

A landlord's depreciable personal property falls into one of two broad categories:
- personal property contained in a rental building or individual apartment, or
- other personal property used in a rental activity.

Personal Property Inside Rental Buildings

Anything inside your rental building that is not a structural component of the building is personal property. Often it is easy to tell whether or not an item is a structural component of a rental building—for example, refrigerators and other kitchen appliances are not structural components, while load-bearing walls obviously are. Other examples of items inside rental buildings that are not structural components include:
- carpeting that is tacked down (but not glued down)
- drapes and blinds
- furniture (only depreciable if you own it)
- personal signs
- moveable and removable partitions
- laundry equipment in a laundry room
- weights and other exercise equipment in an exercise room

- pool tables, ping pong tables, televisions, and other recreational equipment in a recreation room, and
- office furniture and equipment located in a manager's office.

In many cases, however, it can be very difficult to determine whether property is a structural component—for example, is tile flooring a structural component? The IRS says that it is if it is cemented, mudded, or otherwise permanently affixed to the floor. There have been many disputes with the IRS on what constitutes a structural component, resulting in many court decisions, often disagreeing with each other. Refer to Chapter 6 for a detailed discussion of the tests used to determine if property is a structural component of a rental building.

Personal Property Not Inside Rental Buildings

Landlords typically own various items of long-term property that they use in connection with their rental activities, but the items are not actually inside their rental buildings—for example, lawn mowers and other landscaping and maintenance equipment, computers, cell phones, fax machines, office furniture, and automobiles.

As long as this property is not a structural component of a building or other permanent structure, it is personal property for depreciation purposes. For example, a lawn mower is personal property even if it is kept inside a building or other permanent structure such as a storage shed—a lawn mower is obviously not a building component. On the other hand, carpeting in your rental office will not be personal property if it is glued to the floor—such carpeting is a building component, and is considered part of the building for depreciation purposes. See Chapter 6 for detailed guidance on when property is a building component.

When to Depreciate Personal Property

You don't need to separately depreciate all of the personal property you own. However, you may wish to do so.

Personal Property Included in Purchase

When you buy a rental property, you pay one lump sum that covers both the structure and the personal property it contains. When you initially place the property into service, you can simply depreciate the entire property as a whole (as outlined in "How to Depreciate Buildings," above). The IRS requires no separate allocation for, or depreciation of, the personal property in the building. This saves you the time and trouble of having to figure out the basis of each item of personal property the building contains, and keeping separate depreciation records for them.

However, you have the option of depreciating personal property within a rental building separately from the building itself. Such segmented depreciation is advantageous taxwise, because it will give you larger deductions each year. Segmented depreciation is discussed in detail in Chapter 6.

Personal Property Improvements

You must separately depreciate personal property that you add to a building after you place it into service—for example, if you install a new stove or refrigerator in a rental property you've already made available for rent, you'll depreciate it separately from the other appliances already in the unit. Your depreciation begins the year you place the item in service.

Other Personal Property

Depreciate personal property not contained in your rental property, such as computers and office furniture, as you buy it. Depreciate each item separately. However, it might be possible to deduct the full amount of such property in one year under a special tax rule called Section 179.

Do You Depreciate Paper Clips?

Do you have to depreciate paper clips and other inexpensive items that you buy for your rental activity? No. Although paper clips and similar items might be expected to last more than one year, you can treat their cost as a current expense for tax purposes. Most businesses and investors establish a cost threshold for property they depreciate—things that cost more are treated like depreciable property, while items that cost less are treated as currently deductible operating expenses. The IRS has no rules on the amount of the limit, except that it must be reasonable. For a small landlord, a reasonable limit would be $100 to $250. For example, you could treat a $50 bookcase you buy for your office as an operating expense; a $500 bookcase would be a long-term asset.

When Is Personal Property Placed in Service?

Depreciation begins when property is placed in service. Personal property inside or attached to a building is placed in service when it's installed in the building and is available and ready for rental use.

EXAMPLE: On November 22, Jack purchased a dishwasher for his vacant rental property. The appliance was delivered, installed, and ready for use on December 7. However, he did not rent out the apartment until February of the following year. The dishwasher was placed in service on December 7, even though it was not actually used by his tenant until February.

Personal property you use yourself for your rental activity is placed in service when it is available for your use.

EXAMPLE: Stan purchases a new computer to help him with the bookkeeping for his many rental properties. The computer is placed in service when Stan sets it up in his office for his use.

Keep copies of sales receipts showing when personal property was delivered.

Determining the Basis of Personal Property

Usually, your basis in personal property is whatever you paid for it. Its cost includes not only the purchase price, but also sales tax, delivery charges, installation, and testing fees, if any. You may depreciate the entire cost, no matter how you paid for the property—in cash, on a credit card, or with a bank loan.

EXAMPLE: Victor buys a new refrigerator and stove for a duplex he's been renting for several years. The purchase price for the items was $900, plus $100 sales tax, and $100 for delivery and installation. Victor puts the entire amount on his credit card, except for the delivery charge, which he pays in cash. His basis in the items is $1,100.

There are certain situations, however, when you can't use the cost basis method for personal property.

Property Converted to Rental Use

If you convert property you have been using personally to use in your rental activity, your starting basis is equal to the property's fair market value when you start using it for rental purposes.

EXAMPLE: Jeff wants to add some furniture to a vacant apartment he's trying to rent. Rather than buying new furniture, he moves in some old furniture from his personal residence, including a sofa, dinette set, and bed. The fair market value of these items when Jeff places them in his rental is $400. This is his starting basis when he begins to depreciate the property.

You determine your property's fair market value by figuring out how much someone would be willing to pay for it. If the property is new, or fairly new, you can use the cost to replace it. If the property is older, you'll need to figure out the value based on the new price minus an amount for the wear and tear the property has undergone. Look at classified ads and listings for similar property on eBay, or call people who buy and sell the type of property involved. If you think the property is extremely valuable, get an appraisal from an expert. Keep records of how you calculated the property's value.

Most personal property that you convert to rental use probably won't be worth much. You can't claim inflated values for old property just to maximize your depreciation deductions.

Property Bought With a Trade-In

If you buy property with a trade-in, your starting basis is equal to the adjusted basis in the trade-in property, plus any cash you pay for the new property.

EXAMPLE: Phil owns a pickup truck he uses exclusively for his rental business. He trades in the truck for a new model, for which he pays $10,000. His old truck's adjusted basis was $3,000. His starting basis in the new truck is $13,000. This is so even though the new truck's list price was only $10,000.

Inherited and Gifted Personal Property

The starting basis of inherited personal property is its fair market value on the day the owner died. Your starting basis in gifted property is its fair market value at the time of the gift.

Mixed-Use Property

You may take a depreciation deduction for personal property you use both for your rental activity and personal purposes. Reduce your depreciable basis in the property by the percentage of your personal use. This will, of course, reduce the amount you can depreciate.

> **EXAMPLE:** Miranda owns a $400 lawn mower that she uses 75% of the time for her rental business and 25% of the time to mow her own lawn. Her depreciable basis in the mower is reduced by 25%, so her basis is $300 instead of $400 (75% x $400 = $300). Miranda can depreciate $300 over the asset's depreciation period.

You can take a depreciation deduction even if you use an asset only 1% of the time for business. (However, special rules apply if you use cars and other types of listed property less than 50% of the time for business—see "Listed Property," below.)

If you use property for both business and personal purposes, you must keep a diary or log listing the dates, times, and reasons the property was used in order to distinguish business from personal use. (See Chapter 17.)

Depreciation Period

Virtually all of the personal property you use in your rental activity will have a five- or seven-year depreciation period. The depreciation periods for most types of personal property used by landlords are listed below. These periods are also called recovery classes; all property that comes within a period is said to belong to that class. For example, computers have a five-year depreciation period and thus fall within the five-year class, along with automobiles and office equipment.

Type of Property	Depreciation Period
Computer software (Software included in the price of a computer is depreciated as part of the computer, unless you're billed separately for the software; other software is separately depreciated.)	3 years
Computers and their peripheral equipment Office machinery, such as typewriters, calculators, and copiers Automobiles Light trucks (actual weight less than 13,000 pounds) Appliances, such as stoves, refrigerators, and dishwashers Carpets Furniture used in rental property Drapes and blinds	5 years
Office furniture and equipment, such as desks and files Any property that does not have a class life and that has not been designated by law as being in any other class	7 years
Shrubbery Permanent fences Sidewalks Driveways Paved parking areas Landscaping Sewer and drainage facilities Swimming pools	15 years

Depreciation the First Year

The IRS has established certain rules (called conventions) that govern how many months of depreciation you can take for the first year that you own an asset. The conventions for personal property are different than those for real property.

Half-Year Convention

The basic rule is that, no matter when you buy personal property, you treat it as being placed in service on July 1—the mid-point of the year. This means that you can take half a year of depreciation for the first year that you own personal property you use for your rental activity.

> **EXAMPLE:** Sam owns a small apartment building. In January, he purchases a new carpet for one of his rentals. In March, he buys a new stove for another rental unit. In December, he installs a new dishwasher in the same unit. Sam treats all these items as having been placed in service on July 1.

Mid-Quarter Convention

You are not allowed to use the half-year convention if more than 40% of the long-term personal property you buy during the year is placed in service during the last three months of the year. The 40% figure is determined by adding together the basis of all the depreciable property you bought during the year and comparing that to the basis of all of the property you bought during the fourth quarter.

If you exceed the 40% ceiling, you must use the mid-quarter convention. Group all of the property that you purchased during the year by quarter (depending on when you bought it) and treat it as if you had placed it in service at the mid-point of that quarter. (A quarter is a three-month period. The first quarter is January through March; the second quarter is April through June; the third quarter is July through September; and the fourth quarter is October through December.)

> **EXAMPLE:** Sam buys a $500 stove in January, a $500 refrigerator in October, and a $500 carpet in December. The basis for all three items he bought during the year is $1,500. He paid $1,000 of this amount during the fourth quarter, so more than 40% of his purchases were made in the fourth quarter of the year. Sam must use the mid-quarter convention. He must treat the stove he bought as being placed in service on February 15—the midpoint of the first quarter. The refrigerator and carpet must be treated as being placed in service on November 15—the midpoint of the fourth quarter. As a result, Sam gets very little depreciation that year for the refrigerator and carpet.

It's usually best to avoid having to use the mid-quarter convention, which means you'll want to buy more than 60% of your total depreciable personal property for your rental activity before September 30 of the year.

Depreciation Methods

Personal property is usually depreciated using the Modified Accelerated Cost Recovery System, or MACRS. (A slightly different system, called the Alternative Depreciation system or ADS, applies to certain property—see "Depreciating Listed Property," below). You can ordinarily use three different methods to calculate personal property depreciation under MACRS: straight-line depreciation or one of two accelerated depreciation methods. Once you choose your method, you're stuck with it for the entire life of the asset.

In addition, you must use the same method for all property of the same class that you purchase during the year. For example, if you use the straight-line method to depreciate a computer, you must use that method to depreciate any other property in the same class as computers. Computers fall within the five-year class, so you must use the straight-line method for all other five-year property you buy during the year, such as office equipment.

Straight-Line Method

You can use the straight-line method to depreciate any type of depreciable property. (This is the method that you must use to depreciate real property.) Most people don't choose this method for personal property, however, because you can deduct items faster using one of the accelerated depreciation methods described below.

Under the straight-line method, you deduct an equal amount each year over the useful life of an asset. If the mid-year convention applies (as it often does), you deduct only a half-year's worth of depreciation in the first year. You make up for this by taking an extra one-half year of depreciation at the end.

> **EXAMPLE:** Sally buys a $1,000 printer-fax-copy machine for her rental business in 2008. It has a useful life of five years. (See the chart in "Depreciation Period," above). Because she bought more than 60% of her depreciable personal property for the year before September 30, she can use the mid-year convention. She decides to use the straight-line method and depreciate the asset over six years—the five years of the printer's useful life, plus an extra year to allow her to make up for the partial deduction she takes for the first year. Her annual depreciation deductions are as follows:

2008	$ 100
2009	200
2010	200
2011	200
2012	200
2013	100
Total	$1,000

Accelerated Depreciation Methods

Most people use accelerated depreciation to depreciate personal property. As the name implies, this method provides faster depreciation than the straight-line method. It does not increase your total depreciation deduction, but it permits you to take larger deductions in the first few years after you buy an asset. You make up for this by taking smaller deductions in later years.

The fastest and most commonly used form of accelerated depreciation is the double declining balance method. This is a confusing name, but all it means is that you get double the deduction that you would get for the first full year under the straight-line method. You then get less in later years. However, in later years, you may switch to the straight-line method (which will give you a larger deduction than using accelerated depreciation). This is built into the IRS depreciation tables. You may use this method to depreciate virtually all of the tangible personal property you buy for your rental activity. However, accelerated depreciation may not be used for real property.

EXAMPLE: Sally decides to use the double declining balance method to depreciate the $1,000 printer-fax-copier machine she buys for her rental business. Her annual depreciation deductions are as follows:

2008	$ 200
2009	320
2010	192
2011	115
2012	115
2013	58
Total	$1,000

An alternative to the double declining method is the 150% declining balance method. This method gives you one-and-one-half times the deduction in the first year that you would otherwise get using the straight-line method. The 150% method may be used for three-, five-, seven-, ten-, 15-, and 20-year personal property.

> **EXAMPLE:** Sally decides to use the 150% declining balance method to depreciate her $1,000 printer-fax-copier. This gives her a smaller deduction in the first year than the double declining balance method, but larger deductions in later years.

2008	$ 150
2009	255
2010	178
2011	167
2012	167
2013	83
Total	$1,000

Using accelerated depreciation is not necessarily a good idea if you expect your income to go up in future years. There are also some restrictions on when you can use accelerated depreciation. For example, you can't use it for cars, computers, and certain other property that you use for your rental activity less than 50% of the time (see "Listed Property," below).

Depreciation Tables

You can figure out the amount of your yearly depreciation deduction using depreciation tables prepared by the IRS. These tables factor in the depreciation convention and method. They are all available in IRS Publication 946, *How to Depreciate Property.*

> **EXAMPLE:** In 2008, Joe buys a $2,000 computer for his rental business. He wants to depreciate it using the double declining balance method so he can get the largest possible deduction during the first year. He uses the property 100% for business and can use the mid-year convention because he didn't buy more than 40% of his business property during the last three months of 2008. To figure his depreciation, he can use the applicable IRS depreciation table from Publication 946, which is reprinted below:

200% Declining Balance Depreciation Method
Convention: Half-year

Year	If the recovery period is: 3 years	5 years	7 years	10 years	15 years	20 years
1	33.33%	20.00%	14.29%	10.00%	5.00%	3.750%
2	44.45	32.00	24.49	18.00	9.50	7.219
3	14.81	19.20	17.49	14.40	8.55	6.677
4	7.41	11.52	12.49	11.52	7.70	6.177
5		11.52	8.93	9.22	6.93	5.713
6		5.76	8.92	7.37	6.23	5.285
7			8.93	6.55	5.90	4.888
8			4.46	6.55	5.90	4.522
9				6.56	5.91	4.462
10				6.55	5.90	4.461
11				3.28	5.91	4.462
12					5.90	4.461
13					5.91	4.462
14					5.90	4.461
15					5.91	4.462
16					2.95	4.461
17						4.462
18						4.461
19						4.462
20						4.461
21						2.231

You can see from the table that for five-year property (like the computer), Joe gets 20% of his total depreciation deduction in the first year. To figure the deduction for the computer, Joe multiplies $2,000 by 20%, resulting in a $400 deduction in 2008. In 2009, the deduction will be $640 (32% x $2,000). The deduction for 2008 is smaller than for 2009 because of the mid-year convention—that is, Joe gets only half of the first year's depreciation because the IRS assumes the property was purchased on July 1. This is factored into the table.

Appendix A of Publication 946 contains 18 different depreciation tables—one for each type of depreciation you can take.

Listed Property

Fearing that taxpayers might claim depreciation for listed property but actually use it for personal reasons, the IRS imposes special rules on certain personal property that can easily be used for personal as well as business or investment purposes. These items, called listed property, include:

- cars and certain other vehicles
- motorcycles, boats, and airplanes
- computers
- cellular phones, and
- any other property generally used for entertainment, recreation, or amusement—for example, televisions VCRs, cameras, stereos, and camcorders.

To prevent this kind of behavior, the IRS requires you to document your use of listed property. You can satisfy this requirement by keeping a logbook showing when and how the property is used. (See Chapter 17 for more on record keeping.)

These rules apply only to listed property that you use yourself in your rental activity—for example, a computer you use to do your rental bookkeeping. They do not apply to personal property contained in a rental unit—for example, a television you place in a rental unit for a tenant's use.

Exception for Computers

You generally have to document your use of listed property even if you use it 100% for business. However, there is an exception to this rule for computers: If you use a computer or computer peripheral (such as a printer) only for business and keep it at your office, you need not comply with the record-keeping requirement. This includes computers that you keep at your home office, as long as the office qualifies for the home office deduction. (See Chapter 9.)

This exception does not apply to items other than computers and computer peripheral equipment—for example, it doesn't apply to calculators, copiers, fax machines, or typewriters.

Depreciating Listed Property

If you use listed property for your rental activity more than 50% of the time, you may deduct its cost just like any other long-term personal property under the normal depreciation rules. However, if you use listed property 50% or less of the time for your rental activity, you must use the straight-line method—the slowest method of depreciation. In addition, you are not allowed to use the normal depreciation periods allowed under the MACRS depreciation system. Instead, you must use the depreciation periods provided for by the Alternative Depreciation System (ADS for short). These are generally longer than the ordinary MACRS periods. However, you may still depreciate cars, trucks, and computers over five years. The main ADS depreciation periods for listed property are provided in the following chart.

ADS Depreciation Periods	
Property	**Depreciation Period**
Cars and light trucks	5 years
Computers and peripheral equipment	5 years
Communication equipment	10 years
Personal property with no class life	12 years

If you start out using accelerated depreciation and in a later year your business use drops to 50% or less, you have to switch to the straight-line method and ADS period for that year and subsequent years. In addition, you are subject to depreciation recapture for the prior years—that is, you must calculate how much more depreciation you got in the prior years by using accelerated depreciation and count that amount as ordinary taxable income for the current year. This will, of course, increase your tax bill for the year.

Section 179 Expensing

Section 179 of the tax code is one of the greatest tax boons available for owners of most types of small businesses. Under Section 179, business owners can deduct the entire cost of long-term personal property that they use in their business, rather than having to depreciate the cost over several years. This is called first-year expensing or Section 179 expensing. Unfortunately, because of restrictions on how it may be used, Section 179 has relatively little importance for most landlords.

What Property Can Be Deducted

A business can use Section 179 to deduct tangible, long-term personal property. However, Section 179 specifically excludes personal property used in residential rental property. This means that landlords can't use Section 179 to deduct the cost of items they purchase for use inside rental units—for example, kitchen appliances, carpets, drapes, or blinds. The only exception is for property in hotels, motels, or vacation homes where the guests stay less than 30 days (see Chapter 15 for a discussion of vacation homes).

In addition, you can't use Section 179 to deduct the cost of:

- land
- permanent structures attached to land, including buildings and their structural components, fences, swimming pools, or paved parking areas
- inventory
- intangible property such as patents, copyrights, and trademarks
- property used outside the United States, or
- air conditioning and heating units.

So, what can a landlord use Section 179 for? Only for personal property not contained in your rental property, such as computers, office equipment, and office furniture you use in your office or other place of business. You can also use it for cars and other vehicles.

Other Restrictions

Section 179 expensing may be used only for used or new property that you purchase for cash (cash includes amounts you borrow). It may not be used for leased property or property you inherit or are given. Nor may it be used for property you buy from a relative, or from a corporation or other organization you control.

If you use property both for business and personal purposes, you may deduct it under Section 179 only if you use it for business purposes more than half of the time. Reduce the amount of your deduction by the percentage of personal use. You'll need to keep records showing your business use of such property. If you use an item for business less than half the time, you must depreciate it.

Deduction Limit

There is a limit on the total amount of business property expenses you can deduct each year using Section 179. In 2003, the limit increased from $24,000 to $100,000 and was increased again in 2007 to $125,000. It will stay at $125,000, with annual adjustments for inflation, until 2011, when it is scheduled to go down to $25,000.

Congress could decide to make the higher limit permanent, but at this point no one knows what will happen. So, if you're planning on buying over $25,000 worth of property that can be expensed for your business in a year and want to deduct the whole amount under Section 179, you should make your purchases before 2011.

This dollar limit applies to all your businesses together, not to each business you own and run. You do not have to claim the full amount. It's up to you to decide how much of the cost of property you want to deduct. But you don't lose out on the remainder; you can depreciate any cost you do not deduct under Section 179.

If you purchase more than one item of Section 179 property during the year, you can divide the deduction among all the items in any way, as long as the total deduction is not more than the Section 179 limit. It's usually best to apply Section 179 to property that has the longest useful life and therefore the longest depreciation period. This reduces the total time you have to wait to get your deductions.

Because Section 179 is intended to help smaller businesses, there is also a limit on the total amount of Section 179 property you can purchase each year. You must reduce your Section 179 deduction by one dollar for every dollar your annual purchases exceed the applicable limit. For 2007 through 2010, the limit is $500,000, plus an amount to be added for inflation. In 2011 and later, the limit is scheduled to go down to $200,000. Thus, for example, if you purchase $550,000 of Section 179 property in 2007, your Section 179 deduction for the year will be limited to $75,000 ($550,000 – $500,000 = $50,000; $125,000 deduction limit – $50,000 = $75,000).

Year	Section 179 Deduction Limit	Property Value Limit
2006	$108,000	$430,000
2007	$125,000	$500,000
2008–2010	$125,000 + annual inflation adjustment	$500,000 + annual inflation adjustment
2011	$25,000	$200,000

Income Limit on Section 179 Deduction

Here's yet another big limitation: You can't use Section 179 to deduct more in one year than the total of your profit from all of your businesses and your salary (if you have one). If you're married and file a joint tax return, you can include your spouse's salary and business income in this total as well. You can't count investment income—for example, interest you earn on your savings.

You can't use Section 179 to reduce your taxable income below zero. But you can carry to the next tax year any amount you cannot use as a Section 179 deduction and possibly deduct it then.

> **EXAMPLE:** In 2008, Amelia earned a $5,000 profit from her rental house and $10,000 from a part-time job. She spent $17,000 for computer and office equipment. She can use Section 179 to deduct $15,000 (her total profit and salary for the year) for 2008 and she can deduct the remaining $2,000 the next year.

Minimum Period of Business Use

When you deduct an asset under Section 179, you must continue to use it for business at least 50% of the time for as many years it would have been depreciated. For example, if you use Section 179 for a computer, you must use it for business at least 50% of the time for five years, because computers have a five-year depreciation period.

If you don't meet these rules, you'll have to report as income part of the deduction you took under Section 179 in the prior year. This is called recapture.

⚠️ **Make sure your rental activity qualifies as a business before you use Section 179.** If someone else does all the work for you, your rental activity may be an investment, not a business. Make sure you qualify as a business before you even think about using Section 179. This topic is covered in detail in Chapter 2.

When You Sell Your Property

When you sell your property, you'll have to pay tax on any gain (profit) you earn ("recognize," in tax lingo), unless you do a like-kind exchange. If you lose money, you'll be able to deduct the loss, subject to important limitations covered in Chapter 16. Whether you have a gain or loss depends on your adjusted basis in the property.

Adjusted Basis

Your basis in property is not fixed. It changes over time to reflect the true amount of your investment. This new basis is called the adjusted basis because it reflects adjustments from your starting basis.

Reductions in Basis

Each year, you must subtract from the property's basis the amount of depreciation allowed for the property—this is true regardless of whether you actually claimed any depreciation on your tax return. If you hold on to your property for the full recovery period—27.5 years for residential rental property—your adjusted basis will be reduced to zero, and there will be nothing left to depreciate.

Your starting basis in property must also be reduced by any items that represent a return of your cost. These include:

- the amount of any insurance or other payment you receive as the result of a casualty or theft loss
- any deductible casualty loss not covered by insurance (see Chapter 13), and
- any amount you receive for granting an easement.

Your basis is also reduced if you took the wrong amount of depreciation on your tax return. If you claimed too little depreciation, you must decrease the basis by the amount you should have taken. If you took too much depreciation, you must decrease your basis by the amount you should have deducted, plus the part of the excess you deducted that actually lowered your tax liability for any year.

Increases in Basis

You must increase the basis of any property by:

- the cost of any additions or improvements
- amounts spent to restore property after it is damaged or lost due to theft, fire, flood, storm, or other casualty (see Chapter 13)
- the cost of extending utility service lines to the property, and
- legal fees relating to the property, such as the cost of defending and perfecting title.

In addition, assessments for items that tend to increase the value of your property, such as streets and sidewalks, must be added to its basis. For example, if your city installs curbing on the street in front of your rental house, and assesses you for the cost, you must add the assessment to the basis of your property.

Effect of Adjusted Basis When You Sell

When you sell your rental property, your gain or loss for tax purposes is determined by subtracting its adjusted basis on the date of sale from the sales price (plus sales expenses, such as real estate commissions). Thus, reductions in basis can increase your tax liability when you sell your property because they will increase your gain. Increases in basis will reduce your gain and therefore your tax liability.

> **EXAMPLE:** Viola bought a small apartment building in January 2003 and sold it for $300,000 in December 2008. Her starting basis was $200,000. The following chart shows her adjusted basis for each year.

Year	Depreciation Deduction	Increases in Basis	Adjusted Basis (+ increases – reductions)
Original Cost			$200,000
2003	$ 6,970	None	193,030
2004	7,272	None	185,758
2005	7,272	None	178,486
2006	7,272	None	171,214
2007	7,272	None	163,942
2008	6,969	$13,027 for new roof	170,000
Total depreciation	$ 43,027		

> Viola calculates her taxable gain on the property by subtracting her adjusted basis in 2008 from the sales price: $300,000 – $170,000 = $130,000.

As you can see, when you sell your property, you effectively give back the depreciation deductions you took on it. Since they reduce your adjusted basis, they increase your taxable gain. Thus, Viola's taxable gain was increased by the $43,027 in depreciation deductions she took. The amount of your gain attributable to the depreciation deductions you took in prior years is taxed at a single 25% rate. Viola, for example, would have to pay a 25% tax on the $43,027 in depreciation deductions she received. The remaining gain on the sale is taxed at capital gains rates (usually 15%).

		Tax Rate	Tax
Sales price	$ 300,000		
Adjusted basis	170,000		
Total gain (sales price – adjusted basis)	$ 130,000		
Gain due to prior depreciation	43,027 X 25%	= $ 10,757	
Remaining capital gain (total gain – depreciation)	$ 86,973 X 15%	= 13,046	
Total Tax			$ 23,803

You can't avoid this result by failing to take depreciation deductions each year. The IRS will treat you as if you had taken the depreciation and reduce your adjusted basis accordingly. Thus, you'll end up paying tax on depreciation deductions you never claimed. A true tax disaster!

Like-Kind Exchanges: Deferring Taxes on Rental Property

In a like-kind exchange (also called a Section 1031 exchange), you can defer paying taxes upon the sale of property by swapping your property for similar property owned by someone else. The property you receive in a like-kind exchange is treated as if it were a continuation of the property you gave up. The result is that you postpone the recognition (taxation) of gain by shifting the basis of old property to the new property. So you defer paying taxes on any profit you would have received and own new property instead.

⚠ **Like-kind exchanges are one of the most complex areas of taxation.** There are many rules that are strictly enforced by the IRS. These exchanges should be done only with professional assistance.

> **EXAMPLE:** Eve exchanges a rental house with an adjusted basis of $250,000 for other real estate held for investment. The fair market value of both properties is $500,000. The basis of Eve's new property is the same as the basis of the old ($250,000). No gain is recognized on the transaction.

You may only exchange property for other similar property, called like-kind property by the IRS. Like-kind properties have the same nature or character, even if they differ in grade or quality. All real estate owned for investment or business use in the United States is considered to be like kind with all other such real estate in the United States, no matter the type or location. For example, an apartment building in New York is like kind to an office building in California.

If you keep exchanging your property for property worth at least as much as yours, you'll never recognize any gain on which you must pay tax. However, sooner or later you'll probably want to sell the replacement property for cash, not exchange it for another property. When this occurs, the original deferred gain, plus any additional gain realized since the purchase of the replacement property, is subject to tax. For this reason, a like-kind exchange is tax deferred, not tax free.

> **EXAMPLE 1:** Assume that five years after the exchange described in the above example, Eve sells her rental house for $800,000 cash. Now she has to pay tax—and quite a lot at that—because she has a $550,000 long-term capital gain. Her gain is $550,000 because her basis in the property is only $250,000 (the basis of the property she exchanged for the building five years earlier). The $800,000 sales price minus $250,000 basis = $550,000 gain. However, if you convert the last property you exchange into your personal residence, you can permanently exclude up to $500,000 of your gain from its sale. You must own the property for at least five years and live in it for at least two years to qualify for this exclusion.

> **EXAMPLE 2:** Assume that Eve rents out her house for all of 2006 and 2007. On April 15, 2008, she moves into the house and uses it as her personal residence. She can sell the property any time after April 14, 2011 (after five

years of ownership and living there for two years), and pay no tax at all on up to $500,000 of her gain because she is a married taxpayer filing jointly (the exclusion is only $250,000 for single taxpayers).

In practice, it's rarely the case that two people want to swap their properties with each other. Instead, one of the property owners usually wants cash for his or her property, not a swap. This transaction can still be structured as a like-kind exchange. This is often done with the help of a third party called a qualified intermediary or QI, in the business of facilitating like-kind exchanges.

EXAMPLE: Abe owns a rental triplex he bought for $400,000 and is now worth $500,000. He wants to exchange it for other property instead of selling it and having to pay tax on his $100,000 profit. He puts his property up for sale and in the meantime contacts Carl, a qualified intermediary. Carl locates a small apartment building for sale that Abe likes. Bob, the owner of the building, however, has no interest in exchanging it for other property. Carl and Abe enter into an exchange agreement. Carl purchases Bob's building for $200,000 cash that he borrows and then exchanges it for Abe's triplex. Carl receives a fee for facilitating the exchange and sells Abe's triplex to repay the funds he borrowed to buy Bob's property. With Carl's help, Abe has exchanged his triplex for Bob's building, even though Bob didn't want to do an exchange.

There are strict time limits on such delayed exchanges which can be more complicated than the above example, involving as many as four parties. You must identify the replacement property for your property within 45 days of its sale. And your replacement property purchase must be completed within 180 days of the initial sale. Because of these time limits, it's a good idea to have a replacement property lined up before you sell your property. Professional exchange companies (also called accommodators or facilitators) can help you find replacement property and handle the transaction for you. You can find listings for such companies through the website of the Federation of Exchange Accommodators at www.1031.org.

For more information on real property exchanges, see IRS Publication 544, *Sales and Other Disposition of Assets*, and IRS Form 8824, *Instructions, Like-Kind Exchanges*. Also, refer to *The Real Estate Investor's Tax Guide*, by Vernon Hoven (Dearborn).

Tax Reporting and Record Keeping for Depreciation

You must report depreciation on IRS Form 4562, Depreciation and Amortization. Carry over the amount of your depreciation to your Schedule E and subtract it from your gross rental income along with your other rental expenses.

Use a tax software program for Form 4562. Form 4562 is one of the most complex and confusing IRS forms. If you want to complete it yourself, do yourself a favor and use a tax preparation program.

You need to keep accurate records for each asset you depreciate showing:
- a description of the asset
- when and how you purchased the property
- the date it was placed in service
- its original cost
- the percentage of time you use it for business
- the amount of depreciation you took for the asset in prior years, if any
- the asset's depreciable basis
- the depreciation method used
- the length of the depreciation period, and
- the amount of depreciation you deducted for the year.

If you use tax preparation software, it should create a worksheet containing this information. Be sure to check these carefully and save them. You can also use an accounting program such as *QuickBooks* to keep track of your depreciating assets. (Simple checkbook programs like *Quicken* and *MSMoney* are not designed to track depreciation.) You may also use a spreadsheet program to create your own depreciation worksheet. Spreadsheet templates are available for this purpose. Of course, you can also do the job by hand.

The instructions to IRS Form 4562 contain a blank worksheet you can use.

An example of a filled-out worksheet is shown below.

Depreciation Worksheet

Description of Property	Date Placed in Service	Cost or Other Basis	Business/Investment Use Percentage	Section 179 Deduction and Special Allowance
House 666 First St.	2/10/05	$200,000	100%	0
New roof 123 Main St.	4/10/03	$10,000	100%	0

continued below

continued from above

Depreciation In Prior Years	Basis for Depreciation	Method/ Convention	Recovery Period	Rate or Table Percentage	Depreciation Deduction
0	$200,000	SL/MM	27.5	3.182%	$6,364
$258	$10,000	SL/MM	27.5	3.636%	$364

Be sure to keep all the documents you have showing the cost of your depreciable assets. This includes:

- your real property purchase agreement
- the settlement statement and closing statement you receive from the escrow company when your property purchase is completed
- canceled checks and receipts for all the expenses you paid for the purchase
- receipts and canceled checks for all improvements you make to the property
- property tax bills, and
- evidence for the improvement ratio (see Chapter 6).

If you use segmented depreciation (see Chapter 6), you need evidence of the personal property that was included with your purchase and its age—this includes carpeting, stove, refrigerator, dishwasher, drapes and other window coverings, washers, and dryers. You can include this information in your purchase agreement or a separate statement signed by the seller.

Chapter 6

Maximizing Your Depreciation Deductions

This chapter shows you two important ways to maximize your depreciation deductions. First, you'll learn how to best determine the value of your rental buildings and nondepreciable land. Next, you'll see how you can use segmented depreciation to greatly increase the depreciation deductions you get each year during the first few years you own rental property.

Do You Really Need a Larger Depreciation Deduction?

Using the methods described in this chapter to increase your depreciation deductions will be a pointless exercise if you can't make use of the deductions. This will be the case if more deductions will only increase your real estate losses and the passive activity loss rules prevent you from currently deducting any more losses than you already are deducting (or deducting any losses at all). If you're uncertain about whether you can make use of more rental activity deductions, carefully read Chapter 16. If you can't benefit from more deductions, don't bother using segmented depreciation.

Determining the Value of Your Land and Buildings

As discussed in Chapter 5, you can't depreciate land because it lasts forever. However, when you buy a rental property, you usually pay one lump sum that covers the cost of both the land and buildings it contains. To determine the depreciable value of the buildings (their basis), you must allocate the purchase price between the land and buildings and other depreciable property.

How you do this allocation is the single most important factor that will determine how much depreciation you may deduct each year and in total. The more your land is worth, the less your basis in the property and the less depreciation you will receive.

EXAMPLE: Miranda owns a duplex that cost $200,000. If the land is worth $50,000, she'll have a $150,000 depreciable basis for the building. If the land is worth $20,000, her basis in the building will be $180,000. The chart below illustrates the difference in the depreciation deductions she'll receive assuming the property was placed in service in January. She receives over $1,000 more in depreciation each year with the lower land valuation.

Year	Depreciation: $150,000 basis ($50,000 land value)	Depreciation: $180,000 basis ($20,000 land value)
1	$5,228	$6,264
2–27	$5,454	$6,555
28	$2,955	$3,546

It's up to you (or your accountant or tax preparer) to decide how much your land and buildings are worth in the first year you depreciate your property. You don't need to provide your allocation or explain how you arrived at it on the forms you file with the IRS to claim depreciation—you simply list your property's depreciable basis. However, the IRS can review your determination if you're audited. In that event, you'll need to explain how you arrived at your basis.

If the IRS determines that your valuation is too low, you'll have to pay back some of the depreciation you received, along with interest and, in some cases, tax penalties. (See "Tax Penalties for Unreasonable Valuations," below.)

Most people don't give their land valuation much thought; they simply use a standard formula or their property tax bill to determine its value. But, as explained below, there are other ways to value your land and buildings that may yield much better results.

Get it right the first time! You'll likely have to live with the depreciation valuations you come up with on the initial tax return you file for your rental property for the entire time you own the property. If you decide you made a mistake on your initial return and want to redo how you figured your depreciation, you will have to get permission from the IRS to amend your tax return (see Chapter 19). Your request can be denied and making the request may increase your chances of being audited. Thus, it pays to get it right the first time. You have plenty of time to work on your depreciation valuations—you don't need to file the first tax return for a rental property you buy until April 15 of the following year (and you can even get an extension until October 15, provided you pay all the tax you owe by April 15).

Tax Penalties for Unreasonable Valuations

The IRS may impose tax penalties if it determines that you overstated the value of your buildings and other depreciable property—and correspondingly, understated the value of your land. The penalty is equal to 20% of the amount of tax you underpaid. However, the penalty may be imposed only if you over-stated the value of your depreciable property by at least 200% over the correct amount and the overstatement resulted in an underpayment of tax of at least $5,000. Few small landlords ever overstate the value of their property by this much. Moreover, even if you do overstate your values by this amount, the IRS must waive the penalty if you had a "reasonable basis" for your valuation and acted in good faith. (IRC Sec. 6662.) The fact that your property valuations must be wildly inflated before you'll be subject to tax penalties gives you an idea of how much leeway you have in deciding what depreciable rental property is worth.

There Is No One Way to Determine Land and Building Values

The IRS gives landlords virtually no guidance on how to go about calculating the value of their land and buildings for depreciation purposes. Its regulations simply provide that "In the case of the acquisition ... of a combination of depreciable and nondepreciable property for a lump sum, as for example, buildings and land, the basis for depreciation cannot exceed an amount which bears the same proportion to the lump sum as the value of the depreciable property at the time of acquisition bears to the value of the entire property at that time." (IRS Reg. 1.167(a)-5.)

In other words, the basis of the nondepreciable land and the depreciable buildings and other improvements must be allocated in proportion to their relative values. But how do you arrive at these relative values? There is no single method to determine how much any property is worth, and the IRS does not require you to use any particular method. Different methods can yield very different results. The methods you may employ include using:

- your property tax bill
- the replacement cost of your building and improvements
- buyer–seller valuations, or
- comparable land sales.

You can try all these methods and use the best result, or average the various results you obtain. Remember, your valuation doesn't have to be precise, it just has to be a reasonable ballpark figure.

Figuring Your Improvement Ratio

The easy way to determine how much of the value of the property you can depreciate is to figure your property's improvement ratio (also called the land-to-building ratio or land-to-improvement ratio). This is the amount the improvements (buildings) are worth compared to the value of the total property, expressed as a percentage. This a mathematical way to show the relative values of the land and improvements, as the IRS regulation requires.

For example, if you determine that the correct improvement ratio for your property is 80%, you multiply the total cost of the property by this amount to determine your depreciable basis. If your total cost (purchase price + certain depreciable expenses of the sale) is $100,000, the amount you can depreciate is $80,000 ($100,000 x 80% = $80,000). The other $20,000 is the value of the land, which may not be depreciated.

Improvement ratios vary from 85% to 40% or less depending on the location of the property. Obviously, land values vary widely—for example, land in Manhattan or San Francisco is worth much more than the same amount of land in Kansas City or Portland. Thus, an apartment building in San Francisco may have a 40% improvement ratio, while the same structure in Portland would have an 80% ratio.

It's important to understand that there's no such thing as a precise improvement ratio for a property. This is because land value is not a fact, like the size of a lot; rather, it's based on someone's opinion or calculations based on certain assumptions. Different opinions or assumptions can lead to different ratios. You want your improvement ratio to be as high as possible, but not so high that the IRS will likely conclude it's unreasonable if you're audited.

Don't Use a Standard Improvement Ratio

Many accountants and tax preparers use a standard ratio for every property—for example, 75% or 80%. They don't bother to look at any evidence of the property's value, such as the county tax assessor's valuation or lender's appraisal. Don't use this method—it leaves much to be desired. If the IRS audits you and questions the ratio, you'll have no evidence to back it up.

Property Tax Bill

Most landlords determine their improvement ratios by using their property tax bill. The bill usually provides a valuation of the land and buildings together, and a value for each alone, or for just the buildings alone. The ratio is determined by dividing the assessed improvement value by the total assessed value of the property (assessed improvement value ÷ total assessed value = improvement ratio).

If you don't have a copy of your tax bill handy, you may be able to find the assessor's valuation at its website. The following websites provide links to local tax assessor websites in the various states:

- Property assessment databases: http://homepage.mac.com/researchventures, and
- Tax assessor database: www.pulawski.com

Often, the values listed on your property tax bill do not reflect the true market value of your property. This is not important, however, for purposes of determining your improvement ratio.

> **EXAMPLE:** Suzy buys a rental duplex with a total basis of $200,000 (purchase price + depreciable sale expenses). The property tax bill lists the property's total value at $160,000, and provides that the improvements are worth $110,000 and the land $50,000. According to the county tax assessor, therefore, the property has a 69% improvement ratio. ($110,000 ÷ $160,000 = 69%). Using this percentage, her depreciable basis is $110,400. (69% x $160,000 = $110,400.) She may use this amount to determine her depreciation each year.

This is a very easy and simple way to calculate the value of your land and buildings. It is what most people do, and the IRS will almost never object if you use this method. However, improvement ratios determined from a property tax assessment often do not reflect reality. County tax assessors aren't greatly concerned about arriving at an accurate breakdown of the relative values of your land and improvements. This is because it has no effect on your property tax bill—your tax is based on the total assessed value of your property. Often, county assessors apply a standard percentage to all property in the area—for example, 70%. Or, they may use sales data from previous years which is out of date.

As a general rule, tax assessor improvement ratios are on the low side. You can usually do better using a different means to determine your basis.

You Don't Have to Use the Assessor's Valuation

Many people believe they have to use their county tax assessor's valuations to calculate their basis. This is not the case. There is nothing in the tax law or IRS regulations that requires you to use a county tax assessor valuation or hire an appraiser to do a valuation. Indeed, in at least one case, the tax court found that the improvement ratio derived from the county assessor's valuation should not be used, declaring that there was no evidence that "the assessor's allocations of value between land and building comport with reality." (*Meiers v. Comm'r.*, T.C. Memo 1982-5.) This is a good case to point out to any IRS auditor who says you have to use your county tax assessor's valuation.

Replacement Cost

Another way to determine your improvement ratio is to use the replacement cost of your building and other improvements. The replacement cost is the cost to build a brand new structure that is identical with the structure currently on your land.

EXAMPLE: Steven Meiers purchased two condominiums in 1977. His property tax bill gave an improvement ratio of 55%—that is, the land was worth 45% of the purchase price and the building 55%. Meiers didn't think this was good enough. He investigated the replacement costs for his buildings, and determined that a fair improvement ratio was 80%. This, of course, gave him a much higher depreciable basis. Meiers was audited by the IRS, which insisted that he should use the tax assessor's ratio. Meiers appealed to the tax court and won. The court found that Meier's 80% ratio was reasonable and should be used. How did Meier's calculate his ratio? He used the replacement cost of the buildings. (*Meiers v. Comm'r.*, T.C. Memo 1982-5.)

There are several ways to determine replacement cost:
- appraisal
- your own calculations
- expert opinion, or
- construction records.

Appraisal

If you borrowed money from a bank or other lender to acquire the property, the lender almost certainly required an appraisal before approving your loan. You should make sure to obtain and keep a copy of the appraisal. It should contain the appraiser's estimate of how much it would cost to replace the structure and how much the land is worth. This may be in the section of the appraisal report called cost approach. The appraiser provides an estimate of how much it would cost to replace the structure with an identical new structure, and then reduces this amount with an allowance for depreciation, depending on the age of the building. The appraiser also gives an estimate of the cost of replacing improvements other than the building—for example, walkways. These are added together to come up with the total replacement cost—often called indicated value by cost approach. The IRS will probably accept the appraiser's valuation, unless it's clearly unreasonable.

You calculate your improvement ratio by dividing the amount of the appraiser's replacement cost by the appraised value of the entire property (structures and land). In other words, appraiser's replacement cost of building and land improvements ÷ appraised value of entire property = improvement ratio.

> **EXAMPLE:** Recall Miranda from the first example who bought a rental duplex for $200,000. Her lender's appraisal provides that the value of the entire property is $210,000. The cost method section says that the replacement cost of the duplex and other property improvements is $150,000. This gives Miranda an improvement ratio of 75% ($150,000 ÷ $200,000 = 75%.) This is better than the 69% improvement ratio the county assessor's valuation provided.

Calculating Replacement Value Yourself

Appraisers are not infallible. An appraisal is just one person's opinion as to how much a property is worth. Appraisals of the same property by different appraisers can and do differ. Your lender's appraisal of the replacement cost may have been poorly done or been too conservative. Like county tax assessors, lenders' appraisers are more concerned with the total value of the property than the relative values of the land and structures; so they may not have given the replacement cost calculation all the time and attention you would like.

If you think this is the case, you can hire an appraiser to do a new valuation of your property. An appraisal for a single-family residence costs about $375 to $400. Appraising an income property of two or more units costs at least $800 to $1,000. Your appraisal will carry the most weight with the IRS if it's done by a well-qualified appraiser. Well-qualified real estate appraisers ordinarily belong to the Appraisal Institute and use the initials MAI (Member of the Appraisal Institute). You can find a directory of MAI appraisers at www.appraisalinstitute.org.

If you want to pay for an appraisal, go ahead. However, you don't have to hire an expensive appraiser to determine your property's replacement cost. You can do it yourself. This is what Steven Meiers in the above example did. This will require that you spend a little time and effort, but will enable you to cheaply double check the replacement cost determined by the lender's appraiser.

Figuring out the replacement cost for a building might sound hard, but it really isn't. The Marshall and Swift Valuation Service has a website that will calculate the replacement cost of a building for you (www.swiftestimator.com). All you have to do is plug in detailed information about the structure—its size, buildings materials, age, location, and so forth. It is very inexpensive to use—just a few dollars per estimate.

If you don't want to use a website, you can calculate your building's replacement cost by using one of the many readily available publications that provide estimates of how much it costs to build any type of structure. These include:

- The *National Building Cost Manual* (Craftsman Book Company; www.costbook.com)
- The *National Construction Cost Estimator* (Craftsman Book Company), and
- *Walker's Building Estimator's Reference Book* (Frank R. Walker Co.).

You should be able to find one or more of these in your public library. Make sure to use the current edition. These books are updated each year.

EXAMPLE: Miranda wants to figure the replacement value of her duplex herself. She refers to the *National Building Cost Manual* book in her local library. It tells her that the cost to build a four-unit building like hers of average quality is $60 per square foot. Her building contains 3,000 square feet, resulting in a $180,000 replacement cost. However, the $180,000 amount represents the cost to build a brand new building. Miranda's building is five years old. The *National Building Cost Manual* tells Miranda that a building like hers has approximately a 55-year useful life and will be worth 88% of its original cost after five years. 88% of $180,000 equals $158,400. This is the true approximate value of Miranda's building. This amount gives her an improvement ratio of 79% ($158,400 ÷ $200,000 = 79%). This is better than the 75% improvement ratio she obtained using the appraiser's valuation. She decides to use this improvement ratio to calculate her depreciation. She takes care to keep all the documentation showing how she calculated her duplex's replacement value, including making copies of the relevant pages from the *National Building Cost Manual.*

Expert Opinion

Another, perhaps easier, way to figure out a building's replacement cost yourself is to ask your insurance company. They insure buildings, so they need to know accurately how much they are worth. Ask your insurance agent when you purchase the insurance for your property. Local builders can also tell you how much it would cost to rebuild a structure like yours. Ideally, you should have the insurance agent or builder write down the estimate on his or her letterhead, and date and sign it. Be sure to keep it in your records.

Construction Records

Alternatively, if you built the building yourself, or bought it from a seller who built it, you may have ready access to construction documentation showing exactly how much it cost to build the structure. This will make it easy to figure the replacement value—use the original cost less a reduction for depreciation that you can calculate using the references listed above.

Buyer–Seller Valuation

When you buy real estate, you usually pay one lump sum for everything on the property. However, you and the seller could agree on how much the land and buildings are worth and list the values in your purchase agreement.

EXAMPLE: Charles Nicholson had the following language added to the escrow instructions for commercial property he purchased in Northern California: "80% of the real estate value is attributed to the building and 20% to land." Unfortunately for Nicholson, the IRS didn't agree with this allocation and neither did the tax court. The court found that there wasn't a shred of evidence that the building was worth 80% of the property's purchase price. Instead, it concluded that a 10% improvement ratio was proper. (*Nicholson v. Comm'r.,* T.C. Memo 1993-183.)

As the *Nicholson* case shows, any allocation you and the seller agree on probably isn't worth much. Sellers ordinarily don't care about the cost allocation between the land and building—they're only concerned with the total purchase price. Thus, they are likely to agree to any allocation the buyer wants. This makes such allocations inherently suspect in the eyes of the IRS and courts.

However, this doesn't mean that it's necessarily a bad idea to allocate the purchase price between the land and buildings in your purchase agreement. It costs nothing to do so and the allocation could impress an IRS auditor who doesn't know what he or she is doing (more than a few fall into this category). Make sure, though, that your allocation is not unreasonable, or the IRS will likely ignore it.

Comparable Land Sales

An entirely different way to determine your depreciable basis is to estimate the value of your land alone by seeing what comparable unimproved real estate in the area sells for. To do this, you look at the selling prices of a number of vacant lots, calculate their average per-square-foot cost, and apply it to your land. Be warned, however, that this approach often leads to inflated land values.

> **EXAMPLE:** Miranda's rental duplex has a 10,000 square foot lot. She looks at three similar vacant lots in the area that sold in the past two years. Their total square footage was 25,000, and the total sales price for the lots was $150,000. This results in an average per-square-foot cost of $6. By applying this average cost to her property, Miranda determines that her land is worth $60,000 ($6 x 10,000 square feet = $60,000). This is, by far, the worst result Miranda achieved with any of the methods she used. Even using the assessed valuation, her land was worth only $50,000.

You can look for comparable lots offered for sale in the area in the multiple listing service, or check the county recorder's office. However, it may be hard to find any comparable unimproved land if your property is in a highly urban area. Also, you need to make sure to compare the prices only of unimproved lots—that is, lots that don't have underground utilities, sidewalks, or grading. Improvements such as these increase land values, so you'll get an inflated result.

Segmented Depreciation

When you purchase a rental property—whether a house, duplex, apartment building, or condominium—you pay a single lump sum to the owner, but you are actually purchasing more than one asset. Rental property consists of:

- the land the building sits on, as well as any other surrounding land included with the purchase
- improvements that have been made to the land, such as landscaping
- the building itself, and
- personal property items inside the building that are not building components—for example, refrigerators, stoves, dishwashers, and carpeting.

Most landlords depreciate all these items together (excluding the land, which is not depreciable), using the 27.5-year recovery period for buildings and the straight-line depreciation method—which is how buildings must be depreciated (see Chapter 5).

However, you have the option of depreciating each asset separately. (*Hospital Corporation of America*, 109 T.C. 21 (1997).) This depreciation method is more complicated, and will require more record keeping, but it will result in a larger total depreciation deduction each year during the first several years you own the property. This is because personal property and land improvements have much shorter depreciation periods than residential real property and can be depreciated using accelerated depreciation. Your total depreciation deduction won't be any different, but you'll get it much more quickly.

The technical name for this type of depreciation is cost segregation. For convenience, we'll refer to it as segmented depreciation.

Cost Segregation Study

You may wish to hire an engineer to conduct a cost segregation study to determine how to classify and value your property's various components. The engineer should inspect the property and, wherever possible, use construction-based documents such as blueprints and specifications to determine the value of the building components. When estimates are required, they should be based on costing data from contractors or reliable published sources. The engineer should prepare a detailed written report that you can show to the IRS if you are audited and it questions your valuations. Such a study can be expensive—typically $10,000 to $25,000, but the cost is a tax deductible business expense. Whether paying for such a study makes sense for you depends on how much your rental property is worth. The speedier depreciation you'll obtain may justify the expense if your property is worth $750,000 or more.

Identifying Your Personal Property

It is to your advantage to identify as many items of personal property inside and outside your rental building as you can. This way, you can depreciate them separately from your building and land improvements using accelerated depreciation and shorter recovery periods.

Any tangible property inside, or attached to, your rental building, that is not a structural component, is personal property for depreciation purposes. IRS regulations define structural components as:

- "all parts of a building," and
- "all other components relating to the operation or maintenance of a building." (IRS Reg. 1.48-1(e)(2).

Ordinarily, a building is planned, designed, and constructed with the expectation that the structural components will remain in place indefinitely. They are usually integrated with the building during the construction phase and are permanent parts of the building. They are not installed merely to meet the peculiar needs of a tenant. As a general rule, they are for the operation or maintenance of a building and "cannot be removed or relocated without doing at least temporary damage to the building itself." (*Metro Nat'l. Corp. v. Comm'r.*, T.C. Memo. 1987-38.)

The tax court developed six questions designed to determine whether a particular asset qualifies as personal property:

1. Can the property be moved and has it been moved? A "yes" indicates the item is personal property.

2. Is the property designed or constructed to remain permanently in place? A "yes" indicates the property is a building component.

3. Are there circumstances that show that the property may or will have to be moved? A "yes" indicates the item is personal property.

4. Is the property readily movable? A "yes" indicates the item is personal property.

5. How much damage will the property sustain when it is removed? The less damage, the more likely the property is personal property.

6. How is the property affixed to land? The more permanently affixed, the more likely the property is a building component. (*Whiteco Industries, Inc. v. Comm'r.*, 65 T.C. 664, 672-673 (1975).)

The following tables list common types of assets inside rental buildings that are structural components and personal property.

Personal Property
Kitchen appliances, such as stoves, refrigerators, dishwashers, microwaves, and trash compactors (IRS Reg. 1.48-1(c))
Removable partitions (Senate Report 95-163; (*Metro Nat'l. Corp. v. Comm'r.*, T.C. Memo. 1987-38))
Carpeting that is tacked down, not glued to the floor (Senate Report 95-163)
Tile flooring applied with adhesives designed to ease its removal—not cemented, mudded, or otherwise permanently affixed to the building floor (Senate Report 95-163)
Clothes washers and dryers (*Mandler v. Comm'r.*, 65 T.C. 586)
Furniture owned by the landlord (Rev. Rul. 81-133)
Ornamental fixtures (Senate Report 95-163)
Drapes, curtains, and window blinds (IRS Reg. 1.48-1(c))
False balconies (Senate Report 95-163)

Personal Property (continued)

Awnings and canopies (PLR 7102269400A)

Fire extinguishers (Rev. Rul. 67-417)

Portable space heaters (Rev. Rul. 70-103)

Lighting to illuminate the exterior of a building, but not lighting for parking areas (Senate Report 95-163)

Decorative lighting, such as chandeliers and décor wall lights *(Morrison, Inc. v. Comm'r.,* T.C. Memo. 1986)

Fire extinguishers (Rev. Rul. 67-417)

Plants inside a building *(Texas Instruments, Inc. v. Comm'r.,* T.C. Memo. 1992-306)

Advertising signs *(Whiteco Industries, Inc. v. Comm'r.,* 65 T.C. 664, 672-673 (1975)

Portable window air conditioners *(Film N' Photos v. Comm'r.,* 37 TCM 709.)

Moveable storage sheds (PLR 7102269400A)

Building Components

Walls and nonmoveable partitions and permanent coverings for them, such as paneling (IRS Reg. 1.48-1(e)(2))

Floors and permanent coverings for them, such as tiling that has been cemented or glued to the floor (IRS Reg. 1.48-1(e)(2))

Ceilings, including suspended ceilings (IRS Reg. 1.48-1(e)(2); *Boddie-Noelle Enters. v. United States,* 96-2 USTC ¶ 50,627 (Fed. Cl. 1996))

Windows and doors (IRS Reg. 1.48-1(e)(2))

All components of a central air conditioning or heating system, including motors, compressors, pipes, and ducts (whether in, on, or adjacent to the building) (IRS Reg. 1.48-1(e)(2))

Plumbing and plumbing fixtures, such as sinks and bathtubs (IRS Reg. 1.48-1(e)(2))

Electric wiring and lighting fixtures (IRS Reg. 1.48-1(e)(2))

Chimneys and fireplaces (IRS Reg. 1.48-1(e)(2))

Stairways and elevators (IRS Reg. 1.48-1(e)(2))

Sprinkler systems (IRS Reg. 1.48-1(e)(2))

Fire escapes (IRS Reg. 1.48-1(e)(2))

Determining Fair Market Value of Personal Property

The tax basis of personal property you purchase as part of a rental property is its fair market value. If the property is new, or fairly new, you can use the cost to replace it. The new prices for any type of personal property can easily be researched on the Internet, or using publications such as the Sears catalog.

If the property is older, you'll need to figure out the value based on the new price minus an amount for the wear and tear the property has undergone. Look at classified ads and listings for similar property on eBay, or call people who buy and sell the type of property involved. If you think the property is extremely valuable, get an appraisal from an expert. Keep records of how you calculated the property's value.

If you don't want to spend a huge amount of time calculating fair market values, you can limit your segmented depreciation to big ticket items, such as kitchen appliances and carpets. But, the more personal property you separately depreciate, the faster you'll get your deductions for the property.

Steps to Calculate Segmented Depreciation

You must calculate segmented depreciation in the proper order, or you'll get less than you should. Here are the steps:

Step 1: Determine the cost of your property as a whole—this is the purchase price plus certain other expenses (see Chapter 5).

Step 2: Determine the fair market value of the personal property included with the purchase and deduct it from your total cost. (See "Determining the Value of Your Land and Buildings," above.) We'll call this amount (cost minus personal property) your preliminary basis.

Step 3: Determine your improvement ratio (see "Determining the Value of Your Land and Buildings," above) and multiply it by your preliminary basis. This amount is the basis in your building and land improvements together.

Step 4: Determine the value of the depreciable land improvements on your property and deduct it from your basis. The remainder is the depreciable basis of your building alone. How to value land improvements is covered in Chapter 5. This can take some time and effort. If you want, you can skip this step and include the land improvements with your building for depreciation purposes. However, be aware that when you do this, it will take you over twice as long to fully depreciate your land improvements.

Step 5: Create three different depreciation schedules: one each for your personal property, land improvements, and building. (You don't need a schedule for land improvements if you don't separately depreciate them.)

EXAMPLE: Jack purchases a small rental house in January. He determines his depreciation deductions as follows:

1. He figures the total cost of the house—he paid $150,000 for the house, plus the following amounts:

Escrow fee	$ 375
Document preparation fee	150
Notary fee	30
Recording fee	145
Survey fee	50
Title insurance	900
Total	$1,650

This gives Jack a total cost for the property of $151,650.

2. Jack determines the fair market value of the personal property included with the house. This consists of:

Wall-to-wall carpet (new)	$4,830
Stove (10 years old)	100
Refrigerator (5 years old)	200
Dishwasher (new)	707
Venetian blinds (3 years old)	500
Total	$6,337

Jack deducts this amount from his total cost to determine his preliminary basis ($151,650 − $6,337 = $145,313).

3. Jack determines his improvement ratio to be 80%, based on the replacement cost of the house. He multiplies this by his preliminary basis to determine the basis for his building and improvements together (80% x $145,313 = $116,250). This is the value of his house and improvements, not counting the land they occupy.

4. Jack determines the cost of the land improvements on his property:

Landscaping	$ 1,000
Fence	2,000
Driveway	1,200
Walkway	800
Total	$ 5,000

Jack deducts the value of the land improvements from the basis for the house and improvements he calculated in Step 3 ($116,250 − $5,000 = $111,250). This is the depreciable basis for the house alone.

5. Jack creates separate depreciation schedules for the personal property, land improvements, and house.

Year	House ($111,250 basis; 27.5-year recovery period; straight-line method; property placed in service in January)	Land improvements ($5,000 basis; 15-year recovery period; 150% declining balance method)	Personal property ($6,337 basis; 5-year recovery period; 200% declining balance method)	Total
1	$3,877	250	1,267	$5,394
2	4,045	475	2,028	6,528
3	4,045	428	1,217	5,625
4	4,045	385	730	5,160
5	4,045	347	730	5,122
6	4,045	312	365	4,722
7–15	4,045	295		4,340
16	4,045	148		4,093
17–27	4,045			4,045
28	2,192			2,192

In contrast, if Jack simply depreciated the house, improvements, and personal property together, his depreciation schedule would look like this:

80% improvement ratio x $151,650 cost = $121,320 basis

Year	Depreciation
1	$4,186
2–27	$4,411
28	$2,390

As you can see, for the first six years Jack owns the house, he gets substantially larger depreciation deductions by using segmented depreciation.

Chapter 7

Interest

nterest is often a landlord's single biggest expense. This chapter explains when and how it can be deducted.

Interest Landlords Can (and Can't) Deduct

As a general rule, you may deduct interest on money you borrow for a business or investment activity, including being a landlord. A landlord's most common deductible interest payments are:

- mortgage interest payments to banks and other financial institutions on loans used to acquire rental property
- mortgage interest payments to financial institutions on loans used to improve rental property
- interest on credit cards for goods or services used in a rental activity, and
- personal loans for any item used in a rental activity.

The limitations on when and how these interest payments may be deducted are explained in more detail below.

No deduction for money kept in the bank. You get no rental deduction for interest you pay on loan proceeds that you keep in the bank. Your rental interest deduction begins only when you spend the money on your rental activity. Money kept in the bank is considered an investment—at best you might be able to deduct the interest you pay on the money as investment interest.

Certain types of interest can't be deducted under any circumstances:

Interest on money you don't owe. You may only deduct interest for money you legally owe. If you are liable for part of a debt, you can deduct only your share of the total interest paid or accrued.

EXAMPLE: Sandra and her daughter, Sally, purchase a rental house together. Both their names are on the deed, but only Sally's name is on the mortgage. Because Sandra is not legally liable for the mortgage, she cannot deduct any interest she pays on it; only Sally gets this deduction.

Interest paid with funds borrowed from original lender. You cannot deduct interest you pay with funds borrowed from the original lender through a second loan, an advance, or any other arrangement similar to a loan. You can deduct the interest expense once you start making payments on the new loan. When you make a payment on the new loan, you first apply the payment to interest and then to the principal.

> **EXAMPLE:** Phil obtains a $20,000 high-interest, short-term loan from the Acme Finance Company to pay for repairs to get his aged rental building up to code and avoid a condemnation. Phil is personally liable for the loan. He falls behind in his loan payments. To avoid having Acme take his bank accounts or personal property, he obtains a second loan from Acme for $5,000, secured by his own house. He uses the second loan to pay $5,000 in overdue payments on his original loan from Acme. The $5,000 payment, which is almost all for interest charges, is not a deductible interest payment. Six months later, Phil pays back the $5,000 loan with interest. He can deduct the interest he pays on this loan.

Interest on income tax. Interest charged on income tax assessed on your individual income tax return is not deductible even though the tax due is related to income from your rental activity.

Mortgage Interest

Landlords typically borrow money from banks or other financial institutions to purchase their rental properties. Indeed, it's not uncommon for a landlord to make a down payment of as little as 10%, 5%, or even 0% of the purchase price to buy a rental property, financing the remainder with one or more loans. The ability to borrow so much to purchase real estate is one of its great attractions as an investment. The more leverage you have, the more money you can make for each dollar invested. (Leverage means using borrowed funds to increase your total purchasing power.)

You can deduct the mortgage interest you pay for a rental property each year as it is paid. You list the deduction on Schedule E, on the line labeled "Mortgage interest paid to banks, etc."

Interest, Not Principal, Is Deductible

You only deduct the interest you pay on a loan to purchase or improve a rental property. You may not deduct payments of principal—that is, your repayments of the amount you borrowed. The principal is ordinarily added to the basis of your property and depreciated over 27.5 years. (See Chapter 5.)

EXAMPLE: Ken takes out a $10,000 second mortgage on his rental house to remodel the kitchen. This is a home improvement loan. The $10,000 loan amount is not deductible. Instead, it is added to Ken's basis in the home and depreciated over 27.5 years.

In contrast, if you borrow money to repair your rental property, you may deduct the principal amount of the loan in the year in which it is incurred as an operating expense. You deduct the interest as it is paid each year. (See Chapter 4 for a detailed discussion of the difference between a repair and an improvement.)

EXAMPLE: Ken later takes out a $10,000 third mortgage on his rental home to repair the roof. This expense is a repair, not an improvement. The $10,000 principal amount of the loan is deductible in full in the year Ken takes out the loan. He deducts the interest on the loan as he pays it each year.

It's easy to keep track of how much of your loan payments are for interest and how much for principal. If you paid $600 or more of mortgage interest (including certain points) during the year on any one mortgage, you will receive an IRS Form 1098 from the lender listing how much you paid in interest during the year.

Depending on the length of the loan, your first few years' payments will be mostly for interest, not principal. For example, with a 20-year self-amortizing loan at a 6% interest rate, you would pay off only 15% of the principal over the first five years; the other 85% of the monthly payments pay off interest, which is deductible. However, as a loan becomes "seasoned" (gets older) more and more of the loan payments are for repayment of principal, not interest, and are therefore not deductible. When your loan is paid off, you'll get no more interest deductions. This is something to keep in mind when you figure the value of your tax deduction for a rental property.

Expenses to Obtain a Mortgage

You can't deduct as interest any expenses you pay to obtain a mortgage on your rental property. Instead, these expenses are added to your basis in the property and depreciated along with the property itself (see Chapter 5). These basis adjustments include:

- abstract fees
- charges for installing utility services
- legal fees

- mortgage commissions
- recording fees
- surveys
- transfer taxes
- title insurance, and
- any amounts the seller owes that you agree to pay, such as back taxes or interest, recording or mortgage fees, charges for improvements or repairs, and sales commissions.

Private Mortgage Insurance

Private mortgage insurance (PMI) is a special insurance policy that protects the lender if the borrower defaults on the loan. A landlord can deduct any PMI premiums he or she pays on rental property as they are paid each year. You list the deduction on Line 9 of Schedule E—write "PMI" on the dotted line.

Mortgage Refinancing

One way to use real estate to get cash is to do a "cash-out refinancing"—obtain a new loan to pay off your old loan, plus borrow more money to end up with cash in your pocket. However, you may not deduct the interest on the cash-out portion of the loan unless you use the money to do real estate improvements (or to pay for certain medical or education expenses).

> **EXAMPLE:** Tim owes $100,000 on his rental duplex, which has a fair market value of $200,000. He obtains a new $150,000 loan on the property. He pays off the original $100,000 loan and puts the other $50,000 in his pocket to use for a vacation, new car, and other personal purposes. He may only deduct two-thirds of the interest he pays on the new loan because the other third was a cash-out that he used for personal purposes. However, if Tim used the $50,000 to pay for new improvements to his duplex, he could deduct all of the interest.

Mixed-Use Properties

If you live in a multiunit building and rent out the other units, you claim the home mortgage deduction for the portion you live in and deduct the remainder as a landlord expense on your Schedule E. If you receive one bill, you should prorate the rental portion based on square footage.

> **EXAMPLE:** Samantha owns a duplex and lives in one unit and rents out the other. She has a $100,000 home loan on the entire property, for which she paid $6,000 in interest this year. Both units are the same size, so Samantha deducts 50% of her interest payment as a personal itemized deduction on her Schedule A, and the other 50% as a landlord expense on her Schedule E.

Other Interest Expenses

Landlords aren't just limited to deducting interest on mortgages. Other interest is also deductible.

Credit Cards and Loans

If you use your credit card or take out a loan to purchase goods or services for your rental activity, you can deduct the interest you pay to the credit card company or lender, even if you have to depreciate the principal amount of the purchase. This is considered trade or business interest because the borrowed money is used to help carry on your business. A typical example is interest on a credit card (or bank loan) used to purchase supplies for your rental activity.

Business interest is fully deductible in the year in which it is paid (or incurred in the case of accrual basis taxpayers; see Chapter 17).

> **EXAMPLE:** Andre uses his credit card to purchase and install a $900 dishwasher in a rental duplex he owns. The credit card interest he pays on the $900 is deductible as it is paid. However, the $900 cost of the dishwasher must be depreciated over five years. (See Chapter 5.)

It's a very good idea to use a separate credit card to buy things for your rental activity. If you use a credit card to buy rental-related items and personal items, you'll have to figure out how much of the monthly credit card interest you pay is for the rental items and how much for the personal items—often, a math nightmare.

Car Loans

If you use your car for your rental activity, you can deduct the interest that you pay on your car loan as an interest expense. You can take this deduction whether you deduct your car expenses using the actual expense method or the standard mileage rate, because the standard mileage rate was not intended to encompass interest on a car loan. The amount you can deduct depends on how much you use the car for business—for example, if you use it 25% of the time for your rental business, you may deduct 25% of your car loan interest payments. (See Chapter 10.)

Home Offices

If you take the home office deduction, you can deduct the home office percentage of your home mortgage interest as a business expense, instead of an itemized personal deduction. (See Chapter 9 for more on the home office deduction.)

Home Equity Loans

In some cases, it could be advantageous taxwise to use a home equity loan for landlord purposes. A home equity loan is a loan for which you use your main home or second home as collateral. Interest on home equity loans of less than $100,000 is deductible as an itemized personal deduction. This is so regardless of how the money is spent—for example, you could spend the money on your rental activities and still deduct the interest as a personal deduction.

This could be favorable for a landlord because these loans are not subject to the passive activity rules discussed in Chapter 16. Thus, you can deduct the interest regardless of whether the passive loss rules prevent you from deducting your other rental expenses.

Points and Prepaid Interest

If you are a cash basis taxpayer (the vast majority of small landlords are—see Chapter 17), you may not deduct interest that you prepay in a single year. Instead, you must allocate the interest over the tax years to which it applies and deduct it in those years.

The most common type of prepaid interest is points. The term points is often used to describe some of the charges paid by a borrower when the borrower takes out a loan or a mortgage. A point is equal to 1% of the loan amount—for example, one point on a $100,000 loan is $1,000. These charges are also called loan origination fees, maximum loan charges, loan discounts, or premium charges. If any of these charges (points) are solely for the use of money, they are interest for tax purposes. Because points are prepaid interest, you cannot deduct the full amount in the year paid. (However, there is an exception for points paid on your home mortgage—see IRS Publication 936, *Home Mortgage Interest Deduction*, for details.) Instead, you must allocate the interest payment portion over the term of the loan and only deduct for payments allocated for that tax year.

You deduct points in equal amounts over the life of the loan. You divide the points by the number of payments over the term of the loan and deduct points for the year according to the number of payments made in that year. This process is called amortization. If the loan ends prematurely, due to a payoff or refinancing, for example, then the remaining points are deducted in that year.

> **EXAMPLE:** Assume that you take out a 20-year loan in January to purchase a rental house. You pay $3,000 in points to obtain the mortgage. A 20-year loan has 240 payments (20 years x 12 months = 240). $3,000 ÷ 240 = $12.50. Thus, you deduct $12.50 for each month you pay off your loan. If you pay the loan for a full year, you get a $150 deduction for that year. If you sell the house after five years, you deduct the remaining $2,250 that year.

Some real estate loans are structured with balloon payments: The monthly loan payments are based on a relatively lengthy time period, which keeps the payments lower, but the entire loan must be paid off at an earlier date. In this event, you can amortize any loan points over the earlier time period.

> **EXAMPLE:** Vic obtained a $200,000 mortgage to buy a small apartment building. He pays three points for the loan ($6,000). His monthly payments are based on a 20-year term. However, he must pay off the entire loan with a balloon payment at the end of 60 months. He can deduct his points over 60 months instead of 240 months (20 years). This enables him to deduct $100 per month, instead of $25.

The first year you deduct points, you must list the amount in the amortization section of IRS Form 4562, Depreciation and Amortization. You then add the amount to your other mortgage interest deductions you list on IRS Schedule E (see Chapter 18).

Interest on Construction Loans

If you borrow money to construct a rental property, you may currently deduct as an operating expense the interest you pay before construction begins and after it ends. However, you may not deduct the interest you pay during the construction period. Instead, this cost must be added to the basis of your property and depreciated over 27.5 years. (See Chapter 5.) (IRC Sec. 263A(f)(1).)

The construction period for real property begins when physical construction starts. Physical construction includes:

- clearing, grading, or excavating land
- demolishing or gutting an existing building
- construction of infrastructure such as sidewalks, sewers, cables, and wiring
- structural, mechanical, or electrical work on a building, and
- landscaping.

The construction period ends when all production activities reasonably expected to be done are completed and the property is placed in service—that is, made available for rent.

Activities such as planning and design, preparing architectural blueprints, or obtaining building permits do not constitute physical construction. Thus, interest paid while these activities are going on, but before physical construction is done, can be currently deducted as an operating expense.

> **EXAMPLE:** Jennifer obtains a $100,000 loan to construct a rental house. She gets the loan on January 15 and starts paying interest on February 1. Because of problems in obtaining final approval for a building permit, physical construction of the house does not begin until June 1. Jennifer may deduct the interest she paid during February through May. She cannot, however, deduct the interest she pays while the house is being constructed from May through October. Instead, she must add it to the tax basis of the house and depreciate it over 27.5 years. The interest Jennifer pays after the house is completed and offered for rent she can currently deduct as she pays it each year.

Loans With Low or No Interest

One way a person who sells real property and finances all or part of the sale him- or herself can save on taxes is to charge little or no interest on the amount the buyer borrows. To make up for the low or no interest, the seller increases the property's purchase price. This is advantageous for the seller because interest payments are taxed at ordinary income tax rates, while the gain on the sale of real property owned for more than one year is taxed at lower capital gains rates (usually 20%).

EXAMPLE: Joe owns a rental house with a fair market value of $100,000. He sells the property to Jean. Jean pays $120,000. She puts down $20,000 and Joe finances the remainder himself, charging Jean only 2% interest. He pays 20% capital gains tax on his gain on the sale ($120,000 minus his $60,000 basis), and ordinary income tax on the interest payments Jean will make—taxed at Joe's top 28% income tax rate. Joe comes out ahead on the deal by getting a higher sales price for the property and charging less interest.

Unfortunately for sellers, the IRS is well aware of this scheme. If an installment sale contract does not provide for adequate interest, part of the sales price must be treated as interest for tax purposes. This amount is called "unstated interest" or "original issue discount," depending upon the circumstances. The seller must reduce the stated sales price, and increase his or her annual interest income, by this interest amount. For the buyer, the property's basis is the stated purchase price, less the amount considered to be unstated interest.

How much interest is too little? Generally, an interest rate is inadequate if it is less than the applicable federal rate of interest (AFR). The AFR is set by the IRS each month. You can find it on the IRS website at www.irs.gov (look for the Index of Applicable Federal Rates). For example, in June 2005, the AFR for a loan of over nine years paid monthly was 4.48%.

Calculating how much additional interest must be paid is very complicated. Refer to IRS Publication 537, *Installment Sales*, for more information; or, better yet, see an accountant.

Loans on Rental Property Used for Nonrental Purposes

You can take out a loan secured by your rental property and use the proceeds for nonrental purposes. If you do this, you can't deduct interest you pay on the loan as a rental expense. Whether it is deductible at all, and to what extent, depends on what you use the money for:

- **Personal purposes.** You get no deduction if you use the loan proceeds to buy something for your personal use—for example, you take a vacation or buy new appliances for your residence. Personal interest is not deductible, except for interest paid for a mortgage for a personal residence or second home (and some interest on student loans). You'd be much better off using a home equity loan for such expenses because then you can deduct the interest (up to a $100,000 loan) as an itemized personal deduction.

- **Investment purposes.** You may get a deduction if you use the loan for investment purposes—for example, to purchase stocks or bonds or some other investment. You can deduct investment interest as an itemized personal deduction. However, you can deduct investment interest only from investment income. Thus, if you have no investment income, you get no deduction. If your interest expense exceeds your investment income, you cannot deduct the overage. You must carry it forward to deduct in a future year when you have enough investment income.

- **Business purposes.** You can deduct the interest if you use the loan proceeds for a business other than renting residential property—for example, a landlord borrows money on his rental property to purchase equipment for his construction business. You can fully deduct business interest as a business expense in the year in which it is paid (or incurred in the case of accrual basis taxpayers; see Chapter 17). Sole proprietors (people who individually own their businesses) deduct interest expenses on IRS Schedule C, Profit or Loss From Business.

Keeping Track of Borrowed Money

Here's a simple rule you should follow whenever you borrow money for your rental activity: NEVER, NEVER commingle borrowed funds with money that is not for, or from, your rental activity. Instead, deposit the money in a separate rental bank account.

If you don't follow this rule, you could be in for trouble: If you deposit borrowed money in a bank account that you use to pay bills for both landlord and other purposes, it could be difficult to determine what you spent the money on.

> **EXAMPLE:** Linda borrows $10,000 from the bank to remodel her rental house. She deposits the money in her personal checking account. The account already contains $5,000. Over the next several months, she writes checks to pay for food, her home mortgage, personal clothing, and an architect to remodel her rental. How does Linda know whether the money she borrowed was used for her rental house or personal expenses? She could have avoided this problem had she deposited the money in a separate rental account.

If you do commingle borrowed funds, you'll have to deal with the following IRS rules on tracing loan proceeds.

30-Day Rule

If you buy something for your rental activity within 30 days of borrowing money, the IRS presumes that the payment was made from those loan proceeds (up to the amount of the loan). This is true regardless of the method or bank account you use to pay the rental expense. If you receive the loan proceeds in cash, you can treat the payment as made on the date you receive the cash instead of the date you actually make the payment.

> **EXAMPLE:** Frank gets a loan of $1,000 on August 4 and receives the proceeds in cash. Frank deposits $1,500 in his bank account on August 18 and on August 28 writes a check on the account for a landlord expense. Also, Frank deposits his paycheck and other loan proceeds into the account, and pays his personal bills from the account during the same period. Regardless of these other transactions, Frank can treat $1,000 of the deposit he made on August 18 as being paid on August 4 from the loan proceeds. In addition, Frank can treat the landlord expense he paid on August 28 as made from the $1,000 loan proceeds deposited in the account.

Allocation Rules

If you don't satisfy the 30-day rule, special allocation rules determine how loan proceeds deposited in a bank account were spent for tax purposes. Generally, the IRS will assume that loan proceeds were used (spent) before:
- any unborrowed amounts held in the same account, and
- any amounts deposited after the loan proceeds.

> **EXAMPLE:** On January 9, Edith opened a checking account, depositing a $5,000 bank loan and $1,000 in unborrowed money. On February 13, Edith takes $1,000 from the account for personal purposes. On February 15, she takes out $5,000 to pay for a repair to the roof of her rental property. Edith must treat the $1,000 used for personal purposes as made from the loan proceeds, leaving only $4,000 of the loan in the account for tax purposes. As a result, she may deduct as a landlord expense the interest she pays on only $4,000 of the $5,000 she used to pay for the repair.

Chapter 8

Start-Up Expenses

L andlords often need to spend money to get their rental business started. Costs you incur before you are actually in business are called start-up expenses. Special tax rules govern the deduction of these costs. If you are a landlord who is already actively engaged in the residential rental business, you may not need to read this chapter. But if you aren't yet in business or are considering expanding your residential rental business into new geographic areas, this material explains what type of expenditures are start-up expenses and how you can deduct these costs.

What Are Start-Up Expenses?

Start-up expenses are the costs you incur to get your rental business up and running. Any expense that would be deductible as an operating expense by an ongoing business is a start-up expense when it's incurred before a business begins. Common start-up expenses for landlords include:

- minor or incidental repairs to get a rental property ready to rent
- outside office expenses paid for before a rental business begins, such as office rent, telephone service, utilities, office supplies, and office equipment rental
- home office expenses
- the cost of investigating what it will take to create a successful residential rental business, including research on potential real estate markets
- attending real estate seminars or conferences or other educational programs or classes
- insurance premiums (but not title insurance)
- maintenance costs for a rental property paid for before the property is offered for rent—for example, landscaping and utilities (but not the cost of connecting utilities)
- costs for recruiting and training employees before the business opens—for example, hiring and training an apartment manager
- fees paid to a market research firm to analyze the demographics, traffic patterns, and general economic conditions of a neighborhood
- business licenses, permits, and other fees, and
- fees paid to lawyers, accountants, consultants, and others for professional services; however, legal and other fees paid to purchase a rental property are not start-up expenses.

Unlike operating expenses, start-up expenses cannot automatically be deducted in a single year. This is because the money you spend to start a rental (or any other) business is a capital expense—a cost that will benefit you for more than one year. Normally, you can't deduct these types of capital expenses until you sell or otherwise dispose of the business. However, a special tax rule allows you to deduct up to $5,000 in start-up expenses the first year you are in business, and then deduct the remainder, if any, in equal amounts over the next 15 years. (IRC § 195.)

EXAMPLE: Ed, a Los Angeles resident, is thinking about purchasing a rental house in Las Vegas. He has never been a landlord before, but he thinks it might be a good investment. To find out more about it, he attends a seminar about real estate investing offered by a famed real estate guru. He then starts looking for a house to buy. However, he discovers that it is not so easy to find a suitable property. He makes six trips to Las Vegas over the next year. He incurs substantial travel expense but finds no property he likes. Then, on the seventh trip, he discovers his dream rental house. He quickly buys it and takes title on September 1. The house is vacant but requires some repairs. Ed hires a handyman to do the work and arranges for a gardener to take care of the lawn and landscaping on a weekly basis. On November 1, he lists the property for rent by taking out an ad in the local newspaper. He finds a tenant who moves in on December 1.

Before November 1 (the date he offered the house for rent) Ed paid the following expenses:

Real estate seminar	$ 300
Travel, lodging, and food for six unsuccessful trips to Las Vegas	3,000
Travel, lodging, and food for one successful Las Vegas trip	500
Gardener	100
Utilities	100
Repairs	2,500
Total	$ 6,500

All of these expenses are start-up expenses except for the travel costs to find the property Ed ended up buying. Those costs must be added to the property's tax basis and depreciated. This leaves $6,000 in deductible start-up expenses. Ed may deduct $5,000 of the $6,000 on his tax return for the current year. He can deduct the remaining $1,000 in equal installments over the first 180 months (15 years) he's in business, starting with the month his rental business began (November). He deducts $66.67 for every full year he's in business until he has completely deducted the $1,000 (assuming his rental business lasts that long).

Obviously, you want to spend no more than $5,000 on start-up expenses so you don't have to wait 15 years to get all of your money back. There are ways you can avoid spending more than the $5,000 limit. These are described in more detail below. But first, you need to understand when a rental business begins for tax purposes.

Determining Your Business Start Date

A crucial moment in your tax life as a landlord is when your rental business begins. Once your business is up and running, the start-up expense rule will not apply. Until then, you need to count every penny you spend to make sure you don't go over the $5,000 limit for currently deductible start-up expenses.

Rental Business Begins When You Offer Property for Rent

The general rule is that a new business begins for tax purposes when it starts to function as a going concern and performs the activities for which it was organized. (*Richmond Television Corp. v. U.S.*, 345 F.2d 901 (4th Cir. 1965).) For a rental business, this is when you first offer property for rent. You don't have to actually rent out your property—that is, have it occupied by tenants; you only have to put it on the rental market. (*Francis v. Comm'r*, T.C. Memo 1977-170.)

> **EXAMPLE:** In 1993, Freddie and Sarah Charlton bought lakefront property in Texas that contained several vacant and run-down rental cabins. They began to rehabilitate the cabins in late 1994. They deducted $27,724 on their 1994 tax return for supplies, taxes, travel, utilities, legal and professional expenses, and car and truck expenses for the cabin rental activity. However, the cabins weren't offered for rent or actually rented out until 1998. Both the IRS and tax court denied the deductions. The court held that the Charltons' rental activity didn't become a business until 1998 when the cabins were offered for rent. Thus, the $27,724 was not a business operating expense and could not all be deducted in one year. Instead, it had to be deducted as

a start-up expense after the Charltons' rental business began. (*Charlton v. Comm'r.*, 114 TC 333.)

The date you offer your property for rent is an important one that you should plan for and make careful note of. You should also be prepared to prove you offered your property for rent on the date you claim.

Have Proof of When Your Rental Business Began

Being able to show the IRS a copy of an advertisement to rent your property is a great way to prove your property was available for rent. You don't need to buy an expensive ad—a free ad in the local penny saver will do. Or a copy of a free rental listing with an apartment rental service or local college or university will also establish that your property was available. Another way to show property was offered for rent is to place a For Sale sign on the property and take a picture of it. The picture must be date stamped. If you purchase a property that is already occupied by a tenant, you can use a copy of your first rent check to establish when you were in business.

Expanding an Existing Rental Business

If you've never owned a rental property, it's easy to tell when your rental business begins—the date you offer your first property for rent. But what if you already own rental property and decide to purchase additional rental property? The cost of expanding an existing business is a business operating expense, not a start-up expense. As long as business expansion costs are ordinary and necessary, they are currently deductible.

EXAMPLE: Alex owns an apartment building that he has rented out for over two years. This rental (which qualifies as a business) has been so successful that he decides to purchase another apartment building next door. He spends $10,000 on repairs, advertising, and other expenses to get the building ready to rent. Because Alex is already in business, these costs are currently deductible as business operating expenses—they are not start-up expenses.

However, your expenses will be currently deductible only if the expansion involves an activity that is "within the compass" of your existing rental business. In other words, it must be part of "the normal expansion" of your business. (*Malmstedt v. Comm'r.*, 578 F.2d 520 (4th Cir. 1978).) The costs of expanding into a *new* business are start-up expenses, not operating expenses.

The IRS and tax court have taken a very narrow view of what constitutes a rental business. They have held that a landlord's rental business only exists in the geographic area where the property is located. Thus, a landlord who buys (or seeks to buy) property in a different area is starting a new rental business. This means the expenses for expanding in the new location are start-up expenses.

> **EXAMPLE:** Patrick O'Donnell was a Chicago resident who owned two apartments in Las Vegas. He took a two-day trip to Miami to investigate buying a rental property there. However, he decided not to go through with the deal. Both the IRS and tax court denied him a deduction for his travel expenses. The court found that, even though O'Donnell was in the rental business in Las Vegas, his business did not extend to Miami, so he couldn't deduct the trip as an operating expense. (*O'Donnell v. Comm'r.*, 62 T.C. 781.) Had O'Donnell purchased the property, his travel expenses would have been neither operating expenses nor start-up costs; instead, he would have had to add them to the basis of the property and depreciate them over 27.5 years. (See Chapter 5.)

In another case, the tax court held that a husband and wife who owned several rental properties in North Carolina started a new rental business (as opposed to expanded their existing rental business) when they purchased a rental house in Richmond, Virginia. This was so, even though they lived in Richmond. (*Odom v. Comm'r.*, T.C. Memo. 1982-531.)

Forming New Business Entities

Another situation where a landlord could be viewed as starting a new rental business, not expanding an existing one, is where a new business entity such as a limited liability company or partnership is formed to own the new property. This is often done in an attempt to limit a landlord's legal liability. (See Chapter 1.)

> **EXAMPLE:** Harriet and her husband own an LLC that, in turn, owns an apartment building. They decide to purchase a new apartment building. They form a second LLC, unrelated to the first, to own this property, hoping separate ownership entities will insulate each property from debts or lawsuits arising from the other property. The second LLC could be viewed by the IRS as an entirely new rental business. Any costs the second LLC incurs before the new apartment building is offered for rent would be start-up expenses.

Avoiding the Start-Up Rule's Bite

The start-up tax rule will adversely affect you only if you spend more than $5,000 before your rental business begins. Amounts over the $5,000 limit will have to be deducted over 15 years. So, if possible, you want to stay under the $5,000 limit. To do this, you will need to keep careful track of how much you spend. If you go near or over the $5,000 limit, cut back on your spending until your rental business begins.

As a landlord, there are many expenses you can put off paying until after you are in business. For example, you can hold off on expensive repairs you don't absolutely have to do before you list the property for rent. Repairs you pay for after the property is available for rent will be currently deductible operating expenses, not start-up expenses.

If you must spend more than $5,000 on start-up expenses, go ahead and do it. But at least try to keep your total start-up expenses below $50,000. This is because your first-year $5,000 deduction limit will be reduced by any amount you spend over $50,000 on start-up expenses.

> ⚠ **Don't wait on repairs that significantly affect your tenants.** If you hold off on major repair work, your tenant may reasonably object to living in a construction zone, and may request alternate housing or a rent reduction. Consider taking care of major work that needs to be done before you offer your property for rent—the tax advantages of waiting may begin to appear less attractive once you have to deal with unhappy tenants. A better approach may be to plan to do work at turnover time, when the unit is vacant. At turnover, you are still in business because you've previously rented or offered the property for rent.

If you've already spent $5,000 on start-up items, but you have to buy something more before you start your rental business, try to postpone paying for it until after your business begins. That way, you can currently deduct the expense, if it qualifies as a business operating expense. (This assumes you're a cash basis taxpayer—someone who reports income and expenses on the date they are actually paid, not on the date when an agreement to pay is made. The vast majority of landlords use cash basis accounting; see Chapter 17.) If you can get your rental business started quickly, your creditors should not have to wait long to be paid.

How to Deduct Start-Up Expenses

You can deduct $5,000 in start-up expenses the first year you're in business. You'll have to deduct any expenses in excess of $5,000 in equal amounts over the first 180 months (15 years) you're in business. This process is called amortization. The 180 months is the minimum amortization period; you can choose a longer period if you wish (almost no one does).

However, you won't be entitled to the full $5,000 deduction if you have more than $50,000 in start-up expenses. Your $5,000 deduction is reduced by the amount by which such start-up expenditures exceed $50,000. For example, if you have $53,000 in start-up expenses, you may only deduct $2,000 the first year, instead of $5,000. If you have $55,000 or more in start-up expenses, you get no current deduction. The whole amount must be deducted over 180 months.

> ⚠ **Investors can't deduct start-up expenses.** Only people engaged in a business can deduct start-up expenses. Investors in real estate are not considered to be "in business" for tax purposes. (*Sorrell v. Comm'r.*, 882 F.2d 484 (11th Cir. 1989).) (See Chapter 2 for a detailed discussion of investors versus landlords for tax purposes.)

If Your Rental Business Began in 2004

The start-up expense provision of the tax law (IRC § 195) was amended by Congress in 2004 to permit $5,000 of start-up expenses to be deducted the first year a business is in operation. Before the change, all start-up expenses had to be deducted over the first 60 months a business was in operation. The amendment took effect on October 22, 2004. If your business began before this date, the old rule applies to you. Deduct all your start-up expenses in equal monthly installments for the first 60 months you're in business.

Expenses You Can Deduct

You can deduct as start-up expenses any costs that would be currently deductible as operating expenses after your rental business begins. This means the expenses must be ordinary, necessary, directly related to the business, and reasonable in amount. (See Chapter 3 for a discussion of operating expenses.) For example, you can't deduct the cost of pleasure travel or entertainment unrelated to your rental business. These expenses would not be deductible as operating expenses by an ongoing rental business, so you can't deduct them as start-up expenses either. See "What Are Start-Up Expenses," above, for common examples of deductible start-up expenses for landlords.

Costs That Are Not Start-Up Expenses

Some costs related to opening a rental business are not considered start-up expenses. Many of these costs are still deductible, but different rules apply to them.

Real Property and Other Long-Term Assets

Real property and other long-term assets you purchase for your rental business that will last for more than one year are not considered part of your start-up costs. This includes the property you buy to rent and any long-term personal property you purchase for your rental property, such as appliances, carpeting, furniture, or lawn mowers. It also includes any long-term property you buy to run your business, such as computers, office furniture and equipment, and cars and other vehicles. These items are capital assets and their costs are capital expenses.

You must depreciate the cost of this property over its useful life—27.5 years for residential real property and five or seven years for most personal property. (In the case of some personal property, you have the option of deducting the cost in one year under Section 179—see Chapter 5 for more on Section 179). Chapter 5 explains how to depreciate long-term assets. However, you can't take depreciation deductions until your property is placed in service—for example, you can't begin to depreciate a rental building until you make it available for rent.

Ordinarily, the largest single expense you will have that you cannot deduct as a start-up expense is the cost of your rental property—for example, the house or apartment building that you purchase to rent. For tax purposes, the cost of the rental property includes not just the purchase price, but expenses related to the purchase, including:

- abstract fees (the fee for obtaining a summary of the ownership and legal history of a real estate parcel)
- attorneys' fees
- charges for installing utility services
- closing costs
- escrow fees
- travel expenses (see Chapter 11)
- improvements (the difference between real property improvements and repairs is discussed in Chapter 4)
- legal fees
- recording fees
- repairs already contracted for by the seller
- termite inspection fees
- surveys
- transfer taxes
- title insurance, and
- any amounts the seller owes that you agree to pay, such as back taxes or interest, recording or mortgage fees, and sales commissions.

You cannot deduct any of these expenses as start-up expenses. Instead, you add these costs to the rental property's basis (the property's value for tax purposes) and then depreciate the property's cost (including these amounts) over 27.5 years.

Some costs associated with purchasing property might be start-up expenses. There are certain expenses related to buying real property that you can deduct as start-up expenses if you meet all the requirements. These expenses include:

- fire insurance premiums
- mortgage insurance premiums (private mortgage insurance)
- loan assumption fees
- credit report costs, and
- fees for an appraisal required by a lender.

Real Property Improvements

The cost of improvements you make to rental property are not start-up or operating expenses. Instead, these are capital expenses that you must depreciate. The cost of any repairs you make to rental property, on the other hand, are start-up expenses before your rental business begins and operating expenses after you are in business. The difference between an improvement and a repair is that a repair merely keeps property in good operating condition, while an improvement makes it more valuable, useful, or long-lived. For example, fixing a crack in an existing foundation is a repair; but adding a new foundation to a building is an improvement. Telling the difference between a repair and an improvement can be difficult. (See Chapter 4.)

Travel Expenses

Travel expenses to get your rental business going are deductible start-up expenses with one important exception: Travel costs to buy a particular rental property are not start-up expenses. Instead, they are capital expenses that must be added to the cost of the property and depreciated. (See Chapter 11.)

Interest and Taxes

You cannot deduct interest on a rental property mortgage (or any other interest) or real estate taxes as start-up expenses. Points you pay to obtain a mortgage are considered interest. You can deduct these costs as you pay them, once your real estate business begins. (See Chapter 7.)

Organizational Costs

Costs you pay to form a partnership, limited liability company, or corporation are not part of your start-up costs. However, under a different rule, you can deduct $5,000 of these costs the first year you are in business and any amount remaining over the first 180 months you are in business. (I.R.C. § 248.)

Making a Section 195 Election

You must indicate that you want to deduct start-up costs on your tax return by making a Section 195 election. (Section 195 is the tax law governing start-up expenses.) You must attach a statement (called a Section 195 statement) to your tax return listing your start-up expenses, the dates you paid them, the date your business began, and a description of your business. If you have more than $5,000 in start-up expenses, you'll have to deduct the excess over 180 months. You must file IRS Form 4562, Depreciation and Amortization, with your return showing how much you're deducting. You must also list the number of months in the amortization period (180) in your Section 195 statement.

You should add the total of all the start-up expenses you deduct each year to Line 18 of your Schedule E, the line for "Other" expenses.

If you forget to list all of your start-up costs in your Section 195 statement, you can file an amended statement later listing any items you omitted. However, you may not list any expenses that you have already claimed were deductible under other tax laws—for example, as ordinary and necessary operating expenses.

> **EXAMPLE:** Ed failed to list a $500 repair expense as a start-up expense in his Section 195 statement. Instead, he mistakenly deducted the expense as a currently deductible business operating expense. Three years later, he is audited. The auditor says Ed should have listed the expense as a start-up cost, not a currently deductible operating expense, and disallows the deduction. Ed cannot amend his Section 195 statement to add the expense as a start-up expense because he has already claimed, albeit mistakenly, that the expense was deductible under another tax rule. Even though Ed made an innocent mistake, he won't get any deduction for his repair expense.

The moral is this: Be very careful when you prepare your first tax return after your rental business opens. Figure out how to categorize each of your expenses, and make sure to list every start-up expense in your Section 195 election.

⚠ **You must make a timely election to deduct start-up expenses.** If you want to deduct your start-up expenses, you must file your election (IRS Form 4562 and Section 195 statement) on or before the due date for your first tax return after you start your business. For example, if your business begins in 2008, you must file the election with your 2008 tax return, due April 15, 2009 (or later, if you receive an extension). If you miss this deadline, you have one last chance to make your election:

You may file an amended return making the election within six months after the date your original return was due.

If Your Business Doesn't Last 15 Years

Many rental businesses don't last for 180 months. If you had more than $5,000 in start-up expenses and are in the process of deducting the excess amount, you don't lose the value of your deductions if you sell or close your rental business before you have had a chance to deduct all of your start-up expenses. You can deduct any leftover start-up expenses as ordinary business losses. (IRC § 195(b)(2).) This means that you may be able to deduct them from any income you have that year, deduct them in future years, or deduct them from previous years' taxes. However, there are rules that limit deductions for losses from a real estate activity. (See Chapter 16.)

Keep Good Expense Records

You should keep careful track of every expense you pay before your rental business begins. Obviously, you should keep receipts and canceled checks. You should also keep evidence that will help show that the money went to investigate your new business—for example, correspondence and emails with real estate brokers, lenders, accountants, and attorneys, and copies of advertisements. You will need these records to calculate your deductions and prove your expenses to the IRS if you face an audit.

If Your Business Never Begins

Many people investigate starting a rental business, but the venture never gets off the ground. General start-up costs are expenses you pay before you decide to start a new business or acquire a specific existing business. They include all of the costs of doing a general search for, or preliminary investigation of, a business—for example, costs to analyze potential markets. If you never start the business, these costs are personal (and not deductible). In other words, they are a dead loss.

One intended effect of this rule is that you can't deduct travel, entertainment, or other "fun" expenses by claiming that you incurred them to investigate a rental business unless you actually start the business. Otherwise, it would be pretty tough for the IRS to figure out whether you were really considering a new venture or just having a good time.

EXAMPLE: Kim spends $5,000 on a two-week Hawaii vacation. While there, she attends a one-hour seminar on how to make money by buying rental properties. However, she never starts a rental business. The cost of her trip is not a start-up expense.

■

The Home Office Deduction

The federal government helps out business owners by letting them deduct their home office expenses from their taxable income. This is true whether you own your home or apartment or are a renter. If you own the home where your home office is located (as most landlords do), the home office deduction isn't as valuable as it is for those who are renters. This is because your mortgage interest is deductible whether or not you have a home office, while rent is not deductible without a home office. Still, homeowners who qualify for the deduction will be able to recoup some of their business-related costs by understanding and using this deduction.

Qualifying for the Home Office Deduction

In the past, the IRS took the position that landlords couldn't take the home office deduction. However, the tax court has held that landlords who meet the requirements may take the deduction, and landlords have successfully done so.

> **EXAMPLE:** Edwin Curphey, a dermatologist, owned six rental properties in Hawaii that he managed by himself. He converted a bedroom in his home into an office that he used exclusively for bookkeeping and other activities related to management of his rental properties. The room was furnished with a desk, bookcase, filing cabinet, calculators, and answering machine. The closet of the room was used only to store items used for the rental properties, such as lamps, carpets, and other furnishings, For Rent signs, and a tool box. Because Curphey met the requirements for the deduction, the tax court held he could deduct his home office expenses. (*Curphey v. Comm'r.*, 73 T.C. 766 (1980).)

Moreover, changes in the tax law that took effect in 1999 make it easier than it has ever been for landlords (and other business owners) to take the home office deduction, and harder for the IRS to successfully object. Still, the IRS doesn't go out of its way to encourage landlords to take the deduction. Indeed, you won't find a single word about it in any IRS publication or form.

There are strict requirements you must meet to qualify for the home office deduction. You are entitled to the home office deduction if:

- your rental activities qualify as a business
- you use your home office exclusively for your rental business, and
- you use your home office for rental business on a regular basis.

After you meet these three threshold requirements, you must also satisfy *any* *one* of the following four requirements:

- you regularly and exclusively use your home office for administrative or management activities for your rental business and have no other fixed location where you regularly perform such activities
- you perform your most important rental activities at your home office
- you meet business-related visitors, such as tenants, at your home office, or
- you use a separate structure on your property exclusively for rental business purposes.

Will Taking the Deduction Increase Your Audit Chances?

Some people believe that taking the home office deduction invites an IRS audit. The IRS denies this. But even if taking the deduction increases your audit chances, the risk of an audit is still low (see Chapter 1). Moreover, you have nothing to fear from an audit if you're entitled to take the deduction and you keep good records to prove it.

Threshold Requirements

To take the home office deduction, you must have a home office—that is, an office or other workplace in your home that you use regularly and exclusively for your rental business. Your home may be a house, apartment, condominium, mobile home, or even a boat. Your home can even be a part of your rental property—for example, an apartment in a multiunit apartment building you own, or one-half of a duplex—but, you must actually live in it.

Your office may be all or part of a bedroom, den, or other space in your home that is physically and functionally part of your residence. You can also take the deduction for separate structures on your property that you use for business, such as an unattached garage or workshop. Any space that is not part of your residence is not subject to these rules—for example, space inside your rental building that you use for office work, maintenance, storage, or other landlord purposes.

Your Rental Activities Must Be a Business

Your rental activities must qualify as a business for tax purposes if you want to take the home office deduction. The deduction is not available if your rental activity qualifies only as an investment. Whether your rental activity is a business depends on how much time and effort you put into it. To be a business, you must be actively involved in managing your property on a regular, systematic, and continuous basis. You don't have to work full-time as a landlord—in fact, you can have only a single rental unit and still be a business for tax purposes. You just must be able to show that you are actively involved in managing the rental. (See Chapter 2 for more on when a rental activity constitutes a business for tax purposes.)

You Must Use Your Home Office Exclusively for Business

You can't take the home office deduction unless you use part of your home exclusively for your rental business. In other words, you must use your home office *only for your rental business*. The more space you devote exclusively to your business, the more your home office deduction will be worth.

If you use part of your home—such as a bedroom—as your rental business office, and you use that same space for personal purposes, you won't qualify for the home office deduction.

> **EXAMPLE 1:** Johnny has a den at home furnished with a desk, chair, book-shelf, filing cabinet, and a bed for visiting guests. He uses the desk and chair for both his rental business and personal reasons. The bookshelf contains both personal and rental business books, the filing cabinet contains both personal and rental business files, and the bed is used only for personal reasons. Johnny can't claim a business deduction for the den because he does not use it, or any part of it, exclusively for his rental business.

> **EXAMPLE 2:** Paul keeps his desk, chair, bookshelf, computer, and filing cabinet in one part of his den and uses them exclusively for his rental business. The remainder of the room—one-third of the space—is used to store a bed for house guests. Paul can take a home office deduction for the two-thirds of the room that he uses exclusively as an office.

If you use the same room (or rooms) for your office and for other purposes, you'll have to arrange your furniture and belongings so that a portion of the room is devoted exclusively to your business. Place only your business furniture and other business items in the office portion of the room. Business furniture includes anything that you use for your business, such as standard office furniture like a desk and chair, and tools and other items you use in your rental business.

The IRS does not require you to physically separate the space you use for business from the rest of the room. However, doing so will help you satisfy the exclusive-use test. For example, if you use part of your living room as an office, you could separate it from the rest of the room with folding screens or bookcases.

How Big (or Small) Can Your Home Office Be?

Your home office can be as big or small as you want or need it to be. You are not required to use as small a space as possible. If you like plenty of office space, you can spread out and use more than one room. But remember, you may use your home office space only for business. You aren't supposed to use it for any other purpose—even personal business, such as writing personal checks.

Although the IRS probably won't be inspecting your home office, your deduction must still make sense. If you live in a one-bedroom apartment and claim the entire bedroom as a home office, you'll have to have an answer ready when the IRS asks where you sleep.

The easiest way to meet the exclusive use test is to devote an entire room in your home to your rental business—for example, by using an extra bedroom as your office. However, not everybody has a room to spare—and the IRS recognizes this. You can still claim the deduction even if you use just part of a room as your office, as long as you devote that portion of the room exclusively to your rental business.

Although you must use your home office exclusively for your rental business, you and other family members or visitors may walk through it to get to other rooms in your residence.

As a practical matter, the IRS doesn't have spies checking to see whether you're using your home office just for business. However, complying with the rules from the beginning means you won't have to worry if you are audited.

Can the IRS Enter Your Home?

IRS auditors may not enter your home unless you or another lawful occupant gives them permission. The only exception is if the IRS obtains a court order to enter your home, which is very rare. In the absence of such a court order, an IRS auditor must ask permission to come to your home to verify your home office deduction. You don't have to grant permission for the visit—but if you don't, the auditor will probably disallow your deduction.

You Must Use Your Home Office Regularly

It's not enough to use a part of your home exclusively for business; you must also use it regularly. For example, you can't place a desk in a corner of a room and claim the home office deduction if you almost never use the desk for your business.

Unfortunately, the IRS doesn't offer a clear definition of regular use. The agency has stated only that you must use a portion of your home for business on a continuing basis—not just for occasional or incidental business. One court has held that 12 hours of use a week is sufficient. (*Green v. Comm'r.*, 79 TC 428 (1982).)

Many landlords probably spend less than 12 hours per week working in their home offices. As long as they work regularly, they probably pass muster with the IRS. Thus, for example, even in the case of Edwin Curphey (see example at the beginning of "Qualifying for the Home Office Deduction," above), who owned only six rental units but had clearly defined home office space, the IRS didn't raise the issue of how much time he spent in his home office (it couldn't have been much).

Additional Requirements

Using a home office exclusively and regularly for your rental business is not enough to qualify for the home office deduction: You must also satisfy at least one of the additional three tests described below.

You Perform Administrative and Management Work at Your Home Office

You qualify for the home office deduction if:

- you regularly and exclusively use your home office for administrative or management activities for your rental business, and

- there is no other fixed location where you regularly conduct these activities.

Home offices that meet these requirements are deemed to qualify as the principal place of business for your rental activity. Administrative or management activities include, but are not limited to: keeping books and records, ordering supplies, scheduling appointments, talking to tenants or a resident manager on the phone, arranging for repairs, or writing a rental advertisement. Provided you have no other fixed location where you regularly do these things—for example, an outside office—you'll get the deduction. This makes it easy for almost any landlord to qualify for the deduction. All you have to do is set up a home office that you regularly and exclusively use to manage or administer your rental business.

Under these rules, you can even have an outside office or workplace and still qualify for the home office deduction, as long as you use your home office to perform management tasks and you don't perform substantial management tasks at your outside office.

> **EXAMPLE:** Bill owns a six-unit apartment building. He has a small workshop in the building's basement that he uses to perform repairs and other maintenance work. He also has a home office where he takes care of all the management tasks for his rental business, such as record keeping. Bill may take the home office deduction.

You may also perform some management tasks in a place other than a fixed location, such as your car.

You Perform Your Most Important Rental Activities at Home

If you can't satisfy the requirements discussed above, you can still qualify for the home office deduction if you perform your most important rental business activities—those activities that most directly generate your rental income—at home.

If you do, your home office qualifies as your principal place of business. This leads to the question: How do landlords decide where they do their most important work? The IRS might argue that they do their most important work at their rental properties, not in their home offices. After all, this is where their tenants live, where they show their properties, perform maintenance, and so forth. On the other hand, a landlord could argue that the bookkeeping and management activities he or she performs from home are most important. This is an unanswered question.

> **EXAMPLE:** Charles is a lawyer who owns a large apartment building. He performs some bookkeeping work for his rental business from his law office. Thus, he doesn't satisfy the rules discussed above. However, Charles concludes that his home office still qualifies as his principal place of business because it is the place where he performs his most important rental business-related work. Charles employs a resident manger to take care of his building, so he rarely goes there. He deals with his manager and performs the bulk of his bookkeeping from his home office, so he reasonably claims that it is the location from which he earns most of his rental income. The IRS is unlikely to challenge this.

If the work landlords do at their home offices and at their rental properties is of equal importance, then their principal place of business is where they spend more than half of their time. If you can show that you spend more time at your home office than at your rental properties, your home should qualify as your principal place of business.

You Meet Business Visitors at Home

Even if your home office is not your principal place of business, you may deduct your expenses for any part of your home that you use exclusively to meet with tenants, maintenance workers, vendors, or others involved with your rental business. You must physically meet with others in this home location—phoning them from there is not sufficient. And the meetings must be a regular part of your rental business; occasional meetings don't qualify.

It's not entirely clear how often you must meet these people at home for those meetings to be considered regular. However, the IRS has indicated that meeting people one or two days a week is sufficient. Exclusive use means you use the space where you meet tenants and others only for your rental business. You are free to use the space for business purposes other than meeting tenants—for example, doing your rental business bookkeeping or other paperwork. But you cannot use the space for personal purposes, such as watching television.

If you want to qualify under this part of the rule, keep a log or appointment book showing all the visits by your tenants and others.

You Use a Separate Structure for Rental Business

You can also deduct expenses for a separate freestanding structure, such as a garage or shed, if you use it exclusively and regularly for your rental business. The structure does not have to be your principal place of business, and you do not have to meet tenants there.

Exclusive use means that you use the structure only for your rental business.

> **EXAMPLE:** Gina uses a storage shed in the rear of her house exclusively to store tools and supplies she uses for her rental business. She may take the home office deduction for the shed.

Calculating the Home Office Deduction

This is the fun part—figuring out how much the home office deduction will save you in taxes.

How Much of Your Home Is Used for Your Rental Business?

To calculate your home office deduction, you need to determine what percentage of your home you use for your rental business. The law says you can use "any reasonable method" to do this. Obviously, you want to use the method that will give you the largest home office deduction. To do this, you want to maximize the percentage of your home that you claim as your office. There is no single way to do this for every home office. Try both methods described below and use the one that gives you the largest deduction.

Square Footage Method

The most precise method of measuring your office space is to divide the square footage of your home office by the total square footage of your home. For example, if your home is 1,600 square feet and you use 400 square feet for your home office, 25% of the total area is used for business. Of course, you must know the square footage of your entire home and your office to make this calculation. Your home's total square footage may be listed on real estate documents or plans; you'll have to measure your office space yourself. You don't need to use a tape measure; you can just pace off the measurements.

You are allowed to subtract the square footage of common areas such as hallways, entries, stairs, and landings from the total area that you are measuring.

You can also exclude attics and garages from your total space if you don't use them for business purposes. You aren't required to deduct the common area footage, but doing so will give you a larger deduction because your overall percentage of business use will be higher.

Room Method

Another way to measure is the room method. You can use this method only if all of the rooms in your home are about the same size. Using this method, you divide the number of rooms used for business by the total number of rooms in the home. Don't include bathrooms, closets, or other storage areas. You may also leave out garages and attics if you don't use them for business. For example, if you use one room in a five-room house for your rental business, your office takes up 20% of your home.

The room method often yields a larger deduction. Even though IRS Form 8829, *Expenses for Business Use of Your Home* (the form you must file to claim the home office deduction), seems to require you to use the square footage method, this isn't the case. As long as all of the rooms in your home are about the same size, you can use the room method. Using the room method will often result in a larger deduction.

EXAMPLE: Rich owns a six-room house in San Francisco and uses one bedroom as his home office for his rental business. Using the square footage method, Rich measures his entire house and finds it is 2,000 square feet. His home office is 250 square feet. Using these figures, his home office percentage is 12.5% (250 divided by 2,000 = 12.5%). However, he wants to do better than this, so he measures his common areas, such as hallways and stairways, which amount to 200 square feet. He subtracts this amount from the 2,000 total square feet, which leaves 1,800 square feet. This gives him a home office percentage of 14% (250 divided by 1,800 = 14%.)

Rich then tries the room method to see whether this provides a better result. His house has six rooms—three bedrooms, a living room, a dining room, and a kitchen. He doesn't count the bathroom, garage, or attic. Because he uses one entire room as his home office, he divides one by six, leaving 16.7% as his home office percentage. Rich uses this amount to figure his home office deduction.

Square Footage Method (Total Area)

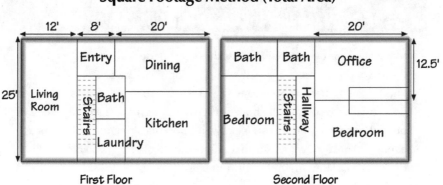

First Floor   Second Floor

Square Footage Method (Excluding Common Areas)

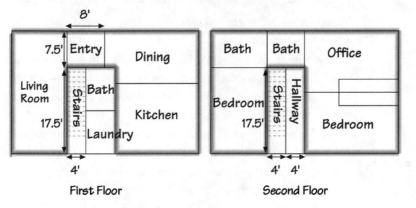

First Floor   Second Floor

Room Method

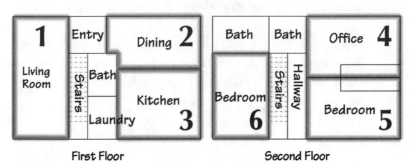

First Floor   Second Floor

You Can Deduct Business Expenses Even If You Don't Qualify for the Home Office Deduction

Many business owners believe that they can't deduct any expenses they incur while working at home unless they qualify for the home office deduction. This is a myth that has cost many taxpayers valuable deductions. Even if you don't qualify for or take the home office deduction, you can still take tax deductions for expenses you incur while working at your rental business at home. These are expenses that arise from the fact that you are doing business as a landlord, not from your use of the home itself.

These include:

- **Telephone expenses.** You can't deduct the basic cost of a single telephone line into your home, but you can deduct the cost of long-distance rental business calls and special phone services that you use for your business (such as call waiting or message center). You can also deduct the entire cost of a second phone line that you use just for your rental business.

- **Business equipment and furniture.** The cost of office furniture, copiers, fax machines, and other personal property you use for your rental business and keep at home is deductible, whether or not you qualify for the home office deduction. If you purchase these items specifically for your rental business, you can expense them (deduct them in one year) under Section 179 or depreciate them over several years. If you convert personal property you already own to business use, you may depreciate the fair market value. If you use the property for both business and personal reasons, the IRS requires you to keep records showing when the item was used for business or personal reasons—for example, a diary or log with the dates, times, and reasons the item was used. See Chapter 5 for a detailed discussion of these rules.

- **Supplies.** Supplies for your rental business are currently deductible as an operating expense if they have a useful life of less than one year (see Chapter 3). Otherwise, you must depreciate them or expense them under Section 179, as explained in Chapter 5.

What Expenses Can You Deduct?

The home office deduction is not one deduction, but many. Most costs associated with maintaining and running your home office are deductible. However, because your office is in your home, some of the money you spend also benefits you personally. For example, your utility bill pays to heat your home office, but it also keeps the rest of your living space warm. The IRS deals with this issue by dividing home office expenses into two categories: direct expenses, which benefit only your home office, and indirect expenses, which benefit both your office and the rest of your home.

Types of Home Expenses		
Expense	**Description**	**Deductibility**
Direct	Things you buy only for your home office	Deductible in full
Indirect	Things you buy to keep your entire home up and running	Deductible based on the percentage of your home used as a business office
Unrelated	Things you buy only for parts of your home that are not used for business	Not deductible

Direct Expenses

You have a direct home office expense when you pay for something just for the home office portion of your home. This includes, for example, the cost of painting your home office, carpeting it, or hiring someone to clean it. The entire amount of a direct home office expense is deductible.

> **EXAMPLE:** Jean pays a housepainter $400 to paint her home office. She may deduct this entire amount as a home office deduction.

Virtually anything you buy for your office is deductible. However, you may have to depreciate permanent improvements to your home over 39 years, rather than deduct them in the year when you pay for them. Permanent improvements are changes that go beyond simple repairs, such as adding a new room to your home to serve as your office. (See Chapter 4 for more information on improvements versus repairs.)

Indirect Expenses

An indirect expense is a payment for something that benefits your *entire home*, including both the home office portion and your personal space. You may deduct only a portion of this expense—the home office percentage of the total.

> **EXAMPLE:** Instead of just painting her home office, Jean decides to paint her entire home for $1,600. She uses 25% of her home as an office, so she may deduct 25% of the cost, or $400.

Most of your home office expenses will be indirect expenses, including:

- **Rent.** If you rent your home or apartment, you can use the home office deduction to deduct part of your rent—a substantial expense that is ordinarily not deductible. Your tax savings will be particularly great if you live in a high-rent area.

  > **EXAMPLE:** Sam uses 20% of his two-bedroom Manhattan apartment as a home office for his rental business. He pays $2,000 per month in rent, and may therefore deduct $400 of his rent per month ($4,800 per year) as a home office expense. This saves him over $2,000 in federal, state, and self-employment taxes.

- **Mortgage interest and property taxes.** Whether or not you have a home office, you can deduct your monthly mortgage interest and property tax payments as a personal itemized income tax deduction on your Schedule A, Itemized Deductions (the tax form where you list your personal income tax deductions). But if you have a home office, you have the option of deducting the home office percentage of your mortgage interest and property tax payments on Schedule E as part of your home office deduction. If you do this, you may not deduct this amount on your Schedule A (you can't deduct the same item twice). There is no great tax advantage for a landlord to do this; it just switches the deduction from one tax form to another.

- **Depreciation.** If you own your home, you're also entitled to a depreciation deduction for the office portion of your home. See Chapter 5 for a detailed discussion of depreciation.
- **Utilities.** You may deduct your home office percentage of your utility bills for your entire home, including electricity, gas, water, heating oil, and trash removal.
- **Insurance.** Both homeowner's and renter's insurance are partly deductible as indirect home office expenses. However, special insurance coverage you buy just for your home office—for example, insurance for your computer or other rental business equipment—is fully deductible as a direct expense.
- **Home maintenance.** You can deduct the home office percentage of home maintenance expenses that benefit your entire home, such as housecleaning of your entire house, roof and furnace repairs, and exterior painting. These costs are deductible whether you hire someone or do them yourself. If you do the work yourself, however, you can deduct only the cost of materials, not the cost of your own labor. Termite inspection, pest extermination fees, and snow removal costs are also deductible. Home maintenance costs that don't benefit your home office—for example, painting your kitchen—are not deductible at all.
- **Casualty losses.** Casualty losses are damage to your home caused by such things as fire, floods, or theft. Casualty losses that affect your entire house—for example, a leak that floods your entire home—are deductible in the amount of your home office percentage. Casualty losses that affect only your home office for example, a leak that floods only the home office area of the house are fully deductible direct expenses. Casualty losses that don't affect your home office—for example, if only your kitchen floods—are not deductible as business expenses. However, they may be deductible as itemized personal deductions. (See Chapter 13 for a detailed discussion of casualty losses.)
- **Condominium association fees.** These fees (often substantial) are partly deductible as an indirect expense if you have a home office.
- **Security system costs.** Security system costs are partly deductible as an indirect expense if your security system protects your entire home. If you have a security system that protects only your home office, the cost is a fully deductible direct expense.

Sam Creates a Home Office

Sam converts one of the bedrooms of his two-bedroom condominium into a home office to use for his rental business. He goes on something of a shopping spree, purchasing the following items:

- carpeting for his office
- a separate telephone for the office
- office supplies, such as a stapler and paper
- a new desk for his office
- a new computer for his office (and one for his family).

He also moves a fancy chair he already owns to his office and uses it solely for his business. In the meantime, Sam's wife has their kitchen repainted and hires someone to clean the entire condo twice a month. Sam and his wife pay $2,000 each month on mortgage interest, real estate taxes, and homeowner's insurance.

The chart below shows which of these expenses are direct and indirect home office expenses, business operating expenses that are deductible whether or not Sam qualifies for the home office deduction, long-term asset expenses that are also deductible without regard to the home office deduction, and expenses that are not deductible.

Direct Home Office Expenses (100% Deductible)	Indirect Home Office Expenses (Deductible in Amount of Home Office Percentage)	Business Operating Expenses	Long-Term Asset Expenses	Not Deductible
Carpet for home office	Mortgage interest and real estate taxes	Office supplies	Office desk	Kitchen repainting
	Utilities (electricity and heat)	Business telephone	Office chair	Computer for children
	Cleaning service		Computer for business	
	Homeowner's insurance			

- **Local travel expenses.** If your home office is your principal place of business, you can deduct the cost of traveling from your home to other work locations for your rental business. For example, you can deduct the cost of driving from home to perform maintenance at your rental property. If you don't have a home office, these costs are not deductible. See Chapter 10 for a detailed discussion of the business mileage deduction.
- **Computer equipment.** Computers and peripheral equipment (such as printers) you use for your rental business are deductible whether or not you qualify for the home office deduction. However, if you don't qualify for the home office deduction, you must prove that you use your computer more than half of the time for business by keeping a log of your usage. (See Chapter 5 for more information on this requirement.) If you qualify for the home office deduction, you don't need to keep track of how much time you spend using your computer for business.
- **Supplies and materials.** Office supplies and materials you use for your rental business are not part of the home office deduction. They are deductible whether or not you qualify for the home office deduction.

Profit Limit on Deductions

The tax code significantly limits the size of any home office deduction: You cannot deduct more than the net profit you earn from a business you run from your home office. If your rental business earns a substantial profit, this won't pose a problem. But if your business earns very little or loses money, the limitation could prevent you from deducting part or even all of your home office expenses in the current year.

If your deductions exceed your profits, you can deduct the excess in the following year and in each succeeding year until you deduct the entire amount, assuming you earn profits in these years. There is no limit on how far into the future you can deduct these expenses; you can claim them even if you are no longer living in the home where they were incurred.

So, whether or not your business is making money, you should keep track of your home office expenses and claim the deduction on your tax return. The profit limitation applies only to the home office deduction. It does not apply to rental business expenses that you can deduct under other provisions of the tax code.

For these purposes, your profit is the gross income you earn from your rental business minus your rental business deductions other than your home office deduction. You must also subtract the home office portion of your mortgage interest, real estate taxes, and casualty losses.

Tax preparation software can calculate your profit for home office deduction purposes, but it's a good idea to understand how it works.

First, start with your gross income from your rental business—this is all the rent you receive each year. Next, figure out how much money you earn from using your home office. If you do all of your work at home, this will be 100% of your rental business income. But if you work in several locations—for example, at home and at your rental properties—you must determine the portion of your gross income that comes from working in your home office. To do this, consider how much time you spend working in your home office and the type of work you do at home.

Then, subtract from this amount:

- the business percentage of your mortgage interest and real estate taxes (you'll have these expenses only if you own your home), plus any casualty losses, and
- all of your rental business expenses that are not part of the home office deduction—for example, interest paid on rental properties, repairs, depreciation, utilities, insurance, car expenses, business phone, and supplies. You deduct these separately from the home office deduction.
- The remainder is your net profit—the most you can deduct for using your home office.

EXAMPLE: Sam uses 10% of his home to run his rental business. In one year, his gross income from the business was $25,000 and he had $20,000 in expenses separate from his home office deduction. He paid $10,000 in mortgage interest and real estate taxes on his home for the year. His home office deduction for the year is limited to $4,000. He calculates this as follows:

Gross income from rental business	$	25,000
Minus business portion of mortgage interest and taxes ($10,000 x 10%)		1,000
Balance	$	24,000
Minus direct business expenses		20,000
Home office deduction limit	$	4,000

Sam's total home office expenses for the year amount to $6,000. This includes $1,000 in mortgage interest and real estate taxes, plus $5,000 in other expenses, such as utilities, depreciation of his home, and a new carpet for and painting of his home office. Sam first deducts the $5,000 in home office expenses that are not deductible as personal itemized deductions—everything other than mortgage interest, real estate taxes, and casualty losses. He can deduct $4,000 of this $5,000 amount because his home office deduction profit limit is $4,000. Sam reached his $4,000 profit limit so he can't deduct $1,000 of his home office expenses that can't be itemized or any portion of his $1,000 mortgage interest and real estate tax expenses as a home office deduction. However, he may deduct his mortgage interest and real estate taxes as personal itemized deductions on Schedule A. He can deduct the $1,000 in unused home office expenses the following year, if he has sufficient income from his rental business.

Special Concerns for Homeowners

Until recently, homeowners who took the home office deduction were subject to a special tax trap: If they took a home office deduction for more than three of the five years before they sold their house, they had to pay capital gains taxes on the profit from the home office portion of their home. For example, if you made a $50,000 profit on the sale of your house, but your home office took up 20% of the space, you would have had to pay a tax on $10,000 of your profit (20% x $50,000 = $10,000).

Fortunately, IRS rules no longer require this. As long as you live in your home for at least two out of the five years before you sell it, the profit you make on the sale—up to $250,000 for single taxpayers and $500,000 for married taxpayers filing jointly—is not taxable. (See IRS Publication 523, *Selling Your Home.*) If you sold your house after May 6, 1997 and paid capital gains tax on the home office portion, you may be entitled to amend your return for the year you sold the house and receive a tax refund from the IRS. (See Chapter 19 for information on amending tax returns for prior years.)

However, you will have to pay a capital gains tax on the depreciation deductions you took after May 6, 1997 for your home office. This is the deduction you are allowed for the yearly decline in value due to wear and tear of the portion of the building that contains your home office. (See Chapter 5 for more information on depreciation deductions.) These recaptured deductions are taxed at a 25% rate (unless your income tax bracket is lower than 25%).

EXAMPLE: Sally bought a $200,000 home in 2002 and used one of her bedrooms as her home office for her rental business. She sold her home in 2007 for $300,000, realizing a $100,000 gain (profit). Her depreciation deductions for her home office from 2002 through 2007 totaled $2,000. She must pay a tax of 25% of $2,000, or $500.

Having to pay a 25% tax on the depreciation deductions you took in the years before you sold your house is actually not a bad deal. This is probably no more—and is often less—tax than you would have had to pay if you hadn't taken the deductions in the first place and instead paid tax on your additional taxable income at ordinary income tax rates.

IRS Reporting Requirements

Reporting your home office deduction is simple. First, you figure out the amount of your deduction. You can do this by using the IRS worksheet contained in Publication 587, *Business Use of Your Home*. If you have enough rental income to take a home office deduction this year (Line 32 of the worksheet), report the amount (up to the profit limit) on Line 18 of your Schedule E. Write "Business Use of Home" on the dotted line beside the entry. If you don't have enough rental income to take a home office deduction this year, write nothing in your Schedule E. Keep your record of your home office expenses to use in a future year when you have more rental income.

You need not file IRS Form 8829, Expenses for Business Use of Your Home. This form is only filed by taxpayers who file IRS Schedule C, Profit or Loss From Business. Landlords do not file Schedule C (see Chapter 1.)

The IRS worksheet contained in Publication 587 is reproduced below.

Audit-Proofing Your Home Office Deduction

If the IRS audits you and questions your home office deduction, you want to be able to prove that you:
• qualify for the deduction, and
• have correctly reported the amount of your home office expenses.
If you can do both those things, you should be home free.

Worksheet To Figure the Deduction for Business Use of Your Home
Use this worksheet if you file Schedule F (Form 1040) or you are an employee or a partner.

PART 1—Part of Your Home Used for Business:
1) Area of home used for business . . . .   1) _____
2) Total area of home . . . .   2) _____
3) Percentage of home used for business (divide line 1 by line 2 and show result as percentage) . . . .   3) _____ %

PART 2—Figure Your Allowable Deduction
4) Gross income from business (see instructions) . . . .   4) _____

	(a) Direct Expenses	(b) Indirect Expenses
5) Casualty losses . . . . 5)	_____	_____
6) Deductible mortgage interest . . . . 6)	_____	_____
7) Real estate taxes . . . . 7)	_____	_____
8) Total of lines 5 through 7 . . . . 8)	_____	_____

9) Multiply line 8, column (b), by line 3 . . . .   9) _____
10) Add line 8, column (a), and line 9 . . . .   10) _____
11) Business expenses not from business use of home (see instructions) . . . .   11) _____
12) Add lines 10 and 11 . . . .   12) _____
13) Deduction limit. Subtract line 12 from line 4 . . . .   13) _____

14) Excess mortgage interest . . . . 14)	_____	_____
15) Insurance . . . . 15)	_____	_____
16) Repairs and maintenance . . . . 16)	_____	_____
17) Utilities . . . . 17)	_____	_____
18) Other expenses . . . . 18)	_____	_____
19) Add lines 14 through 18 . . . . 19)	_____	_____

20) Multiply line 19, column (b) by line 3 . . . .   20) _____
21) Carryover of operating expenses from prior year (see instructions) . . . .   21) _____
22) Add line 19, column (a), line 20, and line 21 . . . .   22) _____
23) Allowable operating expenses. Enter the **smaller** of line 13 or line 22 . . . .   23) _____
24) Limit on excess casualty losses and depreciation. Subtract line 23 from line 13 . . . .   24) _____
25) Excess casualty losses (see instructions) . . . .   25) _____
26) Depreciation of your home from line 38 below . . . .   26) _____
27) Carryover of excess casualty losses and depreciation from prior year (see instructions) . .   27) _____
28) Add lines 25 through 27 . . . .   28) _____
29) Allowable excess casualty losses and depreciation. Enter the **smaller** of line 24 or line 28 . . . .   29) _____
30) Add lines 10, 23, and 29 . . . .   30) _____
31) Casualty losses included on lines 10 and 29 (see instructions) . . . .   31) _____
32) Allowable expenses for business use of your home. (Subtract line 31 from line 30.) See instructions for where to enter on your return . . . .   32) _____

PART 3—Depreciation of Your Home
33) Smaller of adjusted basis or fair market value of home (see instructions) . . . .   33) _____
34) Basis of land . . . .   34) _____
35) Basis of building (subtract line 34 from line 33) . . . .   35) _____
36) Business basis of building (multiply line 35 by line 3) . . . .   36) _____
37) Depreciation percentage (from applicable table or method) . . . .   37) _____ %
38) Depreciation allowable (multiply line 36 by line 37) . . . .   38) _____

PART 4—Carryover of Unallowed Expenses to Next Year
39) Operating expenses. Subtract line 23 from line 22. If less than zero, enter −0− . . . .   39) _____
40) Excess casualty losses and depreciation. Subtract line 29 from line 28. If less than zero, enter −0− . . . .   40) _____

Prove That You Are Following the Rules

Here are some ways to convince the IRS that you qualify for the home office deduction.

- Take a picture of your home office and draw up a diagram showing your home office as a portion of your home. Do not send the photo or diagram to the IRS. Just keep it in your files to use in case you're audited. The picture should have a date on it—a digital camera can impose a date, or you can have your film date stamped by a developer.

- Have all of your rental business mail sent to your home office.
- Use your home office address on all of your rental business cards, stationery, and advertising.
- Get a separate phone line for your rental business and keep that phone in your home office.
- Keep a log of the time you spend working in your home office. This doesn't have to be fancy; notes on your calendar will do.

Keep Good Expense Records

Be sure to keep copies of your bills and receipts for home office expenses, including:

- IRS Form 1098, Mortgage Interest Statement (sent by whomever holds your mortgage), showing the interest you paid on your mortgage for the year
- property tax bills and your canceled checks as proof of payment
- utility bills, insurance bills, and receipts for payments for repairs to your office area, along with your canceled checks paying for these items, and
- if you're a renter, a copy of your lease and rent receipts or your canceled rent checks.

Deducting an Outside Office

If you have an outside office for your rental activities, your tax life is simpler than if you use a home office. In addition, landlords who are investors, as well as business owners, can deduct expenses for an outside office.

Renting an Office

The rent and other expenses you pay for an outside office or other work space you use for your rental activity may be deducted the year they are paid as ordinary and necessary business expenses. None of the home office deduction rules apply to outside offices. You may deduct the rent you pay your landlord to use the property during the year. You may also deduct other expenses you pay the landlord, such as a portion of the landlord's property taxes or utility bills. Of course, you can deduct your own utility bills. You may deduct the cost of repairs you pay for, but permanent improvements to the property must be depreciated over several years. For example, you can currently deduct the cost of fixing the furnace, but you'd have to depreciate the cost of buying a new furnace. (See Chapter 5.)

Rental expenses for an outside office are reported on your Schedule E, the same as any other rental operating expense. List them on Line 18.

Using an Office in Your Rental Building

Many landlords use space inside their rental buildings as an office, workshop, or for storage. You may deduct the utilities you pay for the space, but you get no deduction for the rent you lose by not renting the space to tenants. You may depreciate the space along with the rest of your building. Use the 27.5-year depreciation period for residential property, if 80% of your total rentals from the building come from the dwelling units. Otherwise, you must use the 39-year term for nonresidential property. When you use a space in your building as an office, you use the fair rental value of the space to calculate this percentage.

> **EXAMPLE:** Sam owns several rental properties, including a duplex with two small one-bedroom units of equal size. He rents one side of the duplex to a tenant to live in and uses the other side as his office for his rental activities. He charges his tenant $800 per month rent, which is also the fair rental value of his office. Less than 80% of the gross rental income from the duplex comes from dwelling units—$800 is 50% of $1,600. As a result, Sam must depreciate the entire duplex using the 39-year term for nonresidential property. He may deduct the full amount he spends for utilities for his office and for repairs.

See Chapter 5 for a detailed discussion of depreciation.

Buying a Separate Office Building

If you buy a separate building that is not a residential rental to use as your office, you may currently deduct as ordinary and necessary business expenses your mortgage interest and real estate taxes and expenses associated with the sale. In addition, you may depreciate the value of the real estate (not including the land) over 39 years. The cost of repairs may be currently deducted, but permanent improvements to the property must be depreciated. (See Chapter 4 for more on repairs versus improvements.)

Chapter 10

Car and Local Transportation Expenses

This chapter shows you how to deduct expenses for local transportation—that is, trips that don't require you to stay away from home overnight. These rules apply to local trips using any means of transportation, but this chapter focuses primarily on car expenses, the most common type of deduction for local travel. Overnight trips (whether by car or other means) are covered in Chapter 11.

⚠ Transportation expenses are a red flag for the IRS. Car and other local transportation expenses are always a key item for IRS auditors. It is easy to overstate them, so, if you're audited, the IRS will probably look carefully to make sure that you're not bending the rules. Your first line of defense against an audit is to keep good records to back up your deductions. This is something no tax preparation program or accountant can do for you—you must develop good record-keeping habits and follow them faithfully to stay out of trouble with the IRS.

Deductible Local Transportation Expenses

Local transportation costs are deductible in the year in which they are incurred as operating expenses if they are ordinary and necessary for your rental activity—meaning common, helpful, and appropriate for your activity. (See Chapter 3 for a detailed discussion of the ordinary and necessary requirement.) It makes no difference what type of transportation you use to make the local trips—car, van, pickup, truck, motorcycle, taxi, bus, or train—or whether the vehicle you use is owned or leased. You can deduct these costs as long as they are ordinary and necessary and meet the other requirements discussed below.

You can deduct local transportation expenses if your rental activity qualifies as a business or an investment for tax purposes. (*Horowitz v. Comm'r.*, T.C. Memo 1979-27.) If you do a lot of driving for your rental activity, however, there's a good chance you are engaged in a business, not an investment. Investors usually don't do much driving to or from their rental properties or for other business purposes because (by definition) they are not actively involved in the management of their rental properties. (See Chapter 2 for a detailed discussion of whether you qualify as a business or investor for tax purposes.)

Travel Must Be for Rental Activities

You can deduct only local trips that are for your rental activities. Personal trips—for example, to the supermarket or the gym—are not deductible as transportation expenses. For example, you can deduct the cost of driving to:

- your rental property
- where you have your principal place of business for your rental activity, including a home office
- places where you meet with tenants, suppliers, vendors, repairpeople, attorneys, accountants, real estate brokers, real estate managers, and other people who help in your rental activity
- the bank where you do banking for your real estate activity
- the garbage dump where you haul refuse from your rental property
- a local college where you take landlord-related classes (educational expenses are deductible only if your rental activities qualify as a business; see Chapter 14), or
- a store where you buy supplies or materials for your real estate activity.

Moreover, you don't have to do all the driving yourself to get a car expense deduction. Any use of your car by another person qualifies as a deductible business expense if it is directly connected with your business. Thus, for example, you can count as business mileage a car trip your employee, spouse, or child takes to deliver an item for your rental business or for any other business purpose.

Travel Costs Before You Become a Landlord

The cost of local travel you do before you become a landlord, such as travel to investigate purchasing a rental property, is not a currently deductible operating expense. If your rental activity becomes a business, such travel is a start-up expense. Up to $5,000 in start-up expenses may be deducted the first year your rental business is in operation. Any amount over $5,000 must be deducted in equal installments over the first 180 months you're in business. Landlords who are only investors may not deduct such start-up expenses. (See Chapter 2.)

Driving From and to Home

Most local trips that landlords make for their rental activities start and end at home. Whether driving from home is deductible as an operating expense depends on whether you have a home office for your rental activity, and where you drive to.

You Have a Home Office

If you have a home office that qualifies as your principal place of business, you can deduct the cost of any trips you make from home to another location for your rental activity. You can get a lot of travel deductions this way. For example, you can deduct the cost of driving from home to your rental property or to the bank.

To deduct the cost of driving to and from your home office, it must qualify as your principal place of business. The rules for the home office deduction are used to determine whether a home office is a person's principal place of business. Under these rules, a home office qualifies if it is the place where you perform management or administrative tasks. Practically any landlord can set up a home office to perform such tasks—but you may not use the office for any other purpose.

> **EXAMPLE:** Kim owns five rental houses scattered throughout Southern California. She maintains a home office where she does bookkeeping and other administrative and management work for her rental business. She can deduct all of her rental-business-related trips from her home office, including trips she makes from home to any of her rental properties. Thanks to her home office, she can usually deduct 200 miles per month as a business trip expense.

You might think that landlords whose rental activities qualify as an investment (not a business) have no principal place of business since they are not in business. This is not the case, however. Landlords who are investors get the same transportation deductions as landlords who are in business, as long as their home office meets the requirements for the home office deduction. If it does, then their home office is treated as their principal place of business for the transportation deduction. This is so, even though the home office deduction itself is limited to landlords who are in business. (See Chapter 9 for more on the home office deduction.)

You Don't Have a Home Office

If you don't have a home office that qualifies as your principal place of business, your transportation deductions will be limited by the commuting rule. Commuting expenses are nondeductible personal expenses. Commuting means driving from where you live to your main or regular place of work for your rental activity. For landlords, this means driving from home to their rental properties or to their outside office (if they have one).

> **EXAMPLE:** Sue, an accountant, lives in a Chicago suburb and owns a five-unit apartment building in downtown Chicago, about 10 miles away. Sue does no work for her rental activity from home. Instead, she does all of her rental-related bookkeeping and other management tasks from her accounting office. Because of the commuting rule, Sue may not deduct the cost of driving from her home to her rental properties, or to her accounting office to perform rental-related work.

Even if a trip from home has a business purpose—for example, to haul tools or supplies from home to your rental property—it is still considered commuting and is not deductible. (You may, however, deduct the cost of renting a trailer or any other extraordinary expenses you incur to haul the tools or supplies from your home.)

Once you arrive at your rental office or rental property, you may deduct trips to other rental-related locations. But not trips back home.

> **EXAMPLE:** Sue drives directly from home to her rental property to supervise a repair. She then drives directly to her office, and drives back home later that day. She may deduct the trip from her rental property to her rental office, but none of her other trips.

Travel to a Temporary Work Location

Even if you don't have a home office, some trips from home may be deductible. Remember, commuting occurs when you go from home to a permanent work location—either:

- your office or other principal place of business for your rental activity, or
- your rental property, or any other place where you have worked or expect to work for more than one year.

Travel between your home and a temporary work location is not considered commuting and is therefore deductible. A temporary work location is any place where you realistically expect to work less than one year. This may include the bank, post office, building supply store, local college where you take real estate courses, and similar places.

> **EXAMPLE:** Sue travels from her home to a building supply store to pick up a part for a repair to her rental property. This is not commuting and is deductible.

However, a place will cease to be a temporary work location if you continue to go there for more than one year.

> **EXAMPLE:** Sue goes from her house to the building supply store almost every week for over a year. The store is no longer a temporary work location, and her trips there from home are nondeductible commuting expenses.

You can convert a nondeductible commute into a deductible local business trip by making a stop at a temporary work location on your way to your office. Stopping at a temporary work location converts the entire trip into a deductible travel expense.

> **EXAMPLE:** One morning, Sue leaves home, stops off at the local newspaper office to place a rental advertisement, and then goes to her office. The entire trip is deductible because she stopped at a temporary work location on her way to her office.

Keep in mind, though, that making such stops is necessary only if you *don't* have a home office. If Sue had a home office, the commuting rule wouldn't apply and the trip would be deductible with or without the stop.

The Standard Mileage Rate

If you drive a car, SUV, van, pickup, or panel truck for your rental activity (as most landlords do), you have two options for deducting your vehicle expenses: You can use the standard mileage rate or you can deduct your actual expenses. Let's start with the easy one—the standard mileage rate.

How the Standard Mileage Rate Works

To use the standard mileage rate, you deduct a specified number of cents for every mile you drive for your rental activity. The IRS sets the standard mileage rate each year. In 2007, the rate was 48.5 cents per mile. You can find the current rate in IRS Publication 463, *Travel, Entertainment, Gift, and Car Expenses*. You can download it from the IRS website at www.irs.gov, or obtain a hard copy by calling 800-TAX-FORM.

To figure out your deduction, simply multiply your rental business activity miles by the standard mileage rate that applies for that period of use. The rate is the same whether you own or lease your car.

> **EXAMPLE:** Ed drove his car 1,000 miles for his rental activity in 2007. To determine his car expense deduction, he multiplies the total rental activity miles he drove (1,000) by 48.5 cents. This gives him a $485 deduction.

The big advantage of the standard mileage rate is that it requires very little record keeping. You only need to keep track of how many rental activity miles you drive, not the actual expenses for your car, such as gas, maintenance, or repairs. However, unless you drive a very inexpensive car which qualifies for very little depreciation, the standard mileage rate will usually give you a smaller deduction than the actual expense method.

If you choose the standard mileage rate, you cannot deduct actual car operating expenses—for example, maintenance and repairs, gasoline and its taxes, oil, insurance, and vehicle registration fees. All of these items are factored into the rate set by the IRS. And you can't deduct the cost of the car through depreciation or Section 179 expensing, because the car's depreciation is also factored into the standard mileage rate (as are lease payments for a leased car).

The only actual expenses you can deduct (because these costs aren't included in the standard mileage rate) are:

- parking fees and tolls for rental-related trips (but you can't deduct parking ticket fines or the cost of parking your car at your place of work)
- interest on a car loan, and
- personal property tax you paid when you bought the vehicle, based on its value—this is often included as part of your auto registration fee.

If, like most landlords, you use your car for both rental-related and personal trips, you can deduct only the rental use percentage of the above-mentioned interest and taxes.

EXAMPLE: Ralph uses his car 50% for his rental activity and 50% for personal trips. He uses the standard mileage rate to deduct his car expenses. He pays $3,000 a year in interest on his car loan. He may deduct 50% of this amount, or $1,500, as an operating expense in addition to his rental activity mileage deduction.

Requirements to Use the Standard Mileage Rate

Not everyone can use the standard mileage rate. You won't be able to use it (and will have to use the actual expense method instead) if you can't meet the following two requirements.

First-Year Rule

You must use the standard mileage rate in the first year you use a car for your rental activity or you are forever foreclosed from using that method for that car. If you use the standard mileage rate the first year, you can switch to the actual expense method a later year, and then switch back and forth between the two methods after that, provided the requirements listed below are met. For this reason, if you're not sure which method you want to use, it's a good idea to use the standard mileage rate the first year you use the car for business. This leaves all your options open for later years. However, this rule does not apply to leased cars.

There are some restrictions on switching back to the standard mileage rate after you have used the actual expense method. You can switch back to the standard mileage rate only if you used the straight-line method of depreciation during the years you used the actual expense method. This depreciation method gives you equal depreciation deductions every year, rather than the larger deductions you get in the early years using accelerated depreciation methods. You can't switch back to the standard mileage rate after using the actual expense method if you took accelerated depreciation, a Section 179 deduction, or bonus depreciation.

Five-Car Rule

You can't use the standard mileage rate if you have five or more cars that you use for your rental activity simultaneously. (Before 2004, the IRS didn't allow people who used more than one car at the same time to use the standard mileage rate.)

The Actual Expense Method

Instead of using the standard mileage rate, you can deduct the actual cost of using your car for your rental activity. Although it requires more record keeping, you'll often get a larger deduction if you use the actual expense method instead of the standard mileage rate. The American Automobile Association estimated that the average cost of owning a car in 2007 was 62 cents per mile. This is substantially more than the IRS allowed to be deducted under the standard mileage rate in 2007—48.5 cents per mile.

Nevertheless, many taxpayers choose the standard mileage rate because it's easier. You only need to keep track of how many miles you drive for your rental activity, instead of keeping track of how much you spend for gas, oil, repairs, and all your other car expenses. Moreover, if you don't drive many miles each year for your rental activity, the extra deduction you get from the actual expense method may not be worth the record keeping required.

For example, if you drive 1,000 miles a year for your rental activity in 2007, you'll get a $485 deduction using the standard mileage rate. If you use the actual expense method, you should get about $620, based on the AAA figures. That small a difference may not be worth the extra paperwork and record keeping.

Travel by Motorcycle

You must use the actual expense method if you ride a motorcycle—the standard mileage rate is for passenger vehicles only. However, the limits on depreciation for passenger automobiles (discussed below) do not apply to bicycles or motorcycles. You may depreciate these items just like any other rental activity property. Or, if your rental activity qualifies as a business, you can deduct the full cost of a motorcycle or bicycle in the year that you purchase it under Section 179. (See Chapter 5 for more on depreciation and Section 179.)

How the Actual Expense Method Works

As the name implies, under the actual expense method, you deduct the actual costs you incur each year to operate your car, plus depreciation. If you use this method, you must keep careful track of all of your car expenses during the year, including:

- gas and oil
- repairs and maintenance
- depreciation of your original vehicle and improvements
- car repair tools
- license fees
- parking fees for rental activity trips
- registration fees
- tires
- insurance
- garage rent
- tolls for rental activity trips
- car washing
- lease payments
- interest on car loans
- towing charges, and
- auto club dues.

Watch Those Tickets

You may not deduct the cost of driving violations or parking tickets, even if you were on rental-related business when you got the ticket. Government fines and penalties are never deductible as a matter of public policy.

When you do your taxes, add up the cost of all these items. For everything but parking fees and tolls, multiply the total cost of each item by the percentage of time you use your car for your rental activity. For parking fees and tolls that are rental activity related, include (and deduct) the full cost. The total is your deductible transportation expense for the year.

EXAMPLE: Laura owns several rental houses in the Miami area. In one recent year, she drove her car 1,000 miles for her rental activity and 9,000 miles for personal purposes. She can deduct 10% of the actual costs of operating her car, plus the full cost of any rental-related tolls and parking fees. Her expenses amount to $10,000 for the year, so she gets a $1,000 deduction, plus $50 in tolls and parking.

If you have a car that you use only for your rental activity, you may deduct 100% of your actual car costs. Be careful here. If you own just one car, it's hard to successfully claim that you use it only for your rental activity. The IRS is not likely to believe that you walk or take public transportation everywhere, except when you drive for your rental activity. (The IRS will know whether you have more than one vehicle available for personal use; people who claim transportation expenses must provide this information on their tax returns.)

Record-Keeping Requirements

When you deduct actual car expenses, you must keep records of all the costs of owning and operating your car. This includes not only the number of rental activity miles and total miles you drive, but also gas, repair, parking, insurance, tolls, and any other car expenses. (You'll find more information on record-keeping requirements in Chapter 17.)

Vehicle Depreciation Deductions

Using the actual expense method, you can deduct the cost of your vehicle. However, you can't deduct the entire cost in the year when you purchase your car. Instead, you must deduct the cost a portion at a time over several years, using a process called depreciation. (For more on depreciation generally, see Chapter 5.) Although the general concept of depreciation is the same for every type of property, special rules apply to depreciation deductions for cars. These rules give you a lower deduction for cars than you'd be entitled to using the normal depreciation rules.

This section focuses on the depreciation rules for passenger automobiles, as defined by the IRS. This category of vehicles includes almost all automobiles and other passenger vehicles—cars, trucks, pickups, vans, and SUVs. To understand the depreciation rules discussed in this section, you will need to be familiar with the general depreciation rules covered in Chapter 5.

Is Your Vehicle a Passenger Automobile?

First, you must figure out whether your vehicle is a passenger automobile as defined by the IRS. A passenger automobile is any four-wheeled vehicle made primarily for use on public streets and highways that has an unloaded gross weight of 6,000 pounds or less. This definition includes virtually all automobiles.

However, if your vehicle is a truck, SUV, or van, or has a truck base (as do most SUVs), it is a passenger automobile only if it has a gross loaded vehicle weight of 6,000 pounds or less. The gross loaded weight is based on how much the manufacturer says the vehicle can carry and is different from unloaded weight— that is, the vehicle's weight without any passengers or cargo.

You can find out your vehicle's gross loaded and unloaded weight by looking at the metal plate in the driver's-side door jamb, looking at your owner's manual, checking the manufacturer's website or sales brochure, or asking an auto dealer. The gross loaded weight is usually called the Gross Vehicle Weight Rating (GVWR for short). The gross unloaded weight is often called the curb weight.

Trucks that weigh 14,000 pounds or less when fully loaded are subject to the same rules as passenger automobiles, unless the vehicle is not likely to be used for personal purposes (as is true of moving vans, construction vehicles, tractors, and utility repair trucks). In that case, the vehicles are not considered passenger automobiles, and the limitations on depreciation discussed in this section don't apply. Instead, such vehicles are depreciated like any other personal property as described in Chapter 5.

Passenger Automobiles Are Listed Property

The IRS classifies all passenger automobiles as listed property—property that is often used for personal purposes. As explained in Chapter 5, the IRS imposes more stringent requirements on deductions for listed property to discourage fraudulent deduction claims. Because passenger automobiles are listed property, you must keep mileage records showing how much you use your car for rental activity and personal purposes. You must also file IRS Form 4562, Depreciation and Amortization, with your annual tax return.

What You Can Depreciate

You can depreciate your entire investment in a car (also called your basis). If you buy a passenger automobile and use it for your rental activity that same year, your basis is its cost. You may depreciate the entire cost, even if you financed part of the purchase with a car loan. The cost also includes sales taxes, destination charges, and other fees the seller charges. It does not, however, include auto license and registration fees.

If you trade in your old car to a dealer to purchase a new car, your basis in the car you purchase is the adjusted basis of the trade-in car, plus the cash you pay (whether out of your own pocket or financed with a car loan).

EXAMPLE: Brenda buys a new pickup that she uses part of the time for her rental business. The pickup has a $20,000 sticker price. She trades in her old pickup and pays the dealer $15,000, all of which she finances with a car loan from her bank. Her trade-in has a $3,000 basis. Her basis in the new pickup is $18,000 ($3,000 + $15,000), even though the sticker price on the new pickup was $20,000.

If you convert a car that you previously owned for just personal use to use in your rental activity, your basis is the lower of what you originally paid for it (when you purchased it for personal use) or its fair market value at the time you convert it to rental activity use. Your basis will usually be its fair market value, as this is usually the lower number.

You can determine the fair market value of your car on the date of conversion by checking used car value guides, such as the *Kelley Blue Book*. These guides often give more than one value—for example, the *Kelley Blue Book* gives a private party value and a retail value. Using the highest value will give you the largest deduction. The best-known used car price guides (available free on the Internet) are:

- *Kelley Blue Book*: www.kbb.com
- Edmunds: www.edmunds.com, and
- NADA guides: www.nadaguides.com

Look at more than one guide, because the prices can vary.

Depreciation Methods for Passenger Automobiles

Most landlords who own a small number of rental units don't use a single car 100% of the time for their rental activity. Instead, they use their car both for personal and rental activity purposes. If you use a passenger automobile for your rental activity less than 50% of the time, you must depreciate it using the straight-line method. This method gives you equal deductions each year except for the first and last year. It is explained in detail in Chapter 5.

If you use your car more than 50% of the time for your rental activity, you may use accelerated depreciation, which gives you larger deductions the first few years you own your car. But, if you start out using a car more than 50% for your rental activity and your rental use falls below 50% in a later year, you must give back any extra depreciation you received using accelerated depreciation in the prior years. In other words, you must recalculate all of your deductions for the car using the straight-line method, and repay any difference between this amount and the deductions you actually took using another method.

The following table shows how much of the cost of an automobile may be depreciated each year using the three different depreciation methods and applying the half-year convention. (If more than 40% of all the depreciable property you placed in service during the year was placed in service during the last quarter of the year, you'll have to use the mid-quarter convention; see Chapter 5.)

	Automobile Depreciation Table		
Year	200% Declining Balance Method (mid-year convention)	150% Declining Balance Method (mid-year convention)	Straight-Line Method (mid-year convention)
1	20%	15%	10%
2	32%	25.5%	20%
3	19.2%	17.85%	20%
4	11.5%	16.66%	20%
5	11.5%	16.66%	20%
6	5.76%	8.33%	10%

Depreciation Limits for Passenger Automobiles

Passenger automobiles have a five-year class life (but it takes six calendar years to depreciate a car; see "Depreciating Personal Property" in Chapter 5). As a result, you'd think it would take at most six years to fully depreciate a car. Unfortunately, this is usually not the case. Depreciating a passenger automobile is unique in one very important way: The annual depreciation deduction for automobiles is limited to a set dollar amount each year. The annual limit applies to all passenger vehicles, no matter how much they cost. Because the limits are so low, it can take many years to fully depreciate a car, far longer than the six years it takes to depreciate other assets with a five-year class life.

In 2003, the IRS established two different sets of deduction limits for passenger automobiles: one for passenger automobiles other than trucks and vans, and one for trucks and vans that qualify as passenger automobiles (based on their weight) and are built on a truck chassis. This includes minivans and many sports utility vehicles (as long as they meet the weight limit).

The charts below show the maximum annual depreciation deduction allowed for passenger automobiles and trucks and vans placed in service in 2007. Both charts assume 100% rental activity use of the vehicle. You can find the current deduction limits in IRS Publication 946, *How to Depreciate Property,* and Publication 463, *Travel, Entertainment, Gift, and Car Expenses.*

These figures are the maximum amount you can deduct each year, regardless of what depreciation method you use. The depreciation limits are not reduced if a car is in service for less than a full year. This means that the limit is not reduced when the automobile is either placed in service or disposed of during the year.

Depreciation Limits for Passenger Automobiles Placed in Service During 2007	
1st tax year	$3,060
2nd tax year	$4,900
3rd tax year	$2,850
Each succeeding year	$1,775

Depreciation Limits for Trucks and Vans Placed in Service During 2007	
1st tax year	$3,260
2nd tax year	$5,200
3rd tax year	$3,050
Each succeeding year	$1,875

EXAMPLE: Mario pays $50,000 for a new passenger automobile on June 1, 2007, and uses it only for his rental activity. He may depreciate a maximum of $3,060 the first year he owns the car, $4,900 the second, and $2,850 the third.

The deduction limits in the above tables are based on 100% rental activity use of the vehicle. If, like most landlords, you don't use your car solely for your rental activity, the limits are reduced based on your percentage of personal use.

EXAMPLE: Mario uses his new car 20% of the time for his rental activity. His first-year deduction is limited to $612 (20% x $3,060 = $612).

Determining Your Business Miles for Depreciation

As shown above, your total depreciation deduction depends on the percentage of the time you use your car for business. For example, if you drive 1,000 miles for your rental business and 9,000 for personal purposes in a year, you'll have 10% business use and you'll only qualify for 10% of the total allowable depreciation deduction for that year. Thus, if the total allowable deduction was $3,060, you would only get $306. Obviously, you want to have as many business miles as possible. A little-known IRS rule can help you rack up more business mileage. When you determine your business mileage for purposes of your depreciation deduction, you may include miles you drove for investment or other income-producing purposes—for example, to attend an investment seminar. This rule applies only when you figure your total allowable automobile depreciation deduction.

Section 179

If you use your passenger vehicle more than 50% of the time for your rental activity, you could be entitled to use Section 179 expensing. Section 179 permits you to deduct the full cost of personal property you use at least 51% of the time for your rental activity. Your rental activity must qualify as a business for you to use Section 179. This deduction is discussed in detail in Chapter 5. If you qualify, you may combine Section 179 expensing with regular depreciation.

EXAMPLE: Billie buys a used Yugo in February 2007 and uses it 100% for her rental business. The car costs $5,000—her tax basis for depreciation purposes. Using the fastest form of regular depreciation (200% declining balance method), the most Billie can deduct the first year is $1,000 (20% x $5,000), which is far less than the $3,060 annual limit for auto depreciation. She decides to combine depreciation with Section 179 expensing instead. First, she deducts $2,060 using Section 179, then she deducts the remaining $1,000 using regular depreciation. This way, she gets to use the full $3,060 auto depreciation deduction, instead of just $1,000.

You can use Section 179 expensing for both new and used cars you purchase. However, if you use a car for personal travel, then later decide to convert it to a business vehicle, you cannot use the Section 179 deduction.

Remember, this deduction is available only if you use your car more than 50% for your rental activity each year. You can't get around this rule by using it more than 50% for your rental activity in the first year and less in subsequent years. If your use falls below 50% during any year in the five-year period, you'll have to repay to the IRS the extra money you saved by taking a Section 179 deduction. (This process is called recapture—see Chapter 5 for more information.)

Depreciation Beyond the Five-Year Limit

Because of the annual limits on depreciation deductions for passenger automobiles, you usually won't be able to deduct the entire cost of a car over the five-year depreciation period. Don't worry—as long as you continue to use your car for business, you can keep taking annual deductions after the five-year depreciation period ends, until you recover your full basis in the car.

Special Rule for Heavy Vehicles

The annual dollar limits in the charts above don't apply if you use Section 179 to deduct the cost of a vehicle that is not a passenger vehicle. They don't apply to trucks, pickups, RVs, vans, SUVs, and other vehicles that don't come within the passenger automobile definition—that is, vehicles with a gross loaded weight of more than 6,000 pounds (see "Is Your Vehicle a Passenger Automobile? above). This means that you could buy an SUV (or van, truck, pickup, or RV) weighing more than 6,000 pounds for your rental business and deduct the cost in the first year, up to the Section 179 limit.

The normal Section 179 limit for 2007 through 2010 is $125,000, plus inflation adjustments. However, a law enacted at the end of 2004 limits the Section 179 deduction for SUVs to a maximum of $25,000.

For example, suppose Terry, in 2007, pays $40,000 for a 7,000 lb. SUV that she uses 100% of the time for her rental business. Terry may deduct $25,000 of the SUV's cost in 2007 using Section 179. She may deduct the remaining $15,000 of her SUV's cost using regular depreciation.

Caution: As this book went to press, legislation was pending in Congress to eliminate the Section 179 deduction for most SUVs. Before purchasing an SUV be sure to check and see if this new law has been enacted.

Auto Repairs and Improvements

Auto repairs and maintenance costs are fully deductible in the year you pay them. Add these costs to your other annual expenses when you use the actual expense method. (You get no extra deduction for repairs when you use the standard mileage rate.) If you fix your car yourself, you may deduct the cost of parts and depreciate or deduct tools, but you can't take a deduction for your time or labor.

Unlike repairs, improvements to your car must be depreciated over several years, not deducted all in the year when you pay for them. What's the difference between a repair and an improvement? Unlike a repair, an improvement:

- increases the value of your car
- makes the car more useful, or
- lengthens your car's useful life.

These are the exact same rules that are used to determine if a change to rental property is a repair or improvement. (See Chapter 4.)

EXAMPLE 1: Doug spends $100 to fix his car's carburetor. This is a currently deductible repair because it doesn't increase the value of his car or lengthen its useful life. The repair merely allows the car to last for a normal time.

EXAMPLE 2: Doug spends $2,000 on a brand new engine for his car. This is an improvement that must be depreciated because the new engine increases the car's value and useful life.

Improvements must be depreciated separately from the vehicle itself—that is, they are treated as a separate item of depreciable property. The same rules, however, apply to depreciating improvements as regular auto depreciation. Combine the cost of the original vehicle and the improvements for purposes of the annual automobile depreciation limit. The recovery period begins when the improvement is placed in service.

Leasing a Car

If you lease a car that you use in your rental activity, you can use the actual expense method to deduct the portion of each lease payment that reflects the rental activity percentage use of the car. You cannot deduct any part of a lease payment that is for commuting or personal use of the car.

EXAMPLE: John pays $400 a month to lease a Lexus. He uses it 10% for his rental activity and 90% for personal purposes. He may deduct 10% of his lease payments ($40 a month) as a local transportation expense for his sales business.

Leasing companies typically require you to make an advance or down payment to lease a car. You can deduct this cost as well, but you must spread the deduction out equally over the entire lease period.

You may use either the actual expense method or the standard mileage rate when you lease a car for business. However, if you want to use the standard mileage rate, you must use it the first year you lease the car and continue to use it for the entire lease term. If you use the standard mileage method, you can't deduct any portion of your lease payments. Instead, this cost is covered by the standard mileage rate set by the IRS.

Is It Really a Lease?

Some transactions that are called auto leases are really not leases at all. Instead, they are installment purchases—that is, you pay for the car over time, and by the end of the lease term you own all or part of the car. You cannot deduct any payments you make to buy a car, even if the payments are called lease payments. Instead, you have to depreciate the cost of the car as described above.

Leasing Luxury Cars

If you lease what the IRS considers to be a luxury car for more than 30 days, you may have to reduce your lease deduction. The purpose of this rule is to prevent people from leasing very expensive cars to get around the limitations on depreciation deductions for cars that they purchase (see "Vehicle Depreciation Deductions," above). A luxury car is currently defined as one with a fair market value of more than $15,500.

The amount by which you must reduce your deduction (called an inclusion amount) is based on the fair market value of your car and the percentage of time that you use it for business. The IRS recalculates it each year. You can find the inclusion amount for the current year in the tables published in IRS Publication 463, *Travel, Entertainment, Gift, and Car Expenses*. The amount is usually fairly modest. For example, if you leased a $40,000 car in 2007 and used it solely for business that year, you would have to reduce your car expense deduction by $172 for the year. If you used the car only 50% for business, the reduction would be $86. Prorate the inclusion amount for the first year based on the month when you start using the car for business.

Should You Lease or Buy Your Car?

When you lease a car, you are paying rent for it—a set fee each month for the use of the car. At the end of the lease term, you give the car back to the leasing company and own nothing. As a general rule, leasing a car instead of buying it makes economic sense only if you absolutely must have a new car every two or three years and drive no more than 12,000 to 15,000 miles per year. If you drive more than 15,000 miles a year, leasing becomes an economic disaster because most leases penalize you for higher mileage.

There are numerous financial calculators available on the Internet that can help you determine how much it will cost to lease a car rather than buy one. Be careful when you use these calculators—their design is based on certain assumptions about how much cars depreciate each year and other matters, and different calculators can give different answers. For a detailed consumer guide to auto leasing created by the Federal Reserve Board, go to the Board's website at www.federalreserve.gov/pubs/leasing.

Other Local Transportation Expenses

You don't have to drive a car or other vehicle to get a tax deduction for local trips. You can deduct the cost of travel by bus or other public transit, taxi, train, ferry, motorcycle, bicycle, or any other means. However, all the rules limiting deductions for travel by car also apply to other transportation methods. The same record-keeping requirements apply as well.

Reporting Transportation Expenses on Your Tax Return

Report your local transportation deduction on Line 6 of IRS Schedule E. Combine it with your travel expenses (see Chapter 18). You must also complete and file

Part V of IRS Form 4562, Depreciation and Amortization. This form requires that you answer the following questions about your vehicle use:

- total business/investment miles driven during the year
- total commuting miles driven during the year
- total other personal (noncommuting) miles driven during the year, and
- whether you had another vehicle available for personal use.

As you can see, by looking at your answers to these questions, the IRS can determine what percentage of the time you claim to use your car for your rental activity and for personal use. The IRS will likely think something is wrong if you claim to use your car 100% of the time for your rental activity, but say you have no other car available for personal use.

■

Travel Expenses

f you travel overnight for your rental activity, you can deduct your airfare, hotel bills, meals, and other expenses. If you plan your trip carefully, you can even mix landlord business with pleasure and still take a deduction. However, IRS auditors closely scrutinize deductions for overnight travel and many taxpayers get caught claiming these deductions without proper records to back them up. To stay within the law (and avoid unwanted attention from the IRS), you need to know how this deduction works and how to properly document your travel expenses.

What Are Travel Expenses?

For tax purposes, travel expenses are the amounts you spend when you travel away from your tax home overnight for your business (rental) activity. You don't have to travel any set distance to take a travel expense deduction. However, you can't take this deduction if you just spend the night in a motel across town. You must travel outside your city limits. If you don't live in a city, you must go outside the general area where your tax home is located.

You must stay away overnight or at least long enough to require a stop for sleep or rest. You cannot satisfy the rest requirement by merely napping in your car.

> **EXAMPLE:** Phyllis lives in Los Angeles. She flies to San Francisco to deal with a repair problem in a rental house she owns there. She spends the night in a hotel, and returns home the following day. Her trip is a deductible travel expense.

If you don't stay overnight, your trip will not qualify as travel. However, this does not necessarily mean that you can't take a tax deduction. Local trips for your rental activity are also deductible (see Chapter 10), but you are entitled to deduct only your transportation expenses—the cost of driving or using some other means of transportation. You may not deduct meals or other expenses like you can when you travel and stay overnight.

> **EXAMPLE:** Philip drives from his home in Los Angeles to San Diego to show his rental property to prospective tenants and returns home that same day. His 200-mile round trip is a deductible local trip. He may deduct his expenses for the 200 miles he drove, but he can't deduct the breakfast he bought on the way to San Diego.

How to deduct local travel. For a detailed discussion of tax deductions for local travel, see Chapter 10.

Where Is Your Tax Home?

Your tax home is the entire city or general area where your principal place of business for your rental activity is located. If you run your rental activity out of your residence, your tax home is the city or area where you live.

The IRS doesn't care how far you travel for business. You'll get a deduction as long as you travel outside your tax home's city limits and stay overnight. Thus, even if you're just traveling across town, you'll qualify for a deduction if you manage to stay outside your city limits.

> **EXAMPLE:** Pete's tax home is in San Francisco. He drives to Oakland to check up on an apartment building he owns. He decides to spend the night in an Oakland hotel rather than brave the traffic back to San Francisco. Pete's stay qualifies as a deductible travel expense even though the distance between San Francisco and Oakland is only eight miles. Pete can deduct his hotel and meal expenses.

If you don't live in a city, your tax home covers the general area where you typically reside—the area within about 40 miles of your home.

Your Trip Must Be for Business

In order to deduct the cost of your trip, it must be primarily for your rental activity. This means that you must have a rental purpose in mind before starting out, and you must actually do something for your rental activity while you're away. Examples of rental business purposes include:

- traveling to your rental property to deal with tenants, maintenance, repairs, or improvements
- traveling to building supply stores or other places to obtain materials and supplies for your rental activity
- traveling to your rental property to show it to prospective tenants
- learning new skills to help in your rental activity, by attending landlord-related classes, seminars, conventions, or trade shows, and

- traveling to see people who can help you operate your rental activity, such as attorneys, accountants, or real estate brokers.

On the other hand, rental-related activities do not include:

- sightseeing
- recreational activities that you attend by yourself or with family or friends, or
- attending personal investment seminars or political events.

Use common sense when deciding whether to claim that a trip is for your rental activity. If you're audited, the IRS is likely to question any trip that doesn't have some logical connection to your rental activity.

Travel Must Be Ordinary and Necessary

To be deductible, your travel expenses must be ordinary and necessary. This means that the trip and the expenses you incur must be helpful and appropriate for your rental activity, not necessarily indispensable. Traveling to a rental property is not always ordinary and necessary.

> **EXAMPLE:** Rayford Strickland owned two parcels of real estate about 500 miles from his tax home in Texas. During a two-year period, he made 80 trips to the property at a claimed cost of $11,000. The properties generated a total of $1,653 in income during this time. The IRS and tax court disallowed Strickland's travel expense deductions. The court found that the 80 trips were not an ordinary and necessary expense because Strickland was unable to provide any explanation of why it was necessary to make so many trips to the two properties. (*Strickland v. Comm'r*, 43 T.C.M. 1061.)

Travel Before You Become a Landlord

You must be involved in an ongoing rental activity to deduct your business trips. Trips you take to investigate acquiring your first rental property are not currently deductible business travel expenses.

> **EXAMPLE:** Michelle, a San Francisco resident, has never owned any rental property, but would like to buy some. She has heard that there are good buys in Reno, Nevada, so she takes several trips there to search for income properties. She can't currently deduct her travel expenses because she is not yet in business.

Travel to View Rental Properties for Sale

There are several hurdles to deducting travel expenses you incur while looking at rental properties to purchase. You may not deduct expenses you incur to find new properties to buy if your rental activity is an investment, instead of a business, for tax purposes. Investors may not deduct expenses incurred to find new investments. Most landlords are in business. (*Frank v. Comm'r*, 20 T.C. 511.) (See Chapter 2 for a detailed discussion of whether a rental activity qualifies as a business or investment.)

If your rental activity is a business, travel costs to look for properties to purchase fall into two categories:

- expenses incurred to look at properties you purchase, and
- expenses incurred to look at properties you don't purchase.

Expenses you incur to look at a property you end up buying must be added to the basis of your property and depreciated over 27.5 years along with the rest of the property. (Rev. Rul. 77-254.) This means it will take a long time to fully deduct your travel expenses for a property you buy.

If you look at rental property on a trip, but don't buy it, your travel expenses can be currently deductible as an operating expense, but only if you are already engaged in a rental business in the geographic area where the property is located. Unfortunately for landlords who like to travel, the IRS and courts have taken a restrictive view of the geographic area in which a small landlord is in business, holding that it extends only to the area where the landlord already owns property.

EXAMPLE: Patrick O'Donnell, a Chicago resident who owned two apartments in Las Vegas, took a two-day trip to Miami to investigate buying a rental property there. However, he decided not to go through with the deal. Both the IRS and tax court denied him a deduction for his travel expenses. The court found that, even though O'Donnell was in the rental business in Las Vegas, his business did not extend to Miami. Because he was not in business in Miami, he couldn't deduct as a business operating expense his costs to travel there to look at properties. If he had actually bought a rental property in Miami, his travel expenses to purchase it would still not currently be deductible. Instead, he would have to add the cost to the property's basis and depreciate it over 27.5 years. However, if he had also incurred expenses to look at properties he didn't buy before finding the property he did buy, those expenses could be deducted as business start-up expenses. (See Chapter 8.) (*O'Donnell v. Comm'r*, 62 T.C. 781.)

It's unclear exactly how large an area the IRS and tax court would say a small landlord does business in. For example, would O'Donnell in the above example have been able to deduct the expenses of looking for rental properties in Reno, Nevada, or Los Angeles? No one knows. It is clear, however, that your best case for being able to deduct travel expenses is where you look for property in or near an area where you already own rental real estate. Once you start traveling outside of the area where you already own rental property, you'll have a tougher time claiming the deduction with the IRS, especially if you travel to a vacation destination like Miami or Hawaii.

If you travel outside your area of business to look at new rental properties and decide to take your chances with the IRS and claim the deduction, be sure to properly document your expenses and the time you spend looking for rental properties on your trip. You'll have a problem only if you're audited. But, claiming large travel deductions as a landlord will definitely increase your chance of getting audited.

Deductible Travel Expenses

Subject to the limits covered in "How Much You Can Deduct," below, virtually all of your travel expenses are deductible. These costs fall into two broad categories: your transportation expenses and the expenses you incur at your destination.

Transportation expenses are the costs of getting to and from your destination—for example:

- fares for airplanes, trains, or buses
- driving expenses, including car rentals
- shipping costs for your personal luggage or other things you need for your rental activity, and
- meals, beverages, and lodging expenses you incur while en route to your final destination.

If you drive your own car to your destination, you may deduct your costs using the standard mileage rate, or you can deduct your actual expenses. You may also deduct your mileage while at your destination. (See Chapter 10 for more on mileage deductions.)

You may also deduct your food and lodging expenses while at your destination. Destination expenses include:

- hotel or other lodging expenses for days you work at your rental activity
- 50% of meal and beverage expenses

- taxi, public transportation, and car rental expenses at your destination
- telephone, Internet, and fax expenses
- computer rental fees
- laundry and dry cleaning expenses, and
- tips you pay on any of the other costs.

You may deduct 50% of your entertainment expenses if you incur them for your rental activity. You can't deduct entertainment expenses for activities that you attend alone; this solo entertainment obviously wouldn't be for business purposes. (See Chapter 14 for a detailed discussion of the special rules that apply to deductions for entertainment expenses.)

Traveling First Class or Steerage

You may not deduct lavish or extravagant expenses, but the IRS gives you a great deal of leeway here. You may, if you wish, travel first class, stay at four-star hotels, and eat at expensive restaurants. On the other hand, you're also entitled to be a cheapskate—for example, you could stay with a friend or relative at your destination to save on hotel charges and still deduct your meals and other expenses.

Taking People With You

You may deduct the expenses you pay for a person who travels with you only if he or she:

- is your employee
- has a genuine business reason for going on the trip with you, and
- would otherwise be allowed to deduct the travel expenses.

These rules apply to your family as well. This means you can deduct the expense of taking your spouse, child, or other relative only if the person is your employee and his or her presence is essential to your rental activity.

> **EXAMPLE:** Jason lives in Dallas and owns an apartment building in Tulsa, Oklahoma. He hires his son Dave to assist him in doing repairs for his property. He may deduct the cost of traveling to Tulsa with Dave to do repairs.

In addition, you may deduct the travel costs of your spouse or any other relative who is a co-owner of the rental property you travel to visit, provided that he or she spends sufficient time on rental activities.

If you bring your family along simply to enjoy the trip, you may still deduct your own business expenses as if you were traveling alone—and you don't have to reduce your deductions, even if others get a free ride with you. For example, if you drive to your destination, you can deduct the entire cost of the drive, even if your family rides along with you. Similarly, you can deduct the full cost of a single hotel room even if you obtain a larger, more expensive room for your whole family.

How Much You Can Deduct

If you spend all of your time at your destination on rental business, you may deduct 100% of your expenses (except meal expenses, which are only 50% deductible—see below). However, things get more complicated if you mix business and pleasure. Different rules apply to your transportation expenses and the expenses you incur while at your destination (destination expenses).

Travel Within the United States

Travel within the United States is subject to an all or nothing rule: You may deduct 100% of your transportation expenses only if you spend *more than half of your time* on rental activities while at your destination. In other words, your rental activity days must outnumber your personal days. If you spend more time on personal activities than on rental activities, you get no transportation deduction.

You may also deduct the destination expenses you incur on days when you do rental-related tasks. Expenses incurred on personal days at your destination are nondeductible personal expenses. (The rules used to determine what constitutes a rental activity day are discussed below.)

> **EXAMPLE:** Tom's tax home is in Atlanta, but he owns an apartment building in New Orleans. He takes the train to New Orleans to supervise extensive remodeling of his property. He spends six days in New Orleans, where he spends all of his time on rental business, and spends $900 for his hotel, meals, and other living expenses. On the way home, he stops in Mobile for three days to visit his parents and spends $100 for lodging and meals there. His round-trip train fare is $250. Tom's trip consisted of six rental activity

days and three personal days, so he spent more than half of the trip on rental activities. He can deduct 100% of his train fare and the entire $900 he spent while on business in New Orleans. He may not, however, deduct the $100 he spent while visiting his parents.

If your trip is primarily a vacation—that is, you spend more than half of your time on personal activities—the entire cost of the trip is a nondeductible personal expense. However, you may deduct destination expenses that are directly related to your rental activity. This includes things like phone calls or faxes. It doesn't include transportation, lodging, or food.

As long as your trip is primarily for your rental activity, you can add a vacation to the end of the trip, make a side trip purely for fun, or enjoy evenings at the theater or ballet, and still deduct your entire airfare. What you spend while having fun is not deductible, but you can deduct all of your rental activity and transportation expenses.

> **EXAMPLE:** Bill flies to Miami where he spends four days working on his rental property. He spends three extra days in Miami swimming and enjoying the sights. Because he spent over half his time on rental business—four days out of seven—the cost of his flight is entirely deductible, as are his hotel and meal costs while he worked on his rental property. He may not deduct his hotel, meal, or other expenses during his vacation days.

Travel Outside the United States

Travel outside the United States for a rental activity can be deductible. In one case, for example, a landlord who lived in Seattle was permitted to deduct travel expenses he incurred to oversee extensive repairs to a 31-unit apartment building he owned in Berlin, Germany that had been severely damaged in World War II. (*Reisner v. Comm'r*, 34 T.C. 1122.) However, as explained above, it's unlikely the IRS would permit you to deduct expenses of traveling to a foreign country unless you already own rental property there.

Travel outside the United States is subject to different rules than travel within the country. The rules for deducting your transportation expenses depend on how long you stay at your destination.

Trips for Up to Seven Days

If you travel outside the United States for no more than seven days, you can deduct 100% of your airfare or other transportation expenses, as long as you spend part of the time on rental activities. You can spend a majority of your time on personal activities, as long as you spend at least some time on rental activities. Seven days means seven consecutive days, not counting the day you leave but counting the day you return to the United States. You may also deduct the destination expenses you incur on the days you do rental-related work.

> **EXAMPLE:** Billie lives in Portland, Oregon, and owns a rental property in Vancouver, Canada. She spends four days sightseeing in Vancouver and one day dealing with a repair for her rental. She may deduct 100% of her airfare, but she can deduct her lodging, meals, and other expenses from her stay in Vancouver only for the one day when she was involved with her rental.

Trips for More Than Seven Days

The IRS does not want to subsidize foreign vacations, so more stringent rules apply if your foreign trip lasts more than one week. For these longer trips, the magic number is 75%: If you spend more than 75% of your time on rental activities at your foreign destination, you can deduct what it would have cost to make the trip if you had not engaged in any personal activities. This means you may deduct 100% of your airfare or other transportation expenses, plus your living expenses while you were on rental business and any other rental-related expenses.

> **EXAMPLE:** Sean flies from Boston to Dublin, Ireland, where he owns an apartment building he inherited from his mother. He spends one day sightseeing and nine days overseeing extensive remodeling of the aged building. He has spent 90% of his time on rental activities, so he may deduct 100% of his airfare to Dublin and all of the living and other expenses he incurred during the nine days he spent on rental activities. He may not deduct any of his expenses (including hotel charges) for the day he spent sightseeing.

If you spend more than 50%—but less than 75%—of your time on rental activities, you can deduct only the rental activity percentage of your transportation and other costs. You figure out this percentage by counting the number of rental activity days and the number of personal days to come up with a fraction. The number of rental activity days is the numerator (top number) and the total number of days away from home is the denominator (bottom number). For ease in determining the dollar amount of your deduction, you can convert this fraction into a percentage.

> **EXAMPLE:** Sam flies from Las Vegas to London, where he spends six days dealing with his rental property and four days sightseeing. He spent 6/10 (or 60%) of his total time away from home on rental activities. He can deduct 60% of his travel costs—that is, 60% of his round-trip airfare, hotel, and other expenses. The trip cost him $3,000, so he gets a $1,800 deduction.

If you spend 50% or less of your time on rental activities on a foreign trip that lasts more than seven days, you cannot deduct any of your costs.

What all this means is that you must spend a great deal of time on rental activities to deduct all or part of a foreign trip that lasts more than 14 days. You can't spend much time sightseeing or at the beach. As explained in detail below, you must work on rental activities over four hours a day for that day to count as a rental activity day. Travel days also count as rental activity days. So, if, for example, you own rental property in Aruba or some other vacation spot, you can forget about flying there, spending all your time lying in the sun, and then deducting your travel costs as a rental activity expense.

Conventions

A convention is an assembly of people who meet for a common purpose—good examples are the political conventions held every four years by the Democrats and Republicans.

If your rental activity is a business, you may deduct the cost of traveling to a convention just like the cost of any other business trip, as long as you satisfy the following rules.

Conventions Within North America

You may deduct the expense of attending a convention in North America if your attendance benefits your rental business. You may not, however, deduct any expenses for your spouse or other family unless they are co-owners of your rental property.

How do you know if a convention benefits your rental business? Look at the convention agenda or program (and be sure to save a copy). Any convention specifically for landlords should pass muster with the IRS. Examples of conventions that are not deductible include those for investment, political, or social purposes.

You probably learned in school that North America consists of the United States, Canada, and Mexico. However, for convention expense purposes, North America includes much of the Caribbean and many other great vacation destinations, including: American Samoa, Antigua and Barbuda, Aruba, Baker Island, Barbados, Canada, Costa Rica, Dominica, Dominican Republic, Grenada, Guam, Guyana, Honduras, Howland Island, Jamaica, Jarvis Island, Johnston Island, Kingman Reef, Marshall Islands, Mexico, Micronesia, Midway Islands, Netherlands Antilles, Northern Mariana Islands, Palau, Palmyra, Puerto Rico, Saint Lucia, Trinidad and Tobago, United States (the 50 states and Washington, D.C.), U.S. Virgin Islands, and Wake Island.

Foreign Conventions

More stringent rules apply if you attend a convention outside of North America (as defined above). You can take a deduction for a foreign convention only if:

- the convention is directly related to your rental business (rather than merely benefiting it), and
- it's as reasonable for the convention to be held outside of North America as in North America.

To determine whether it's reasonable to hold the convention outside of North America, the IRS looks at the purposes of the meeting and the sponsoring group, the activities at the convention, where the sponsors live, and where other meetings have been or will be held. It's highly unlikely the IRS would permit a landlord to deduct the cost of attending a foreign convention unless he or she owned property in the foreign country—for example, a landlord who owns rental property in Canada could probably deduct the costs of traveling to a convention for landlords in Toronto. As a general rule, if you want a tax deduction, avoid attending a convention outside of North America.

Travel by Ship

Travel by ship can be deductible if a convention or other rental business event is conducted on board; or, more rarely, if you use a ship as a means of transportation. The following rules apply to sea travel.

What Is Foreign Travel?

Because different deduction rules apply to travel within the United States and foreign travel, it's important to know which is which. For IRS purposes, foreign travel means travel outside of the United States. Thus, for example, a trip to Puerto Rico would be a foreign trip, even though it is a United States possession. Travel outside the United States does not include travel from one point in the United States to another point in the United States.

If you travel by plane, train, or other public transportation, any place in the United States where your plane or other means of transportation makes a scheduled stop is a point in the United States. Your foreign trip begins at the last scheduled stop in the United States.

> **EXAMPLE:** Ben flies from Chicago to Miami, changes planes, and then flies to Puerto Rico. The flight from Chicago to Miami is within the United States, so the domestic travel rules apply. The flight from Miami to Puerto Rico is outside the United States, so the foreign travel rules apply. Ben then returns to Chicago on a nonstop flight from Puerto Rico. All of the return trip counts as foreign travel because there are no scheduled stops in the United States.

If you travel by private car to a foreign destination, the portion of the trip that is within the United States is governed by the domestic travel rules.

> **EXAMPLE:** Bart travels by car from Denver to Mexico City and returns. His travel between Denver and the United States border is travel within the United States. The foreign travel rules apply only to the portion of his trip within Mexico.

If you travel by private airplane, any flight (or portion thereof) that both takes off and lands in the United States is travel within the United States, even if the plane flies over a foreign country.

> **EXAMPLE:** Brenda flies her private plane nonstop from Seattle to Juneau, Alaska. Because she took off and landed in the United States, the trip is within the United States for tax purposes—even though she had to fly over Canada on the way to Juneau. However, if she makes a scheduled stop in Vancouver, Canada, both legs of the flight are considered travel outside the United States, and are subject to the foreign travel rules.

Shipboard Conventions and Seminars

If your rental activity qualifies as a business, you may be able to deduct the cost of attending shipboard conventions or seminars that directly benefit your rental business. However, forget about taking a tax deduction for a pure pleasure cruise. Nor can you deduct personal investment or financial planning seminars. Landlords who are not in business get no deductions for shipboard conventions, seminars, or similar meetings.

If you meet the requirements, there is one major restriction: You must travel on a U.S.-registered ship that stops only in ports in the United States or its possessions, such as Puerto Rico or the U.S. Virgin Islands. If a cruise sponsor promises you'll be able to deduct your trip, investigate carefully to make sure it meets these requirements.

To deduct your rental business-related cruise expenses, you must file a signed note with your tax return from the meeting or seminar sponsor listing the business meetings scheduled each day aboard ship and certifying how many hours you spent in attendance. Make sure to get this statement from the meeting sponsor. Your annual deduction for attending conventions, seminars, or similar meetings on ships cannot exceed $2,000.

Transportation by Ship

You can get a deduction if you use an ocean liner, cruise ship, or other vessel solely as a means of transportation to a destination you travel to for your rental activity. This isn't very common these days, but it can be done. In this situation, your deduction for each travel day is limited to twice the highest amount federal workers are paid each day (called the per diem rate) for their living expenses while traveling inside the U.S. on government business. You can find the latest rates in IRS Publication 1542, *Per Diem Rates*.

> **EXAMPLE:** In 2007, Caroline travels by ocean liner from Los Angeles to Juneau, Alaska, where she owns a rental property. She pays $5,000 for the six-day cruise. However, she may deduct only up to twice the highest federal per diem amount for each day of the cruise. This amount is $338, so she can deduct up to $676 per day. Caroline's deduction for the cruise cannot exceed $4,056 (6 days x $676 = $4,056).

You may take this deduction where your rental activity qualifies as a business or investment for tax purposes.

Calculating Time Spent on Rental Activities

To calculate how much time you spend on rental activities while on a trip, compare the number of days you spend on rental-related work to the number of days you spend on personal activities. You spend a day on rental activities if you:

- spend more than four hours doing rental-related work
- are not at a particular place for your rental activity—for example, to show a vacant rental unit even if you spend most of the day on personal activities
- spend more than four hours on travel for your rental activity (travel time begins when you leave home and ends when you reach your hotel, or vice versa)
- drive at least 300 miles for your rental activity. You can average your mileage. For example, if you drive 600 miles to your destination in two days, you may claim two 300-mile days, even if you drove 500 miles on one day and 100 miles on the other.
- spend more than four hours on some combination of travel and your rental activities
- are prevented from working rental activities because of circumstances beyond your control, such as a transit strike or terrorist act, and
- stay at your destination between days you work on rental activities, if it would have cost more to go home and return than to remain where you are. This sandwich rule allows you to count weekends as rental activity days, if you work at your travel destination during the previous and following week.

EXAMPLE: Mike lives in New Orleans and owns several rental properties in Denver. Mike drives from his home to Denver, making the 1,100 mile drive in three days. He arrives in Denver on Saturday night. Mike rests and attends church on Sunday. On Monday, he deals with repairs for one of his rental houses. Mike works on this for five hours on Monday and three hours on Tuesday, spending the rest of his time resting and sightseeing. On Wednesday, he spends about two hours working at his rental property and spends the rest of the day sightseeing. He spends Thursday and Friday sightseeing. He then drives straight home on Saturday, taking another three days. Mike's trip consisted of eight rental activity days: six travel days, one sandwiched day (the Sunday before the Monday he worked on his rental property), and the one day he worked more than four hours. He had four personal days—the two days he worked less than four hours and the two days he spent sightseeing.

Be sure to keep track of your time while you're away. You can do this by taking notes on your calendar or travel diary. (See Chapter 17 for a detailed discussion of record keeping while traveling.)

50% Limit on Meal Expenses

You may deduct the cost of meals you eat on traveling days and days you spend working on your rental activity, as defined in the previous section. However, the IRS figures that you have to eat, whether you're at home or away on a trip for your rental activity. Because meals you eat at home ordinarily aren't deductible, the IRS won't let you deduct all of your food expenses while traveling. Instead, you can deduct only 50% of your meal expenses while on a trip. There are two ways to calculate your meal expense deduction: You can keep track of your actual expenses or use a daily rate set by the federal government.

Deducting Actual Meal Expenses

If you use the actual expense method, you must keep track of what you spend on meals (including tips and tax) while traveling and at your destination. When you do your taxes, you add these amounts together and deduct half of the total.

> **EXAMPLE:** Frank travels from his home in Santa Fe, New Mexico, to Reno, Nevada, to deal with a vacant rental unit. He gets there by car. While on the road, he spends $200 for meals. In Reno, he spends another $200 on the days he spends more than four hours dealing with his rental. His total meal expense for the trip is $400. He may deduct half of this amount, or $200.

Meals that constitute entertainment (for example, if you take a rental-business partner to a business lunch) are subject to the rules on entertainment expenses covered in Chapter 14.

You do not necessarily have to keep every receipt for your meals, but you need to keep careful track of what you spend, and you should be able to prove that the meal was for business. (See Chapter 14 for a detailed discussion of record keeping for meal expenses.)

Using the Standard Meal Allowance

When you use the actual expense method, you must keep track of what you spend for each meal. This can be a lot of work, so the IRS provides an alternative method of deducting meals: Instead of deducting your actual expenses, you can deduct a set amount for each day of your trip. This amount is called the standard meal allowance. It covers your expenses for meals, beverages, tax, and tips. The amount of the allowance depends on where and when you travel.

The advantage of using the standard meal allowance is that you don't have to keep track of how much you spend on meals and tips. However, you have to keep records to prove the time, place, and rental purpose of your travel. (See Chapter 17 for more on record keeping.)

The disadvantage is that the standard meal allowance is one-half of what federal workers are allowed to charge for meals while traveling, and is therefore relatively modest. In 2007, the full rate federal workers could charge for domestic travel ranged from $39 per day for travel in the least expensive areas to up to $64 for high-cost areas, which includes most major cities. And because you can generally deduct only half of your meal and entertainment expenses, your deduction is limited to one-half of the federal meal allowance. If you use the standard meal allowance and spend more than the allowance, you get no deduction for the overage.

The standard meal allowance includes $3 per day for incidental expenses—tips you pay to porters, bellhops, maids, and transportation workers. If you wish, you can use the actual expense method for your meal costs and the $3 incidental expense rate for your tips. However, you'd have to be a pretty stingy tipper for this amount to be adequate.

The standard meal allowance is revised each year. You can find the current rates for travel within the United States on the Internet at www.gsa.gov (look for the link to "Per Diem Rates" in the "Featured Topics" section), or in IRS Publication 1542, *Per Diem Rates (for Travel Within the Continental United States)*. The rates for foreign travel are set by the U.S. State Department, and can be found at www.state.gov. You want to check the "M & IE Rate"—short for meals and incidental expenses. Rates are also provided for lodging, but these don't apply to nongovernmental travelers.

You can claim the standard meal allowance only for days you work on rental activities. If you travel to more than one location in one day, use the rate in effect for the area where you spend the night. Remember, you are allowed to deduct only 50% of the federal worker rate as a business expense.

EXAMPLE: Art travels from Los Angeles to Chicago, where he spends five days showing a vacant rental unit to prospective tenants. Chicago is a high-cost locality, so the daily meal and incidental expense (M&IE) rate is $64. Art figures his deduction by multiplying the daily rate by five and dividing this in half: 5 days x $64 = $320; $320 x 50% = $160.

If you use the standard meal allowance, you must use it for *all of the rental-related trips you take during the year.* You can't use it for some trips and use the actual expense method for others. For example, you can't use the standard allowance when you go to an inexpensive destination and the actual expense method when you go to a pricey one.

Because the standard meal allowance is relatively small, it's better to use it only if you travel exclusively to low-cost areas, or if you are simply unable or unwilling to keep track of what you actually spend for meals.

Maximizing Your Travel Deductions

Here are some simple strategies you can use to maximize your business travel deductions.

Plan Ahead

Plan your itinerary carefully before you leave to make sure your trip qualifies as a tax deductible trip. This means you must spend more than half of your days on rental activities for your transportation to be deductible. If you know you're going to spend three days on rental activities, arrange to spend no more than two days on personal activities so that your trip meets the requirements. If you're traveling overseas for more than 14 days, you'll have to spend at least 75% of your days on rental activities to deduct your transportation—you may be able to do this by using strategies to maximize your rental activity days.

Make a Paper Trail

If the IRS audits you, they will probably question you about travel deductions. Of course, you'll need to have records showing what you spent for your trips. However, you'll also need documents proving that your trip was for your existing rental activity. You can do this by:

- making a note in your calendar or daily planner of all rental-related work you do—be sure to note the time you spend on each rental activity
- obtaining and saving business cards from anyone you meet while dealing with rental problems—for example, contractors or repair people
- noting in your calendar or daily planner the names of all the people you meet for your rental activity on your trip
- keeping the programs or agendas from any conventions or training seminars you attend, as well as any notes you made, and
- keeping copies of rental-related correspondence or e-mails you sent or received before the trip.

Maximize Your Rental Activity Days

If you mix business with pleasure on your trip, you have to make sure that you have enough rental activity days to deduct your transportation costs. You'll need to spend more than 50% of your days on your rental activity on domestic trips and more than 75% for foreign trips of more than 14 days.

You don't have to work all day for that day to count as a rental activity day: Any day in which you work at least four hours on rental matters is a rental activity day, even if you goof off the rest of time. The day will count as a rental activity day for purposes of determining whether your transportation expenses are deductible, and you can deduct your lodging, meal, and other expenses during the day, even though you only worked four hours.

You can easily maximize your rental activity days by taking advantage of this rule. For example, you can:

- work no more than four hours on rental activities in any one day whenever possible
- spread your work over several days—for example, if you need to do a repair that takes 12 hours, spread the work over three days instead of one or two, and
- avoid using the fastest form of transportation to your destination—travel days count as rental activity days, so you'll add rental activity days to your trip if you drive instead of fly. Remember, there's no law that says you have to take the quickest means of transportation to your destination.

However, you can't work super slowly just to be able to claim you spent more than four hours a day on rental activities. Your work schedule must be believable and reasonable.

EXAMPLE: Otto Harris lived in St. Louis, Missouri and owned investment real property in Charlotte, North Carolina, where he also had relatives. Over the course of a year, he made three trips to Charlotte. He claimed that during the first two trips he worked on the property seven to nine hours a day, six days a week, clearing underbrush, cutting down thick foliage, chopping dead wood, raking leaves, and cleaning up trash. During his last trip of the year, which occurred over Christmas and lasted 11 days, he claimed he spent his time neatly stacking the wood he had cut on his previous trips into neat one-foot piles as required by a local ordinance. The tax court permitted Harris to deduct the travel costs for his first two trips, but not the third. It found that it was credible that Harris worked six to nine hours a day on the first two trips to clear his property. However, the court simply could not believe that it could take him 11 days to stack some wood. The court concluded that it was likely that Harris had actually spent the majority of his time celebrating Christmas with his relatives. (*Harris v. Comm'r*, T.C. Memo 1978-332.)

Take Advantage of the Sandwich Day Rule

Days when you do no rental-related work still count as rental activity days if they are sandwiched between rental activity days, as long as it was cheaper to spend that day away than to go back home for the off days. If you work on Friday and Monday, this rule allows you to count Saturday and Sunday as rental activity days, even if you don't do any work.

EXAMPLE: Kim lives in Boston and owns a rental condominium in Miami. She flies to Miami to deal with repairs and show her unit to prospective renters. She arrives on Wednesday and returns the following Wednesday. She does not engage in any rental activities over the weekend and goes to the beach instead. Nevertheless, because it was cheaper for her to stay in Miami than to fly back to Boston for the weekend and return to Miami, she may count Saturday and Sunday as rental activity days. This means she can deduct her lodging and meal expenses for those days.

Hiring Help

Whenever you hire a worker to help you with your rental business, you will be faced with a number of tax-related questions:

- Are your payments to the worker deductible?
- Is the worker an employee or independent contractor?
- If the worker is an independent contractor, what tax-reporting requirements do you have?
- If the worker is an employee, what payroll tax rules must you comply with?
- Are there special rules that apply when you hire a family member?

This chapter goes over the host of tax rules that apply to landlords who hire people to help them with their rental business and explains how you can comply with those rules.

Deducting Payments to Workers

You may deduct all or most of what you pay a person who performs services for your rental activity. It doesn't matter how you measure or make the payments. You can pay a salary or a set fee for a job, or you can pay by the hour. You can even provide free rent in exchange for services.

The money you pay a worker will fall into one of the following three categories of deductible rental expenses:

- operating expenses
- start-up expenses, or
- depreciation.

The general rules for each of these types of expenses are discussed in earlier chapters; this section explains how workers' pay falls into all of these categories.

Operating Expenses

Most of the time, amounts you pay workers will be operating expenses. These expenses are currently deductible as long as they are:

- ordinary and necessary
- reasonable in amount
- paid for services actually performed, and
- actually paid or incurred in the year the deduction is claimed (as shown by your payroll records).

A worker's services are ordinary and necessary if they are common, accepted, helpful, and appropriate for your rental activity—they don't have to be indispensable. A worker's pay is reasonable if the amount is within the range that other landlords pay for similar services. These requirements usually won't pose a problem when you hire a worker to perform any legitimate function for your rental activity.

> **EXAMPLE:** Ken hires Karen, a gardener, to perform gardening work on his three rental houses. He pays her $200 per month—what similar workers are typically paid in the area. Ken can deduct his monthly payments to Karen as an operating expense. If Karen works a full year, Ken will get a $2,400 deduction.

Payments to workers for personal services are not deductible as business expenses.

> **EXAMPLE:** Ken also hires Karen to perform gardening services for his personal residence. These services are personal, not related to Ken's rental activity. Thus, Ken may not deduct her pay as an operating expense. Indeed, such payments are not deductible at all.

Special rules (described below) apply if you hire family members to work in your rental activity.

See Chapter 3 for more on operating expenses.

Start-Up Expenses

Amounts you pay workers for services performed during the start-up phase of your rental activity are start-up expenses. Up to $5,000 in start-up expenses may be deducted in the first year in which your rental activity is in operation. Any amount over $5,000 must be deducted in equal installments over the first 180 months you're in business. (See Chapter 8 for more on deducting start-up costs.)

> **EXAMPLE:** Michelle purchases her first rental property—a small house in need of a new paint job. She hires Al, a professional painter, to paint the house. After Al completes his work, Michelle lists the house for rent. Michelle paid Al $2,000 to paint her house. His fee is a start-up expense

because it was incurred before Michelle's rental activity had begun—that is, before she offered the property for rent. Michelle may deduct the $2,000 the first year she is in business.

Depreciation Expenses

Amounts you pay workers to help purchase, transport, install, or improve long-term assets, are not business operating expenses. Instead, these costs are added to the basis (cost) of the asset and get depreciated over time with the asset. In certain situations, you may be able to currently deduct these costs under Section 179.

> **EXAMPLE:** John buys a dilapidated apartment building for $250,000. He pays Jackie, a licensed contractor, $50,000 to refurbish the building. John paid Jackie the money to improve a long-term asset—a building. Thus, he may not currently deduct the $50,000. Instead, once the building is offered for rent, he may depreciate the cost over 27.5 years. He gets to deduct $1,818 per year, except for the first and last years.

Employees Versus Independent Contractors

As far as the IRS is concerned, there are only two types of people you can hire to help in your rental activity: employees and independent contractors (ICs). It's very important to understand the difference between these two categories because the tax rules for each are very different. If you hire an employee, you become subject to a wide array of state and federal tax requirements. You may have to withhold taxes from your employees' earnings and pay other taxes for them out of your own pocket. You must also comply with complex and burdensome bookkeeping and reporting requirements. If you hire an independent contractor, none of these requirements apply.

Initially, it's up to you to determine whether any person you hire to help in your rental activity is an employee or an IC. However, your decision about how to classify a worker is subject to review by various government agencies, including:

- the IRS
- your state's tax department
- your state's unemployment compensation insurance agency, and
- your state's workers' compensation insurance agency.

These agencies are mostly interested in whether you have classified workers as independent contractors when you should have classified them as employees. The reason is that you must pay money to each of these agencies for employees, but not for independent contractors. As more workers are classified as employees, the more money flows into the agencies' coffers. In the case of taxing agencies, employers must withhold tax from employees' paychecks and hand it over to the government; ICs pay their own taxes, which means the government must wait longer to get its money and faces the possibility that ICs won't declare their income or will otherwise cheat on their taxes. If an agency determines that you misclassified an employee as an IC, you may have to pay back taxes, fines, and penalties.

Independent Contractors Are Not the Same as Construction Contractors

The terms independent contractor and construction contractor are often confused. The two are not the same. A construction contractor (often simply called a contractor) is a self-employed person who performs construction work or building remodeling work for customers. An independent contractor is any person who performs services for others without being classified as an employee for legal purposes. Most construction contractors are independent contractors, but many people besides construction contractors are independent contractors.

Tests to Determine Workers' Tax Status

Scrutinizing agencies use various tests to determine whether a worker is an IC or an employee. The determining factor is usually whether you have the right to control the worker. If you have the right to *direct and control* the way a worker performs—both the final results of the job and the details of when, where, and how the work is done—then the worker is your employee. On the other hand, if you have only the right to accept or reject the final results the worker achieves, then that person is an IC.

An employer may not always exercise its right of control. For example, if an employee is experienced and well trained, the employer may not feel the need to closely supervise him or her. But the employer still has the right to step in at any time, which distinguishes an employment relationship from an IC arrangement.

> **EXAMPLE:** Anne hires John to serve as resident manager for her triplex. John works ten hours per week. Anne has full control over the work John does. She must approve any repair he makes and provide any tools or supplies he needs to perform his maintenance duties. Anne has the right to fire John at any time if she is unhappy with his performance.
>
> If John proves to be an able and conscientious worker, Anne may choose not to supervise him very closely. But Anne has the right to do so at any time. John is Anne's employee.

In contrast, a worker is an independent contractor if the landlord does not have the right to control the person on the job. Because the worker is an independent businessperson not solely dependent on you (the hiring party) for a living, your control is limited to accepting or rejecting the final results the IC achieves.

> **EXAMPLE:** Anne hires Mary, a real estate manager, to keep track of her rental income and expenses and to help with her taxes. Anne is only one of Mary's many clients. Anne doesn't tell Mary how to do her accounting tasks; Mary is a professional who already knows how to do her work. Mary sets her own hours, provides her own equipment, and works from her own home office. Mary is an independent contractor.

Because Mary is clearly running her own business, it's virtually certain that Anne does not have the right to control the way Mary performs her accounting services. Anne's control is limited to accepting or rejecting the final result. If Anne doesn't like the work Mary has done, she can refuse to pay her.

There's no clear-cut way for auditors to figure out whether you have the right to control a worker you hire. After all, they can't look into your mind to see whether you are controlling a worker (or whether you believe that you have the right to do so). They rely instead on indirect or circumstantial evidence indicating control or lack of it—for example, whether you provide a worker with tools and equipment, where the work is performed, how the worker is paid, and whether you can fire the worker. The following chart shows the primary factors used by the IRS and most other government agencies to determine if you have the right to control a worker.

IRS Test for Worker Status		
	IC Factors	**Employee Factors**
Behavioral Control	Workers will more likely be considered ICs if you: • do not give them instructions • do not provide them with training	Workers will more likely be considered employees if you: • give them instructions they must follow about how to do the work • give them detailed training
Financial Control	Workers will more likely be considered ICs if they: • have a significant investment in equipment and facilities • pay business or travel expenses themselves • make their services available to the public • are paid by the job • have opportunity for profit or loss	Workers will more likely be considered employees if: • you provide them with equipment and facilities free of charge • you reimburse their business or travel expenses • they make no effort to market their services to the public • you pay them by the hour or other unit of time • they have no opportunity for profit or loss—for example, because they're paid by the hour and have all expenses reimbursed
Relationship Between You and the Worker	Workers will more likely be considered ICs if they: • don't receive employee benefits such as health insurance • sign a client agreement with the hiring firm • can't quit or be fired at will • perform services that are not part of your regular business activities	Workers will more likely be considered employees if they: • receive employee benefits • have no written client agreement • can quit at any time without incurring any liability to you • can be fired at any time • perform services that are part of your core business

⚠ **Part-time workers and temps can be employees.** Don't assume that a person you hire to work part-time or for a short period automatically qualifies as an IC. People who work for you only temporarily or part-time are your employees if you have the right to control the way they work.

Common Classifications for Workers

Let's apply the IRS rules for worker status to the type of people landlords commonly hire.

People Who Offer Services to the Public

People who offer their services to the general public are almost always independent contractors. This includes most of the people landlords hire—for example:

- repairmen
- construction contractors
- gardeners
- plumbers
- electricians
- carpet layers
- painters
- roofers, and
- people who provide professional services to the public, such as real estate brokers, real estate appraisers, architects, real estate management companies, lawyers, accountants, and bookkeepers.

Virtually all the factors listed in the chart above will ordinarily point to IC status whenever a person provides services such as these to the public at large.

EXAMPLE: Janet owns a four-unit apartment building. The toilet in one of the apartments becomes stopped up. Janet hires Ralph, a plumber, to fix the toilet. Ralph provides plumbing repair services to the public. Janet is just one of his many customers. He makes his services available to the public by advertising and maintaining a website. He provides his own tools, and hires his own assistants. He receives no instructions or training from Janet on how to perform his plumbing services—she knows nothing about plumbing, that's why she hired Ralph. He is paid by the hour. He must pay various expenses to maintain his plumbing business, such as rent, salaries, and insurance. Because he has monthly expenses, he'll lose money if he doesn't earn enough from his plumbing business. Here's how these factors stack up in the IC–employee equation:

IC Factors	Employee Factors
Receives no instructions	Is paid by the hour
Receives no training	
Offers services to the public	
Provides own tools and training	
Hires own assistants	
Has business expenses and risk of loss	

Ralph is clearly an IC. If he charged by the job, instead of by the hour, not one factor would point to employee status. However, many ICs like Ralph charge by the hour.

People Who Work Solely for You

Any person who works just for you will likely be your employee. These will usually be family members, but not always.

EXAMPLE: Janet hires Tom, her 17-year-old son, to perform gardening and maintenance services for her apartment building. Janet provides Tom with all the tools he needs to do his work, such as a lawnmower, hedge trimmer, and building repair tools. She trains him on how to do yard work properly. When Tom first begins work, Janet accompanies him and closely supervises him. Later, she doesn't accompany him, but requires that he give her detailed progress reports on his work. Tom does not offer his services to the public; he only works for his mother. He has no expenses and, thus, no risk of loss. Janet pays Tom by the hour, and pays any expenses Tom incurs, such as the cost of cleaning supplies he buys. Let's see how these factors look on the following chart:

IC Factors	Employee Factors
	Receives instructions and training
	Provides progress reports
	Has no tools
	Does not offer services to public
	Has no expenses and no risk of loss
	Is paid by the hour

Tom is clearly Janet's employee. Even if Tom performed garden services for some other people besides Janet, he would likely still be Janet's employee because she controls him so closely.

Need more information about independent contractors? For a detailed discussion of the practical and legal issues business owners face when hiring ICs, see *Working with Independent Contractors*, by Stephen Fishman (Nolo).

Tax Rules When Hiring Independent Contractors

As far as taxes are concerned, hiring independent contractors is very simple. When you hire an independent contractor, you don't have to withhold or pay any state or federal payroll taxes on the IC's behalf. In contrast, when you hire an employee you must withhold federal and state taxes and pay one-half of the worker's Social Security and Medicare taxes out of your own pocket. (See "Tax Rules for Employees.") This is one of the great benefits of hiring ICs.

However, there is one tax detail you may have to take care of when you hire an IC: If you pay an unincorporated IC $600 or more during the year for business-related services, you must:

- file IRS Form 1099-MISC telling the IRS how much you paid the worker, and
- obtain the IC's taxpayer identification number.

The IRS imposes these requirements because it is very concerned that to avoid paying taxes, many ICs don't report all the income they earn. To help prevent this, the IRS wants to find out how much you pay ICs you hire and make sure it has their correct tax ID numbers.

Any landlord whose rental activity qualifies as a business must comply with these reporting and tax ID requirements. Landlords who are only investors need not comply. (See Chapter 2 for detailed guidance on when a rental activity is a business or an investment for tax purposes.)

Rental Agents Must Report IC Payments

If a rental agent manages your rental property, the agent must comply with the reporting requirements explained in this section. The agent must also report to the IRS the amount of rent he or she pays you each year. (IRS Reg. 1.6041-1.)

For example, suppose Gale is a rental agent who manages rental property for Howard. Gale finds tenants, arranges leases, collects rent, deals with tenant complaints, and hires and makes payments to repairmen. Gale subtracts her commission and any maintenance payments from the rental payments and remits the remainder to Howard. Gale must comply with the IC reporting requirements when she hires repairmen and others to perform services for Howard's property. In addition, she must file a 1099 form with the IRS each year reporting the amount of rent payments she remits to Howard.

Threshold for IC Income Reporting

You need to obtain an unincorporated IC's taxpayer ID number and file a 1099 form with the IRS only if you pay the IC $600 or more during a year for business-related services. It makes no difference whether the sum was one payment for a single job or the total of many small payments for multiple jobs.

> **EXAMPLE:** Andre hires Leslie to paint a rental house and pays her $1,000. Because Andre paid Leslie more than $599 for rental business-related services, Andre must file Form 1099 with the IRS reporting the payment, and obtain Leslie's taxpayer ID number.

In calculating whether the payments made to an IC total $600 or more during a year, you must include payments you make for parts or materials the IC used in performing the services. For example, if you hire an electrician to rewire a rental building and he charges you separately for the electrical wiring and other materials he installs, the cost must be included in the tally. However, not all payments you make to ICs are counted towards the $600 threshold.

Payments for Merchandise

You don't need to include in the $600 threshold payments you make solely for merchandise.

> **EXAMPLE:** Betty hires Al, an IC electrician, to rewire her apartment building. She pays him $1,000 for new lighting fixtures. The payment need not be counted toward the $600 threshold because the fixtures are merchandise.

Payments for Personal Services

You need only count payments you make to ICs for services they perform in the course of your rental business. You don't count payments for services you make to ICs for personal or household services or repairs—for example, payments to babysitters or gardeners and housekeepers for your personal residence. Running your home is not a business.

> **EXAMPLE:** Landlord Joe pays Mary a total of $1,000 during the year for gardening services for his residence. None of the payments count toward the $600 threshold because they don't relate to Joe's rental business. Joe need not obtain Mary's taxpayer ID number or file a 1099 form reporting the payments to the IRS.

Obtaining Taxpayer Identification Numbers

Some ICs work in the underground economy—that is, they're paid in cash and never pay any taxes or file tax returns. The IRS may not even know they exist. The IRS wants you to help it find these people by supplying the taxpayer ID numbers from all ICs who meet the requirements explained above.

If an IC won't give you his or her number or the IRS informs you that the number the IC gave you is incorrect, the IRS assumes the person isn't going to voluntarily pay taxes. So it requires you to withhold taxes from the compensation you pay the IC and remit them to the IRS. This is called backup withholding. If you fail to backup withhold, the IRS will impose an assessment against you equal to 31% of what you paid the IC.

How to Avoid Backup Withholding

Backup withholding can be a bookkeeping burden for you. Fortunately, it's very easy to avoid it. Have the IC fill out and sign IRS Form W-9, Request for Taxpayer Identification Number, and retain it in your files. (You can obtain a copy of the form by calling the IRS at 800-TAX-FORM, by contacting your local IRS office, or by downloading it from the IRS website at www.irs.gov.)

You don't have to file the W-9 with the IRS. This simple form merely requires the IC to list his or her name and address and taxpayer ID number. Partnerships and sole proprietors with employees must have a federal employer identification number (EIN), which they obtain from the IRS. In the case of sole proprietors without employees, the taxpayer ID number is the IC's Social Security number.

If the IC doesn't already have an EIN, but promises to obtain one, you don't have to backup withhold for 60 days after he or she applies for one. Have the IC fill out and sign the W-9 form, stating "Applied For" in the space where the ID number is supposed to be listed. If you don't receive the IC's ID number within 60 days, start backup withholding.

Backup Withholding Procedure

If you are unable to obtain an IC's taxpayer ID number or the IRS informs you that the number the IC gave you is incorrect, you'll have to do backup withholding. You must begin doing so after you pay an IC $600 or more during the year. You need not backup withhold on payments totaling less than $600.

To backup withhold, deposit with your bank 31% of the IC's compensation every quarter. You must make these deposits separately from any payroll tax deposits you make for employees. Report the amounts withheld on IRS Form 945, Annual Return of Withheld Federal Income Tax. This is an annual return you must file by January 31 of the following year. See the instructions to Form 945 for details. You can obtain a copy of the form by calling the IRS at 800-TAX-FORM, by contacting your local IRS office, or by downloading it from the IRS website at www.irs.gov.

Filing IRS Form 1099

The IRS wants to know how much ICs earn each year so it can make sure they are reporting all their income. This is accomplished by requiring people and companies that hire ICs to report the amount of their payments to the IRS on IRS Form 1099-MISC. You must file a 1099-MISC form for each IC you paid $600 or more during the year. You must obtain original 1099 forms from the IRS for filing. You cannot photocopy this form because it contains several pressure-sensitive copies. Each 1099 form contains three parts and can be used for three different workers. All your 1099 forms must be submitted together along with one copy of Form 1096, which is a transmittal form—the IRS equivalent of a cover letter. You must obtain an original Form 1096 from the IRS; you cannot submit a photocopy. Obtain these forms by calling the IRS at 800-TAX-FORM or by contacting your local IRS office. You can also obtain usable 1099 forms from stationery stores and office supply companies.

Filling out Form 1099-MISC is easy. Follow this step-by-step approach.

- List your name and address in the first box titled Payer's name.
- Enter your taxpayer identification number in the box entitled Payer's Federal identification number.
- The IC you have paid is called the "Recipient" on this form, meaning the person who received the money. Provide the IC's taxpayer identification number, name, and address in the boxes indicated. For sole proprietors, you list the individual's name first, and then you may list a different business name, though this is not required. You may not enter only a business name for a sole proprietor.
- Enter the amount of your payments to the IC in Box 7, entitled Non-employee compensation. Be sure to fill in the right box or the IRS will consider Form 1099-MISC invalid.
- Finally, if you've done backup withholding for an IC who has not provided you with a taxpayer ID number, enter the amount withheld in Box 4.

The Form 1099-MISC contains five copies. These must be filed as follows:

- Copy A, the top copy, must be filed with the IRS no later than February 28 of the year after payment was made to the IC. If you don't use the remaining two spaces for other ICs, leave those spaces blank. Don't cut the page.
- Copy 1 must be filed with your state taxing authority if your state has a state income tax. The filing deadline is probably February 28, but check with your state tax department to make sure. Your state may also have a specific transmittal form or cover letter you must obtain.
- Copy B and Copy 2 must be given to the worker no later than January 31 of the year after payment was made.
- Copy C is for you to retain for your files.

File all the IRS copies of each 1099 form together with Form 1096, the simple transmittal form. Add up all the payments reported on all the 1099 forms and list the total in the box indicated on Form 1096. File the forms with the IRS Service Center listed on the reverse of Form 1096.

Filing 1099s Electronically

You have the option of filing your 1099s with the IRS electronically instead of by postal mail. You must get permission from the IRS to do this by filing IRS Form 4419, Application for Filing Information Returns Magnetically/Electronically. If you file electronically, the deadline for filing 1099s with the IRS is extended to March 31. For more information, visit the IRS website at www.irs.gov (click on "IRS e-file"), or call the IRS Information Reporting Program at 304-263-8700.

You can also send 1099s to independent contractors electronically—that is, by email. However, you may do this only if the contractor agrees. If the contractor doesn't agree, you must deliver a printed copy of the 1099 by mail or in person.

Reporting Requirements Don't Apply to Corporations

The filing and ID requirements discussed above don't apply to corporations, probably because large businesses have a strong legislative lobby. The IRS has attempted to change the law to include corporations, but so far it hasn't succeeded. This means that if you hire an incorporated IC, you don't have to file anything with the IRS.

EXAMPLE: Landlord Bob pays $5,000 to Yvonne, a CPA, to perform accounting services. Yvonne has formed her own one-person corporation called Yvonne's Accounting Services, Inc. Bob pays the corporation, not Yvonne personally. Because Bob is paying a corporation, he doesn't need to report the payment on Form 1099-MISC or obtain Yvonne's personal tax ID number.

There are two exceptions to the rule that you don't have to file 1099 forms for payments to corporations. You must report all payments of $600 or more you make to a doctor or lawyer who is incorporated. This is necessary only where the payments are for your landlord activity—for example, you hire an incorporated attorney to handle a tenant eviction. You don't need to report payments you make to incorporated doctors or lawyers for personal services.

New Hire Reporting Requirements for ICs

Several states require that businesses that hire independent contractors file a report with a state agency providing the contractor's contact information and how much you pay the worker. The purpose of these requirements is to aid in the enforcement of child support orders issued against independent contractors. The following states impose reporting requirements for independent contractors:

State	Contact Information
California	Phone: 916-657-0529 Fax: 916-255-0951 Website: www.edd.ca.gov/taxrep/txner.htm
Connecticut	Phone: 860-263-6310 Fax: 800-816-1108 Website: www.ctnewhires.com Email: ctnewhires@po.state.ct.us
Iowa	Phone: 515-281-5331 Fax: 800-759-5881 Website: https://secure.dhs.state.ia.us/epics
Massachusetts	Phone: 617-626-4154 Fax: 617-887-5049 Website: www.cse.state.ma.us/programs/newhire/nh_temp.htm Email: PDUmail@shore.net
New Jersey	Phone: 888-624-6339 Fax: 800-304-4901 Website: www.nj-newhire.com Email: newjersey@nj-newhire.com
Ohio	Phone: 888-872-1490 Fax: 888-872-1611 Website: www.oh-newhire.com Email: oh-newhire@policy-studies.com

Paying Independent Contractors' Expenses

Independent contractors often incur expenses while performing services for their clients or customers—for example, for travel or materials. Although many ICs want their clients to separately reimburse them for such expenses, it's better for you not to do so. ICs who pay their own expenses are less likely to be viewed as your employees by the IRS or other government agencies. Instead of reimbursing expenses, pay ICs enough so they can cover their own expenses.

However, it's customary in some businesses and professions for the client to reimburse the IC for expenses. For example, a lawyer who handles an eviction or other legal matter for your rental business will usually seek reimbursement for expenses such as photocopying, court reporters, and travel. If this is the case, you may pay these reimbursements without concern about misclassification problems.

When you reimburse an IC for a business-related expense, you get the deduction for the expense, not the IC. You should not include the amount of the reimbursement on the 1099 form you file with the IRS reporting how much you paid the IC, because the reimbursement is not considered income for the IC.

Tax Rules for Employees

Whenever you hire an employee other than your spouse or child, you become an unpaid tax collector for the government. You are required to withhold and pay both federal and state taxes for the worker. These taxes are called payroll taxes or employment taxes. Federal payroll taxes consist of:

- Social Security and Medicare taxes—also known as FICA
- unemployment taxes—also known as FUTA, and
- federal income taxes—also known as FITW.

You must periodically pay FICA, FUTA, and FITW to the IRS, either electronically or by making federal tax deposits at specified banks, which then transmit the money to the IRS. You are entitled to deduct as a business expense payroll taxes that you pay yourself. You get no deductions for taxes you withhold from employees' pay.

Every year, employers must file IRS Form W-2, Wage and Tax Statement, for each of their workers. The form shows the IRS how much the worker was paid and how much tax was withheld.

However, if you hire your spouse or child to work in your rental activity, you may not have to pay some or all of the payroll taxes you must pay when you hire nonrelatives.

Find out more about payroll taxes. IRS Circular E, *Employer's Tax Guide*, provides detailed information on payroll tax requirements. You can get a free copy by calling the IRS at 800-TAX-FORM, by calling or visiting your local IRS office, or by downloading it from the IRS website at www.irs.gov.

Employer's FICA Contributions

FICA is an acronym for Federal Income Contributions Act, the law requiring employers and employees to pay Social Security and Medicare taxes. FICA consists of:

- a 12.4% Social Security tax on an employee's wages up to an annual wage ceiling or cap (in 2007, the cap was $97,500 per year), and
- a 2.9% Medicare tax on all employee wages paid.

This adds up to a 15.3% tax, up to the Social Security tax ceiling. Employers must pay half of this—7.65%—out of their own pockets. They must withhold the other half from their employees' pay. You are entitled to deduct (as an operating expense) the portion of the tax that you pay yourself.

The ceiling for the Social Security tax changes annually. You can find out what the Social Security tax ceiling is for the current year from IRS Circular E, *Employer's Tax Guide*; the amount is printed right on the first page.

FUTA

FUTA is an acronym for the Federal Unemployment Tax Act, the law that establishes federal unemployment taxes. Most employers must pay both state and federal unemployment taxes. Even if you're exempt from the state tax, you may still have to pay the federal tax. Employers alone are responsible for FUTA—you may not collect or deduct it from employees' wages.

You must pay FUTA taxes if:

- you pay $1,500 or more to employees during any calendar quarter—that is, any three-month period beginning with January, April, July, or October, or
- you had one or more employees for at least some part of a day in any 20 or more different weeks during the year. The weeks don't have to be consecutive, nor does it have to be the same employee each week.

Technically, the FUTA tax rate is 6.2%, but in practice, you rarely pay this much. You are given a credit of 5.4% if you pay the applicable state unemployment tax in full and on time. This means that the actual FUTA tax rate is usually 0.8%. In 2007, the FUTA tax was assessed on only the first $7,000 of an employee's annual wages. Therefore, the full amount of the tax is $56 per year per employee. This amount is a deductible operating expense.

FITW

FITW is an acronym for federal income tax withholding. You must calculate and withhold federal income tax from your employees' paychecks. Employees are solely responsible for paying federal income tax. Your only responsibility is to withhold the funds and remit them to the government. If you fail to do this, you'll get into big trouble with the IRS. You get no deductions for FITW; it wasn't your money to begin with.

State Payroll Taxes

Employers in every state are required to pay and withhold state payroll taxes. These taxes include:

- state unemployment compensation taxes in all states
- state income tax withholding in most states, and
- state disability taxes in a few states.

Unemployment Compensation

Employers in every state are required to contribute to a state unemployment insurance fund. Employees make no contributions, except in Alaska, New Jersey, Pennsylvania, and Rhode Island, where employers must withhold small employee contributions from employees' paychecks. The employer contributions are a deductible expense.

If your payroll is very small—less than $1,500 per calendar quarter—you probably won't have to pay unemployment compensation taxes. In most states, you must pay state unemployment taxes for employees if you're paying federal unemployment taxes. However, some states have stricter requirements. Contact your state labor department for the exact rules and payroll amounts.

Income Taxes

All states except Alaska, Florida, Nevada, South Dakota, Texas, Washington, and Wyoming have income taxation. If your state has income taxes, you must withhold the applicable amount from your employees' paychecks and pay it to the state taxing authority. Each state has its own income tax withholding forms and procedures. Contact your state tax department for information. Of course, employers get no deductions for withholding their employees' state income taxes.

Disability Insurance

California, Hawaii, New Jersey, New York, and Rhode Island have state disability insurance programs that provide employees with coverage for injuries or illnesses that are not related to work. Employers in these states must withhold their employees' disability insurance contributions from their pay. Employers must also make their own contributions in Hawaii, New Jersey, and New York—these employer contributions are deductible.

Workers' Compensation Insurance

Employers in all states (subject to some important exceptions) must provide their employees with workers' compensation insurance to cover work-related injuries. Workers' compensation is not a payroll tax. Employers purchase a workers' compensation policy from a private insurer or the state workers' compensation fund. Your workers' compensation insurance premiums are deductible as an insurance expense (see Chapter 14.)

Employers in California must withhold for parental leave. California recently became the first state to require paid family leave. Employers in California must withhold money from their employees' paycheck (as part of the state's disability insurance program) to fund this leave program. For more information on the program, go to www.edd.ca.gov/direp/pflind.asp.

Bookkeeping expenses are deductible. Figuring out how much to withhold, doing the necessary record keeping, and filling out the required forms can be complicated. If you have a computer, software programs such as *QuickBooks* can help with all the calculations and print out your employees' checks and IRS forms. The cost of such software is deductible—you can deduct the full cost in one year under Section 179 or depreciate the cost over three years (see Chapter 5). You can also hire a bookkeeper or payroll tax service to do the work. Amounts you pay a bookkeeper or payroll tax service are deductible operating expenses. You can find these listed in the phone book or on the Internet under payroll tax services. You can also find a list of payroll service providers on the IRS website. Be aware, however, that even if you hire a payroll service, you remain personally liable if your payroll taxes are not paid on time. The IRS recommends that employers: (1) keep their company address on file with the IRS, rather than the address of the payroll service provider, so that the company will be contacted by the IRS if there are any problems; (2) require the payroll service provider to post a fiduciary bond in case it defaults on its obligation to pay any penalties and interest due to IRS deficiency notices; and (3) ask the service provider to enroll in and use the Electronic Federal Tax Payment System (EFTPS) so the employer can confirm payments made on its behalf.

Hiring Your Family

Whoever said, "Never hire your relatives" must never have read the tax code. The tax law promotes family togetherness by making it highly advantageous for landlords to hire family members.

Employing Your Children

Believe it or not, your children can be a great tax savings device. If you hire your children as employees to do legitimate work in your rental activity, you may deduct their salaries from your rental income as an operating expense. Your child will have to pay tax on his or her salary only to the extent it exceeds the standard deduction amount for the year—$5,350 in 2007. Moreover, if your child is under the age of 18, you won't have to withhold or pay any FICA (Social Security or Medicare) tax on the salary (subject to a couple of exceptions).

These rules allow you to shift part of your income from your own tax bracket to your child's bracket, which should be much lower than yours (unless you earn little or no income). This can result in substantial tax savings.

The following chart shows the federal income tax brackets for 2007. A child need only pay a 10% tax on taxable income up to $7,825—taxable income means total income minus the standard deduction. Thus, a child could earn up to $13,175 and pay only a 10% income tax. In contrast, if you were married and filed jointly, you'd have to pay a 15% federal income tax on taxable income between $15,561 and $63,700, and a 25% tax on taxable income from $63,701 to $128,500.

2007 Federal Personal Income Tax Brackets

Tax Bracket	Income If Single	Income If Married Filing Jointly
10%	Up to $7,825	Up to $15,560
15%	From $7,826 to $31,850	$15,561 to $63,700
25%	$31,851 to $77,100	$63,701 to $128,500
28%	$77,101 to $160,850	$128,501 to $195,850
33%	$160,851 to $349,700	$195,851 to $349,700
35%	All over $349,700	All over $349,700

EXAMPLE: Carol hires Mark, her 18-year-old son, to perform gardening, repair, and maintenance services for her four-unit apartment building. He works ten hours per week and she pays him $15 per hour (the going rate for such work in her area). Over the course of a year, she pays him a total of $7,200. She need not pay FICA tax for Mark because he's not yet 18. When she does her taxes for the year, she may deduct his $7,200 salary from her rental income as an operating expense. Mark pays tax only on the portion of his income that exceeds the $5,350 standard deduction—so he pays federal income tax only on $1,850 of his $7,200 salary. With such a small amount of income, he is in the lowest federal income tax bracket—10%. He pays $185 in federal income tax for the year. Had Carol not hired Mark and done the work herself, she would have lost her $7,200 deduction and had to pay income tax on this amount—a 25% tax in her tax bracket. Thus, she would have had to pay an additional $1,800 in federal taxes. Depending on the state where Carol lives, she likely would have had to pay a state income tax as well.

What About Child Labor Laws?

You're probably aware that certain types of child labor are illegal under federal and state law. However, these laws generally don't apply to children under the age of 16 who are employed by their parents, unless the child is employed in a hazardous occupation. Hazardous occupations include driving a motor vehicle, being an outside helper on a motor vehicle, and operating various power-driven machines, including machines for woodworking and metal forming, sawing, roofing, wrecking, excavation, and demolition operations.

A child who is at least 16 may be employed in any nonhazardous occupation. Children at least 17 years of age may spend up to 20% of their time driving cars and trucks weighing less than 6,000 pounds as part of their job if they have licenses and no tickets, drive only in daylight hours, and go no more than 30 miles from home. They may not perform dangerous driving maneuvers (such as towing). Also, many states have laws specifying when, and for how long, children may work, limiting the hours and days of the week (and imposing more stringent limits during the school year.) For detailed information, see the Department of Labor website, www.dol.gov.

No Payroll Taxes

One of the advantages of hiring your child is that you need not pay FICA taxes for your child under the age of 18 who works in your trade or business, or your partnership, if it's owned solely by you and your spouse.

Moreover, you need not pay federal unemployment (FUTA) taxes for services performed by your child who is under 21 years old.

However, these rules do not apply—and you must pay both FICA and FUTA—if you hire your child to work for:

- your partnership, unless all the partners are parents of the child, or
- your corporation (few small landlords are incorporated).

No Withholding

In addition, if your child has no unearned income (for example, interest or dividend income), you must withhold income taxes from your child's pay only if it exceeds the standard deduction for the year. The standard deduction was $5,350 in 2007 and is adjusted every year for inflation. Children who are paid less than this amount need not pay any income taxes on their earnings. However, you must withhold income taxes if your child has more than $250 in unearned income for the year and his or her total income exceeds $850 (in 2007).

> **EXAMPLE:** Connie, a 15-year-old girl, is paid $4,000 a year to help out in her parent's rental activity. She has no income from interest or any other unearned income. Her parents need not withhold income taxes from Connie's salary.
>
> If Connie is paid $4,000 in salary and has $500 in interest income, her parents must withhold income taxes from her salary because she has more than $250 in unearned income and her total income for the year was more than $750.

Employing Your Spouse

You don't get the benefits of income shifting when you employ your spouse in your business, because your income is combined when you file a joint tax return. You'll also have to pay FICA taxes on your spouse's wages, so you get no savings there either. However, you need not pay FUTA tax if you employ your spouse in your unincorporated business. This tax is usually only $56 per year, so this is not much of a savings.

The real advantage of hiring your spouse is in the realm of employee benefits. You can provide your spouse with employee benefits such as health and accident insurance. You can take a tax deduction for the cost of the benefit and your spouse doesn't have to declare the benefit as income, provided the IRS requirements are satisfied. This is a particularly valuable tool for health insurance—you can give your spouse health insurance coverage as an employee benefit.

Another benefit of hiring your spouse is that you can take rental-related trips together and deduct the cost as a travel expense, as long as your spouse's presence was necessary (for your rental activity, not for you personally).

Rules to Follow When Employing Your Family

The IRS is well aware of the tax benefits of hiring a child or spouse, so it's on the lookout for taxpayers who claim the benefit without meeting the requirements. If the IRS concludes that your children or spouse aren't really employees, you'll lose your tax deductions for their salary and benefits—and they'll have to pay tax on their benefits. To avoid this, you should follow these simple rules:

Rule 1: Your Child or Spouse Must Be a Real Employee

First of all, your child or spouse must be a bona fide employee. Their work must be ordinary and necessary for your rental activity, and their pay must be compensation for services actually performed. Their services don't have to be indispensable, but they must be common, accepted, helpful, and appropriate for your business. Any real work for your rental can qualify—for example, you could employ your child or spouse to perform yard work or routine maintenance for your rental properties; or they could clean your office, answer the phone, and help with bookkeeping. You get no business deductions when you pay your child for personal services, such as babysitting or mowing your lawn at home.

The IRS won't believe that an extremely young child is a legitimate employee. How young is too young? The IRS has accepted that a seven-year-old child may be an employee (see "Hardworking Seven-Year-Old Was Parents' Employee," below), but probably won't believe that children younger than seven are performing any useful work for your rental activity.

You should keep track of the work and hours your children or spouse perform by having them fill out time sheets or time cards. You can find these in stationery stores or you can create a time sheet yourself. It should list the date, the services performed, and the time spent performing the services. Although not legally required, it's also a good idea to have your spouse or child sign a written employment agreement specifying his or her job duties and hours. These duties should only be related to your business.

Hardworking Seven-Year-Old Was Parents' Employee

Walt and Dorothy Eller owned three trailer parks and a small strip mall in Northern California. They hired their three children, ages seven, 11, and 12, to perform various services for their businesses including pool maintenance, landscaping, reading gas and electric meters, delivering leaflets and messages to tenants, answering phones, doing minor repairs, and sweeping and cleaning trailer pads and parking lots. The children worked after school, on weekends, and during their summer vacations.

The Ellers paid their children a total of $17,800 over a three-year period and deducted the amounts as business expenses. The IRS tried to disallow the deductions, claiming that the children's pay was excessive. The court allowed most of the deductions, noting that these hardworking children performed essential services for their parents' businesses. The court found that the seven-year old was a bona fide employee, but ruled that he should earn somewhat less than his older brother and sister because 11- and 12-year-old children can generally handle greater responsibility and do more work than seven-year-old children. Thus, while the older siblings could be paid $5,700 for their services over the three years in question, the seven-year-old could reasonably be paid only $4,000. (*Eller v. Comm'r.*, 77 T.C. 934 (1981).)

Rule 2: Compensation Must Be Reasonable

When you hire your children, it is advantageous (taxwise) to pay them as much as possible. That way, you can shift more of your income to your children, who are probably in a much lower income tax bracket. Conversely, you want to pay your spouse as little as possible, because you get no benefits from income shifting; you and your spouse are in the same income tax bracket (assuming you file a joint return, as the vast majority of married people do). Moreover, your spouse will have to pay a 7.65% Social Security tax on his or her salary—an amount that is not tax deductible. (As your spouse's employer, you'll have to pay employment taxes on your spouse's salary as well, but these taxes are deductible business expenses.)

However, you can't just pay whatever amount will result in the lowest tax bill: Your spouse's and/or your child's total compensation must be reasonably related to the value of the work performed. Total compensation means the sum of the salary plus all the fringe benefits you provide, including health insurance and medical expense reimbursements, if any. You shouldn't have a problem as long as you don't pay more than you'd pay a stranger for the same work. In other words, don't try paying your child $100 per hour for yard work just to get a big tax deduction. Find out what workers who perform similar services in your area are being paid.

To prove how much you paid (and that you actually paid it), you should pay your child or spouse by check, not cash. Do this once or twice a month, just as you would for any other employee. The funds should be deposited in a bank account in your child's or spouse's name. Your child's bank account may be a trust account.

Rule 3: Comply With Legal Requirements for Employers

You must comply with most of the same legal requirements when you hire a child or spouse as you do when you hire a stranger.

At the time you hire: When you first hire your child or spouse, you must fill out IRS Form W-4. You (the employer) use it to determine how much tax you must withhold from the employee's salary. A child who is exempt from withholding should write "exempt" in the space provided and complete and sign the rest of the form. You must also complete U.S. Citizenship and Immigration Services Form I-9, Employment Eligibility Verification, verifying that the employee is a U.S. citizen or is otherwise eligible to work in the U.S. Keep both forms. You must also record your employee's Social Security number. If your child doesn't have a number, you must apply for one. In addition, you must have an employer identification number (EIN). If you don't have one, you may obtain it by filing IRS Form SS-4.

Every payday: You'll need to withhold income tax from your child's pay only if it exceeds a specified amount. You don't have to withhold FICA taxes for children younger than 18. You must withhold income tax and FICA for your spouse, but not FUTA tax. If the amounts withheld, plus the employer's share of payroll taxes, exceed $2,500 during a calendar quarter, you must deposit the amounts monthly by making federal tax deposits at specified banks or electronically depositing them with the IRS.

Every calendar quarter: If you withhold tax from your child's or spouse's pay, you must deposit it with the IRS or a specified bank. If you deposit more than $1,000 a year, you must file Form 941, Employer's Quarterly Federal Tax Return, with the IRS showing how much the employee was paid during the quarter and how much tax you withheld and deposited. If you need to deposit less than $2,500 during a calendar quarter, you can make your payment along with the Form 941, instead of paying monthly. Employers with total employment tax liability of $1,000 or less may file employment tax returns once a year instead of quarterly. Use new IRS Form 944, *Employer's Annual Federal Tax Return*. You should be notified by the IRS if you're eligible to file Form 944. If you haven't been notified, but believe you qualify to file Form 944, call the IRS at 1-800-829-0115.

Each year: By January 31 of each year, you must complete and give your employee a copy of IRS Form W-2, Wage and Tax Statement, showing how much you paid the employee and how much tax was withheld. You must also file copies with the IRS and Social Security Administration by February 28. You must include IRS Form W-3, Transmittal of Wage and Tax Statements, with the copy you file with the Social Security Administration. If your child is exempt from withholding, a new W-4 form must be completed each year.

You must also file Form 940 or Form 940-EZ, *Employer's Annual Federal Unemployment (FUTA) Tax Return*. The due date is January 31; however, if you deposited all of the FUTA tax when due, you have ten additional days to file. You must file a Form 940 for your child even though you are not required to withhold any unemployment taxes from his or her pay. If your child is your only employee, enter his or her wages as "exempt" from unemployment tax.

Need more information on employing family members? IRS Circular E, *Employer's Tax Guide* and Publication 929, *Tax Rules for Children and Dependents*, provide detailed information on these requirements. You can get free copies by calling the IRS at 800-TAX-FORM, by calling or visiting your local IRS office, or by downloading them from the IRS website at www.irs.gov.

Hiring a Resident Manager

Landlords who don't want to do all the work themselves often hire a resident manager (also called an apartment manager) to handle the day-to-day details of running an apartment building, such as dealing with repairs, showing and renting vacant units, and collecting rent. As the name implies, a resident manager lives at the rental property. In some states and cities—California, for example—resident managers are required if an apartment building exceeds a certain size (16 or more units in California; nine or more units in New York City).

You should have a resident manager sign an employment agreement spelling out his or her duties and pay. Detailed guidance on how to hire a resident manager, including a sample employment agreement, can be found in *Every Landlord's Legal Guide*, by Marcia Stewart, Ralph Warner, and Janet Portman (Nolo).

Resident managers (also called apartment managers) are employees of the landlords who hire them. This is so, whether they are paid a regular salary or are compensated wholly or partly with reduced rent. Not a single court decision or IRS ruling has ever held otherwise. (PLR 8128117.) All of the tax rules for hiring employees discussed in "Tax Rules for Employees," above, apply to resident managers, but there are a couple of special rules you need to know about.

Management Companies Are Not Employees

Instead of, or in addition to, hiring a resident manager, some landlords hire property management companies to manage their rentals. Such companies are often used by owners of large apartment complexes or absentee landlords who live far away from their rental property. Typically, you sign a contract spelling out the management company's duties and fees. Such companies normally charge a fixed percentage—typically five to ten per cent—of the rent collected. Such fees are a deductible rental expense. Schedule E contains a line where they are deducted.

A management company is an independent contractor, not your employee. The people who work for the company are its employees or independent contractors—you are not responsible for their payroll taxes. The rules for independent contractors covered above apply to management companies.

No Payroll Taxes for Free Lodging

If you pay a resident manager a regular salary, you must pay and withhold federal payroll taxes, which consist of Social Security and Medicare taxes, unemployment taxes, and federal income taxes. However, you need not pay or withhold any federal payroll taxes on the value of free lodging you provide a resident manager for a rental property if:

- the lodging is at your rental property—that is, the manager lives in a unit at your rental building
- the lodging is furnished for your convenience, and

- you require the manager to live there as a condition of employment—in other words, the manager has no choice in the matter. (IRC Sec. 119.)

It is not difficult for any landlord who hires a resident manager to satisfy these requirements.

Under the rules, you furnish lodging for your convenience if you do it for a substantial business reason, other than providing the employee with additional pay. Obviously, landlords have a substantial business reason to have someone living at their rental property—they need a person there 24 hours a day to take care of tenants, maintenance, and security. Moreover, as mentioned above, resident managers are required by law in some states.

The condition of employment test is met if you require the employee to accept the lodging because they need to live at your rental property to properly perform their duties. The very nature of resident managers' duties require that they live at the rental property. It's a good idea to have a written employment agreement with a resident manager, including a clause requiring the manager to live at your rental property. This clause can simply say: "In order to properly accomplish the duties of Resident Manager, Employee is required to live at Employer's rental property at [address] as a condition of employment."

EXAMPLE: Anne owns a triplex. She rents two of the units to regular tenants, but she gives John, the tenant of the third unit, an $800 per month reduction in rent in return for his working as her resident manager. John takes care of repairs, maintenance, and gardening for the building. Although John is Anne's employee, she need not withhold or pay any payroll taxes on the $800 in free monthly rent she pays John.

Minimum Wage Requirements

Whether you pay your manager a salary or with a rent reduction, you need to comply with federal and state minimum wage requirements. The federal minimum wage is scheduled to go to up to $7.25 per hour by 2009. This increase will be made in phased increments as shown in the following chart. If your state's minimum wage is higher, you must pay the higher rate.

Date	July 24, 2007	July 24, 2008	July 24, 2009
Minimum Wage	$5.85	$6.55	$7.25

If the total number of hours a manager works, multiplied by the applicable minimum hourly wage, exceeds the rent reduction or other fixed rate of pay, you are in violation of the minimum wage laws. Depending on the state, you may not be able to count the full amount of the rent reduction when making this calculation. For example, in California you can only count two-thirds of the fair market value of the rental you provide a manager for purposes of complying with the minimum wage laws.

Federal wage and hour laws also require employers to pay time-and-a-half if an employee works more than 40 hours per week (with a few exceptions). Some states, most notably California, require overtime to be paid if an employee works more than eight hours in a day, even if the employee works less than 40 hours in a week.

For information on your minimum wage laws, overtime rules, and record-keeping requirements, see the U.S. Department of Labor website at www.dol.gov. You can also contact the nearest office of the U.S. Labor Department's Wage and Hour Division, or a local office of your state's department of labor or employment.

Chapter 13

Casualty and Theft Losses

Bad things can happen to good rental property. If your rental property is damaged or destroyed by a sudden event like a fire or flood, or if you have a loss due to vandalism or theft, you may be able to obtain a tax deduction for all or part of your loss. These types of losses are called casualty losses.

What Is a Casualty?

A casualty is damage, destruction, or loss of property due to an event that is sudden, unexpected, or unusual. Deductible casualty losses can result from many different causes, including, but not limited to:

- earthquakes
- fires
- floods
- government-ordered demolition or relocation of a building that is unsafe to use because of a disaster
- landslides
- sonic booms
- storms, including hurricanes and tornadoes
- terrorist attacks
- vandalism, including vandalism to rental property by tenants, and
- volcanic eruptions.

One thing all the events in the list above have in common is that they are sudden—they happen quickly. Suddenness is the hallmark of a casualty loss. Thus, loss of property due to slow, progressive deterioration is not deductible as a casualty loss. For example, the steady weakening or deterioration of a rental building due to normal wind and weather conditions is not a deductible casualty loss.

Many legal disputes have occurred over whether an event was sufficiently sudden to cause a deductible casualty loss. Some of these are summarized in the following chart:

Casualty Loss	Not a Casualty Loss
Damage to shoreline buildings due to sudden erosion caused by wave or wind action during a storm (Rev. Rul 76-134)	Damage to buildings due to gradual soil erosion or subsidence (Rev. Rul 76-134)
Termite damage occurring in a single year (*Rosenberg v. Comm'r.*, 198 F.2d 46)	Termite damage occurring over three-year period (*Dodge v. Comm'r.*, 25 T.C. 1022)
Death of trees over 10-day period due to massive insect attack (Rev. Rul. 79-174)	Destruction of trees caused by Dutch elm disease (*Burns v. United States*, 174 F. Supp. 203 (D.OH 1959))
Damage and destruction of plants and trees over four-month period caused by a sudden and unusual drought (*Ruecker v. Comm'r.*, T.C. Memo. 1981-257)	Death of trees caused by a three-year-long drought (*Kemper v. Comm'r.*, 30 T.C. 546)
Destruction of barn caused by high winds during a storm (*Stein v. Comm'r.*, T.C. Memo 1955-57)	Collapse of patio roof caused by dry rot, rather than wind (*Chipman v. Comm'r.*, T.C. Memo 1981-194)

Although damage to property due to routine wear and tear over time is not a deductible casualty loss, routine wear and tear can result in a sudden event that causes a casualty loss.

> **EXAMPLE:** Phil owns a rental home with an aged water heater that has deteriorated over time due to routine wear and tear. One day the water heater suddenly bursts causing rust and water damage to rugs and drapes in Phil's property. The damage to the water heater itself is not a casualty loss since it was due to routine wear and tear. But the damage to the rugs and drapes is a deductible casualty loss because it was caused by a sudden, unexpected, and unusual event—a burst water heater.

External Force Required

There must be some external force involved in a casualty loss. Thus, you get no deduction if you simply lose property or it is damaged or destroyed due to your own negligence. However, a deductible casualty loss can be caused by another person's carelessness or negligence. For example, you can deduct as a casualty loss sudden damage caused by a negligent contractor or workman.

EXAMPLE: Richard and Ruth Marx noticed that the roof to their house was leaking and hired a building contractor to repair it. Not long afterward, the roof leaked again during a storm, but this time the leak was much worse: It caused the drywall ceiling of the home to fall in, resulting in substantial damage to the interior. The tax court permitted the Marxes to claim a casualty loss for the damage, finding that the massive leaks were sudden and unexpected, were caused by the contractor's negligence, and were independent of the preexisting minor leak. (*Marx v. Comm'r.*, T.C. Memo 1991-598.)

Theft or Vandalism

You may also obtain a casualty loss deduction if anything on or in your rental property is stolen or vandalized. The taking of property must be illegal under the laws of the state where it occurred and it must have been done with criminal intent. You should file a police report when a theft occurs or if your property is vandalized. You must deduct losses from a theft or vandalism in the tax year in which the loss is discovered.

EXAMPLE: Lorraine, the owner of a four-unit apartment building, is forced to evict one of her tenants for nonpayment of rent. After the tenant moves out, she discovers that he has completely trashed the apartment—among other things, stopping the toilet with diapers, breaking mirrors, staining carpets, and punching holes in the walls. Lorraine can deduct the uninsured portion of the cost of the vandalism as a casualty loss.

Calculating a Casualty Loss Deduction

You usually won't be able to deduct the entire cost of property damaged or destroyed by a casualty. How much you may deduct depends on whether the property involved was stolen, completely destroyed, or partially destroyed, and whether the loss was covered by insurance. You must always reduce your casualty losses by the amount of any insurance proceeds you receive, or reasonably expect to receive in the future. If more than one item is stolen, damaged, or destroyed, you must figure your deduction separately for each.

One good thing about casualty losses is that they are not subject to the restrictions on deducting passive losses discussed in Chapter 16. You can simply ignore the complex passive loss rules when determining how much you may deduct.

Insurance

You may take a deduction for casualty losses to your rental property only to the extent that the loss is not covered by insurance. If the loss is fully covered, you get no deduction. You can't avoid this rule by not filing an insurance claim. If you have insurance coverage, you must timely file a claim, even if it will result in cancellation of your policy or an increase in your premiums. If you have insurance and don't file an insurance claim, you cannot obtain a casualty loss deduction. (IRC Sec. 165(h)(4)(E).)

You must reduce the amount of your claimed casualty loss by any insurance recovery you receive or reasonably expect to receive, even if it hasn't yet been paid. If it later turns out that you receive less insurance than you expected, you can deduct the amount the following year. If you receive more than you expected and claimed as a casualty loss, the extra amount is included as income for the year it is received.

You must also reduce your claimed loss by the amount of any of the following payments or services you receive or expect to receive:

- the cost of any repairs made by a tenant that you don't pay for
- payments to you by the tenant to cover the cost of repairs
- any part of a federal disaster loan that is forgiven
- court awards for damage or theft loss, minus any attorney fees or other expenses incurred to obtain the award, and
- the value of repairs, restoration, or cleanup services provided for free by a relief agency such as the Red Cross.

Property a Total Loss

If the property is completely destroyed or stolen, your deduction is calculated as follows:

Adjusted basis
- Salvage value
- Insurance proceeds
= Deductible loss

Your adjusted basis is the property's original cost, plus the value of any improvements, minus any deductions you took for depreciation or Section 179 expensing—see Chapter 5. You determine the basis for your building, land improvements, and landscaping separately.

Salvage value is the value of whatever remains after the property is destroyed. This usually won't amount to much. For example, if a rental house burns down completely, there may be some leftover bricks, building materials, personal property, and other items with some scrap value. Obviously, if a personal property item is stolen, there will be no salvage value at all.

> **EXAMPLE:** Sean's rental house burns down and is completely destroyed. The house had an adjusted basis of $100,000. Sean only had $50,000 of fire insurance coverage. The house's salvage value is $2,000. Sean's deductible casualty loss is $48,000, calculated as follows:
>
> | | |
> |---|---|
> | Adjusted basis | $ 100,000 |
> | Salvage value of building | –   2,000 |
> | Insurance recovery | –   50,000 |
> | Deductible loss | $ 48,000 |

Property a Partial Loss

If the property is only partly destroyed, your casualty loss deduction is the *lesser* of:

- the decrease in the property's fair market value, or
- its adjusted basis.

You must reduce both amounts by any insurance you receive or expect to receive. Unless you've owned the property for many years, the fair market value measure is usually less and is the one you must use.

If you've experienced a casualty loss, you can use an appraiser to determine the reduction in fair market value of your partly damaged property. However, this is often too expensive or impractical. Instead, most people use the cost of repairing the property to determine the fair market value reduction. To do this, you must actually repair the property to the same condition it was in before the casualty. Repair estimates may not be used.

EXAMPLE: The chimney in Sally's rental duplex collapses during an earthquake. She has no earthquake insurance coverage. She pays $5,000 to a building contractor to repair the chimney back to the condition it was in before the earthquake. She figures her casualty loss deduction as follows:

1. Adjusted basis of duplex before earthquake	$ 96,000
2. Fair market value before earthquake	125,000
3. Fair market value after earthquake	– 120,000
4. Decrease in fair market value (based on cost of repair)	5,000
5. Amount of loss (line 1 or line 4, whichever is less)	5,000
6. Insurance reimbursement	– 0
7. Deductible loss	$ 5,000

The cost of repairing damaged property is not part of a casualty loss, but can be deducted as an operating expense (see Chapter 3). Sally, therefore, can deduct the $5,000 she spent to fix the chimney as a repair expense.

Deducting Separate Components

You must calculate casualty loss to rental property separately for each item that is damaged or destroyed. (IRS Reg. 1.165-7(a)(2)(ii).) This may include a building, land improvements under the building, landscaping, and other land improvements apart from the building. However, you don't need to separately deduct personal property items inside a rental property, such as stoves and refrigerators.

EXAMPLE: Tim's rental house is damaged by a tornado. The twister not only damaged the building, but tore up his landscaping—trees and shrubs—as well. Tim must separately calculate his casualty loss for the building and the landscaping. The adjusted basis of the building is $166,000. The trees and shrubs have an adjusted basis of $4,500. Tim hires an appraiser who determines that the fair market value of the building immediately before the tornado was $200,000, and was $152,000 immediately afterwards. The fair market value of the trees and shrubs immediately before the casualty was $4,000 and afterwards was $400. Tim received $40,000 in insurance to cover the loss to the building.

Tim calculates his casualty loss for the building as follows:

1. Adjusted basis of house before tornado	$166,000
2. Fair market value before tornado	200,000
3. Fair market value after tornado	− 152,000
4. Decrease in fair market value	48,000
5. Amount of loss (line 1 or line 4, whichever is less)	48,000
6. Insurance reimbursement	− 40,000
7. Deductible loss	$ 8,000

Tim separately calculates his loss for the landscaping as follows:

1. Adjusted basis of landscaping before tornado	$4,500
2. Fair market value before tornado	4,000
3. Fair market value after tornado	− 400
4. Decrease in fair market value	3,600
5. Amount of loss (line 1 or line 4, whichever is less)	3,600
6. Insurance reimbursement	− 0
7. Deductible casualty loss	$3,600

Damage to Your Home Office

If you qualify for the home office deduction, you may deduct losses due to damage to, or destruction of, your home office as part of your home office deduction.

You can deduct casualty losses that affect your entire house as an indirect home office expense. The amount of your deduction is based on your home office use percentage.

EXAMPLE: Dana's home, valued at $500,000, is completely destroyed by a fire. Her fire insurance covered only 80% of her loss, or $400,000, leaving her with a $100,000 loss. Her home office took up 20% of her home. She can deduct 20% of her $100,000 loss, or $20,000, as an indirect home office deduction.

You can fully deduct casualty losses that affect only your home office—for example, if only your home office is burned in a fire—as direct home office expenses. However, you can't take a business expense deduction for casualty losses that don't affect your home office at all—for example, if your kitchen is destroyed by fire. (See Chapter 9 for a detailed discussion of the home office deduction.)

If the loss involves property you use for you rental activity that is in your home office but is not part of your home—for example, a burglar steals your home office computer—you can deduct the entire value of that loss directly, rather than as part of the home office deduction.

Effect of Casualty Losses on Basis

Any casualty loss you claim on your taxes reduces the basis of the property. Insurance or other reimbursements you receive also reduce your basis. This will increase your gain when you sell the property (see Chapter 5).

⚠️ **Deduction for damage to personal property not used for rental activity is more limited.** You deduct casualty losses to personal property—that is, property you don't use for your rental activity from your income tax as an itemized personal deduction. However, the deduction is severely limited: You can deduct only the amount of the loss that exceeds 10% of your adjusted gross income for the year. This greatly limits or eliminates many casualty loss deductions. To add insult to injury, you must also subtract $100 from each casualty or theft you suffered during the year. Big exception: The 10% and $100 limitations do not apply to casualty losses caused by Hurricanes Katrina, Rita, or Wilma.

Disaster Area Losses

If you suffer a deductible casualty loss in an area that is declared a federal disaster by the president, you may elect to deduct the loss for your taxes for the previous year. This will provide you with a quick tax refund since you'll get back part of the tax you paid for the prior year. If you have already filed your return for the prior year, you can claim a disaster loss against that year's income by filing an amended return (see Chapter 19).

> **EXAMPLE:** Tom's apartment building is damaged by a flood in August of 2008. Tom suffers a deductible casualty loss of $10,000. The area in which his building is located is declared a federal disaster area. Tom may deduct his $10,000 casualty loss on his 2007 taxes, even though he has already paid

them, by filing an amended return for the year. As a result, he gets a $2,500 tax refund for that year.

Generally, you can carry a net operating loss (NOL) back to the two tax years before the NOL year. However, if your property was located in the Gulf Opportunity Zone—the area destroyed by Hurricane Katrina—your NOL can be carried back up to five years.

You can determine if an area has been declared a disaster area by checking the Federal Emergency Management Administration (FEMA) website at www.fema. gov/news/disasters.fema.

Casualty Gains

In some cases, the insurance reimbursement you receive will exceed the value of the property that is damaged or destroyed. In this event, you have a casualty gain, not a deductible loss.

> **EXAMPLE:** In 1970, Rick bought a rental house for $18,000. He made no further improvements or additions to the property. When a storm destroyed the house in January 2008, the house was worth $250,000. Rick received $146,000 from the insurance company in March. Rick had a gain of $128,000 ($146,000 – $18,000).

If you have a gain, you might have to pay tax on that gain. If you owned the property one year or more, the gain is a capital gain taxed at capital gains rates. Gains on property owned less than one year are taxed at ordinary income tax rates. (Ordinary rates are higher than capital gains rates for everyone except taxpayers in the lowest tax brackets; see Chapter 1.)

However, if you have a gain on damaged property, you can postpone paying tax on it if you replace or restore the property. You must replace the property with new property that is similar or related in service or use to the property it replaces. For example, you can replace a rental house with another rental house or apartment building; but you can't replace it with a home you live in.

You do not have to use the same funds you receive as reimbursement for your old property to acquire the replacement property. If you spend the money you receive from the insurance company for other purposes, and borrow money to buy replacement property, you can still postpone reporting the gain if you meet the other requirements.

The cost of restoring or replacing the property must be at least as much as the reimbursement you receive. If the cost is less than the reimbursement, you must include the gain in your income up to the amount of the unspent reimbursement.

> **EXAMPLE:** Rick from the above example spent $144,000 to rebuild his rental house. Because this is $2,000 less than the insurance proceeds he received ($146,000), he must include $2,000 in his taxable income for the year.

To postpone reporting your gain, you must restore or replace the damaged or destroyed property within two years after the close of the first tax year in which any part of your gain is realized. If the property is in a federal disaster area, this period is increased to four years. If it is located in the Hurricane Katrina disaster area, the replacement period is increased to five years.

Tax Reporting and Record Keeping for Casualty Losses

Casualty losses are a hot ticket item for the IRS. Claiming them will increase your chances of being audited. Make sure you can document your losses. You'll need to have:

- documents showing that you owned each asset you claimed was damaged, stolen, or destroyed—for example, a deed or receipt
- contracts or purchase receipts showing the original cost of the item, plus any improvements you made to it
- copies of your old tax returns showing all your depreciation and Section 179 deductions for the property, and
- evidence of the property's fair market value, such as insurance records, an appraisal, or receipts for the cost of repairing it.

You report casualty losses to rental property on part B of IRS Form 4684, Casualties and Thefts, and then transfer the deductible casualty loss to Form 4797, Sales of Business Property, and the first page of your Form 1040. The amount of your deductible casualty loss is subtracted from your adjusted gross income for the year. These reporting requirements differ from those for other deductions covered in this book, which are reported on IRS Schedule E, Form 1040.

■

Chapter 14

Additional Deductions

This chapter looks at some common deductible operating expenses that you are likely to incur in the course of your rental activity, such as real estate taxes, insurance, and legal fees. You can deduct these costs as operating expenses as long as they are ordinary, necessary, and reasonable in amount—and meet the additional requirements discussed below.

Dues and Subscriptions

Dues you pay to professional, business, and civic organizations are deductible expenses, as long as the organization's main purpose is not to provide entertainment facilities to members. You can deduct dues paid to:

- apartment owner associations
- real estate boards
- local chambers of commerce and business leagues, and
- civic or public service organizations, such as a Rotary or Lions club.

You get no deduction for dues you pay to belong to other types of social, business, or recreational clubs—for example, country clubs or athletic clubs. For this reason, it's best not to use the word dues on your tax return because the IRS may question the expense. Use other words to describe the deduction— for example, if you're deducting membership dues for an apartment owners' organization, list the expense as apartment owners' association membership fees.

You may also deduct the cost of publications you read for your rental activity—magazines or journals on real estate, taxation, law, or finance. Subscription websites dealing with real estate are also deductible. (Don't forget to deduct the cost of this book!)

Education Expenses

You may deduct your expenses for landlord-related education—for example, a seminar or course on buying or operating rental property. You may also deduct the cost of attending a real-estate-related convention or meeting as an education expense. To qualify for an education deduction, you must be able to show the education:

- maintains or improves skills required to be a successful landlord, or
- is required by law or regulation to maintain your professional status.

EXAMPLE 1: Jerry owns three rental houses. He attends a one-day seminar on how to make more money from rental property offered by The Learning Annex, a company that produces educational seminars on various taxes. The cost is deductible as an education expense.

EXAMPLE 2: Herb is a landlord and licensed real estate broker. Every year, he is required by his state real estate licensing board to take 30 hours of continuing education to maintain his status as a licensed broker. He may deduct the cost as an education expense.

Deductible education expenses include tuition, fees, books, and other learning materials. They also include transportation and travel (see below). You may also deduct expenses you pay to educate or train your employees.

Before You Are in Business

You cannot currently deduct education expenses you incur before your rental activity begins. For example, if you have never owned rental property and attend a course on how to be a successful landlord, you may not deduct the expense as an education expense. However, if you do end up buying rental property, you may deduct the expense as a start-up expense. Up to $5,000 in start-up expenses may be deducted the first year your rental activity is in operation. Any amount over $5,000 must be deducted in equal installments over the first 180 months you're in business. (See Chapter 8.)

Likewise, if you're not already involved in the real estate field, you may not deduct the cost of attending courses to become a licensed real estate broker. (IRS Reg. 1.162-5(a).)

Traveling for Education

Transportation expenses you pay to travel to and from a deductible educational activity are deductible. This includes transportation between your home and the educational activity. Going to or from home to an educational activity does not constitute nondeductible commuting. If you drive, you may deduct your actual expenses or use the standard mileage rate. (See Chapter 10 for more on deducting car expenses.)

There's no law that says you must take your education courses as close to home as possible. You can travel outside your geographic area for education, even if the same or a similar educational activity is available near your home or place of business. Companies and groups that sponsor educational events are well aware of this rule and take advantage of it by offering courses and seminars at resorts and other enjoyable vacation spots such as Hawaii and California. Deductible travel expenses can include airfare or other transportation, lodging, and meals. (See Chapter 11 for more on deducting travel expenses.)

Lifetime Learning Credit

Instead of taking a tax deduction for your rental business-related education expenses, you may qualify for the lifetime learning credit. A tax credit is a dollar-for-dollar reduction in your tax liability, so it's even better than a tax deduction.

The lifetime learning credit can be used to help pay for any undergraduate or graduate level education, including nondegree education to acquire or improve job skills (for example a continuing education course. If you qualify, your credit equals 20% of the first $10,000 of post-secondary tuition and fees you pay during the year, for a maximum credit of $2,000 per tax return. However, the credit is phased out and then eliminated at certain income levels: It begins to go down if your modified adjusted gross income is over $47,000 ($94,000 for a joint return) and you cannot claim the credit at all if your MAGI is over $57,000 ($114,000 for a joint return).

You can take this credit not only for yourself, but for a dependent child (or children) for whom you claim a tax exemption, or your spouse as well (if you file jointly). And it can be taken any number of times. However, you can't take the credit if you've already deducted the education cost as a business expense.

EXAMPLE: Bill, a self-employed real estate broker with a $40,000 AGI, spends $2,000 on continuing real estate education courses during 2008. He may take a $400 lifetime learning credit (20% x $2,000 = $400).

Gifts

You may deduct the cost of gifts you make in the course of your rental business—for example, to thank or maintain goodwill with a vendor, tenant, or employee. This includes holiday gifts to tenants. However, the gift expense deduction is limited to $25 per person per year. Any amount over the $25 limit is not deductible. If this amount seems low, that's because it was established in 1954! In addition, there are special record-keeping requirements for gifts. (See Chapter 17.)

> **EXAMPLE:** Landlord Lisa gives a $60 Christmas gift to the gardener who takes care of her rental properties. She may deduct $25 of the cost.

The $25 limit applies only to gifts to individuals. It doesn't apply if you give a gift to an entire company. Such companywide gifts are deductible in any amount, as long as they are reasonable. However, the $25 limit does apply if the gift is intended for a particular person or group of people within the company.

If you give a gift to a family member of a tenant, the gift is considered to be an indirect gift to the tenant and is subject to the $25 limit. Thus, you are limited to a single $25 gift deduction for each tenant and his or her entire family.

Insurance for Your Rental Activity

You can deduct the premiums you pay for almost any insurance related to your rental activity. This includes fire, theft, and flood insurance for rental property, as well as landlord liability insurance. If you have employees, you may deduct the cost of their health and workers' compensation insurance. Unemployment insurance contributions you make for your employees are deducted either as insurance costs or as taxes, depending on how they are characterized by your state's laws.

The one type of insurance that may not be deducted as an operating expense is title insurance you obtain when you purchase rental property. Its cost is added to the basis of the property and depreciated over 27.5 years. The same rule applies to insurance premiums you pay on property under construction. (See Chapter 5.)

Homeowner's Insurance for Your Home Office

If you have a home office and qualify for the home office deduction, you may deduct the home office percentage of your homeowner's or renter's insurance premiums. For example, if your home office takes up 20% of your home, you may deduct 20% of the premiums. You can deduct 100% of any coverage that you add to your homeowner's policy specifically for your home office and/or rental property. For example, if you add an endorsement to your policy to cover business property, you can deduct 100% of the cost.

Car Insurance

If you use the actual expense method to deduct your car expenses, you can deduct the cost of insurance that covers liability, damages, and other losses for vehicles used in your rental activity as an operating expense. If you use a vehicle only for your rental activity, you can deduct 100% of your insurance costs. If you operate a vehicle for both your rental activity and for personal use, you can deduct only the part of the insurance premiums that applies to the rental use of your vehicle. For example, if you use a car 10% for your rental activity and 90% for personal reasons, you can deduct 10% of your insurance costs.

If you use the standard mileage rate to deduct your car expenses, you can't take a separate deduction for insurance. The standard rate is intended to cover all your automobile costs, including insurance. (See Chapter 10 for more on vehicle deductions.)

Prepaying Your Insurance Premiums

Many landlords make a single payment for an entire year of insurance coverage. The insurance company charges you less when you do this. However, if you are a calendar year taxpayer, as are the vast majority of small landlords, this will have a tax consequence. Any portion of an insurance premium payment that applies to insurance coverage for the following calendar year can't be deducted until that year. Thus, you'll have to wait an extra year to deduct the amount. (Rev. Rul. 70-413.)

> **EXAMPLE:** Irving obtains a new insurance policy for his rental building on July 1, 2008. He pays $1,000 for 12 months of insurance coverage. Because Irving's tax year is the calendar year, he may deduct only six months, or 50%, of the premium in 2008. He may deduct the remainder in 2009.

Legal and Professional Services

You can deduct fees that you pay to attorneys, accountants, property management companies, real estate investment advisors, and other professionals as operating expenses if the fees are for work related to your rental activity.

EXAMPLE: Landlord Ira hires attorney Jake to evict a deadbeat tenant. The legal fees Ira pays Jake are a deductible operating expense.

Legal and professional fees that you pay for personal purposes generally are not deductible. For example, you can't deduct the legal fees you incur if you get divorced or you sue someone for a traffic accident injury. Nor are the fees that you pay to write your will deductible, even if the will covers rental property that you own.

Buying Long-Term Property

If you pay legal or other fees in the course of buying real estate or other long-term property, you must add the amount of the fee to the tax basis (cost) of the property. You deduct this cost over several years, through depreciation. This rule also applies to attorney fees incurred in legal disputes over who holds title to real estate, or in boundary disputes or condemnation proceedings.

Management Fees

The fees you pay a real estate management company to manage your property are deductible operating expenses. But be careful if you hire your child, spouse, or other relatives to serve as your manager. If you pay a relative more than the going market rate and you are audited, the IRS can deny your deduction for the excess amount. (IRS Reg. 1.162-1(a).)

Starting a Business

Legal and accounting fees that you pay to start a rental business are deductible only as business start-up expenses. You may deduct them over the first 60 months you are in business. The same holds true for incorporation fees or fees that you pay to form a partnership or LLC. You may not deduct such fees if your rental activity is an investment for tax purposes, not a business. (See Chapter 8 for more on deducting start-up costs.)

Accounting Fees

You may deduct any accounting fees that you pay for your rental activity as a deductible operating expense—for example, fees you pay an accountant to set up or keep your books, prepare your tax return, or give you tax advice for your rental activity.

You may also deduct the cost of having an accountant or other tax professional complete the rental portion of your tax return—Schedule E and other rental activity tax forms—but you cannot deduct the time the preparer spends on the personal part of your return. Make sure that you get an itemized bill showing the portion of the tax preparation fee allocated to preparing your Schedule E.

Meals and Entertainment

Meal and entertainment expenses are usually not a big deduction item for a person running a small rental business. However, if you do spend money to take people out to lunch or dinner for your rental business, or treat them to a ballgame or play, you can deduct part of your entertainment expense if you satisfy strict IRS requirements.

Find out more about meal and entertainment expenses. For detailed guidance about deducting meal and entertainment expenses, refer to IRS Publication 463, *Travel, Entertainment, Gift, and Car Expenses*. You can download it from www.irs.gov or call 800-TAX-FORM.

Who Can You Entertain?

The entertainment deduction is, understandably, a great temptation for landlords who want to mix work with pleasure—and enjoy as much of the latter as possible. To prevent abuses, the IRS has something to say about your guest list. To obtain a deduction when entertaining, you must be with at least one person who can benefit your rental activity in some way. This could include:

- prospective buyers of your rental property
- investors or prospective investors in your real estate activity
- tenants or prospective tenants (not very common for residential real estate)
- suppliers
- employees
- independent contractors, such as construction contractors, architects, and repairmen

- government officials
- real estate agents
- real estate managers
- partners, or
- professional advisors such as your attorney or accountant.

If people who can't benefit your rental activity are also present and you pay their expenses, you can't deduct the cost.

You Must Discuss Your Rental Activity

Rental business entertainment expenses, like all operating expenses, are deductible only if they are ordinary and necessary. This means that the expense must be common, helpful, and appropriate for your rental activity. Moreover, you must have a discussion relating to your rental activity either before, during, or after a social event if you want to claim an entertainment deduction.

The IRS doesn't have spies lurking in restaurants, theaters, or other places of entertainment, so it has no way of knowing whether you really talk about your rental activity. You're pretty much on the honor system here. However, be aware that if you're audited, the IRS closely scrutinizes this deduction because many taxpayers cheat when they take it. You'll also have to comply with stringent record-keeping requirements. (See Chapter 17.)

Calculating Your Deduction

Expenses that you incur for entertainment can include meals (with beverages, tax, and tips), your transportation expenses (including parking), tickets to entertainment or sporting events, catering costs for parties, cover charges for admission to night clubs, and rent you pay for a room in which to hold a dinner or cocktail party. As long as they meet the requirements explained above, they are deductible—but not in full. The tax rules specify that you may deduct only 50% of your entertainment expenses. For example, if you spend $50 for a meal in a restaurant, you can deduct $25. (Even though you can deduct only half of the expense, you must keep track of everything you spend and report the entire amount on your tax return.) The only exception to the 50% rule is for transportation expenses, which are 100% deductible.

Ordinarily, you cannot deduct the cost of entertaining your spouse or the spouse of a rental business associate. However, if your spouse is co-owner of the rental property involved, you may deduct his or her expenses.

Taxes

Most taxes that you pay in the course of your rental activity are currently deductible operating expenses.

Real Property Taxes

You can fully deduct your current year state and local property taxes on rental real property as an operating expense. However, if you prepay the next year's property taxes, you may not deduct the prepaid amount until the following year.

When you buy your rental property, the property taxes due for the year must be divided between the buyer and seller according to how many days of the tax year each held ownership of the property. You'll usually find information on this in the settlement statement you receive at the property closing.

Local Benefit Taxes and Special Assessments

Water bills, sewer charges, and other service charges assessed against your rental property are not real estate taxes, but they are deductible as operating expenses. (If a tenant pays these expenses, as sometimes happens with single-family house rentals, the landlord gets no deduction unless he or she reimburses the tenant. The tenant gets no deduction because these are personal expenses for the tenant.)

However, real estate taxes imposed to fund specific local benefits for property, such as streets, sidewalks, sewer lines, and water mains, are not currently deductible as operating expenses where they are imposed only on the property owners who will benefit from them. Because these benefits increase the value of your property, you must add what you pay for them to the tax basis of your property and depreciate them. (IRC Sec. 164(c)(1).) Most of these improvements can be depreciated over 15 years as land improvements (see Chapter 5.)

However, there is an exception to this rule: Any part of a special assessment you pay that is for maintenance, repairs, or an interest charge for a local benefit for your property is deductible as an operating expense. You may claim this deduction only if the taxing authority sends you an itemized tax bill separately listing the amounts you must pay for construction, interest, and maintenance. (IRS Reg. 1.164-4(b)(1).)

EXAMPLE: A city assessed a front foot benefit charge against property that was benefited by construction of a water system. The city's tax bill itemized the charge, showing how much was assessed for construction of the water system, interest, and maintenance costs. Taxpayers were allowed to currently deduct the amounts for interest and maintenance. (Rev. Rul. 79-201.)

Real Estate Transfer Taxes

When you purchase rental property, you must ordinarily pay state and local real estate transfer taxes. You cannot deduct these taxes in the year in which you paid them. Instead, add them to the basis of your property and depreciate them over time, as explained in Chapter 5.

Employment Taxes

If you have employees, you must pay half of their Social Security and Medicare taxes from your own funds and withhold the other half from their pay. These taxes consist of a 12.4% Social Security tax, up to an annual salary cap ($97,500 in 2007); and a 2.9% Medicare tax on all employees' pay. You may deduct half of this amount as a business expense. You should treat the taxes you withhold from your employees' pay as wages paid to your employees on your tax return. However, you need not pay employment taxes when you hire your children. (See Chapter 12.)

Unpaid Rent

If tenants fail to pay the rent owed you, can you deduct the loss? The short answer for the vast majority of small landlords is no. (Some bad debts are deductible, but unpaid rent is almost never one of them.) Here's why:

IRS regulations provide that a worthless debt arising from unpaid rent is deductible only if you report the amount of rent you were supposed to be paid as income for that year (or a prior year). (IRS Reg. 1.166-1(e).) Landlords who can report this kind of yet-uncollected rent are operating on an accrual accounting basis (if you are an accrual basis taxpayer, you report rent as income as it becomes due, not when it's actually paid). The great majority of small landlords operate on a cash basis, which means they report rent as income only when it is actually paid to them by their tenants. Since cash basis landlords do not report rent that has never been paid on their tax returns, it's not deductible. (See Chapter 17 for a detailed discussion of accounting methods.)

EXAMPLE: John and Margaret Kopunek rented a house in Sarasota, Florida, to a new tenant who stopped paying rent after a few months and moved out. After they kept the tenant's security deposit, the Kopenuks were left with $750 in unpaid rent. Because they were cash basis taxpayers, they did not report the $750 of rent that they never received as income on their tax return for the year. When they deducted the $750 from their taxes for the year as a bad debt, they were audited by the IRS and the deduction was denied. The tax court held that the IRS had acted properly. Having never reported the unpaid rent as income, the hapless Kopuneks could not deduct it as a bad debt. (*Kopunek v. Comm'r.*, T.C. Memo 1987-417.)

So, in order to deduct unpaid rent, you must report unpaid rent as income on your tax return for the year the rent was due—in other words, you'd have to adopt an accrual method of accounting. However, the deduction merely offsets the income you've already reported. Thus, there is no point in switching to the accrual method of accounting just to be able to write off unpaid rent; you won't save an extra penny in taxes.

Nor can you deduct unpaid rent as a casualty loss (see Chapter 13). The Kopuneks, from the example above, tried this and failed. (*Kopunek v. Comm'r.*, T.C. Memo 1987-417.)

The moral for landlords is clear: If you have deadbeat tenants, evict them as soon as possible and find a new tenant who will pay the rent. The legal fees to evict a tenant are deductible (see "Legal and Professional Services," above). You can obtain a court judgment against a defaulting tenant for the amount of the unpaid rent (less any security deposit you've retained). However, unless the tenant has money, earns a salary, or has assets you can get your hands on, such a judgment will be worthless. Courts do not collect such judgments for you, you must do it yourself.

■

Chapter 15

Vacation Homes

Millions of Americans own, or think about owning, a vacation home. Often-times, people help pay for the cost of owning a second home by renting it out for part of the year. While this can help defray some of the costs, there are significant tax consequences when you rent out a vacation home that you or your family also use. These rules are complicated and different rules apply depending on how much time you use the home and how much time you rent it out. If you bought your vacation home simply to have fun and don't want tax concerns to ruin your vacations, you can skip this chapter. On the other hand, if you want to save all the taxes you can—even when you're on vacation—you need to read it carefully.

The Vacation Home Tax Morass

You're entitled to deduct operating expenses and depreciation for a rental property, but not for a home, condominium, or other real property that you or your family use as a personal residence. So, what do you do if you use the same property as both a rental and a vacation home or second home during the year?

Unfortunately for vacation homeowners, Congress has decided that they should not be allowed to deduct operating expenses and depreciation costs for the time they use a second home as a personal residence. There are complicated tax rules homeowners must follow to ensure that they don't deduct too much for their second home. If a home is used as both a rental property and a residence, these rules require that you allocate expenses between the two types of uses. The rules differ depending on the amount of time the property is used as a rental and a residence.

The rules apply to any type of dwelling—this is defined quite broadly: It includes a house, condominium, mobile home, or even a boat. However, hotels, motels, and other short-term rentals are not dwellings for these purposes. Nor does the term apply if you rent a room in your home to a short-term paying guest, and never use the room yourself.

To figure out what deductions you can take for a vacation home, you must determine what tax category your home falls into. For tax purposes, a vacation or second home can be a:
- regular rental property
- tax-free vacation home
- vacation home used as rental property, or
- vacation home used as a residence.

Some of these categories receive much more favorable tax treatment than others, so it's important to understand the differences among them. That way, you'll be able to plan your use of your vacation home to receive more favorable treatment.

Every vacation home or second home in America falls into one of the tax categories listed in the chart below. The farther down you go in the chart, the worse tax treatment you receive.

Vacation Home Tax Categories		
Personal Use	Rental Use	Tax Category
0 days	Any number of days	Regular rental property
15 days or more	Fewer than 15 days	Tax-free vacation home
Fewer than 15 days *or* no more than 10% of the rental days	15 days or more	Vacation home used as rental property
More than 15 days *or* more than 10% of the rental days	15 days or more	Vacation home used as residence

Regular Rental Property

If you have a second home that you rent out 100% of the time and never use yourself or permit family members to use, the home is treated like any other rental property described in this book. You can skip to "Calculating Personal and Rental Use," below. This type of rental property is not really a vacation home or second home because its owner does not live in it at all.

Tax-Free Vacation Home

At the other end of the spectrum from a 100% rental property, is a vacation home or second home that you use most of the time for your own personal use and you rent out for only a handful of days during the year. Such homes are treated as personal second homes, not rental properties, for tax purposes. Your vacation home falls within this category if, during the year:

- you rent out your home for fewer than 15 days, and
- the home is used personally for 15 days or more (see "Calculating Personal and Rental Use" for what constitutes personal use). (IRC Sec. 280A(g).)

EXAMPLE: Claudia rents her Florida beachfront condominium for 14 days during the summer. She lives in the condo herself for two months during the year. Her condo qualifies as a tax-free vacation home.

No Tax Due On Rental Income

Here's the great thing about vacation homes in this category: All the rental income you receive from them is tax-free, no matter how much you earn.

EXAMPLE: Claudia earned $2,000 from renting out her Florida condo for two weeks. She doesn't have to pay any federal income tax on this income.

This rule can provide you with a real windfall if, like Claudia, you own a vacation home in a desirable area where people are looking for short-term rentals.

Tax Deductions

The tax deduction rules applicable to any personal vacation home or second home apply to homes in this category. Under these rules, all your real estate taxes are deducted as a personal itemized deduction on your IRS Schedule A. There is no dollar limit on the deduction, or any limit on how many vacation homes you can claim the deduction for each year. You may also deduct your mortgage interest as an itemized deduction (for a mortgage up to $1 million). If you are lucky enough to have more than one vacation home, you must select the one to be treated as the second home for purposes of the mortgage interest deduction. This selection is made anew each year, so that one vacation home may be selected as the second home one year, and another selected the next year.

Because the home is treated as a personal residence for tax purposes, you may not deduct any operating expenses for the property or take any depreciation deduction. You don't file Schedule E, the tax form landlords file to report their income and expenses, because your home is not considered a rental property for tax purposes.

EXAMPLE: Assume that Claudia paid $5,000 in mortgage interest and $2,000 in taxes for her condo. She also incurred $600 in operating expenses—this was the fee she paid to a real estate management company to rent and take care of her condo. She may deduct the taxes and interest as an itemized deduction on her Schedule A. She gets no deduction for the $600 in operating expenses, and no depreciation deduction.

Tax-free treatment also applies to personal residences. The tax-free income tax treatment discussed in this section applies to your main residence, as well as a vacation or second home. Thus, you can rent your house up to 14 days a year and pocket the proceeds free of tax.

Vacation Home Used as Rental Property

The next category of vacation homes are those that are rented out 15 days or more each year and not used very often by their owners. You fall into this category if you rent your property for at least 15 days each year and make personal use of the property:

- fewer than 15 days during the year, or
- no more than 10% of the number of days during the year the property is rented for a fair rental.

EXAMPLE 1: Miranda owns a vacation home in Aspen, Colorado. She uses it for 14 days during the year for a ski vacation. She rents it out to other vacationers for a total of 210 days during the year. Because she used the home fewer than 15 days and rented it out more than 15 days, it falls into the category of vacation home used as rental property.

EXAMPLE 2: Assume that Miranda uses her home for 21 days during the year. The home is still in this category because her personal use does not equal more than 10% of the time she rented it out: 10% of 210 rental days = 21 days, so Miranda would have to use her home for more than 21 days not to qualify.

Taxpayers who make little personal use of their vacation homes receive relatively favorable tax treatment. The home is treated as a rental property for tax purposes. Unlike the case with tax-free vacation homes, you must report and pay tax on your rental income. But you may deduct your rental expenses.

You file Schedule E, the tax form for landlords, to report your rental income and expenses.

Deducting Expenses

How you deduct your expenses depends on whether they are direct expenses or other expenses from your rental activity.

Direct Expenses

Direct rental expenses consist of the money you spend to rent the vacation home and run your rental activity. These include fees charged by a management company you hire to handle your rental, advertising, broker's fees, listing fees, credit checks, office supplies for your rental activity, and depreciation or Section 179 expensing for office equipment you use for your rental activity (such as a computer). You can deduct the full amount of these expenses from your rental income on your Schedule E.

All Other Expenses

All other expenses are other costs you have left. These apply to the entire home, and consist of:

- real estate taxes
- mortgage interest for the vacation home
- operating expenses for the home, including repairs, maintenance, cleaning, insurance, and utilities, and
- depreciation.

You must allocate these expenses according to the amount of time the property was rented and the time it was used personally. This is based on the total number of days the property was used during the year. Expenses allocated to the rental period may be deducted on IRS Schedule E, the same as any other rental expense. In addition, you may take an itemized personal deduction for real estate taxes paid during the period of personal use. However, interest on a mortgage secured by the vacation home and allocatable to personal use is nondeductible personal interest. (IRC Sec. 163(h)(4)(A)(i)(II).)

> **EXAMPLE:** Miranda's vacation home was used a total of 231 days during the year: Miranda used it for 21 days and she rented it out for 210 days The allocation would be 21/231 for personal use and 210/231 for rental use. Converted to percentages, this comes to 9% personal use and 91% rental

use. These percentages must be used to allocate Miranda's deductions. Miranda may deduct the following amounts on her Schedule E:

Expense	Amount	Deduction Percentage	Deduction Amount
Direct expenses (advertising, broker's fee)	$ 500	100%	$ 500
Real estate taxes	3,000	91	2,730
Mortgage interest	12,000	91	10,920
Operating expenses (utilities, repairs, insurance)	2,000	91	1,820
Depreciation	5,000	91	4,550
Total	$ 22,500		$ 20,520

In addition, Miranda can deduct 9% of her real estate taxes as a personal itemized deduction on her Schedule A. This is a $270 deduction. $1,980 of her expenses for the year are not deductible because these are expenses other than taxes allocated to the time she personally used the vacation home.

The Hobby Loss and Passive Loss Rules

There are two sets of tax rules that may prevent you from deducting all or part of your expenses from a vacation home used as a rental: the passive loss rules and the hobby loss rules.

Passive Loss Rules

List the rental income you receive from a vacation home used as a rental property on your Schedule E. You may deduct your rental expenses against this income. If you have expenses left over, you've incurred a loss on the property—in other words, you've spent more on your rental property than you earned on rent during the year.

EXAMPLE: Miranda had deductible rental expenses of $20,520 for her vacation home used as a rental property. She earned $16,000 in rent from the vacation house during the year. This leaves her with a $4,520 annual loss.

Vacation home owners like Miranda would like to deduct their annual losses from the income they earn during the year from other sources, such as job or investments. That way, they can lower their tax bill for the year. However, losses from vacation rentals are subject to draconian rules limiting their deductibility—these rules are called the passive loss rules. Many small landlords can avoid the rules under exceptions provided for them in the tax law, but it can be particularly difficult for owners of vacation homes to do so. See Chapter 16 for a detailed discussion of the passive loss rules.

Hobby Loss Rules

The hobby loss rules are another set of rules that apply to vacation homes used as rentals. If the IRS determines that the primary motive you have for renting your vacation home is something other than to earn a profit, it will conclude that the home is a hobby. In this event, you'll only be able to deduct your income from the home from the expenses you pay for it. These rules have the same impact as the passive loss rules, but are even worse because there are no exceptions from them if they apply. To avoid being subject to these rules, you must behave so that the IRS will believe that you want to earn a profit from your vacation home, rather than owning it just for pleasure or some other purpose not motivated by the desire for profit. See Chapter 2 for a detailed discussion on profit motive.

Vacation Home Used as Residence

The final category is for vacation home owners who rent their property 15 days or more during the year, but use it primarily as a residence. These homeowners get hammered by special vacation home tax rules. Your vacation home falls within this category if you rent it at least 15 days and it is used personally:

* more than 14 days during the year, or
* more than 10% of the number of days during the year the property is rented for a fair rental.

EXAMPLE 1: Paul owns a vacation home in Lake Tahoe. He rents it during the summer for 30 days and uses it himself for 90 days during the rest of the year. He used the property more than 14 days and more than 10% of the number of days it was rented out (10% x 30 rental days = 3 days).

EXAMPLE 2: Assume that Paul used the vacation home for 30 days, but rented it out for 330 days. He would avoid the vacation home used as residence category because his use equaled less than 10% of the number of days the property was rented (10% x 330 = 33 days).

If at all possible, you want to avoid flunking the 14-day/10% test. Keep careful track of how much time you spend at your vacation home. If you must spend more than 14 days at the home, you must rent it out enough so you can come within the 10% threshold.

How Will the IRS Know That Your Home Is a Vacation Home Used as a Rental?

The IRS will know whether your vacation home falls within this category because you must tell it. Line 2 of Schedule E specifically asks whether you use the property more than 14 days or 10% of the days it was rented. You must answer yes or no. If you answer yes, the vacation home tax rules discussed below apply.

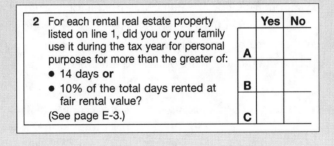

You Cannot Deduct Losses

First of all, your deductions for the vacation home are limited to your rental income from the home. If your expenses exceed your income, you may not deduct the loss from other income you earn that year. The tax law says that such a loss can be carried forward to future years and deducted from your rental income from the property, if you have enough. In real life, however, this rarely happens because the property does not generate enough income. The passive loss rules and the exception to them, (discussed in Chapter 16) do not apply to homes in this category.

Calculating Your Deductions

You are allowed to deduct your expenses from your rental income, but there are strict limitations designed to ensure that you don't deduct personal expenses as rental expenses. To begin with, you must deduct your expenses from your rental income in the following order:

- first, deduct your mortgage interest and real estate taxes
- next, deduct direct rental expenses—expenses that apply only to renting, such as management fees, advertising, rental fees or commissions, and credit checks
- then, you deduct your operating expenses, such as repairs, utilities, insurance, maintenance, and cleaning, and
- finally, if you have any rental income left, you deduct depreciation, as described in Chapter 5.

In addition, you must allocate all of your expenses—other than direct expenses from your rental activity—only to the extent that the property served as a rental, compared to the total time it was used during the year.

EXAMPLE: Paul uses his vacation home for 30 days during the year and rents it out for 90 days. Thus it was used a total of 120 days. Since 90/120 = 75%, he can deduct 75% of his general expenses up to the amount of rental income he earned from the house, which was $10,000. He deducts his expenses in the following order and amounts:

Expense	Amount	Allocation to Rental Use %	Allocation to Rental Use Amount	Amount Deducted This Year	Remaining Rental Income ($10,000 total)	Unused Deduction Carried Forward to Future Years
Property tax	$ 2,000	75%	$ 1,500	$ 1,500	$ 8,500	$ 0
Mortgage interest	10,000	75	7,500	7,500	1,000	0
Direct expenses	1,000	100	1,000	1,000	0	0
Operating expenses	6,000	75	4,500	0	0	4,500
Depreciation	6,000	75	4,500	0	0	4,500
Total	$ 25,000		$19,000	$ 10,000	$ 0	$9,000

Paul deducts his rental income and expenses on Schedule E. Paul may also deduct 25% of his property tax and mortgage interest as a personal itemized deduction on his Schedule A. This is the amount of taxes and rent allocated to the time he personally used the vacation home. This amounts to a $3,000 deduction.

All in all, this is not a good result for Paul. He had $25,000 in expenses, but can deduct only $10,000. He has $9,000 in unused deductions he must carry forward to the next year.

One way to improve this outcome is to increase the amount of property tax and mortgage interest deducted as a personal itemized deduction on Schedule A. This way, more of your operating expenses and depreciation can be deducted from rental income. You can do this by using a different allocation formula for property taxes and interest. Instead of using the number of days the property was used during the year to figure your rental percentage, you use 365 days. This is not the way the IRS would like you to allocate these expenses, but courts have permitted it, reasoning that interest and taxes are paid for an entire year, not just when a vacation home is used. (*Bolton v. Comm'r.*, 694 F.2d 556 (9th Cir. 1982).)

EXAMPLE: If Paul used this alternate method, his allocation percentage for his tax and interest would be 25% instead of 75% (90/365 = 25%). Thus, Paul would deduct only $500 of his property tax and $2,500 of his interest from his $10,000 in rental income. This would let him deduct an additional $5,000 in operating expenses and depreciation. He could deduct the other 75% of his taxes and interest as a $9,000 itemized deduction on his Schedule A. His Schedule E deductions would look like this:

Expense	Amount	Allocation to Rental Use %	Amount	Amount Deducted This Year	Remaining Rental Income ($10,000 total)	Unused Deduction Carried Forward to Future Years
Property tax	$ 2,000	25%	$ 500	$ 500	$ 9,500	$ 0
Mortgage interest	10,000	25	2,500	2,500	7,000	0
Direct expenses	1,000	100	1,000	1,000	6,000	0
Operating expenses	6,000	75	4,500	4,500	1,500	0
Depreciation	6,000	75	4,500	1,500	0	3,000
Total	$ 25,000		$ 13,000	$ 10,000	$ 0	$ 3,000

Another way to increase your deduction is to reduce your mortgage interest expense. Take out a home equity loan on your main home to purchase your vacation home. You can borrow up to $100,000 on your home and deduct the interest as an itemized deduction on your Schedule A. This interest expense won't count when you figure your deduction for your vacation home because the loan is on your main home, not your vacation home. This allows you to deduct more of your operating expenses and depreciation against your vacation rental income.

EXAMPLE: if Paul had taken out a $100,000 home equity loan on his main home to purchase his $160,000 vacation home, he would have reduced the annual mortgage interest on his vacation home from $10,000 to $3,500. His deductions would look like this:

Expense	Amount	Allocation to Rental Use %	Allocation to Rental Use Amount	Amount Deducted This Year	Remaining Rental Income ($10,000 total)	Unused Deduction Carried Forward to Future Years
Property tax	$ 2,000	25%	$ 500	$ 500	$ 9,500	$ 0
Mortgage interest	3,500	25%	875	875	8,625	0
Direct expenses	1,000	100%	1,000	1,000	7,625	0
Operating expenses	6,000	75%	4,500	4,500	3,125	0
Depreciation	6,000	75%	4,500	3,125	0	1,375
Total	$ 18,500		$11,375	$ 10,000	0	$ 1,375

Calculating Personal and Rental Use

The tax category that a vacation home falls into depends on how many days during the year it is used for personal use by the owner and how many days it's rented. As you might expect, there are tax rules for determining this.

Calculating Personal Use

A day of personal use of a vacation home is any day that it is used by:
- you or any co-owner of the property
- a member of your family or a member of the family of any co-owner (unless the family member uses the home as his or her main home and pays a fair rental price)

- anyone under an arrangement that lets you use some other home, or
- anyone at less than a fair rental price.

For these purposes, family members include your brothers and sisters, half-brothers and half-sisters, spouse, ancestors (parents, grandparents, and so on) and lineal descendants (children, grandchildren, and so on). However, renting your vacation home to your aunts, uncles, nieces, nephews, cousins, or friends does not count as personal use. If you rent your vacation home to anyone in this group of people *for a fair market price*, it is considered rental use.

The following examples were created by the IRS to help show how to determine days of personal use. (IRS Publication 527, *Residential Rental Property.*)

EXAMPLE 1: You and your neighbor are co-owners of a condominium at the beach. You rent the unit to vacationers whenever possible. The unit is not used as a main home by anyone. Your neighbor uses the unit for two weeks every year. Because your neighbor is co-owner of the unit, both of you are considered to have used the unit for personal purposes during those two weeks.

EXAMPLE 2: You own a rental property that you rent to your son. Your son has no interest in this property. He uses it as his main home. He pays you a fair rental price for the property. Your son's use of the property is not personal use by you because your son is using it as his main home, he has no interest in the property, and he is paying you a fair rental price. This rental is treated like any other normal rental.

EXAMPLE 3: You rent your beach house to Rosa. Rosa rents her house in the mountains to you. You each pay a fair rental price. You are using your house for personal purposes on the days that Rosa uses it because your house is used by Rosa under an arrangement that allows you to use her house.

EXAMPLE 4: You rent an apartment to your mother at less than a fair rental price. You are using the apartment for personal purposes on the days that your mother rents it because you rent it for less than a fair rental price.

Days Used for Repairs and Maintenance

Any day that you spend working substantially full-time repairing and maintaining your property is not counted as a day of personal use. You don't have to count such a day as a day of personal use even if family members use the property for recreation on the same day.

> **EXAMPLE:** You own a cabin in the mountains that you rent during the summer. You spend three days at the cabin each May, working full-time to repair anything that was damaged over the winter and to get the cabin ready for the summer. You also spend three days each September, working full-time to repair any damage done by renters and getting the cabin ready for the winter. These six days do not count as days of personal use even if your family uses the cabin while you are repairing it.

You also don't need to count days you spend seeking tenants or dealing with realtors as personal days.

Deduct Your Travel Expenses

You may deduct your travel expenses when you journey to your vacation home to do repairs, maintenance, or deal with tenants or realtors. These consist of car expenses, airfare, or other transportation expenses if you don't travel by car, and meals eaten along the way. (See Chapter 11 for a detailed discussion.)

The best way to determine a fair rental price is to obtain a written opinion from a real estate professional familiar with the vacation home rental market in the area. If you can't do this, look at rental listings for similar properties. Be sure to keep records of how you determined the fair rental price.

Trouble with Timeshares

A timeshare property is a vacation home that several people own together and share the use of. Ordinarily, you can rent your timeshare interest, but you can forget about obtaining the favorable tax treatment given to vacation homes used as rentals discussed above. This is because personal use by any owner of a timeshare is considered personal use by all of the owners—for example, if you use your timeshare zero days, but the other owners use it 300 days, you have 300 days of personal use. This makes it virtually impossible for you to satisfy the fewer-than-15-days or 10% personal use tests. Thus, a timeshare you rent out will almost certainly fall within the vacation home used as residence category—the least favorable of the vacation home categories.

Calculating Rental Use

Any day you rent your vacation home at a fair market rent is a day of rental use no matter who you rent it to, unless it's a family member who doesn't live there full-time. Any day you rent your vacation home to anyone for less than a fair rental price is considered a day of personal use.

A fair rental price for your property is the amount of rent that a person who is not related to you would be willing to pay. The rent you charge is not a fair rental price if it is substantially less than the rents charged for other properties that are similar to your property.

Putting Your Calculations Together

Let's look at a comprehensive example to see how these rules operate. Dick owns a vacation home that he used himself for 14 days and rented as follows:
- two days to his brother, who paid a fair rental price, but doesn't live in the home full-time
- four days to his mother, who paid nothing
- 14 days to a stranger who paid a fair market rental, and
- two days to a friend from the office who paid a below-fair-market price.

Dick's own use is personal use. The two days he rented it his brother are also personal days because his brother doesn't live there full-time. The four days his mother used the house are also personal days. The 14 days he rented it to strangers for a fair market price are rental days. The two days he let a friend use it for a below-market rental are personal days. His totals for the year are:
- Rental days = 14
- Personal days = 22

The vacation home qualifies as a tax-free vacation home because it was used personally more than 14 days and rented fewer than 15 days. This means Dick need not pay any income tax on the rental income he received. Had Dick rented it to the strangers for one more day, the house would have come within the vacation home used as residence category with very different tax results.

Converting Your Home to a Rental Property

The vacation home tax rules do not apply when you convert your main home to a rental property—that is, it is used only by renters, not shared by you and renters. Instead, you treat the home like any other rental property as described in the other chapters of this book.

This is so if:

- you rented or tried to rent the property for 12 or more consecutive months, or
- you rented or tried to rent the property for less than 12 consecutive months and the period ended because you sold the property.

In this event, you check the "no" boxes in Section 2 of Schedule E where the IRS asks if you made personal use of the home more than 14 days or 10% of the rental days.

> **EXAMPLE 1:** On February 28, 2008, Mark moved out of the house he had lived in for six years because he accepted a job in another town. He rented his house at a fair rental price on April 1, signing a one-year lease with his tenant. Mark need not treat the house as a vacation home on his 2008 taxes, even though both he and renters lived in it. He may deduct his operating expenses, taxes, interest and depreciation for the period it was rented during the year.

> **EXAMPLE 2:** On January 31, Melissa moved out of the condominium where she had lived for three years. She offered it for rent at a fair rental price beginning on February 1. She was unable to rent it until April. On September 15, she sold the condominium. Melissa need not treat the condo as a vacation home. Instead, she treats the condo as a rental for tax purposes while she offered it for rent and actually rented it. Thus, she may deduct the operating expenses, taxes, interest, and depreciation she incurred from February 1 until September 15.

Chapter 16

Deducting Rental Losses

I f, like many landlords, your tax deductions from your rental properties exceed your rental income, this is the single most important chapter in this book. Complex IRS rules may prevent you from deducting all or part of your rental losses from the other income you earn during the year, which could end up costing you thousands of dollars in extra taxes. However, there are also important exceptions to the rules that were created to help small landlords and others in the real estate industry.

Even if you're fortunate enough to earn a profit each year from your rentals, you still need to know about these rules and how they affect you. This chapter explains the rules in detail.

What Are Rental Losses?

You have a rental loss if all the deductions from a rental property you own exceed the annual rent and other money you receive from the property. If you own multiple properties, the annual income or losses from each property are combined (netted) to determine if you have income or loss from all your rental activities for the year. You report your rental income and deductible expenses on IRS Schedule E.

EXAMPLE: Tanya owns two rental houses. She receives $24,000 annually in rent from each house. She reports her annual expenses for the properties on Schedule E as follows:

Expense	Amount—House A	Amount—House B
Advertising	$ 100	$ 0
Auto and travel	200	200
Cleaning and maintenance	1,500	500
Insurance	2,000	1,800
Mortgage interest	10,000	7,000
Other interest	700	0
Repairs	600	1,000
Supplies	2,000	1,500
Taxes	2,400	2,000
Utilities	2,500	2,000
Depreciation	8,000	7,000
Total Expenses	$ 30,000	$23,000
Rents Received	$ 24,000	$24,000
Total Expenses	− 30,000	− 23,000
Income or (Loss)	$ (6,000)	$ 1,000

Tanya's deductible expenses for House A exceeded the $24,000 in rent she received by $6,000. Thus, she had a $6,000 rental loss for the year for the property. She had $1,000 of income on House B—her expenses for that property were $23,000 and she received $24,000 rent. Tanya subtracts her rental losses (the $6,000 loss on House A) from her rental income (the $1,000 profit on House B), leaving her with a $5,000 loss for the year from all her rental activities.

It is extremely common for landlords to have rental losses, especially in the first few years they own a property. Indeed, IRS statistics show that in the year 2003, over half of the filed Schedule E forms reporting rental income and expenses showed a loss. So if you have a rental loss, you have plenty of company.

Often, you have a loss for tax purposes even if your rental income exceeds your operating expenses. This is because your depreciation deduction is included as an expense for these purposes (even though depreciation is not an operating expense—see Chapter 3 for more on operating expenses). Without the depreciation deduction, Tanya (in the above example) would have had income of $2,000 from House A, instead of a $6,000 loss.

If you have a rental loss for the year, you become subject to two sets of tax rules:

- the passive loss rules, and
- the at-risk rules.

The passive loss rules are by far the most important for most landlords, so we will discuss those rules first.

Overview of the Passive Loss Rules

Fasten your seat belts: We are about to embark on one of the most complicated, confusing, and frightening journeys a rental property owner can take—into the realm of the passive activity loss rules (PAL rules, for short). These rules can make you or break you come tax time.

What Are the PAL Rules For?

Twenty years ago, landlords could freely deduct their rental losses from all of the other income they or their spouses earned during the year (assuming they filed a joint return). However, the unfettered deductibility of real estate losses led to enormous abuses. In the 1980s, wealthy individuals invested in real estate limited partnerships and other tax shelters created solely to generate large losses through depreciation, interest, and other deductions. The investors in these tax shelters would use the losses to offset their other income. The tax benefits obtained could far exceed the amount of money invested in the tax shelter.

All this came to an abrupt end in 1986, when Congress enacted the passive activity loss rules. (IRC Sec. 469.) These rules were designed to limit a taxpayer's ability to use rental or business losses to offset other income. The PAL rules apply to all business activities, but are particularly strict for rental real estate because real estate was the primary tax shelter.

How the PAL Rules Work

Most landlords earn income and incur expenses from more than one source—in addition to income and expenses from their rental property, they may earn a salary from a job, or make money from a business they own. They may also have investments other than rental property, such as stocks and bonds.

For purposes of the PAL rules, all the income you earn, and losses you incur, are divided into three separate categories:

- **Active income or loss.** Income or loss from any business activity, other than real estate rentals, in which you materially participate (actively manage); see "The Real Estate Professional Exemption" for a detailed discussion of material participation. This includes salary and other income from a job, a business you run, or the money you earn from selling your personal services. Social Security benefits are included as well.
- **Passive income or loss.** Income or loss from (1) businesses in which you don't materially participate, and (2) all rental properties you own. Under the rules, income and loss from rental activities are automatically passive, whether or not the landlord materially participates in the rental activity. (Casualty losses from rental property are not passive losses—see Chapter 13).
- **Portfolio income or loss.** Income or loss from investments, such as interest earned on savings, or dividends earned on stocks; gains or losses when investments are sold; expenses paid for investments.

Imagine three buckets, one for each of the three kinds of income or loss. Every penny you earn during the year must go into one of three buckets. In addition, all the money you spend on investments or business activities, such as a rental real estate business, any business you actively manage, or any self-employment activity, also goes into one of the buckets. Money you spend for personal purposes, such as food and clothing, is not counted.

Active income or loss. Income or loss from your job or business activities (other than real estate rentals) in which you materially participate.

Passive income or loss. Income or loss from rental properties or businesses in which you don't materially participate.

Portfolio income or loss. Income or loss from any investments.

Here's the key to the PAL rules: The contents of the passive bucket must always stay in that bucket. You cannot use passive losses to offset income in the other two buckets. Nor can you use passive income to offset losses from the other buckets.

> **EXAMPLE:** Sidney is a successful doctor. This year, he has $200,000 in income from his practice and also earns $50,000 in income from investments. Sidney invests $25,000 in a real estate limited partnership tax shelter. The partnership owns several rental properties that operate at a substantial loss. At the end of the year, the partnership informs Sidney that his share of the partnership's annual operating loss is $75,000. Sidney's three buckets look like this:

Active	**Passive**	**Portfolio**
$200,000 medical practice income	$75,000 rental loss	$50,000 investment income

Sidney invested in the limited partnership because he wanted to use his share of the losses it generated to reduce his taxable income from his medical practice. However, come tax time, he's in for a shock. Because income or loss must stay in the passive bucket, Sidney cannot deduct his $75,000 passive loss from his medical practice income or his investment income. Because he earned no passive income during the year, he can't use his passive loss at all this year. His real estate tax shelter turned out to be useless.

This is what the PAL rules are intended to do: prevent you from deducting your passive losses (such as from rental activities) from your active or portfolio income. Thus, there is no point in investing in real estate rentals just to incur tax losses because you won't be able to use these losses to offset your other non-real estate income.

The PAL rules have accomplished their purpose of preventing wealthy people from investing in rental real estate solely to create tax losses. But the rules apply to all owners of rental property, even landlords who are in the business of renting properties to earn a living and have no interest in obtaining tax losses. To prevent undue economic hardship on these people, special rules were created that wholly or partly exempt many small landlords and people active in the real estate industry from the PAL rules. These are:

- the $25,000 offset, and
- the real estate professional exemption.

➡ **Owners of vacation homes and other short-term rentals aren't subject to the PAL rental activity rules.** If you own only these types of properties, you can skip ahead to "Vacation Homes."

The $25,000 Offset

Congress felt it was unfair to prevent landlords with moderate incomes from deducting their rental losses from their nonrental income. Thus, a special exception—the $25,000 offset—was fashioned for them. It permits landlords to deduct up to $25,000 in rental losses from any other nonpassive income they earn during the year. The offset applies to all rental properties that a landlord owns—that is, you don't get a separate $25,000 for each property you own. (IRC Sec. 469(i).)

> **EXAMPLE:** Recall Tanya from the example at the beginning of the chapter. She owned two rental houses and had a $6,000 loss from one and $1,000 in income from the other. She also has a job that pays her an $80,000 salary. In addition, Tanya earned $10,000 in dividends from stocks and incurred $1,000 in investment expenses (stockbroker commissions), leaving her with $9,000 in investment income. Her three buckets look like this:

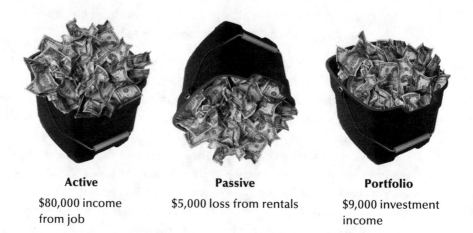

Active	Passive	Portfolio
$80,000 income from job	$5,000 loss from rentals	$9,000 investment income

If Tanya were not a landlord, the PAL rules would bar her from deducting her passive loss from her rentals from her active or portfolio income. However, if Tanya qualifies for the $25,000 offset, which is available only for landlords, she can deduct her $5,000 loss from her nonpassive income that includes her salary and investment income.

The $25,000 offset is particularly important to small landlords. If your income isn't much over $100,000 and your annual rental losses are less than $25,000, it can give you complete relief from the onerous PAL rules.

Requirements

To qualify for the $25,000 offset, you must:

- actively participate in your rental activity
- come within the income limits, and
- be at least a 10% owner of the rental activity.

Any individual who meets these requirements may use the $25,000 offset. This is so whether he or she owns rental property alone or with one or more co-owners. General partners in partnerships that own rental property may use the exemption, but not limited partners. Nor can it be used for property owned by a corporation or trust.

Active Participation

You qualify for the $25,000 offset only if you actively participate in the running of your rental real estate. This is very easy to do. You don't have to work any set number of hours to actively participate; you simply have to be the person who makes the final decisions about approving tenants, arranging for repairs, setting rents, and other management tasks. If you manage your rentals yourself, you'll satisfy this requirement without any problem. The IRS probably won't even raise the issue if you're audited. Management tasks performed by your spouse are also counted in determining if you actively participate. (IRC Sec. 469(i)(6)(D).)

The only time you could have trouble with this requirement is if you hire a resident or nonresident manager or management company to manage your property for you. You cannot simply let the manager do everything. To actively participate, you or your spouse must exercise independent judgment, and not simply okay the actions of a manager or management company. For example, you must be the one who makes such important decisions as what the rent will be and whether to do a major repair or improvement. The manager can make recommendations about such matters, but the final decision must be yours. (S. Rep. No. 313, 99th Cong., 2d Sess. 738 (1986).)

Some management firms automatically issue letters to their clients stating that the client is "actively involved in management of the rental" and approves tenants, arranges for repairs, sets rental fees, and so on. IRS training materials advise IRS auditors to ignore such letters. Instead, if an IRS auditor questions whether you actively participate, he or she is instructed to ask to see a copy of your contract with your management company—the contract should show who has the right to make the final decisions. (Market Segment Specialization Program, *Passive Activity Losses Reference Guide*, pp. 2–7.)

Read your management contract and make sure it provides that you make the final decisions on important rental matters. It should read something like this: "Client shall make all major management decisions for the property, including final approval of all new tenants, rental rates, and repairs over $_____."

Although a well-drafted contract will help show that you actively participate, be sure to document and keep copies of any correspondence with the management company (including emails) that establish your involvement in decision making and the management of the property.

Income (MAGI) Limits

The $25,000 offset is intended for landlords who earn moderate incomes. If your modified adjusted gross income (MAGI) is less than $100,000, you're entitled to the full $25,000 offset. It goes down as your MAGI increases, and is eliminated completely once your modified adjusted gross income exceeds $150,000. (IRC Sec. 469(i)(3).)

Your MAGI consists of all your taxable income for the year, not including taxable Social Security benefits and passive activity income or loss, minus the following expenses:

- self-employed health insurance premiums paid during the year
- contributions to SIMPLE retirement plans and Keogh retirement plans
- alimony paid during the year
- deductible tuition, fees, and student loan interest, and
- penalties for early withdrawal of savings. (IRC Sec. 469(i)(3)(F).)

For most taxpayers, their MAGI is all of their income, not counting their passive income or loss. If you get Social Security, you also deduct this amount from your income. Not being able to deduct passive losses from your MAGI can make it more difficult to fall within the $100,000 to $150,000 MAGI range.

> **EXAMPLE:** Ronald, a self-employed person, earned $150,000 in net income from his engineering consulting business this year and $5,000 in investment income. He also owned an apartment building that had a $25,000 loss. He can't deduct the $25,000 passive loss from the apartment building from his business or investment income. Because his MAGI is $155,000, he is not eligible for any offset.

The offset amount is $25,000 for both single and married taxpayers filing joint returns. Married people who file separate tax returns and live separately for the entire year are each entitled to a $12,500 offset. However, married people who file separate returns and live together *any time* during the year get no offset at all. (IRC Sec. 469(i)(5)(B).)

The phase-out of the $25,000 offset works as follows. For every dollar your MAGI exceeds $100,000, you reduce your $25,000 offset by 50 cents. For example, if your MAGI is $110,000, you reduce your offset by $5,000 (50 cents x $10,000 = $5,000). In that case, you could deduct only $20,000 in passive losses for the year ($25,000 - $5,000 = $20,000). Once your MAGI is $150,000 or more, your offset disappears entirely (50 cents x $50,000 = $25,000).

There are a few ways you might be able to reduce your MAGI if it exceeds $150,000, or if you want to increase the amount of offset you are eligible for. One way is to defer some of the compensation you're owed to the following year. Another way is to make contributions to a Keogh plan, which you can deduct from your MAGI.

EXAMPLE: Ronald's MAGI for the year is $155,000—he has $150,000 in net income from his engineering consulting business and $5,000 in investment income. He also has a $25,000 loss from an apartment building that he owns. Ronald makes a $15,000 contribution to his Keogh plan and tells one of his clients not to pay the $40,000 the client owes him until the following year. Ronald thereby reduces his MAGI from $155,000 to $100,000 and can now deduct the full $25,000 offset amount.

Lottery Winners Lose Out in Tax Court

Edward and Yolanda Hamilton owned rental property in Los Angeles. They incurred rental losses of $22,000 on the property in 2000. That same year, they won $136,000 in the California state lottery. While they were undoubtedly thrilled to win this money, it had some unexpected tax consequences for them. Without their lottery winnings, their MAGI was under $150,000 and they were eligible for the full $25,000 offset for their rental losses for the year. But when the IRS insisted they add their $136,000 lottery winnings to their MAGI, they were way over the $150,000 limit and became ineligible for the offset. They appealed to the tax court, claiming they shouldn't have to include the lottery winnings in their MAGI because they were not professional gamblers. The court held that they were out of luck. (*Hamilton v. Comm'r.*, T.C. Memo. 2004-161.)

Ownership Requirement

To qualify for the offset, you must own at least 10% of all interests in your real estate activity for the entire year. If you're married, your spouse's ownership interests can be counted too. The ownership percentage is determined by the value of the property. For example, if the rental property is worth $100,000, you must own at least $10,000. If you own more than one rental building, you must own 10% or more of each building. (IRC Sec. 469(i)(6)(A).)

This rule should not pose a problem for most small landlords. However, it eliminates most owners of vacation timeshares, because a person who buys a timeshare usually obtains less than a 10% interest in the property. (*Toups v. Comm'r.*, 66 TCM 370.)

If you own a condominium, you need own only 10% of the value of your particular condominium unit, not 10% of the entire building that contains many separate condominium units.

$25,000 Limit Applies to Tax Credits

Some rental property owners can obtain tax credits by rehabilitating their rental property or from the low-income housing tax credit. A tax credit is subtracted from your tax liability after you calculate your taxes. (See Chapter 1.) Because these credits come from your rental property, they go into your passive income and loss bucket, and are subject to the same passive loss rules as the rental property deduction. However, they get particularly favorable treatment when it comes to the $25,000 offset. You don't need to satisfy the active participation requirement to deduct these credits as part of your offset. In addition, for these credits, the phase-out of the $25,000 offset starts when your modified adjusted gross income exceeds $200,000 ($100,000 if you are a married individual filing a separate return and living apart at all times during the year). There is no phase-out of the $25,000 offset for low-income housing credits for property placed in service after 1989. But there's a catch: You can deduct these credits only to the extent you have taxable passive income for the year—no income, no credit. The credits are suspended to a future year when you have net passive income you must pay income tax on. Use IRS Form 8582-CR, Passive Activity Credit Limitations, to figure your allowable annual credit. (IRC Sec. 469(j)(5).)

Determining Your Offset Deduction

Here's how to determine your deduction from the offset:

- First, subtract your passive activity deductions from your passive income. You should have a net loss; otherwise, you won't need the offset. For example, suppose Tess has two apartment buildings. One earned a $5,000 profit, the other had a $15,000 loss. Tess has a $10,000 passive loss for the year.
- Next, determine the amount of the offset you're eligible for. This will be $25,000 if your MAGI is $100,000 or less. Your offset will be less than

$25,000 if your MAGI is $100,000 to $150,000. You get no offset at all if your MAGI is $150,000 or more. Suppose Tess's MAGI is $75,000. She qualifies for the full $25,000 offset. However, she only has $10,000 in passive losses this year, so she can't use the remaining $15,000 of the offset.

- Then, deduct the applicable amount of your offset from your active or portfolio income. Tess deducts her $10,000 passive loss from her active income, reducing it to $65,000 in taxable income for the year.

The Real Estate Professional Exemption

People in the real estate industry moaned and groaned about the passive loss rules. Because the PAL rules were intended to curtail the use of real estate tax shelters by passive investors, those actively engaged in the real estate business felt it was unfair to have the rules apply to them. Congress agreed and created a special exemption from the passive loss rules for real estate professionals. This rule provides more relief than the $25,000 offset because there is no maximum offset amount or income limit requirements.

People who qualify for the real estate professional exemption can treat all of their losses from rental properties as active losses. This means they can deduct any rental activity losses they have for the year from all of their other income for the year, including active income and portfolio income. (IRC Sec. 469(c)(7).) The exemption is particularly important and useful for people with high incomes or large rental losses.

Make sure the exemption applies to your type of business entity. The real estate professional exemption can be used by landlords who are individuals (including joint tenants and tenants in common), general partnerships, limited liability companies taxed like partnerships (most are), and S corporations. C corporations qualify only if 51% or more of their gross receipts come from real property businesses in which they materially participate. The exemption does not apply to limited partnerships, estates, and most types of trusts.

Do you have to worry about this stuff? The real estate professional exemption involves some very complex tax rules. Not every landlord needs to learn these rules. If, like many small landlords, you (and your spouse if you're married and file a joint return) work fewer than 750 hours at being a landlord and any other real estate activities during the year, you can skip this section. The exemption won't apply to you. On the other hand, if the $25,000 offset doesn't provide you with the relief you need from the PAL rules, you may choose to read this material to see how you can qualify for the exemption in the future.

> ⚠️ **If you're a real estate professional—including a real estate broker, salesperson, developer, contractor, or real property manager—be sure to read this section carefully.** You may very well qualify for the exemption, and, if you do, you must take it. Unlike the $25,000 offset discussed in the previous section, the real estate professional exemption is not optional. If you qualify for it, you must apply it to your income and loss for the year. Usually this is a very good thing, but in some cases it can be costly.

The Three-Part Test

To qualify for the real estate professional exemption, you must satisfy *all* of the following three tests:

- **51% test.** You (or your spouse, if you file a joint return) spend more than half of your working hours during the year working in one or more real property businesses.
- **751-hour test.** You (or your spouse, if you file a joint return) spend more than 751 hours a year in one or more real property businesses.
- **Material participation test.** You and your spouse materially participate in your rental activity and any other real property businesses you use to pass the 51% and 751-hour tests.

For the first two tests, each spouse's time is taken into account separately. Thus, one spouse alone must satisfy the 51% and 751-hour requirements. For the third test, both spouses' time together is counted if they file a joint return.

Small landlords usually have little trouble passing the material participation test. It's the 51% and 751-hour tests that give them problems. To pass them, you or your spouse may need to spend more time working on your rental properties or in some other real estate business.

Because this test is based on number of hours and percentage of time, you'll need to keep track of both the time you spend on real estate activities and other non-real estate work to prove you satisfy these requirements.

51% Test

The exemption is for real estate professionals, so it makes sense that you (or your spouse) must spend more than half (51%) of your working hours during the year running a "real property trade or business." Your working hours are the hours you spend personally working in a trade or business, including the time you spend being a landlord, running another business, or working as an employee. Don't count the time you spend working on your personal investments.

A real property trade or business means any real property development, redevelopment, construction, reconstruction, acquisition, conversion, rental, operation, management, leasing, or brokerage business. (IRC Sec. 469(c)(7)(C).) This covers virtually any real estate business activity. Most people who qualify for the exemption are engaged in one of the following activities:

- real estate rentals
- construction (contractor or builder)
- real estate brokerage work, or
- real property management.

You must be directly involved in one or more of these real property businesses to qualify for the exemption. Thus, for example, an attorney or accountant is not in the real property business, even if he or she advises people who are in the business. Mortgage brokers, lenders, and bankers probably don't qualify either, because it's likely the IRS would view them as involved in the financial services industry, not real estate. Real estate sales agents, on the other hand, probably do qualify for the exemption. This is because they are usually paid on a straight commission basis which makes them independent contractors, not employees, for tax purposes. As independent contractors, they are in business and, therefore, should qualify for the exemption—although neither the IRS nor the courts have yet ruled on the question.

If you are an employee in someone else's real property business, you do not qualify for the real estate professional exemption. You must own your own real property business or be a part owner of a business with more than a 5% ownership interest. If you work as an employee for a corporation, you must own more than 5% of your employer's outstanding stock.

If you work full-time at something other than a real property business, it will be hard to pass the 51% test. For example, if you work 40 hours per week at a non-real property business, you would have to work an average of 41 hours per week at one or more real estate activities to pass the test. This would require you to put in an 81-hour week. The IRS is not likely to believe you do this unless you have extremely convincing documentation. IRS auditors are instructed to look carefully at W-2 forms when they audit a taxpayer who claims the real estate professional exemption. If the W-2 shows that the taxpayer has a job not in real estate, the auditor will question whether the 51% test has been satisfied.

On the other hand, if you're married, you can work full-time at a non–real property business and still meet the test if your spouse spends all (or at least over half) of his or her work time managing your rental properties.

> **EXAMPLE:** Leo and Leona are married and file a joint return. Leo is a physician, and doesn't spend any time working on real estate. Leona spends 100% of her annual work time managing apartment buildings the couple own. The test is satisfied because Leona spends more than half of her time working in the real property business.
>
> If Leo spends 20% of his time managing their rental property and Leona spends 40% of her time on real property business, they will not satisfy the 51% test. To meet the 51% test, one spouse must spend at least 51% of his or her time working at a real property business—you can't combine time to reach the 51%.

If you or your spouse is involved in more than one real property business, you can add the time you spend in each of the businesses to see if you pass the 51% test.

> **EXAMPLE:** John works 800 hours per year as a part-time bookkeeper. He owns rental property on which he works 100 hours per year. He also works 701 hours per year as a real estate broker. John passes the 51% test because he spent a combined 801 hours working in real estate businesses and 800 hours in other activities.

Lawyer Flunks 51% Test

Judy Bailey, an attorney, rented out two condominiums, a house, and a four-unit apartment building. In 1997, she had a total rental loss of more than $34,000. Her efforts to deduct these losses from her nonpassive income were rejected by the IRS and tax court. The court held that she failed to qualify for the real estate professional exemption because her records showed she spent 876 hours practicing law in 1997, but only 828 hours managing her rentals. (*Bailey v. Comm'r*, T.C. Memo 2001-296.)

751-Hour Test

It's not enough that you (or your spouse) spend more than half of your work time in a real property business. After all, if you had no other work, you'd spend more than half your work time on real estate if you spent only one hour a year on it. To avoid this result, you or your spouse must spend at least 751 hours per year working at your real property business or businesses. This amounts to only 14.5 hours a week. Again, if you work in more than one real property business, you may combine the time you spend on each.

> **EXAMPLE:** John worked 200 hours per year on his rental properties and 601 hours as a real estate broker. By combining both of these real estate business activities, John exceeds the 751-hour limit.

People like John, who work full- or parttime as a real estate broker, contractor, developer, or other real estate professional, will likely have little trouble meeting the 751-hour requirement. The people who have trouble passing this test are those whose sole real property business is managing their rentals. If you own only a few units, it's unlikely you will need to spend 751 hours per year dealing with them. (And, ironically, if you have stable, long-term tenants who place few demands on their landlord, you'll have less reason to spend time on that rental.) One real property management expert estimates that landlords who manage their rental properties themselves must spend four hours working on each unit per month. At that rate, you would need to own at least 16 rental units to work 751 hours per year.

You will need to spend far less time on your rentals if you hire a competent resident manager or management company to take care of your property for you—probably as much as 90% less; this is so, even though the time you spend overseeing your manager counts as landlord work hours. In that case, you would probably need to own at least 200 units to spend 751 hours per year on real estate business.

Material Participation Test

Material participation is the ketchup of the real estate professional exemption—it has to cover everything. Material participation is what makes an activity active instead of passive for tax purposes. You (or your spouse) must materially participate in:

- your real property business or businesses, and
- in each rental real estate activity you want to treat as nonpassive.

If you fail to materially participate in a real estate business, you can't count the hours you spend working at it for purposes of the 51% or 751-hour tests. So, even if you work the number of hours and percentage of time necessary for the real estate professional exemption, you will not get the exemption if you can't show that you also materially participate in the real estate activity.

You materially participate in a business only if you are in involved with its day-to-day operations on a regular, continuous, and substantial basis. (IRC Sec. 469(h).) The IRS has created several tests to determine material participation, based on the amount of time you spend working in real estate activities. You only need to pass one of the tests to show material participation. Most people use one or more of the first three tests.

500-hour test. You participated in the activity for more than 500 hours during the year.

You did substantially all the work. You did substantially all the work in the activity during the year. To qualify for this, you will probably need to show that you worked at least 71% of the total hours devoted to the activity by all of the people involved. This includes hours spent working on the property by co-owners, employees, and independent contractors, such as property managers.

101-hour test. You participated in the business for more than 100 hours during the year, and you participated at least as much as any other person (including employees and independent contractors, such as property managers).

Combo test. You spent between 100 to 500 hours on two or more real estate businesses, so that your combined hours in real estate total more than 500.

Past performance test. You satisfy any of the IRS tests for material participation for any five of the last ten years.

Facts and circumstances test. The facts and circumstances show that you materially participated. You can't use this test if (1) you didn't participate in the activity for at least 101 hours; (2) anyone worked more than you; or (3) anyone was paid to manage the activity.

You apply these tests first to all your real estate businesses, including your rental real estate activities; and then to your rental real estate activities alone. The time you spend on real estate businesses other than rentals is not considered when you determine if you materially participated in your rental activity.

If you own more than one rental property, each one is a separate rental activity, unless you designate otherwise. You can file a statement (called an election) with your tax return stating that you want all of your rental activities treated as one single activity. This way, you can combine the time you spend

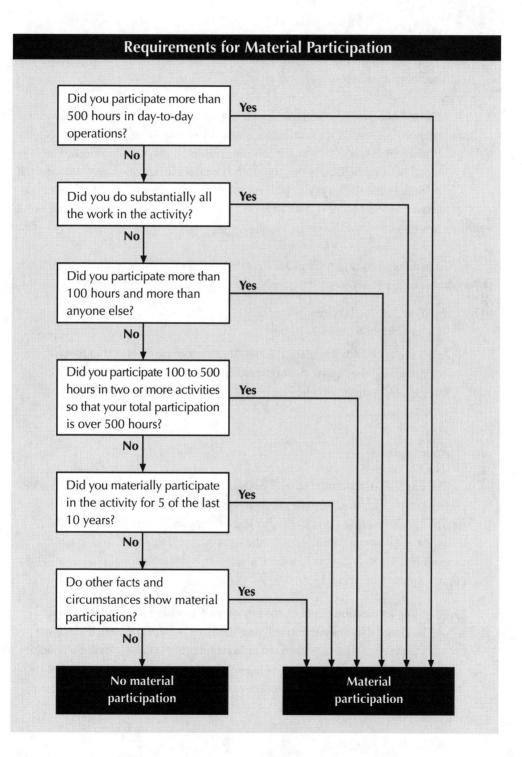

Requirements for Material Participation

Did you participate more than 500 hours in day-to-day operations? — **Yes** → Material participation

No

Did you do substantially all the work in the activity? — **Yes** → Material participation

No

Did you participate more than 100 hours and more than anyone else? — **Yes** → Material participation

No

Did you participate 100 to 500 hours in two or more activities so that your total participation is over 500 hours? — **Yes** → Material participation

No

Did you materially participate in the activity for 5 of the last 10 years? — **Yes** → Material participation

No

Do other facts and circumstances show material participation? — **Yes** → Material participation

No

No material participation

Material participation

working on each rental property to satisfy the material participation tests. If you fail to file the election, you'll have to show that you materially participated in each rental property you own.

> **EXAMPLE:** Dennis owns five rental homes and he does all the work on the properties himself. He works 101 hours a year managing all five properties. If he files an election with his tax return to treat all of his properties as one rental activity, he'll pass the 100 hour material participation test. However, if he fails to file the election, he'll have to materially participate for each house he owns—that is, he'd have to work 101 hours on each house, instead of all five together.

To make an election to treat all your rental activities as one activity, you'll need to draft a statement like the one below and attach it to your tax return:

Tax Year: _____ Taxpayer Name: _____
Taxpayer Identification Number: _____

In accordance with Regulation 1.469-9(g)(3), taxpayer states that he/she is a qualifying real estate professional, and elects under IRC Section 469(c)(7)(A) to treat all interests in real estate as a single rental real estate activity.

_____

Your Signature

The election can be filed in any year in which you qualify for the real estate professional exemption. It only needs to be filed once—it applies automatically to all future years that you qualify for the exemption. It may be revoked only if you have a material change in circumstances. The fact that the election is less advantageous to you in a particular year is not a material change in circumstances. (IRS Reg. 1.469-9(g).)

⚠️ **Filing an election could cause problems if you have suspended losses.** Suspended losses are unused passive losses from prior years. If you have substantial suspended losses from multiple rental properties, think carefully before filing an election to treat them as a single activity. The election could make it difficult for you to deduct your suspended losses when you sell your property.

Activities That Don't Count as Participation

Any work you do for a business that you own, wholly or in part, counts as participation in the business, unless:

- the work is not customarily done by owners of that type of activity, and
- one of your main reasons for doing the work is to avoid application of the PAL rules. (IRS Reg. 1.469-5(f)(2)(i).)

EXAMPLE: Martha has her own small real estate development company, which is co-owned by her husband, Bob. This year, business is slow. Martha figures that she'll end up spending only 500 hours working at the business for the year. To pass the 751 hour test, she hires her husband Bob to work 251 hours answering phones and doing clerical work for the development business. Unfortunately, Bob's time does not count as participation in the real estate activity because answering phones and doing clerical work is not work customarily done by the owner of a real estate development business.

In addition, you do not treat work you do in your capacity as an investor as participation in your real estate activity. This includes:

- studying and reviewing financial statements or reports on the activity's operations—including time spent reading this book!
- preparing or compiling summaries or analyses of the finances or operations of the activity for your own use, and
- monitoring the activity's finances or operations in a nonmanagerial capacity—for example, reviewing rental statements you receive from a rental management company that manages your property for you. (IRS Reg. 1.469-5(f)(2)(ii).)

Courts have held that the time you spend organizing your personal records, preparing your taxes, paying bills, and reviewing monthly statements prepared by a real estate management company all constitute investor activities. (*Barniskis v. Comm'r.*, TC Memo 1999-258.) Time you spend doing these tasks cannot be counted to pass the material participation tests.

Absentee landlords who hire real property managers to do all of their work for them may have difficulty passing the material participation test. To materially participate, a landlord must be involved with the day-to-day operation of the rental property, something absentee landlords often don't do. If you live a substantial distance away from your rental property, the IRS will likely question whether you are really involved in day-to-day operations.

EXAMPLE: Josephine owns two five-unit apartment buildings in Las Vegas, but lives in Houston. She hires a real property management company to manage the properties. She is not involved with the day-to-day management of the buildings. Her involvement is limited to approving the management company's decisions. This year, she spent 50 hours dealing with her management company. She spent another 25 hours reading financial statements and otherwise dealing with her investment. Josephine has not materially participated in her rental activity. None of the time she spends reading financial statements counts as material participation. This leaves her with just 50 hours of work during the year, not enough to materially participate under any of the tests. She clearly doesn't satisfy the 500-hour or 101-hour tests. Nor does she meet the "you-did-all-the-work" test because the management company did most of the work.

If you're married, you combine the time your spouse spends materially participating in the business with your own time. This is so whether or not you and your spouse file a joint return. (IRS Reg. 1.469-9(c)(4).) This can make it much easier to pass one of the material participation tests.

EXAMPLE: Frank and Felicia are married and file a joint return. They own a four-unit apartment building they manage themselves. Felicia does most of the work, spending 400 hours a year dealing with tenants, showing vacant units, handling bookkeeping chores, and so forth. Frank does most of the repair work for the property, spending 120 hours a year on it. Together, Frank and Felicia spent 520 hours materially participating in their rental real estate activity—more than enough to pass the 500 hour test.

If you have more than one real estate activity and you fail to materially participate in one or more of them, you might still be able to deduct your passive losses by using the $25,000 offset. To do this, you need only actively participate in the rental activity. This requires much less time and effort than the more onerous material participation requirement.

Applying the Test

To put it mildly, the rules for the real estate professional exemption are complicated. The easiest way to see if you qualify is to break them down and apply them step-by-step, as shown below.

Step 1: Determine hours you worked in real estate. Figure the number of hours you and your spouse spent on each of your real property businesses during the year, including your rental activity. Do this separately for each activity—for example, your rental activity, real estate brokerage, real property management, or construction. Count only work performed in a real estate business or rental activity in which you or your spouse is a more than 5% owner.

Step 2: Determine if you materially participated in each of your real estate activities. Determine if you and your spouse materially participated in each activity by applying the material participation tests. Combine your hours with those of your spouse to determine material participation in each activity.

Step 3: Determine non–real estate activity hours. Determine the total number of hours you and your wife worked in non-real estate work during the year, whether as an employee, or in a non-real property business you wholly or partly own. Don't consider material participation here. Make separate tallies of the hours for your spouse and yourself.

Step 4: Determine if you pass the 51% test. Compare the total number of hours you worked on real estate activities, including rental activities in which you materially participated, with the number of hours you worked on non-real estate activities. (Don't consider the time you spent working on real estate activities in which you didn't materially participate.) Do the same for your spouse. Unless you or your spouse spent 51% or more of your total work hours on real estate activities, you don't qualify for the exemption.

Step 5: Determine if you pass the 751-hour test. Separately determine the total time you and your spouse each spent working on real property activities during the year in which you materially participated. Don't include the time you or your spouse spent on non-rental real property activities. If you or your spouse spent at least 751 hours on rental real estate activities, you qualify for the real property professional exemption from the PAL rules.

Let's apply this procedure to some typical small landlords, using the five steps we explained just above.

EXAMPLE 1: Max and Maxine are married and own two duplexes they rent out. They have filed an election with their tax return to treat both properties as a single rental activity for tax purposes. Max works full-time (1,800 hours per year) as an accountant. Maxine is a licensed real estate agent. She spends 2,000 hours per year working in this real property business. Max and Maxine both work at managing their rental property. This doesn't take much time.

Max spent 25 hours this year, and Maxine 80 hours. Their total hours are shown in the following charts.

Max's Activities

Real estate activities	Time spent	Non–real estate activities	Time spent
Rental property management	25 hours	Accounting	1,800 hours
Total	25 hours	Total	1,800 hours

Maxine's Activities

Real estate activities	Time spent	Non–real estate activities	Time spent
Real estate agent	1,800 hours	None	0
Rental property management	80 hours		0
Total	1,880 hours	Total	0

Step 1: Determine hours Max and Maxine worked in real estate activities. Max worked only 20 hours. Maxine worked 1,880 hours.

Step 2: Determine if Max and Maxine materially participated in each of their real estate activities. Combine the couple's hours to determine material participation. These landlords engage in two separate activities—managing rental properties and working as a real estate agent. Maxine spent 1,800 hours working at real estate brokerage—more than enough to materially participate under the 501-hour test. Together, the couple spent 105 hours managing their rental property. This is far too little for the 500-hour material participation test; but they qualify under the 101-hour test because no one else worked on their rentals as much as they did.

Step 3: Determine non–real estate activity hours. Max had 1,800 non–real estate hours, Maxine had none.

Step 4: Determine if either Maxine or Max passes the 51% test. Max can't pass the test. He spent almost all his time working at accounting. Maxine passes the test because she spent 100% of her time working on real property activities.

Step 5: Determine if they pass the 751-hour test. Max obviously can't pass this test—he spent only 25 hours working at a real property activity. Maxine easily passes—she put in a whopping 1,880 hours on real property activities.

Max and Maxine qualify for the real estate professional exemption. Now, let's consider another scenario—this time, a married couple manage several rentals, but spend no time in other real estate business. Once again, we'll discover whether these landlords can use the real estate professional exemption by applying our five steps.

EXAMPLE 2: Saul and Sally are married and own three four-unit apartment buildings and four rental houses. They have filed an election with their tax return to treat all seven properties as a single rental activity for tax purposes. Saul works full-time as an attorney. Sally manages the rental properties, spending 800 hours per year. She does no other work. Saul spends no time working on the rental property.

Step 1: Determine the hours Saul and Sally worked in real estate activities. Saul has no real property activity hours, so he is out of the picture for the exemption. Sally spent 800 hours on a single real property activity—rental real estate.

Step 2: Determine if Sally or Saul materially participated in each of their real estate activities. Sally spent well over 500 hours dealing with the day-to-day management of her rental properties, so she satisfies the 500-hour material participation test for her rental real estate activity.

Step 3: Count any non–real estate activity hours. Saul works full-time as an attorney, but Sally does no non–real estate work.

Step 4: Determine if either Sally or Saul passes the 51% test. Sally easily passes the 51% test, because she spent 100% of her work time on her rental real property activity.

Step 5: Determine if Sally or Saul passes the 751-hour test. Sally passes this test as well, because she spent 800 hours on her rental properties.

Saul and Sally qualify for the exemption. But as you'll see in a moment, Bill, below, does not.

EXAMPLE 3: Bill is a retired teacher who owns a small apartment building. He spent 600 hours managing the building this year, and worked at no other activity. His wife does not work and is not involved with the rental.

Step 1: Determine the hours Bill worked in real estate activities. Bill materially participated in his one real property activity—rental property—because he worked over 501 hours.

Step 2: Determine if Bill materially participated in his real estate activities. Bill easily satisfies this test because he worked at no non-real estate activities.

Step 3: Count any non–real estate activity hours. Bill didn't have any.

Step 4: Determine if Bill can pass the 51% test. Again, Bill easily passes this test because he works at no other job.

Step 5: Determine if Bill can pass the 751-hour test. Bill had to spend at least 751 hours working at real property activities to qualify for the exemption. He fails the test because he spent only 600 hours working.

Bill does not qualify for the exemption. Had he been able to spend an additional 151 hours working at his rental activity, he would have gotten the exemption. Alternatively, he could have worked part-time at some other real estate activity, such selling real estate, and combined those hours with his rental activity hours to satisfy the 751-hour threshold.

What Happens If You Qualify for the Exemption?

You must determine anew each year whether you qualify for the real estate professional exemption by applying the three tests discussed above. Any year you qualify, the income and loss from your rental property no longer goes into the passive bucket. It is now nonpassive income or loss. Any loss you have from the property may be deducted from your active or portfolio income, but not from any passive income. Likewise, any income from the property may be placed in the active or portfolio buckets and you can use it to offset any losses in those buckets. However, you may not use the exemption to reduce your income for the year to below zero—that is, to create a net operating loss for the year (see "Overview of the Passive Loss Rules," above).

Now, suppose you incurred passive losses from the property in previous years that you weren't able to deduct because you didn't qualify for the exemption or couldn't use the $25,000 offset. These unused passive losses are called suspended passive losses. They remain passive losses—they stay in your passive bucket. However, you may deduct them from income from your now-exempt rental property income. You can also deduct them from passive income in your passive bucket for the current year, or if you sell the exempt rental property (see "Deducting Suspended Passive Losses"). Because they're in your passive bucket, you can't deduct these suspended losses from your active or portfolio income. (IRC Sec. 469(f)(1)(C).)

> **EXAMPLE:** Jill owns an apartment building. She has $20,000 of rental income in 2008. For the first time, she qualifies for the real estate professional exemption. Jill has $10,000 in suspended rental losses from the property from prior years when she did not qualify for the exemption. She may deduct her $10,000 in suspended losses from her rental property income. This leaves her with $10,000 in rental income for the year.

The Real Estate Professional Exemption Is Not Optional

Usually, qualifying for the real estate professional exemption is highly beneficial taxwise. Indeed, real estate professionals who qualify can have a huge financial advantage over those who aren't so lucky, because they can deduct all their rental losses from any nonpassive income.

However, qualifying for the exemption will not benefit you if you have substantial passive income from non-real estate rental businesses. This is because you can't use your rental losses to offset such passive income. It's left to sit and you can't deduct it until a future year, when you have enough passive losses. If you don't have enough losses, it could sit forever.

> **EXAMPLE:** This year, Felix earns $20,000 in passive income from two limited partnerships. His rental properties have a $20,000 loss. Unfortunately for Felix, he qualifies for the real estate broker exemption from the passive loss rules. This means he must treat the $20,000 in rental losses as nonpassive loss. As a result, he may not deduct it from his $20,000 in passive income.

Unfortunately for people like Felix, the real estate professional exemption is mandatory, not optional. If you qualify, you are not allowed to deduct your losses from your exempt rental real property from passive income. The only way to avoid this is to make sure you don't qualify for the exemption. This is not hard to do—for example, you can hire a management company to manage your rentals for you so you will not materially participate in them. Or, you could just make sure you work fewer than 751 hours per year in real estate activities.

EXAMPLE: Assume that Felix makes sure he does not qualify for the real estate professional exemption by working fewer than 751 hours in real estate this year. Now, his $20,000 in rental losses is passive. He may deduct this amount from his $20,000 in passive income from limited partnerships, leaving him with zero passive income to pay tax on.

Record Keeping for the Real Estate Professional Exemption

To know whether you qualify for the real estate professional exemption, you must know how many hours you (and your spouse, if you're married) spent during the year working in (1) real estate businesses of all kinds, (2) rental real estate activities, and (3) all non–real estate work activities.

If the IRS audits you, you'll need good records of your annual work hours to preserve your real estate professional exemption. Under IRS regulations, you may use any "reasonable means" to keep track of your work time, including daily time reports, logs, appointment books, calendars, or narrative summaries. (IRS Reg. 1.469-5T(f)(4).) The regulations don't require you to keep contemporaneous records—that is, records made at or near the time you did the work involved—but it is a good practice to do so.

Many taxpayers keep few or no records of their time. When they get audited, they sit down and write a narrative summary of work they did during the year, with estimates of the time they spent; or they rely on their oral testimony. This is a good way to lose your exemption.

EXAMPLE: Judy Bailey kept a daily calendar for 1997 that listed the number of visits she made to her many rental properties, but the calendar did not quantify the number of hours that she spent on her rental activities. When the IRS audited Judy, she wrote a summary report, in which she generally explained the activities she performed at the rental properties and estimated the number of hours she spent on each rental property. Both the IRS and tax court found this summary to be inadequate. The court noted that Bailey's estimates were uncorroborated by any other evidence. She assigned hours to activities years after the fact, based solely on her judgment and experience as to how much time the activities must have taken her. The court concluded, therefore, that the summary was an unreliable "ballpark guesstimate." Bailey lost her exemption. (*Bailey v. Comm'r.*, T.C. Memo 2001-296.)

You should learn from Judy Bailey's mistakes. Keep careful track of the actual number of hours you (and your spouse) spend working on each activity during the year. You can note your time on a calendar, appointment book, log, or timesheet. It doesn't matter, as long as your records are accurate and believable.

If you work a regular job, you should have no problem keeping track of those hours. If you work about the same number of hours each week, you can even dispense with a calendar or other record of this time. Make every effort, however, to keep close track of the time you spend on real estate business activities. Remember, to qualify for the exemption, you'll have to show that you spent at least 51% of your time on real estate activities, and that these activities amounted to at least 751 hours.

Get into the habit of writing down the time you perform *any task* related to a real estate activity. This includes, of course, all the time you spend working on your rental properties. For example, you should include the time you spend:

- showing the property for rental
- taking tenant applications
- screening tenants (including ordering credit reports and evaluating them, and calling references)
- preparing and negotiating leases and other rental agreements
- cleaning and preparing units for rent, including "initiation" time you spend welcoming the tenant to the property and explaining your policies
- doing repairs yourself
- doing improvements yourself or arranging for others to do them
- hiring and supervising a resident manager
- hiring and dealing with a rental management company
- purchasing supplies and materials for your rental business
- inspecting the property
- responding to tenant complaints and inquiries
- collecting and depositing rents
- evicting tenants
- writing and placing advertisements
- creating and maintaining a website you use to promote your rentals
- attending seminars or other educational events on how to manage rental property, such as educational events sponsored by your local landlord's association
- time spent attending landlord association meetings, and
- traveling for any of the activities listed above.

If you buy or sell a rental property during the year, keep track of the time involved as well—for example, finding the property, negotiating the purchase, arranging for financing, dealing with escrow, and so forth.

If you have a real estate business other than rentals, keep track of that time as well. For example, if you're a real estate broker, track the time you spend showing properties, marketing your services, and dealing with buyers and sellers.

Landlord Claimed There Were More Than 24 Hours in a Day

Alexander Firsow owned a rental property in a Maryland fishing area. To prove he was entitled to the real estate professional exemption, he prepared a computer spreadsheet for the IRS examiner showing that he had worked on the rental 606 hours in 1999 and 494 hours in 2000. Even though Firsow used a computer to prepare the spreadsheet, the IRS auditor denied the exemption, and the case went to tax court. The court noted that Firsow spent no more than two weeks per year at the rental property, performing maintenance work, but also fishing off the pier. There are only 336 hours in 14 days, so Firsow couldn't have spent more than that much time on his rental even if he had worked 24 hours a day. In effect, Firsow claimed that there were far more than 24 hours in a day! Needless to say, the court held that Firsow was not entitled to the exemption. (*Firsow v. Comm'r.*, T.C. Summary Opinion 2004-112.)

Rental Activities Not Subject to PAL Real Property Rental Rules

Under the PAL rules, all rental activities are automatically deemed passive activities. Thus, all the income or loss you receive from them is passive income or loss unless you qualify for the real estate professional exemption. However, some types of short-term rental activities do not meet the definition of a rental for purposes of the passive loss rules. The income or loss you receive from them is not automatically passive.

Instead, income or loss from these activities is subject to the same test as any other nonrental business income or loss to determine which bucket it falls into—passive or active. Under the rules described above, income or loss from a nonrental business is active only if the owner materially participates in the business. You apply the same material participation rules discussed in "The Real Estate Professional Exemption," above.

Because these short-term rentals are not rental activities for purposes of the PAL rules, you can't use the $25,000 offset or the real property professional exemption. There are no similar exemptions from the PAL rules for activities that don't constitute rental real estate activities.

Rentals for Seven Days or Less

The PAL real property rental rules don't apply if you rent your property for an average period of seven days or less during the year. (IRS Reg. Sec. 1.469-1T(e)(3)(ii)(A).) The average period is figured by dividing the total number of days the property was rented during the year by the number of separate rentals. This exception ordinarily applies to hotels and motels. It can also apply to vacation homes (see below).

Rentals for 30 Days or Less

The PAL real property rental rules also don't apply if the average period of customer use is 30 days or less and significant personal services are provided with the rentals. A hotel with maid service, for example, would not be treated as a rental activity as long as the average rental period does not exceed 30 days. (IRS Reg. 1.469-1T(e)(3)(iv).)

Significant services do not include services commonly provided for high-grade residential rentals, such as repairs, cleaning, maintenance, trash removal, elevators, security, or cable television. (IRS Reg. 1.469-1T(e)(3)(iv)(B)(3).)

Vacation Homes

Many people own second homes that they use as both vacation homes and rental property. How does the tax code treat a vacation home or second home for tax purposes? It depends on how much you and your family use the home and how much you rent it out. (See Chapter 15.) If you use it fewer than 15 days or no more than 10% of the time you rent it out, the home is treated as a rental property for tax purposes. If your average rental period is more than seven days, the rental property passive loss rules covered in this chapter apply. If your average rental is seven days or less, it won't come under the rental property PAL rules—thus, it won't automatically be a passive activity.

EXAMPLE: Glenda rented her Santa Barbara vacation home in 2007 for a total of 35 days. She rented the property five separate times, so she rented her house for seven days or less (35 ÷ 5 = 7). The house does not fall within the rental property PAL rules.

If the rental activity PAL rules do not apply to your second home because you rent it out on average for seven days or less, you may be losing a valuable tax advantage. You won't be able to obtain the $25,000 passive loss offset or the real estate professional exemption. In addition, you are then subject to the passive loss rules for nonrental business activities (assuming your vacation home rental qualifies as a business). This means you'll only be able to treat the income you earn, or loss you incur, from the home as active income or loss if you materially participate in its operation. This can be hard to do for a vacation home, especially if a real property management company manages it for you.

EXAMPLE: Walter Barniskis owned a condominium in a large development on Lake Superior in Minnesota. He and his family used the condo about two weeks a year, and rented it out as much as possible the rest of the time. They hired a real property management company to take care of the unit in return for 45% of the rent it earned. The management company took care of maintenance, making reservations, checking guests in and out, collecting rent, and all the other management details. Barniskis incurred losses from the condo of over $8,000 a year for three straight years. He deducted these losses from his salary income as an engineer, claiming that they were active losses. However, the IRS and tax court disagreed. The court found that Barniskis had not materially participated in the condo because he was not involved in its day-to-day operations or management. The more than 100 hours he claimed to have spent each year organizing his personal records, preparing his taxes for the condo, paying bills, and reviewing the monthly statements of the rentals of the unit were investor activities that didn't count as material participation. (*Barniskis v. Comm'r.*, TC Memo 1999-258.)

If you are unable to deduct losses from a vacation home because of the passive loss rules, it may be desirable, taxwise, to make additional use of the home so that it is treated as residential property. Such vacation homes are not subject to any passive loss rules. Instead, special vacation home tax rules apply.

These permit you to treat much of your mortgage interest as a tax deductible personal interest expense. (See Chapter 15.)

Deducting Suspended Passive Losses

Rental property passive losses you aren't allowed to deduct the year they are incurred are called suspended passive losses. They are not lost. Rather, they are carried forward indefinitely to future years, and may be deducted as follows.

You Must Have Passive Income

You can deduct your suspended losses in any year in which you earn enough passive income. Because they are passive losses, they can't be deducted from your active or portfolio income.

EXAMPLE: Joe has $10,000 in suspended passive losses from prior years. This year, he had $25,000 in income from his rental properties, and only $20,000 in deductions. Thus, he has $5,000 in passive income for the year. He may deduct his prior suspended losses from this income, leaving him no rental income to pay tax on for the year. He also earned $80,000 in salary from his job, but he can't deduct his suspended losses from this active income. He must carry forward his remaining $5,000 in suspended losses to future years.

The $25,000 Offset

Suspended losses may also be deducted by using the $25,000 offset. You can do this for any suspended loss from a property in which you actively participated during the year the loss was incurred.

EXAMPLE: Tom had a $10,000 loss from his rental activities this year. He has $15,000 in suspended losses from the last two years (in both years, he actively participated in his rental activity). Because he qualifies for the $25,000 offset this year, he may deduct his $10,000 passive loss from this year and his $15,000 suspended losses from prior years.

The Real Estate Professional Exemption

If you qualify for the real estate professional exemption to the PAL rules, you may deduct your suspended losses from income you earn from the property.

Profits From Sale of Property

Finally, you may deduct your suspended passive losses from the profit you earn when you sell your rental property. To deduct your suspended losses upon sale, you must:

- sell "substantially all" of your interest in the rental activity
- sell to an unrelated party—that is, a person other than your spouse, brothers, sisters, ancestors (parents, grandparents), lineal descendants (children, grandchildren), or a corporation or partnership in which you own more than 50% (100% of your ownership interest), and
- the sale must be a taxable event—that is you must recognize income or loss for tax purposes; this means tax-deferred Section 1031 exchanges don't count, except to the extent you recognize any taxable income. (IRC Sec. 469(g).)

To deduct your suspended losses from your profit, you must sell substantially all of your rental activity. If you own only one rental property, that property is your entire rental activity. If you own two or more properties, each property will be a separate rental activity unless you elected to group them together. As discussed above, such grouping can help you satisfy the material participation requirement if you want to qualify for the real estate professional exemption from the PAL rules. But it can lead to problems when you sell only one of your grouped properties and try to deduct any suspended losses you have for the property.

> **EXAMPLE:** Connie buys three rental houses in 2000. By 2004, she has $20,000 in suspended losses for each house. She decides she's had enough of the PAL rules and qualifies for the real estate professional exemption by becoming a real estate sales agent. To meet the material participation requirements, she elects in 2004 to treat all three houses as one rental activity. In 2007, she sells one of the houses. She cannot deduct her $20,000 in suspended losses because she has not sold substantially all her rental activity—the activity consists of three houses, and she has sold only one. Had Connie not elected to group her three houses into one activity, each one would be its own rental activity and she could deduct her suspended losses when she sold each one.

It's not entirely clear how much of your activity you must sell to sell substantially all of it—for example, if you own three properties must you sell all three or will two do? If you're presented with this problem, consult a tax professional.

If you meet the requirements for deducting profits from a sale, deduct your suspended losses in the following order:

- first, against income the passive rental activity earned during the year and any gain from its sale
- then, against net income earned during the year from all other passive activities, and lastly
- from any other income—that is, income from nonpassive activities (active and portfolio income). (IRC Sec. 469(g)(1).)

EXAMPLE: Jason owns a rental house from which he has $60,000 in suspended losses. This year, Jason received $5,000 in income from the house, which was passive income. He also earned $90,000 in salary for the year, and $5,000 in passive income from a limited partnership interest he owns. Jason sells his house for a $30,000 profit. He deducts his $60,000 in suspended losses as follows:

First, against the $5,000 passive income he earned from the house and his $30,000 profit from its sale. This leaves $25,000 in suspended losses ($60,000 - $35,000 = $25,000); next, against the income from his other passive activities—this is the $5,000 income he had from his limited partnership interest. This leaves $20,000 in suspended losses; and finally, from his $90,000 salary income, reducing it to $70,000 for the year.

As you can see from the example, if you have enough suspended losses, you may be able to deduct them from nonpassive income, such as salary income, that you earned during the year you sold your rental property.

Tax Reporting for Passive Rental Losses

The IRS wants to know if you have rental losses. They designed Schedule E to show them. The form requires you to separately deduct your expenses from your income for each rental property you own. The form will show if you have net income or loss for each rental property.

You may also have to complete IRS Form 8582, Passive Activity Loss Limitations. This complex tax form requires you to list your current and suspended losses for each rental property, and any other passive activities you are engaged in. You then go through several calculations to figure your deductible passive loss for the year, and the amount of passive loss you must carry forward to future years.

If you qualify for the $25,000 offset, you may not have to file Form 8582. This permits you to deduct up to $25,000 in passive losses from rental property, but your adjusted gross income (modified by some special rules) must be below $150,000. If, like most small landlords, you qualify for the offset, you don't need to file Form 8582 so long as:

- your rental real estate activities were your only passive activities
- you have no suspended losses or tax credits from prior years for your rentals
- your total losses from your rentals were not more than $25,000
- your modified adjusted gross income was not more than $100,000, and
- you don't own any rental real estate as a limited partner.

Thus, before you go to the trouble of filling out Form 8852, determine if you qualify for the $25,000 offset and meet the above requirements.

Strategies for Dealing With the Passive Loss Rules

If you are unable to get full relief from the PAL rules through the $25,000 offset and/or real estate professional exemption, there are some things you can do to limit their impact.

Lower Your Rental Expenses

The PAL rules bar you from deducting your rental expenses from nonpassive income—income from your rental properties or other passive activities. If you don't have enough passive income to deduct all your losses, you can reduce your losses by lowering your expenses. For example, you could:

- pay less mortgage interest on your rental properties by borrowing less money—make a larger down payment when you buy the property or pay down your mortgage. (If you have substantial investments that generate portfolio income, such as stocks and bonds, you could sell them and use the money for this purpose.)
- spend less on repairs and other operating expenses, or
- defer expenses to future years when you might have more passive income.

Use Home Equity Loans

You can borrow up to $100,000 in home equity loans on your main residence and deduct the interest as a personal interest expense on your Schedule A. This is not a rental expense, thus it does not go on your Schedule E. This means the interest is not subject to the PAL rules. You can use the home equity loan to purchase a rental property, pay down an existing mortgage on a rental, or to pay for improvements, repairs, or operating expenses.

Generate More Passive Income

Generate more passive income to soak up your passive losses. There are two ways to do this:

- invest in a rental property or other business that produces passive income (only businesses in which you don't materially participate produce passive income), or
- sell your rental property or another passive activity you own, such as a limited partnership interest.

Some investments are especially designed to produce passive income to soak up passive losses—these are called passive income generators—PIGs for short. Limited partnerships that invest in real estate that generates substantial annual income, such as conference centers, golf courses, and ski resorts, often fall into this category. Such PIGs are syndicated—that is, they're offered to the public through public offerings—and are actively marketed by brokers. If you're interested in investing in a PIG, you'll have no trouble finding out about them from stockbrokers, financial planners, financial publications, or the Internet. Of course, you should be careful when making any investment.

One way you cannot generate more passive income to absorb your rental income is to rent to a business you own or materially participate in. Under the "self-rental rule," such income is recharacterized as nonpassive and can't be used to offset real estate rental losses. (*Beecher v. Comm'r,* 481 F.3d 717 (9th Cir. 2007); Treas. Reg. 1.469-2(f)(6).)

> **EXAMPLE:** Gary and Dolores Beecher are a married couple who owned two corporations engaged in the business of repairing automobile interiors and exteriors. They also owned five rental properties that resulted in substantial annual losses. The Beecher's had a great idea: because they worked out of their home, they would lease their home office to their corporation. They

would use this lease income—ordinarily, passive income—to offset the losses from their rentals. As a result of this combination of income and losses, the Beechers paid no tax on the rental income paid to them by their corporations—this amounted to over $85,000 of tax-free income over three years. Unfortunately, the IRS audited the Beechers and recharacterized their rental income from their corporations as active, not passive, income. Thus, it could not be used to offset their rental losses. Under the self-rental rule, income from the rental of property for use in a trade or business in which the taxpayer materially participates is treated as nonpassive income. The courts upheld the IRS's ruling.

At-Risk Rules

There is yet another set of rules, in addition to the passive loss rules, that may limit your deductions for your rental real estate losses. These are the at-risk rules. Fortunately, these rules aren't nearly as complicated as the PAL rules and they don't apply to most landlords. You usually don't have to worry about the at-risk rules unless you obtain seller financing or a loan from a relative at unusually favorable terms. The rules don't apply at all to rental property placed in service before 1987.

To prevent abusive tax shelters, the at-risk rules limit your annual deductible losses to the amount of money that you have at risk. At risk has nothing to do with insurance, and having insurance will not render you not at risk. At risk means how much money you could lose if a business activity goes belly up. You are at risk to the extent of your investment in the activity.

In the case of rental real estate activities, you are at risk for:

- the total amount of cash you invest—for example, your cash down payment to purchase a rental property
- the adjusted basis (see Chapter 5) of property you contribute to the activity, and
- most loans you obtain to purchase or otherwise operate your rental activity. (IRC Sec. 465.)

Most landlords borrow money to purchase their rental properties, and it is these borrowed funds that make up the great bulk of their at-risk amounts. You may include in your at-risk amount the amount of any type of loan you use for your real estate activity, except for nonrecourse loans from:

- the seller of the property or a person related to the seller
- a person who is related to you and gives you a loan at below-market rates or with other unusually favorable terms, or
- a person who receives a fee due to your investment in the real property or a person related to that person—for example, a real estate broker.

A nonrecourse loan is a loan for which you are not personally liable. The lender's only recourse if you fail to pay is to foreclose on the property and take over ownership. The mortgage document for a nonrecourse loan will contain an exculpatory clause providing that the borrower is not personally liable for the loan. A loan is a recourse loan if you are personally liable if it is not repaid on time—that is, the lender can not only foreclose on the property, but also obtain a deficiency judgment against you for the difference between the property's value at foreclosure and the amount you owe. With this deficiency judgment in hand, the lender can then go after your personal assets, such as your personal bank accounts.

However, you may include in your at-risk amount nonrecourse loans you obtain from banks, savings and loans, and other companies in the business of making real estate loans, or loans obtained from or guaranteed by the government. What all this means is that you may include all your borrowed funds in your at-risk amount unless you obtain seller financing or get a below-market nonrecourse loan from a relative. A person is related to you for these purposes if he or she is your spouse, brother, sister, ancestor (parent, grandparents), or lineal descendant (child or grandchild).

EXAMPLE 1: Stuart buys a rental home by making a $20,000 down payment and borrowing $180,000 from a bank. He is at risk for $200,000. This year, he loses $10,000 on the property. This is far less than his at-risk amount, so it doesn't affect his ability to deduct the loss.

EXAMPLE 2: Assume that, instead of using conventional financing as in the example above, Stuart purchases his home using creative financing. He gives the seller $1,000 cash and a car with an adjusted basis of $4,000. He borrows the remaining $195,000 from the seller, agreeing to a nonrecourse loan. Now, Stuart is at risk for only $5,000, because the $195,000 loan is not included in his at-risk amount. If he loses $10,000 on his property this year, he may only deduct $5,000. The remaining $5,000 loss is suspended and must be carried over to a future year when he has a sufficient amount at risk.

The at-risk rules are applied before the passive loss rules. So, Stuart in the example above, would be left with a $5,000 passive loss. He would then determine if he could deduct this loss by applying the PAL rules and exceptions discussed above.

If the at-risk rules prevent you from deducting a loss, you'll have to fill out IRS Form 6198, At-Risk Limitations.

If you purchase a rental property with seller financing, you need to carefully consider the effect of the at-risk rules. You might consider avoiding or limiting their application by obtaining at least some conventional financing, or by borrowing less by making a larger down payment.

How to Deduct Rental Losses

If, after applying the PAL rules and at-risk rules discussed above, you have a deductible loss from your real estate rentals, transfer it from your Schedule E to the first page of your IRS Form 1040. Use the loss to reduce the taxable income you report on your Form 1040 for the year. If you have other losses, you can deduct those losses from your income for the year as well. Other losses could include:

- casualty losses (see Chapter 13)
- deductible losses from other businesses you're involved in other than real estate, and
- losses incurred when you sell or otherwise dispose of rental or business property.

Calculating Your Net Operating Loss

If your total losses for the year exceed all your annual income from whatever source, you have a net operating loss (NOL, for short). Figuring the amount of a NOL is not as simple as deducting your losses from your annual income. Instead, you start with your adjusted gross income on your tax return for the year reduced by your itemized deductions or standard deduction (but not your personal exemption). This must be a negative number, or you won't have any NOL for the year. Your adjusted gross income already includes all the deductions you have for your losses. You then add back to this amount any nonbusiness deductions you have that exceed your nonbusiness income. These include the standard deduction or itemized deductions, deduction for the personal exemption, nonbusiness capital losses, IRA contributions, and charitable contributions. If the result is still a negative number, you have a NOL for the year. Schedule A of IRS Form 1045, *Application for Tentative Refund,* may be used to calculate a NOL.

> **EXAMPLE:** Glenn Johnson owns several rental properties. He is single and has the following income and deductions on his Form 1040 for the year:

Income:

Wages from part-time job	$ 12,000
Interest on savings	1,425
Total income	$ 13,425

Deductions:

Net loss from rental business (gross income of $67,000 minus expenses of $87,000)	$ 20,000
Standard deduction	5,000
Personal exemption	3,200
Total deductions	$ 28,200

Glenn's deductions exceed his income by $14,775 ($28,200 – $13,425 = $14,775). However, to figure whether he has a NOL, certain deductions are not allowed. He uses Schedule A (Form 1045) to figure his NOL. The following items are not allowed on Schedule A (Form 1045):

Nonbusiness deductions (standard deduction, $5,000) minus nonbusiness income (interest, $1,425)	$ 3,575
Deduction for personal exemption	– 3,200
Total adjustments to net loss	$ 6,775

Glenn's NOL is figured as follows:

Glenn's NOL before adjustment	$ 14,775
Reduced by disallowed items	– 6,775
Glenn's NOL	$ 8,000

Although it may not be pleasant to lose money over an entire year, a NOL has some important tax benefits: You can use it to reduce your taxes for prior or future years. Let's see how that works.

Carrying a Loss Back

Under the IRS's default rules, you must first apply a NOL to the two previous years. This is called carrying back a NOL. To do this, you file an amended tax return deducting the NOL from the income you reported in the prior years, and the IRS will send you a refund of all or part of the taxes you paid for one or both of those years, depending on the size of the NOL and your income for those years. You must first carry the entire NOL to the earliest carryback year. If your NOL is not used up, you can carry the rest to the next closest carryback year.

If you still have part of your NOL left, you then use it to reduce your income in future years—this is called carrying forward a NOL. You can carry forward a NOL for up to 20 years after the NOL year. You start by carrying it to the first tax year after the NOL year. If you do not use it up, you carry the unused part to the next year. You continue to carry any unused part of the NOL forward until the NOL is used up or you complete the 20-year carryforward period.

There are two ways to claim a refund for prior years' taxes from a NOL. You can file IRS Form 1040X, Amended U.S. Individual Income Tax Return, within three years, or you can seek a quicker refund by filing IRS Form 1045, Application for Tentative Refund. If you file Form 1045, the IRS must send your refund within 90 days. However, you must file Form 1045 within one year after the end of the year in which the NOL arose.

Electing to Carry Forward a NOL Instead

Instead of carrying back a NOL as described above, you can elect to carry it forward to future years instead. Some people do this because they are afraid they'll get audited if they carry a NOL back and receive a refund of taxes they've already paid. You may also want to carry a NOL forward if you expect your income to rise substantially in future years and want to use your NOL in the future, when you'll be subject to a higher tax rate.

To make this choice, you must attach a statement to your original return filed by the due date (including extensions) for the NOL year. This statement must show that you are choosing to waive the carryback period under Section 172(b)(3) of the Internal Revenue Code. Write "Filed pursuant to Section 301.9100-2" at the top of the statement. File the amended return at the same address you used for your original return.

Filed pursuant to Section 301.9100-2

Tax Year: _____ Taxpayer Name: _____
Taxpayer Identification Number: _____
Taxpayer elects to waive the carryback period under IRC Section 173(b)(3).

_____

Your Signature

If you filed your return on time but did not file the statement with it, you must file the statement with an amended return for the NOL year within six months of the due date of your original return (excluding extensions). If you do not file this statement on time, you cannot waive the carryback period. Once you elect to waive the carryback period, however, it is irrevocable.

Need to know more about NOLs? Refer to IRS Publication 536, *Net Operating Losses*, for more information. You can download it from the IRS website at www.irs.gov, or obtain a paper copy by calling the IRS at 800-TAX-FORM.

Chapter 17

Record Keeping and Accounting

Your deductions for your rental activities are only as good as the records you keep to back them up. Any deduction you forget to claim on your tax return, or lose after an IRS audit because you lack adequate records, costs you dearly. Every $100 in unclaimed deductions costs the average midlevel-income landlord (in a 25% tax bracket) $25 in additional federal income taxes. This chapter shows you how to document your expenditures and other deductions so you won't end up paying more tax than you have to.

Record Keeping Made Simple

The IRS does not require any special kind of records. You may choose any system that clearly shows your income and expenses. If you own only a few rental units, you don't need a fancy or complex set of books. You don't even need a computerized bookkeeping system, although you can use one if you wish. You can get along very nicely with just a few items:

- a rental checking account and credit card that are separate from your personal accounts and cards (and separate from any other business you might have)
- rental income and expense journals, which list your monthly rental income and expenses
- records for your depreciation deductions, and
- documents that will support your deductions, such as receipts and canceled checks.

In addition, if you have expenses for local or long distance travel, meals, entertainment, or gifts, you'll have to comply with special record-keeping requirements.

Special Concerns When You Hire Employees

If you have employees—such as a resident manager—you must create and keep a number of records, including payroll tax records, withholding records, and employment tax returns. And you must keep these records for four years.

For detailed information, see IRS Circular E, *Employer's Tax Guide*. You can get a free copy by calling the IRS at 800-TAX-FORM, by calling or visiting your local IRS office, or by downloading it from the IRS website at www.irs.gov. Also, contact your state tax agency for your state's requirements. A list of all 50 state tax agency websites can be found at www.taxsites.com/state.html.

If you own more than one rental property, you must separately keep track of your income and expenses for each property—don't mix them together. One reason for this inconvenient rule is that the IRS requires that you separately list your income and expenses for each property on your Schedule E. Also, you'll never know how much money you're making or losing on each property unless you separately track your income and expenses.

An Easy Filing System

You need to establish a system to deal with all your receipts, canceled checks, credit card statements, income and expense journals, and other records. Here's an easy-to-use system:

- Each year, get a separate accordion folder for each rental property you own and label it with the name of the property—for example, 123 Main Street. This folder will contain your records for all your rental units at a single address. (If you wish, you can use a filing cabinet instead of an accordion folder.)

- Place several manila folders in the accordion folder: one for each expense category you have and one folder for your asset records.

- Once a month, file your receipts in the proper manila folders in chronological order—do this at the same time you complete your expense journal. If a receipt applies to more than one property, make copies to file with your receipts for each property.

- Keep your canceled checks for your rental checking account and credit card statements for your rental credit card together in chronological order. Use a separate accordion folder for this with files for each month of the year.

- Keep your income and expense journals and depreciation worksheet in your accordion folder for the appropriate property.

- At the end of the calendar year, safely store your accordion folders to use when you (or your accountant) prepare your tax returns. Make sure it contains all your receipts, income and expense journals, depreciation worksheet, car mileage records, listed property journal, appointment book or calendar, and any other records you'll need to prepare your tax returns.

- Get a new accordion folder and create a new set of records for the new year. (The folders are a tax deductible supplies expense.)

Separate Checkbook and Credit Cards

One of the first things you should do (if you haven't done it already) is set up a separate checking account for your rental activity. Your rental checkbook will serve as your basic source of information for recording your rental expenses and income. Deposit all of your rental income into the account and make rental-related payments by check from the account. Don't use your rental account to pay for personal expenses or your personal account to pay for rental activity items.

Using a separate account will provide these important benefits:

- It will be much easier for you to keep track of your rental income and expenses if you pay them from a separate account.
- Your rental account will clearly separate your personal and rental activity finances; this will prove very helpful if the IRS audits you.
- Your rental account will help convince the IRS that your rental is a for-profit activity. People with not-for-profit activities don't generally have separate bank accounts to fund their pursuits. (See Chapter 2 for more on establishing your tax status.)

⚠️ **Some states require landlords to use a separate account for tenants' security deposits.** Check your state's laws, available online at www.nolo.com and in *Every Landlord's Legal Guide,* by Marcia Stewart, Ralph Warner, and Janet Portman (Nolo). If your state requires a separate account, you may need to establish two accounts for your business—one for general rental activity, and one for deposits.

Setting Up Your Bank Account

You don't have to open your rental checking account at the same bank where you have your personal checking account. Shop around and open your account with the bank that offers you the best services at the lowest price.

When You Write Checks

If you already keep an accurate, updated personal checkbook, do the same for your rental activity checkbook. If, however, you tend to be lax in keeping up your checkbook (as many of us are), you're going to have to change your habits. Now that you're a landlord, you can't afford this kind of carelessness. Unless you write large numbers of rental activity checks, maintaining your checkbook won't take much time.

When you write rental activity checks, you may have to make some extra notations besides the date, number, amount of the check, and the name of the person or company to which the check is written. If the purpose of the payment is not clear from the name of the payee, describe the rental reason for the check—for example, the equipment or service you purchased.

You can use the register that comes with your checkbook and write in all this information manually, or you can use a computerized register. Either way works fine as long as the information is complete and up to date.

Don't Write Checks for Cash

Avoid writing checks payable to cash, because this makes it hard to tell whether you spent the money for a rental purpose. Writing cash checks might lead to questions from the IRS if you're audited. If you must write a check for cash to pay a rental expense, be sure to include the receipt for the cash payment in your records.

Use a Separate Credit Card for Rental Activity Expenses

Use a separate credit card for rental activity expenses instead of putting both personal and rental items on one card. Credit card interest for rental activity purchases is 100% deductible, while interest for personal purchases is not deductible at all (see Chapter 7). Using a separate card for rental-related purchases will make it much easier for you to keep track of how much interest you've paid for such purchases. If you have more than one personal credit card, you can use one for your rental activity only—you don't need to get a special business credit card.

Dealing with Receipts, Canceled Checks, and Other Supporting Documents

The IRS lives by the maxim "Figures lie and liars figure." It knows very well that you can claim anything in your books and on your tax returns, because you create or complete them yourself. For this reason, the IRS requires that you have documents to support the deductions you claim on your tax return. In the absence of a supporting document, an IRS auditor may conclude that an item you claim as a rental activity expense is really a personal expense, or that you never bought the item at all. Either way, your deduction will be disallowed or reduced.

The supporting documents you need depend on the type of deduction. However, at a minimum, every deduction should be supported by documentation showing:

- what you purchased for your rental activity
- how much you paid for it, and
- who (or what company) you bought it from.

You must meet additional record-keeping requirements for local transportation, travel, entertainment, meal, and gift deductions, as well as for certain long-term assets that you buy for your rental activity. (These rules are covered below.)

You can meet the basic requirements by keeping the following types of documentation:

- canceled checks
- sales receipts
- account statements
- credit card sales slips
- invoices, and
- petty cash slips for small cash payments (these are preprinted receipts that say you paid in cash; you can get them at any stationery store).

Canceled Check + Receipt = Proof of Deduction

We're about to disabuse you of a commonly held belief—that a canceled check will prove that you purchased the item it paid for, especially if you note on the check (or on your register) what the check was for. For example, suppose Manny owns three rental houses. He buys a $500 snow blower to use at his rental properties from the local home supply store. He writes a check for the amount and gets a receipt. How does he prove to the IRS that he has a $500 rental expense?

Manny assumes that if he saves his canceled check when it's returned from his bank, that's all the proof he needs. He's wrong. All a canceled check proves is that he spent money for something. It doesn't prove what he bought. Of course, Manny can write a note on his check describing what he purchased, but why should the IRS believe what he writes on his checks himself?

```
MANNY FARBER                                              2345
123 SHADY LANE
ANYTOWN, IL 12345                    Date Feb. 2, 2008    12-34/5780

Pay to the
order of   The Acme Home Supply Store           $  500.00

Five hundred and no cents _____  Dollars

Piggy Bank
100 Main Street
Anytown, IL 12345

Memo   Snow blower                    Manny Farber

⑆ 5780003 58⑆5355⑈05556⑈05555⑈
```

Does Manny's sales receipt prove that he bought his snow blower for his rental activity? Again, no. A sales receipt proves only that somebody purchased the item listed in the receipt. It does not show who purchased it. You could write a note on the receipt stating that you bought the item, but you could easily lie. Indeed, for all the IRS knows, you could hang around stores and pick up receipts people throw away to give yourself tax deductions.

```
Acme Home Supply Store              509257
456 Main Street
Anytown, IL 12345
```

CUSTOMER'S ORDER NO. 14601				DATE February 1, 2008		
NAME Manny Faber						
ADDRESS						
CITY, STATE, ZIP						

SOLD BY SF	CASH	C.O.D.	CHARGE	ON ACCT.	MDSE. RETD.	PAID OUT

	QUAN.	DESCRIPTION	PRICE	AMOUNT
1	1	Snow Blower	500	500
2				
3				
4				
5				
6				
7				
8				
9				
10				
11			Total	500
12				

RECEIVED BY

KEEP THIS SLIP FOR REFERENCE

However, when you put a canceled check together with a sales receipt (or an invoice, a cash register tape, or a similar document), you have concrete proof that you purchased the item listed in the receipt. The check proves that you bought something, and the receipt proves what that something is.

This doesn't necessarily prove that you bought the item for your rental, but it's a good start. Often, the face of a receipt, sales slip, or the payee's name on your canceled check will strongly indicate that the item you purchased was for your rental activity. But if it's not clear, note the purpose of the purchase on the document. Such a note is not proof of how you used the item, but it will be helpful. For some types of items that you use for both rental and personal purposes—computers are one example—you might be required to keep careful records of your use. (See "Asset Records," for the stricter rules that apply to these types of expenses.)

Credit Cards

Using a credit card is a great way to pay rental expenses. The credit card slip will prove that you bought the item listed on the slip. You'll also have a monthly statement to back up your credit card slips.

Account Statements

Sometimes, you'll need to use an account statement to prove an expense. Some banks no longer return canceled checks, or you may pay for something with an ATM card or another electronic funds transfer method. Moreover, you may not always have a credit card slip when you pay by credit card—for example, when you buy an item over the Internet. In these situations, the IRS will accept an account statement as proof that you purchased the item. The chart below shows what type of information you need on an account statement.

Proving Payments with Bank Statements	
If payment is by:	**The statement must show:**
Check	Check number Amount Payee's name Date the check amount was posted to the account by the bank
Electronic funds transfer	Amount transferred Payee's name Date the amount transferred was posted to the account by the bank
Credit card	Amount charged Payee's name Transaction date

Filing Your Receipts

If you pay an expense with a check, note the check number on the receipt. If you pay by credit card, mark it with the code CC. If you own multiple rental properties, indicate which property the receipt is for by marking it with a code. Make up any code that makes sense to you—for example, "Main St." You don't need to note the unit number, even if a check was for an expense for a specific unit. If a receipt applies to all your properties, say so on it (and make duplicates to place in each property's folder). File your receipts by expense category.

Expense Journal

You need to keep track of what you spend on your rental properties. Track your expenses by creating an expense journal—a listing of all your expenses by category. This will show what you buy for your rental activity and how much you spent. It's very easy to do this. You can write your journal out on paper, or you can set up a computer spreadsheet program, such as *Excel* or *Lotus*, to do it. Or, if you already have or would prefer to use a financial computer program such as *Quicken*, you can do that instead. You can also use programs especially designed for landlords, such as *Quicken Rental Property Manager*.

Creating an Expense Journal

You can easily create an expense journal by using paper divided into columns, or by using a professional multicolumn book you can get from any stationery or office supply store. These multicolumn pages are also called ledger sheets. Get ledger sheets with at least 14 columns. Devote a separate column to each major category of expense you have. Alternatively, you can purchase accounting record books with the rental expense categories already printed on them.

Your rental expense categories in your expense journal should be keyed to the categories on IRS Schedule E, the tax form you file to report your rental expenses and income. This is how the IRS wants you to categorize your expenses when you report them on your taxes, so you should use these categories in your records. This way, you simply transfer the totals from your records to your Schedule E when you do your taxes.

Schedule E lists 13 expense categories:

- advertising
- auto and travel
- cleaning and maintenance

Allocating Expenses Among Multiple Properties

If you own more than one rental property, some of the items you buy will benefit more than just one property. Good examples are tools and office supplies you use for all your properties, or legal, accounting, or other professional services that apply to all your properties. In this event, you'll have to allocate the expense among your properties. The IRS does not require that you use any particular method to do this. But whatever method you use must be reasonable and used consistently.

One allocation method is simply to divide the expense involved equally among your properties. This makes sense where the properties generate about the same rental income each year.

For example, suppose Stuart owns three rental houses. He pays $300 for a new lawnmower he will use for all three houses. He allocates $100 of the cost to each rental house.

If your rental properties vary greatly in size, a more reasonable way to allocate expenses is by the gross income they generate. For instance, suppose Marjorie owns a rental house, a duplex, and a four-unit apartment building. She allocates expenses for all the properties according to the monthly rental income she receives from each one, as follows:

House	$1,000
Duplex	2,000
Apartments	4,000
Total	$7,000

She determines an allocation percentage for each property by dividing its monthly rental by the total rental income she receives.

House	$1,000 ÷ $7,000	=	14%
Duplex	$2,000 ÷ $7,000	=	29%
Apartments	$4,000 ÷ $7,000	=	57%

She pays $300 for a lawnmower she will use for all the properties. She allocates the cost as follows:

House	14% X $300	=	$42
Duplex	29% X $300	=	$87
Apartments	57% X $300	=	$171

- commissions
- insurance
- legal and other professional fees
- management fees
- mortgage interest paid to banks
- other interest
- repairs
- supplies
- taxes, and
- utilities.

The ins and outs of Schedule E are discussed in Chapter 18. Refer to that chapter if you need more information about these categories. You may not need to use all of these categories—for example, if you manage your rentals by yourself, you probably don't need the management fees or commissions categories.

The Schedule E categories probably include most of your expenses, but you may have others that are not listed—for example:

- home office expenses
- gifts
- homeowner association dues for rental condominiums and planned-unit developments
- start-up expenses
- entertainment expenses
- telephone or voice mail expenses
- employee expenses
- education expenses
- casualty losses, and
- equipment rental.

You should also have one final category called "miscellaneous" for occasional expenses that don't fit any existing category. However, don't use a miscellaneous category on your Schedule E—it's not allowed. You must have a descriptive category for each expense; you can't claim an expense as miscellaneous.

Don't list your depreciation expenses in your expense journal. These belong in your separate asset records.

You won't need a category for your car expenses unless you use the actual expense method to figure your deduction.

Now, sit down with your bills and receipts and sort them into categorized piles to determine which categories you need in your expense journal. In separate columns, list the check number, date, and name of the person or company paid for each transaction. If you pay by credit card or check, indicate it in the check number column.

Once a month, go through your check register, credit card slips, receipts, and other expense records and record the required information for each transaction. Also, total the amounts for each category when you come to the end of the page and keep a running total of what you've spent for each category for the year to date. After recording the expense, you should file the receipts, checks, and so on in the appropriate manila folder.

The following example shows a page from an expense journal for the month of May.

Rental Expense Journal—1000 Main St.

Date	Check No.	Transaction	Amount	Advertising	Cleaning and maintenance	Insurance
5/1	123	Acme Mortgage Co.	1,000			
5/3	124	Empire Plumbing Co.	200			
5/7	125	Bill's Gardening Service	80		80	
5/10	VISA	Daily Eagle Newspaper	50	50		
5/15	VISA	Gardening World	75			
5/18	126	Gloria Gonzalez	50		50	
5/23	127	County Tax Assessor	400			
5/30	128	Acme Insurance Co.	500			500
Total this page			2,355	50	130	500
Total year to date			8,750	100	450	1,000

continued below

continued from above	Legal and other professional fees	Mortgage interest paid to banks	Other interest	Repairs	Supplies	Taxes	Travel	Miscellaneous
		1,000						
				200				
					75			
						400		
	0	1,000	0	200	75	400	0	0
	500	5,000	100	900	300	400	500	0

Using Computer Financial Programs

Many computer programs are available to help people keep track of their finances. The programs range from relatively simple checkbook programs like *Quicken*, to complex and sophisticated accounting programs like *QuickBooks Pro* and *MYOB*. You can use these in place of the handwritten ledger sheets or simple spreadsheets described above. However, you'll be better off using handwritten ledger sheets, which are easy to create and simple to keep up to date, instead of a complicated computer program that you can't understand or use properly. So, if you're not prepared to invest the time to use a computer program correctly, don't do it!

This book doesn't explain how to use these programs in detail. You'll need to read the manual and use the tutorial that comes with the program you choose. You can also buy books that explain how to use various programs—for example, *Using Quicken In a Business*, by Stephen Nelson, C.P.A. (Redmond Technology Press).

Before You Purchase a Program

You don't want to spend your hard-earned money on an accounting program only to discover that you don't like it. Before you purchase a program:

- talk to other landlords to find out what they use—if they don't like a program, ask them why
- think carefully about how many features you need—the more complex the program, the harder it will be to learn and use it, and
- obtain a free demo version to see if you like it—you can usually download one from the software company's website.

The simplest financial programs are those that work off of a computerized checkbook, like *Quicken* and *MS Money*. Here's how they work: When you buy something for your rental, you write a check using the program. It automatically puts the data into a computerized check register, and you print out the check using your computer (you can also collect payments online). You'll have to input credit card and cash payments separately.

When you set up the system, you create a list of expense categories just like you do when you create a ledger sheet or spreadsheet. Programs like *Quicken* come with preselected categories, but these are not adequate for rentals, so you'll have to create your own—again, use the Schedule E categories as your guide. The program automatically notes the expense category in your register when you write a check.

Now, here's the neat part: The program takes this information (the expense and corresponding expense category) and automatically creates income and expense reports—that is, it will show you how much you've spent or earned for each category. This serves the same function as the expense journal. It can also create profit and loss statements. You can even import these amounts into tax preparation software, such as *TurboTax*, when it's time to do your income taxes. There are also several accounting programs specially designed for landlords.

Rental Income Journal

Of course, you must also keep track of how much money you earn from your rentals and report it to the IRS on your Schedule E. This will primarily consist of the rent you collect. But it could also include:

- fees you charge tenants for paying rent late

- garage or other parking charges
- interest you earn on tenant security deposits
- security deposits you retain to pay for repairs, unpaid rent, or other expenses
- laundry income
- the value of services tenants provide in lieu of rent, or
- payments tenants make to you for repairs or other expenses. (See Chapter 4.)

Any interest you earn on your tenants' security deposits is also rental income, unless state or local law requires you to repay it to your tenants on a yearly basis or when they move out.

Interest you earn on your rental checking account, if any, is not rental income. It is personal interest. Do not include it in your rental income on Schedule E.

As with your rental expenses, you can keep track of your rental income manually by using ledger sheets. You may also use computer spreadsheets, accounting programs like *Quicken*, or programs specially designed for landlords.

Whatever method you use, you must keep separate track of the income you earn for each rental property you own. Thus, you'll have separate ledger sheets, spreadsheets, or computer listings for each property.

Here is an example of an income journal for the month of May, created using ledger sheets. The rental property is a four-unit apartment building.

May Rental Income—123 Main St.

Unit #	Rent	Laundry	Garage	Late fees	Interest	Other	Total income
1	1,000		50			100	1,150
						(payment for	
						broken window	
						pane)	
2	900		50				950
3	1,100			25			1,125
4	1,150						1,150
All Units		160			17		177
Total this page	4,150	160	100	25	17	100	4,552
Total year to date	20,750	800	500	65	72	250	22,437

Asset Records

You need a separate set of records for your long-term assets. These consist primarily of your rental building or buildings, but they also include property such as computers and office furniture, appliances you separately depreciate, and real property improvements. Such long-term property is ordinarily depreciated over several years, not deducted in a single year as are operating expenses. Depreciation is covered in detail in Chapter 5.

When you purchase any property with a useful life of more than one year, you must keep records to verify:

- when and how you acquired the asset
- the purchase price
- how you used the asset
- the cost of any improvements—for example, adding a new roof to a rental building
- Section 179 deductions taken (see Chapter 5)
- deductions taken for depreciation
- when and how you disposed of the asset
- the selling price, and
- expenses of the sale.

You should create a depreciation worksheet showing this information for all your long-term assets, and update it each year. The instructions to IRS Form 4562, Depreciation and Amortization, contain a blank worksheet. You can also use a spreadsheet or computer accounting program such as *QuickBooks*. You don't need to file the worksheet with your tax returns, but it will provide you with all the information you need to claim your depreciation deductions on your taxes. And you will need it if you are audited.

> **EXAMPLE:** Jack purchased a rental house for $145,000 in 2006. He elected to use segmented depreciation in which he separately depreciated the building, land improvements, and personal property in the house. (See Chapter 5, for a detailed discussion of depreciation.)
>
> In April 2007, he added a new roof to the house. In 2007, Jack purchased a lawnmower and computer for his rental business, which he elected to deduct in a single year using Section 179. The chart below shows his 2007 depreciation worksheet.

2007 Depreciation Worksheet

Description of Property	Date Placed in Service	Cost or Other Basis	Business/ Investment Use %	Section 179 Deduction	Depreciation Prior Years	Basis for Depreciation	Depreciation Method/ Convention	Recovery Period	Rate or Table %	Depreciation Deduction
House—building	1/06	$111,250	100%	0	$7,922	$111,240	SL/MM	27.5	3.636%	$4,045
House—land improvements	1/06	5,000	100%	0	725	5,000	150DB/HY	15	8.550%	427
House— personal property	1/06	6,000	100%	0	3,120	6,000	200DB/HY	5	19.200%	1,152
Subtotal— 2005 Property										5,624
House—new roof	3/07	10,000	100%	0	257	10,000	SL/MM	27.5	3.636%	364
Subtotal— 2006 Property										364
Lawnmower	6/07	500	100%	500	0	0				0
Computer	8/07	2,000	100%	2,000	0	0				0
Subtotal— 2007 Property										0
Grand Total— 2007				$2,500						$5,988

Abbreviations Used for Depreciation Methods and Conventions

Straight-Line Depreciation	SL
150% Declining-Balance Depreciation	150DB
200% Declining-Balance Depreciation	200DB
Mid-Month Convention	MM
Half-Year Convention	HY
Mid-Quarter Convention	MQ

Listed Property

The IRS is especially interested in certain kinds of property that taxpayers can easily use personally—yet claim that they purchased for their business. To minimize the chances of abuse, the IRS separates these properties into a list—which is called listed property. Listed property gets extra scrutiny and has special documentation requirements. Listed property includes:

- cars, boats, airplanes, motorcycles, and other vehicles
- computers
- cellular phones, and
- any other property generally used for entertainment, recreation, or amusement—for example, VCRs, cameras, and camcorders.

Keep an appointment book, log book, rental diary, or calendar showing the dates, times, and reasons for which the property is used—both for rental and personal purchases. You also can purchase log books for this purpose at stationery or office supply stores.

> **EXAMPLE:** Bill purchases a computer he uses 50% for rental business and 50% to play games. He must keep a log showing his rental use of the computer. Below is a sample from one week in his log.

Usage Log for Personal Computer

Date	Time of Rental Activity Use	Reason for Use	Time of Personal Use
5/1	2 hours	Rental bookkeeping	
5/2			1 hour
5/3	1 hour	Rental bookkeeping	
5/4			2 hours

You usually have to document your use of listed property even if you use it only for your rental activity. However, there is an exception to this rule for computers: If you use a computer or computer peripheral (such as a printer) only for your rental activity and keep it at your office, you need not comply with the record-keeping requirement. This includes computers that you keep at your home office if the office qualifies for the home office deduction.

> **EXAMPLE:** John owns four rental properties and uses his home office exclusively for his rental activities. The office qualifies for the home office deduction. He buys a $2,000 computer for his office and uses it exclusively for his rental activities. He does not have to keep records showing how he uses the computer.

This exception applies only to computers and computer peripheral equipment. It doesn't apply to other items such as calculators, copiers, fax machines, or typewriters.

Asset Files

You should establish an asset file where you keep all your records supporting your depreciation deductions. This doesn't have to be anything fancy. An accordion file will work fine. Make a separate file for each rental property you own.

Keep your real property closing statements and any documentation showing the cost of the land, such as appraisals and property tax statements.

File your receipts for each long-term asset you purchase, as well as canceled checks or credit card statements proving how much you paid. It's particularly important to keep receipts for real property improvements, because these will affect the tax basis of your real property. (See Chapter 5.)

You need not file any of these supporting documents with your tax returns, but you must have them available in case the IRS audits you and questions your depreciation deductions.

Records Required for Local Travel

If you use a car or other vehicle for rental business purposes, you're entitled to take a deduction for gas and other auto expenses. You can either deduct the actual cost of your gas and other expenses, or take the standard rate deduction based on the number of rental miles you drive.

Either way, you must keep a record of:

- your mileage
- the dates of your rental business trips
- the places you drove for rental business, and
- the rental business purpose for your trips.

The last three items are relatively easy to keep track of. You can record the information in your appointment book, calendar, or day planner. Or, you can record it in a mileage logbook—you can get one for a few dollars from any stationery store and stash it in your car's glove compartment.

Calculating your mileage takes more work. The IRS wants to know the total number of miles you drove during the year for rental business, commuting, and personal driving other than commuting. Commuting is travel between home and your office or other principal place where you conduct your rental activity. If you work from a home office, you'll have no commuting mileage. Personal miles include, for example, trips to the grocery store, personal vacations, or visits to friends or relatives.

There are several ways to keep track of your mileage; some are easy and some are a bit more complicated.

52-Week Mileage Book

The hardest way to track your mileage—and the way the IRS would like you to do it—is to keep track of every mile you drive every day, 52 weeks a year, using a mileage logbook or rental diary. This means you'll list every trip you take, whether for rental or personal reasons. If you enjoy record keeping, go ahead and use this method. But there are easier ways.

Tracking Rental Mileage

An easier way to keep track of your mileage is to record your mileage only when you use your car for your rental activity. Here's what to do:

- obtain a mileage log book and keep it in your car with a pen attached
- note your odometer reading in the logbook at the beginning and end of every year that you use the car for rental purposes. (If you don't know your January 1 odometer reading for this year, you might be able to estimate it by looking at auto repair receipts that note your mileage.)
- record your mileage and note the rental purpose for the trip every time you use your car for rental purposes, and

- add up your rental activity mileage when you get to the end of each page in the logbook. (This way, you'll only have to add the page totals at the end of the year instead of all the individual entries.)

Here's an example of a portion of a page from a mileage logbook.

Date	Destination	Rental Purpose	Mileage at Beginning of Trip	Mileage at End of Trip	Rental Miles	User's Name
5/1	Acme Hardware store, Fresno	Purchase supplies	50,000	50,020	20	Jack S.
5/10	123 Main St., Fresno	Inspect rental property	50,100	50,175	75	Jack S.
5/20	123 Main St., Fresno	Repair rental property	50,500	50,575	75	Jack S.
5/30	Lawyer's office, 666 1st St., Stockton	Consult with lawyer re: eviction	51,000	51,050	50	Jack S.

At the end of the year, your logbook will show the total rental activity miles you drove during the year. Calculate the total miles you drove during the year by subtracting your January 1 odometer reading from your December 31 reading.

If you use the actual expense method, you must also calculate your percentage of rental use of the car. Do this by dividing your rental miles by your total miles.

EXAMPLE: Yolanda owns six rental properties over 100 miles apart. At the beginning of the year her odometer reading was 34,201 miles. On December 31, it was 58,907 miles. Her total mileage for the year was therefore 24,706. She recorded 31 rental trips in her mileage logbook for a total of 4,140 miles. Her rental use percentage of her car is 17% (4,140 ÷ 24,706 = 16.7%).

Record Your Mileage Electronically

If writing your mileage down in a paper mileage logbook seems too primitive, you can keep your records in electronic form with a Palm Pilot or computer. There is special software available for recording rental mileage. However, be warned: Although the IRS's official policy is that electronic records are acceptable, many IRS auditors are old-fashioned. They like to see paper and ink mileage records because they are much harder to alter, forge, or create in a hurry than electronic records.

Sampling Method

The sampling method is the easiest way to track your mileage. Under this method, you keep track of your rental mileage for a sample portion of the year and use your figures for that period to extrapolate your rental mileage for the whole year.

This method assumes that you drive about the same amount for rental purposes throughout the year. To back up this assumption, you must scrupulously keep an appointment book showing your rental activity appointments all year long. If you don't want to keep an appointment book, don't use the sampling method.

Your sample period must be at least 90 days—for example, the first three months of the year. Alternatively, you may sample one week each month—for example, the first week of every month. You don't have to use the first three months of the year or the first week of every month; you could use any other three-month period or the second, third, or fourth week of every month. Use whatever works best for you—you want your sample period to be as representative as possible of the rental travel you do throughout the year.

You must keep track of the total miles you drove during the year by taking odometer readings on January 1 and December 31 and deduct any atypical mileage before applying your sample results.

> **EXAMPLE:** Tom, the owner of three apartment buildings he manages himself, uses the sample method to compute his mileage by keeping track of his rental miles for the first three months of the year. He drove 7,000 miles during that time, and had 1,000 rental activity miles. His rental use percentage of his car was 14%. From his January 1 and December 31 odometer readings, Tom knows he drove a total of 27,000 miles during the year. However, Tom drove to the Grand Canyon for vacation, so he deducts this 1,000 mile trip from his total. This leaves him with 26,000 total miles for the year. To calculate his total rental miles, he multiplies the yearlong total by the rental use percentage of his car: 14% x 26,000 = 3,640. Tom claims 3,640 rental activity miles on his Schedule E.

Keeping Track of Actual Expenses

If you take the deduction for your actual auto expenses instead of using the standard rate (or if you are thinking about switching to this method), keep receipts for all of your auto-related expenses, including gasoline, oil, tires, repairs, and insurance. Create a category for auto expenses in your expense journal. Also, when you figure your depreciation deduction for the year, you'll need to include the amount you're entitled to deduct for depreciation of your auto. (See Chapter 10 for more on using the actual expense method, including vehicle depreciation.)

Allocating Your Rental Miles

You are required to list on Schedule E your car expenses for each rental property you own. This is no problem if you only own one property. But things can get more complicated if you own more than one, because you may make some trips that benefit more than one property at the same time—for example, a trip to the hardware store to purchase supplies you'll use for all your properties. In this event, you must allocate your mileage among your properties. You can split your mileage equally or use a percentage based on the income your properties earn.

Use a Credit Card for Gas

If you use the actual expense method for car expenses, you should use a credit card when you buy gas. It's best to designate a separate card for this purpose. The monthly statements you receive will serve as your gas receipts. If you pay cash for gas, you must either get a receipt or make a note of the amount in your mileage logbook.

Costs for rental-related parking (other than at your office) and for tolls are separately deductible whether you use the standard rate or the actual expense method. Get and keep receipts for these expenses.

Records Required for Long-Distance Travel, Meals, Entertainment, and Gifts

Deductions for travel, meals, entertainment, and gifts are hot-button items for the IRS because they have been greatly abused by many taxpayers. You need to have more records for these expenses than for almost any others, and they will be closely scrutinized if you're audited.

Whenever you incur an expense for rental-related travel, meals, gifts, or entertainment, you must document the following five facts:

- **The date.** The date you incurred the expense will usually be listed on a receipt or credit card slip; appointment books, day planners, and similar documents have the dates preprinted on each page, so entries on the appropriate page automatically date the expense.
- **The amount.** You'll need to be able to prove how much you spent, including tax and tip for meals.
- **The place.** Where you incurred the expense will usually be shown on a receipt, or you can record it in an appointment book.
- **The rental activity purpose.** You'll have to be able to show that the expense was incurred for your rental activity—for example, that you took an out-of-town trip to inspect or repair one of your rental properties.
- **The rental activity relationship.** If entertainment is involved, you should record how the people at the event relate to your rental activity—for example, list their names and occupations and any other information needed to establish their relation to you as a landlord.

The chart below shows the information your records must contain for travel, meal and entertainment, and gift expenses.

The IRS does not require you to keep receipts, canceled checks, credit card slips, or any other supporting documents for travel, meal and entertainment, and gift expenses that cost less than $75. *However, you must still document the five facts listed above.* This exception does not apply to lodging—that is, hotel or similar costs—when you travel for your rental activity. You do need receipts for these expenses, even if they cost less than $75.

All this record keeping is not as hard as it sounds. You can record the five facts you have to document in a variety of ways, and the information doesn't have to be all in one place. Information that is shown on a receipt, canceled check, or other item need not be duplicated in a log, appointment book, calendar, or account book. Thus, for example, you can record the five facts with:

- a receipt, credit card slip, or similar document alone
- a receipt combined with an appointment book entry, or
- an appointment book entry alone (for expenses less than $75).

However you document your expense, you are supposed to do it in a timely manner. You don't need to record the details of every expense on the day you incur it. It is sufficient to record them on a weekly basis. However, if you're prone to forget details, it's best to get everything you need in writing within a day or two.

Proof Required for Travel, Entertainment, and Gift Deductions

Records Must Show	Amount	Time	Place or Description	Rental Purpose and Relationship
Travel	Cost of each separate expense for travel, lodging, and meals. Incidental expenses may be totaled in categories, such as taxis, daily meals, and so on.	Dates you left and returned for each trip, and the number of days spent on rental business	Name of city, town, or other destination	Rental purpose for the expense, or the benefit gained or expected to be gained
Entertainment (including meals)	Cost of each separate expense. Incidental expenses such as taxis, telephones, and so on may be totaled on a daily basis.	Date of entertainment	Name and address or location of entertainment; type of entertainment, if not otherwise apparent	Nature of discussion or activity; for entertainment directly before or after discussion: • date, place, nature, and duration of discussion regarding rental activity • identities of people who took part in discussion and entertainment • occupations or other information (such as names or titles) about the recipients that shows their relationship to you • proof that you or your employee were present at meal
Gifts	Cost of gift	Date of gift	Description of gift	Same as for entertainment

Receipts to Keep	
Type of Expense	**Receipts to Save**
Travel	Airplane, train, or bus ticket stubs, travel agency receipts, rental car receipts, and so on
Meals	Meal check, credit card slip
Lodging	Statement or bill from hotel or other lodging provider; your own written records for cleaning, laundry, telephone charges, tips, and other charges not shown separately on hotel statement
Entertainment	Bill from entertainment provider, ticket stubs for sporting event, theatre, or other event, credit card slips

How Long to Keep Records

You need to have copies of your tax returns and supporting documents available in case the IRS or another taxing agency (such as your state income tax agency) audits you. You might also need them for other purposes—for example, to get a loan, mortgage, or insurance. Keep your records for as long as the IRS has to audit you after you file your returns for the year. These statutes of limitation range from three years to forever—they are listed in the table below.

To be on the safe side, keep your tax returns indefinitely. They usually don't take up much space, so this shouldn't be a big hardship. Your supporting documents probably take up more space. Hang on to these for at least six years after you file your return.

Keep your long-term asset records for as long as you own the property and for three years after you sell or otherwise dispose of it.

Scanning Your Records

If you don't want to keep paper copies of your tax records, you can make digital copies by scanning them and storing them on a computer hard disk or CD-ROM. The IRS has approved the use of electronic storage systems for this purpose. (Rev Proc 97-22, 1997-1 CB 652.)

Record Keeping Made Easy When You Travel

Here's an easy way to keep your travel expense records. When you go on a trip for your rental activity, keep all your receipts in an envelope. When you get back from your trip, sort all your receipts by category—for example, airfare, hotel bills, meals and tips, entertainment, taxis, and car rental.

If your trip was within the United States (as is the vast majority of travel by landlords), you may deduct 100% of your travel expenses (airfare, car expense, and so on) if you spent over half of your time during the trip on rental business. You may deduct your lodging and meal expenses only on the days you spent most of your time on rental business. If you spend over half your trip on personal business, you get virtually no tax deductions. (For more details on travel deduction rules, see Chapter 11.)

Keeping these rules in mind, total your expenses for each category. Do not include nondeductible personal expenses, such as lodging and meals for days you didn't do rental business. Write the totals on the outside of the envelope. Then list the total for all your travel expenses. When figuring this total, only include 50% of your total meal and entertainment expenses because these expenses are only 50% deductible. (See Chapter 14.)

Note on the envelope the dates and place of your trip and the percentage of your time devoted to business. Also note the reason for the trip—the reason should relate to your rental activity. If you have correspondence or other records documenting the purpose, keep them in the envelope as well. Keep a separate envelope for each trip you take.

To make things even simpler, you can avoid having to record the actual cost of your own meals and other incidentals while traveling on business if you use the IRS's standard allowance for these items.

Your final step is to transfer the figures from your envelope to your monthly expense journal. Enter in your journal the total for all your expenses under Travel. Make a note in your journal if you use the IRS standard allowance for meals. Save your envelopes with your travel receipts along with all your other rental activity receipts.

IRS Statute of Limitations	
If:	**The limitations period is:**
You failed to pay all the tax due	3 years
You underreported your gross income for the year by more than 25%	6 years
You filed a fraudulent return	No limit
You did not file a return	No limit

When You Don't Have Proper Tax Records

Because you're human, you may not have kept all the records required to back up your tax deductions. Don't despair, all is not lost—you may be able to fall back on the *Cohan* rule. This rule (named after the Broadway entertainer George M. Cohan, who was involved in a tax case in the 1930s) is the taxpayer's best friend. The *Cohan* rule recognizes that you must spend at least some money when you own rental property, and so you must have at least some deductible expenses, even if you don't have adequate records to back them up.

If you're audited and lack adequate records for a claimed deduction, the IRS can use the *Cohan* rule to make an estimate of how much you must have spent, and allow you to deduct that amount. However, you must provide at least some credible evidence on which to base this estimate, such as receipts, canceled checks, notes in your appointment book, or other records. Moreover, the IRS will allow you to deduct only the smallest amount you might have spent, based on the records you provide. In addition, the *Cohan* rule cannot be used for travel, meal, entertainment, or gift expenses, or for listed property.

If an auditor claims you lack sufficient records to back up a deduction, you should always bring up the *Cohan* rule and argue that you should still get the deduction based on the records you do have. At best, you'll probably get only part of your claimed deductions. If the IRS auditor disallows your deductions entirely or doesn't give you as much as you think you deserve, you can appeal in court and bring up the *Cohan* rule again there. You might have more success with a judge. However, you can't compel an IRS auditor or a court to apply the *Cohan* rule in your favor. They have discretion to decide whether to apply the rule and how large a deduction to give you.

Reconstructing Tax Records

If you can prove that you possessed adequate records at one time, but now lack them due to circumstances beyond your control, you can reconstruct your records for an IRS audit. Circumstances beyond your control include acts of nature such as floods, fires, or earthquakes, or theft. (Treas. Reg. 1.275.5(c)(5).) If you lose your tax records while moving, that doesn't constitute circumstances beyond your control. To reconstruct the needed records, you either create brand-new records just for your audit or obtain other evidence to corroborate your deductions—for example, statements from people or companies from whom you purchased items for your rental activity.

Accounting Methods

An accounting method is a set of rules that you will use to determine when and how to report your income and expenses. Accounting methods might sound like a rather dry subject, but your choice about how to account for your rental expenses and income will have a huge impact on your tax deductions. You don't have to become as expert as a C.P.A. on this topic, but you should understand the basics.

You must choose an accounting method when you file your first tax return for your rental activity. If you later want to change your accounting method, you must get IRS approval. There are two basic methods of accounting: cash basis and accrual basis. Almost all small landlords use the cash method because it's, by far, the simpler of the two.

Cash Method

Most individuals use the cash method for their personal taxes. The cash method is based on this commonsense idea: You haven't earned income for tax purposes until you actually receive the money, and you haven't incurred an expense until you actually pay the money. Using the cash basis method, then, is like maintaining a checkbook. You record income only when the money is received and expenses only when you actually pay them. If you borrow money to pay rental activity expenses, you incur an expense under the cash method only when you make payments on the loan.

The Cash Method of Paying Expenses

Although it's called the cash method, this method for paying business expenses includes payments by check, credit card, or electronic funds transfer, as well as payments by cash. If you pay by check, the amount is deemed paid during the year in which the check is drawn and mailed—for example, a check dated December 31, 2008, is considered paid during 2008 only if it has a December 31, 2008, postmark. If you're using a check to pay a substantial expense, you may wish to mail it by certified mail so you'll have proof of when it was mailed.

EXAMPLE 1: Helen has a vacant rental unit. She signs a lease with a new tenant on December 20, but the tenant does not give her a check for the first month's rent until January 5 of the following year. Using the cash method, Helen records the payment as income in January—when she receives it.

EXAMPLE 2: On December 1, 2008, Helen goes to the Acme home care store and buys a snow blower for her rental business. She buys the item on credit from Acme—she's not required to make any payments until March 1, 2009. Helen does not record the expense until 2009, when she actually pays for the snow blower.

EXAMPLE 3: On December 15, 2008, Helen buys a washer and dryer for the rental property, and pays for it with a credit card. She receives her statement from the bank that issued the card in January. Helen records the expense in December 2008.

Constructive Receipt

Under the cash method, payments are constructively received when an amount is credited to your account or otherwise made available to you without restrictions. Constructive receipt is as good as actual receipt. If you authorize someone to be your agent to receive income for you, you are considered to have received it when your agent receives it. For example, you constructively receive a rental check when your apartment manager receives it from a tenant.

EXAMPLE: Your tenant has his monthly rent checks directly deposited into your rental checking account. Your tenant's January 2008 rent check is credited to your account on December 30, 2007, but you do not withdraw it or enter it into your passbook until January 5, 2008. You must include the amount in gross rental income for 2007—not 2008.

No Postponing Income

You cannot hold checks or other payments from one tax year to another to avoid paying tax on the income. You must report the income in the year you receive the payment or when it's made available to you without restriction.

EXAMPLE: On December 1, 2008, Helen receives a $1,000 rent check from a tenant. She holds the check and doesn't cash it until January 10, 2009. She still has to report the $1,000 as income for 2008 because she constructively received it that year.

No Prepayment of Expenses

The general rule is that you can't prepay expenses when you use the cash method— you can't hurry up the payment of expenses by paying them in advance. An expense you pay in advance can be deducted only in the year to which it applies.

However, there is an important exception to the general rule called the 12-month rule. Under this rule, you may deduct a prepaid expense in the current year if the expense is for a right or benefit that extends no longer than the earlier of:

- 12 months, or
- until the end of the tax year after the tax year in which you made the payment.

EXAMPLE 1: You are a calendar-year taxpayer and you pay $10,000 on July 1, 2008, for a landlord insurance policy that is effective for one year beginning July 1, 2008. The 12-month rule applies because the benefit you've paid for—a landlord insurance policy—extends only 12 months into the future. Therefore, the full $10,000 is deductible in 2008.

EXAMPLE 2: You are a calendar-year taxpayer and you pay $3,000 in 2008 for a landlord insurance policy that is effective for three years, beginning July 1, 2008. This payment does not qualify for the 12-month rule because the benefit extends more than 12 months. Therefore, you must use the general rule: $500 is deductible in 2008, $1,000 is deductible in 2009, $1,000 is deductible in 2010, and $500 is deductible in 2011.

To use the 12-month rule, you must apply it when you first start using the cash method for your rental activity. You must get IRS approval if you haven't been using the rule and want to start doing so. Such approval is granted automatically upon filing IRS Form 3115.

Accrual Method

In accrual basis accounting, you report income or expenses as they are earned or incurred, rather than when they are actually collected or paid. You don't have to wait until you see the money or actually pay money out of your checking account. The accrual method can be difficult to use because complex rules determine when income or expenses accrue.

Expenses

Under the accrual method, you generally deduct a rental expense when:
- you are legally obligated to pay the expense
- the amount you owe can be determined with reasonable accuracy, and
- you have received or used the property or services involved.

EXAMPLE: Bill, the owner of two apartment buildings, borrows $10,000 from his bank to help remodel his rentals. He signs a promissory note on December 15, 2008, and receives the money the same day, but doesn't start making payments to the bank until the following January. Bill can deduct the expense in 2008 because he became legally obligated to pay the expense upon signing the note, the amount of the expense can be determined from the note, and he received the money that day.

Thus, when you use the accrual method, you can take a deduction for an expense you incur, even if you don't actually pay for it until the following year. You can't do this under the cash basis method. There are obvious advantages to getting a tax deduction this year without actually having to shell out any money until a future year. But don't get too excited—the flip side (treatment of income) pretty much cancels out this advantage.

Income

When it comes to income, the accrual method has significant disadvantages compared to the cash method. Under the accrual method, you report an amount in your gross income on the earliest of the following dates:

- when you receive payment
- when the income amount is due to you, or
- when you earn the income.

Thus, you may have to report an amount as income even if you haven't received it. For example, you'd have to report as income rent due even if a tenant has failed to pay it. You could later deduct the amount as a bad debt if it proves uncollectible. (See Chapter 14.) This is one important reason few small landlords use the accrual method.

Obtaining IRS Permission to Change Your Accounting Method

You choose your accounting method by checking a box on your tax form when you file your tax return. Once you choose a method, you can't change it without getting permission from the IRS. Permission is granted automatically for many types of changes, including using the 12-month rule to deduct prepaid expenses. You must file IRS Form 3115, *Application for Change in Accounting Method* with your tax return for the year you want to make the change (if the change is automatically granted).

Automatic approval can also be obtained to change to the cash method if you've been using the accrual method and come within one of the exceptions discussed above. However, changing your accounting method can have serious consequences, so consult a tax professional before doing so.

Tax Years

You are required to pay taxes for a 12-month period, also known as the tax year. Almost all small landlords use the calendar year as their tax year—that is,

January 1 through December 31. Indeed, sole proprietors, partnerships, limited liability companies, and S corporations are required to use the calendar.

However, in some cases it is possible to use a tax year that does not end in December (also known as a fiscal year). You need to get the IRS's permission to use a fiscal year. The IRS might grant you permission if you can show a good reason for it. For example, you rent a condo in a winter resort in January and February, but you incur the bulk of your annual expenses in December of each year because you need to get the condo ready to rent. Using a tax year other than the calendar year will more accurately show your annual income and expenses. To get permission to use a fiscal year, you must file IRS Form 8716, Election to Have a Tax Year Other Than a Required Tax Year.

■

Chapter 18

All About Schedule E

This chapter shows how to fill out IRS Schedule E, the tax form landlords use to report their income and deductions to the IRS. We provide a detailed example to illustrate how the form works in real life.

Who Must File Schedule E?

You must file Schedule E if, like most small landlords, you receive rental income from property that you own as an individual. It doesn't matter whether you own the rental property alone, with your spouse, or with one or more co-owners.

However, if you own or use your rental property in one of the following manners, you do not use Schedule E to report rental income or deductions for the property:

- **Ownership through a business entity.** Partnerships, limited partnerships, LLCs, and small business corporations file IRS Form 8825, Rental Real Estate Income and Expenses of a Partnership or an S Corporation to report rental income and deductions. This form is very similar to Schedule E.
- **Ownership as a real estate dealer.** A real estate dealer buys and sells real property as a business. (See Chapter 2.) Dealers file IRS Schedule C, Profit or Loss From Business, the tax form used by individual business owners other than landlords. However, if a dealer owns rental property as a long-term investment, then he or she must file Schedule E to report the income and expenses for that property.
- **Not-for-profit real property owners.** If your rental activity constitutes a not-for-profit activity for tax purposes, you report any deductible expenses on Schedule A, Itemized Deductions. (See Chapter 2.)
- **Tax-free vacation homes.** If you own a vacation home that you rent out for fewer than 15 days a year and use personally for 15 days or more, you don't need to file a Schedule E. The income from the home is tax free. (See Chapter 15.)
- **Hotels and motels.** If you operate a hotel, motel, or similar property where significant personal services (such as maid services) are provided to guests, you do not file a Schedule E. An individual owner of such a property files Schedule C, Profit or Loss From Business.

SCHEDULE E (Form 1040)	Supplemental Income and Loss	OMB No. 1545-0074

SCHEDULE E (Form 1040)

Department of the Treasury
Internal Revenue Service   (99)

Supplemental Income and Loss

(From rental real estate, royalties, partnerships,
S corporations, estates, trusts, REMICs, etc.)

► Attach to Form 1040, 1040NR, or Form 1041.   ► See Instructions for Schedule E (Form 1040).

OMB No. 1545-0074

2**006**

Attachment
Sequence No. **13**

Name(s) shown on return

Your social security number

Part I   **Income or Loss From Rental Real Estate and Royalties**   **Note.** If you are in the business of renting personal property, use **Schedule C** or **C-EZ** (see page E-3). Report farm rental income or loss from **Form 4835** on page 2, line 40.

1 List the type and location of each **rental real estate property:**

A ....

B ....

C ....

2 For each rental real estate property listed on line 1, did you or your family use it during the tax year for personal purposes for more than the greater of:
- 14 days **or**
- 10% of the total days rented at fair rental value?
(See page E-3.)

	Yes	No
A		
B		
C		

Income:

		Properties			Totals (Add columns A, B, and C.)
		A	B	C	
3 Rents received	3				3
4 Royalties received	4				4

Expenses:

		A	B	C
5 Advertising	5			
6 Auto and travel (see page E-4).	6			
7 Cleaning and maintenance	7			
8 Commissions	8			
9 Insurance	9			
10 Legal and other professional fees	10			
11 Management fees	11			
12 Mortgage interest paid to banks, etc. (see page E-4)	12			
13 Other interest	13			
14 Repairs	14			
15 Supplies	15			
16 Taxes	16			
17 Utilities	17			
18 Other (list) ►	18			

(Line 12 Totals: **12**)

		A	B	C	Totals
19 Add lines 5 through 18	19				19
20 Depreciation expense or depletion (see page E-4)	20				20
21 Total expenses. Add lines 19 and 20	21				
22 Income or (loss) from rental real estate or royalty properties. Subtract line 21 from line 3 (rents) or line 4 (royalties). If the result is a (loss), see page E-5 to find out if you must file **Form 6198**	22				
23 Deductible rental real estate loss. **Caution.** Your rental real estate loss on line 22 may be limited. See page E-5 to find out if you must file **Form 8582**. Real estate professionals must complete line 43 on page 2	23	( )	( )	( )	

24 Income. Add positive amounts shown on line 22. **Do not** include any losses **24**

25 Losses. Add royalty losses from line 22 and rental real estate losses from line 23. Enter total losses here   **25** ( )

26 **Total rental real estate and royalty income or (loss).** Combine lines 24 and 25. Enter the result here. If Parts II, III, IV, and line 40 on page 2 do not apply to you, also enter this amount on Form 1040, line 17, or Form 1040NR, line 18. Otherwise, include this amount in the total on line 41 on page 2   **26**

For Paperwork Reduction Act Notice, see page E-7 of the instructions.   Cat. No. 11344L   **Schedule E (Form 1040) 2006**

Filling Out Schedule E

Completing Schedule E is a relatively straightforward process. You fill out only the first page, which is called Part I. (Part I is also used for royalties, which have nothing to do with rental property.) Parts II-V on the second page are only used by partnerships, S corporations, estates, trusts, and real estate mortgage investment conduits (REMICS, a type of real estate investment).

You separately list on the schedule your income and expenses for each rental property you own. A rental property comprises all the rental units you have at a single address. If you own a multiunit building, you must add together the income and expenses from all the units and list the totals on Schedule E.

Schedule E is designed to be used by up to three rental properties, labeled A, B, and C; there are separate columns for each property. If you have more than three rental properties, complete and attach as many Schedule Es as you need for them all. However, fill in the Totals column on only one Schedule E—the figures in the Totals column on that Schedule E should be the combined totals of all your Schedule Es.

If you own only a part interest in a rental property, report only your share of the property's income and expenses.

EXAMPLE: Betty and Bettina each own a 50% interest in a duplex they rent out. Betty reports 50% of the property's income and expenses on her Schedule E, and Bettina reports the other 50% on her Schedule E.

Use a software program to keep track of your income and expenses. *Quicken Rental Property Manager* is specifically designed to help landlords track and categorize rental income and expenses for Schedule E reporting.

Property Description (Line 1)

You need to describe each rental property in Line 1. You need to show only:
- the kind of property you rented (for example, townhouse)
- the street address, city or town, and state. You do not have to give the ZIP code, and
- your percentage of ownership in the property, if less than 100%.

EXAMPLE: Duplex, 100 Main St, Anytown, IN, 50% owner

Vacation Home Boxes (Line 2)

Line 2 contains Yes or No boxes you must check for each property. These boxes have to do with vacation home and second home rentals. If you check either of the Yes boxes, the vacation home tax rules described in Chapter 15 will apply to you. These greatly limit your tax deductions.

Rental Income (Line 3)

List your total annual rental income for each property in Line 3, and list the total amount for all the properties in the Totals column. This will primarily consist of the rent your tenants pay you. But it could also include:

- laundry income
- fees you charge tenants for paying rent late
- garage or other parking charges
- interest you earn on tenant security deposits
- security deposits you retain to pay for repairs, unpaid rent, or other expenses
- the value of services tenants provide in lieu of rent, or
- payments tenants make to you for repairs or other expenses. (See Chapter 4.)

A security deposit you receive from a tenant is not rental income if you plan to return it when the tenancy ends. But, if you keep all or part of a security deposit when a tenant leaves, the amount you keep is rental income. Any interest you earn on your tenants' security deposits is also rental income, unless you are required to repay it to your tenants when they move out. Some cities require this under their rent control laws.

Interest you earn on your rental checking account, if any, is not rental income. It is personal interest. Do not include it in your rental income on Schedule E.

Expenses (Lines 5–19)

You list your expenses for each property in the Expenses section, Lines 5–18. Your expenses must be broken down into categories; Schedule E lists 13 expense categories:

- **Advertising.** This includes signs, classified ads, and other advertising expenses to rent your property.
- **Auto and travel.** This category includes both local and long-distance travel expenses. (See Chapters 10 and 11.) If you have both types of expenses, you must add them together.

- **Cleaning and maintenance.** This includes janitorial services, gardening, cleaning carpets, drapes, and rugs. Do not include repairs here—repairs are done to fix property after it's broken; maintenance keeps your property in good working order so it won't break down.

- **Commissions.** This category will apply to you only if you hire a rental agency or property management company to help you with your rentals. Such agencies and companies are typically paid a commission—that is, a percentage of the rent they collect (for example, 5% or 10%). Some property managers deduct their commissions from the rents they collect before they send it to the property owner. In this event, be sure to list the total amount of rent charged in the rental income line, not the amount the property manager sends you after deducting the commission.

- **Insurance.** This includes any type of insurance for your rental activity, except for private mortgage insurance and title insurance (see Chapter 14).

- **Legal and other professional fees.** This includes tax advice and preparing tax forms for your rental activity. Some legal fees incurred for buying property aren't deductible; they are added to the property's basis and depreciated. (See Chapter 5.)

- **Management fees.** These are fees charged by rental agencies and property management companies. If you pay such fees, list the total here.

- **Mortgage interest paid to banks.** If you have a mortgage on your rental property, list the amount of interest you paid during the year to banks or other financial institutions. If you paid $600 or more in interest on a mortgage during the year, the financial institution should send you a Form 1098 or similar statement by February showing the total interest received from you. Points, including loan origination fees, charged only for the use of money must be deducted over the life of the loan. (See Chapter 7.) Include the amount you can deduct this year in your mortgage interest total.

- **Other interest.** This is interest you paid to a lender other than a bank or other financial institution—for example, interest on a credit card you use for rental expenses, or interest you pay to the seller of rental property you purchased with creative financing. Also, if you and at least one other person (other than your spouse if you file a joint return) were liable for and paid interest on a mortgage, and the other person received Form 1098, report your share of the deductible interest on this line. Attach a statement to your return showing the name and address of the person who received Form 1098. In the left margin next to the Other interest line, write "See attached."

- **Repairs.** Repairs keep your property in good working order. They do not add significant value to your property or extend its life. Do not include the cost of improvements in this line; they must be depreciated over several years. (See Chapter 4.)

- **Supplies.** This includes office supplies and supplies you use for repairs and maintenance—for example, paint and brushes, or fertilizer. It does not include materials you purchase to undertake improvements—for example, it would not include the cost of the shingles used to install a new roof on your rental property. You must depreciate these materials. (See Chapter 5.)

- **Taxes.** This includes employment taxes you pay if you have employees—for example, a resident manager.

- **Utilities.** This includes charges for water, garbage pickup, gas, and electricity you pay for your rental property. You may also deduct the cost of telephone calls for your rental activities—for example, calls to your renter. However, the base rate (including taxes and other charges) for local telephone service for the first telephone line into your residence is a personal expense that you cannot deduct. Don't include utilities for a home office here.

The Schedule E categories probably include most of your expenses, but you may have others that are not listed—for example:

- home office expenses (Chapter 9)
- travel expenses (Chapter 11)
- car expenses (Chapter 10)
- gifts (Chapter 14)
- homeowner association dues for rental condominiums and planned-unit developments
- start-up expenses (Chapter 8)
- entertainment expenses (Chapter 14)
- wages and salaries for employees
- education expenses (Chapter 14)
- dues and subscriptions (Chapter 14)
- casualty losses (Chapter 13), and
- equipment rental.

If you have expenses for these or other items, list them by category in the Other line. You create your own categories here.

You add up all your expenses for each property and then put the total of all expenses for all properties in the right hand column of Line 19.

Depreciation (Line 20)

You list your total depreciation deduction for each property in the depreciation line and then include the total for all properties in the right-hand column. You must also complete and attach Form 4562, Depreciation and Amortization, if you are claiming:

- depreciation on property first placed in service during the year
- depreciation on listed property including a vehicle, regardless of the date it was placed in service, or
- a Section 179 expense deduction or amortization of costs that began during the year.

You should complete depreciation worksheets for each of your properties. But you don't have to attach them to your return. (See Chapter 5 for a detailed discussion of depreciation.)

Total Income or Loss (Lines 21–22)

Total all your expenses for each property and list the amount in Line 21. Subtract this amount from the rental income you reported in Line 3. The result will either be a net loss or net income for the year. If the amount is a loss, put parentheses around it.

Deductible Loss (Line 23)

If you have a net loss for the year, the amount you can deduct may be limited by the passive activity loss rules. Most small landlords can deduct all or part of their losses by using the $25,000 offset exception to the passive activity rules. If you are able to deduct all your losses by using the offset, you don't need to file Form 8582, Passive Activity Loss Limitations. If you can't deduct all your losses by using the offset, you'll have to complete Form 8582 to figure the amount of loss you can deduct, if any. Enter the deductible amount of your loss, if any, on Line 23. (See Chapter 16 for a detailed discussion of the passive loss rules.)

Total Income and Loss (Lines 24–26)

Add up the total income and losses from all your properties and list the amounts in Lines 24 and 25, respectively. Subtract your total loss from your total income and list the amount in Line 26. This is your total rental real estate activity income or loss for the year. You also enter this amount in the income section of the first page of your Form 1040.

Schedule E Example

Jack rents out a single-family home and a four-unit apartment building. He carefully keeps track of his rental income and expenses throughout the year, using income and expense journals as described in Chapter 17.

At the end of the year, his income journal shows the following income from the apartment building:

December Rental Income—Apartment Building

Unit #	Rent	Laundry	Garage	Late Fees	Interest	Other	Total Income
1	1,000		50			100 (payment for broken window pane)	1,150
2	1,000		50				1,050
3	1,000			25			1,025
4	1,000						1,000
All Units		160			17		177
Total this page	4,000	160	100	25	17	100	4,402
Total year to date	48,000	800	500	65	72	250	49,687

He also earned $15,000 in rent from his house, and had no other income from the property.

Here is his December expense journal for his apartment building, showing his total expenses for the year.

December Rental Expense Journal

Date	Check No.	Transaction	Amount	Advertising	Cleaning and Maintenance	Insurance
12/1	123	Acme Mortgage Co.	3,000			
12/3	124	Empire Plumbing Co.	209			
12/7	125	Bill's Gardening Service	80		80	
12/10	VISA	Daily Eagle Newspaper	50	50		
2/15	VISA	Gardening World	75			
12/18	126	Gloria Gonzalez	50		50	
12/23	127	County Tax Assessor	400			
12/30	128	Acme Insurance Co.	500			500
	129	City Water and Power Co.				
		Total this page	4,364	50	130	500
		Total year to date	33,836	90	500	2,000

The following journal page shows Jack's expenses from his rental house.

December Rental Expense Journal

Date	Check No.	Transaction	Amount	Cleaning and Maintenance	Insurance
12/1	123	Acme Mortgage Co.	800		
12/3	124	Sam Smith	111		
12/15	125	County Tax Assessor	400		
12/25	VISA	Acme Office Supplies	51		
		Total this page	1,362		
		Total year to date	13,159	100	1,015

Jack also drove 1,000 miles for his rental activity. He has an auto mileage log to back up this amount. He uses the standard mileage rate (2006) to figure his deduction, so his deduction is $445 (44.5 cents per mile x 1,000 miles = $445). He allocates this 80% to his apartment building and 20% to his rental house, based on the total rent he earns from the properties.

—Apartment Building

Legal and Other Professional Fees	Mortgage Interest Paid to Banks	Other Interest	Repairs	Supplies	Taxes	Utilities	Miscellaneous
	2,000						
			209				
				75			
					400		
						52	
	2,000		209	75	400	52	290 (casualty loss)
487	24,000	511	1,817	987	2,800	644	290

—House

Legal and Other Professional Fees	Mortgage Interest Paid to Banks	Other Interest	Repairs	Supplies	Taxes
	800				
			111		
					400
				51	
	800		111	51	400
536	9,600	100	922	286	800

Jack also prepares depreciation worksheets to show his depreciation deductions for the properties. He purchased his rental house for $145,000 in 2004, and depreciates the building, land improvements, and personal property separately. He installed a new roof for $10,000 in 2005. He purchased the apartment building for $240,000 in 2005. He concluded it was worth $200,000 without the land. He depreciates it as a whole. He also bought a dishwasher for one of his apartment rental units for $500 in 2005.

2006 Depreciation Worksheet

Description of Property	Date Placed in Service	Cost or Other Basis	Business/ Investment Use %	Section 179 Deduction
House—building	1/04	111,250	100%	0
House—land improvements	1/04	5,010	100%	0
House—personal property	1/04	5,500	100%	0
Subtotal—2004 Property				
House—new roof	3/05	10,000	100%	0
Subtotal—2005 Property				
Subtotal—2006 Property				0
Grand Total—2006				0

2006 Depreciation Worksheet

Description of Property	Date Placed in Service	Cost or Other Basis	Business/ Investment Use %	Section 179 Deduction
Apartment Building	8/05	200,000	100%	0
Dishwasher	5/05	500	100%	0
Subtotal—2005 Property				
Subtotal—2006 Property				0
Grand Total—2006				0

Jack reports his rental income, expenses, and depreciation on Part I of Schedule E. He lists the amount for the house in the column for Property A, and the amounts for the apartment building in the column for Property B. Jack has a casualty loss—an expense not included in the categories on Schedule E. He lists it in the Other line, and writes in "casualty loss."

He need not attach Form 4562, Depreciation and Amortization, to report his depreciation deduction because he didn't purchase any new property or make any new improvements to his existing property in 2006.

—House

Depreciation Prior Years	Basis for Depreciation	Depreciation Method/Convention	Recovery Period	Rate or Table %	Depreciation Deduction
$7,922	$111,240	SL/MM	27.5	3.636%	$4,045
725	5,000	150DB/HY	15	8.550%	428
3,120	6,000	200DB/HY	5	19.200%	1,056
					5,529
652	10,000	SL/MM	27.5	3.636%	364
					364
					0
					$5,893

—Apartment Building

Depreciation Prior Years	Basis for Depreciation	Depreciation Method/Convention	Recovery Period	Rate or Table %	Depreciation Deduction
$2,728	$200,000	SL/MM	27.5	3.636%	$7,272
100		200DB/HY	5	32.000%	160
					7,432
					0
					$7,432

Jack's completed Schedule E is shown below. Jack had a net loss of $4,327 from his house, and net income of $7,829 from his apartment building. This left Jack with a total net rental income for the year of $3,502. He must add this amount to the other income section on the first page of his Form 1040, and pay income tax on it.

Jack need not worry about the passive loss rules because his income from his rental activities exceeded his losses (he had no passive activities other than his rental properties).

SCHEDULE E (Form 1040) Department of the Treasury Internal Revenue Service (99)	**Supplemental Income and Loss** (From rental real estate, royalties, partnerships, S corporations, estates, trusts, REMICs, etc.) ▶ Attach to Form 1040, 1040NR, or Form 1041. ▶ See Instructions for Schedule E (Form 1040).	OMB No. 1545-0074 20**06** Attachment Sequence No. **13**

Name(s) shown on return	Your social security number
Jack Smith	123 45 6789

Part I   Income or Loss From Rental Real Estate and Royalties   Note. If you are in the business of renting personal property, use Schedule C or C-EZ (see page E-3). Report farm rental income or loss from **Form 4835** on page 2, line 40.

1	List the type and location of each **rental real estate property:**		2	For each rental real estate property listed on line 1, did you or your family use it during the tax year for personal purposes for more than the greater of: • 14 days **or** • 10% of the total days rented at fair rental value? (See page E-3.)		Yes	No
A	House 123 Main St.				A		X
B	Apartment Building 1000 1st St.				B		X
C					C		

Income:			Properties				Totals (Add columns A, B, and C.)	
			A	B	C			
3	Rents received	3	15,000	49,687		3	64,687	
4	Royalties received	4				4		
Expenses:								
5	Advertising	5		90				
6	Auto and travel (see page E-4).	6	90	355				
7	Cleaning and maintenance . .	7	100	500				
8	Commissions	8						
9	Insurance	9	1,015	2,000				
10	Legal and other professional fees	10	536	487				
11	Management fees	11						
12	Mortgage interest paid to banks, etc. (see page E-4)	12	9,600	24,000		12	33,600	
13	Other interest	13	100	511				
14	Repairs	14	922	1,817				
15	Supplies	15	286	987				
16	Taxes	16	800	2,800				
17	Utilities	17		644				
18	Other (list) ▶ casualty loss .	18		290				
19	Add lines 5 through 18 . . .	19	13,449	34,481		19	47,930	
20	Depreciation expense or depletion (see page E-4)	20	5,893	7,432		20	13,325	
21	Total expenses. Add lines 19 and 20	21	19,342	41,913				
22	Income or (loss) from rental real estate or royalty properties. Subtract line 21 from line 3 (rents) or line 4 (royalties). If the result is a (loss), see page E-5 to find out if you must file **Form 6198** . .	22	(4,342)	7,884				
23	Deductible rental real estate loss. **Caution.** Your rental real estate loss on line 22 may be limited. See page E-5 to find out if you must file **Form 8582**. Real estate professionals must complete line 43 on page 2	23	(4,342)( )( )					
24	**Income.** Add positive amounts shown on line 22. **Do not** include any losses				24	7,884	
25	**Losses.** Add royalty losses from line 22 and rental real estate losses from line 23. Enter total losses here				25	(4,342)	
26	**Total rental real estate and royalty income or (loss).** Combine lines 24 and 25. Enter the result here. If Parts II, III, IV, and line 40 on page 2 do not apply to you, also enter this amount on Form 1040, line 17, or Form 1040NR, line 18. Otherwise, include this amount in the total on line 41 on page 2				26	3,542	

For Paperwork Reduction Act Notice, see page E-7 of the instructions.   Cat. No. 11344L   Schedule E (Form 1040) 2006

Claiming Tax Deductions for Prior Years

S am, the owner of several rental houses, has managed his rental activities out of his home office for the last four years. However, he has never taken the home office deduction because he was afraid it would increase his chances of being audited. After reading this book, he realizes that he should have claimed the deduction on his last three tax returns. Had he done so, he would have saved thousands on his taxes. But what can he do now?

Fortunately, tax returns are not engraved in stone. If, like Sam, you realize that you failed to claim tax deductions to which you were entitled, you may be able to amend your tax returns for prior years and get the IRS to send you a refund check.

Reasons for Amending Your Tax Return

It's very common for taxpayers to file amended tax returns. Here are some reasons why you might want to amend a tax return:

- you forgot to take a deduction
- you have a net operating loss for the year and want to apply it to prior years
- you claimed a deduction to which you were not entitled
- you entered incorrect information on your return, or
- a retroactive change in the tax laws makes you eligible for an additional deduction.

You need not amend your return if you discover that you made a simple math error. These will be corrected by the IRS computers, and you'll be notified of the change by mail.

However, if you made a mistake in your favor, failed to report income, or took deductions to which you were not entitled, amending your return may avoid all or some fines, interest, and penalties if you're later audited by the IRS.

Filing an amended return makes an audit more likely. You don't have to file an amended return if you don't want to. Filing an amended tax return increases the chances that your tax return for the year involved will be audited by the IRS. Thus, it may not be worth doing unless you are entitled to a substantial refund. If you're not sure whether to amend, consult a tax professional for advice.

Time Limits for Filing Amended Returns

Unfortunately, you can't wait forever to amend a tax return for a prior year. If you wait too long, you'll forever lose your right to file an amended return for the year, even if it means you'll be forced to give up a deduction for that year to which you were legally entitled.

Three-Year Amendment Period

The general rule is that you must file an amended return within three years after the date you filed the original return, or two years after the date you paid the tax, whichever is later. The three-year period applies in most cases. Even if you filed your return for the year before April 15, it is deemed to be filed on that date for amendment purposes. For example, you have until April 15, 2012, to file an amended return for your 2008 taxes, which are deemed to have been filed on April 15, 2009 (even if you filed them earlier).

If you obtain an extension of time to file your original return for the year involved, you may add that time to the three-year period. You can get an automatic extension of time to file your return until October 15.

Section 179 Deductions

In the past, you had very little time to amend your return to claim a Section 179 deduction. (See Chapter 5.) IRS rules required that you file your amended return within six months after the due date for the return for the tax year involved, including any extensions of time you received. Because tax returns are ordinarily due on April 15, you had to file your amended return by October 15 to claim a Section 179 deduction for the prior year, unless you received an extension of time to file your return.

The IRS amended its rules in 2004 to permit taxpayers to amend their returns to claim Section 179 deductions using the same procedures as for any other deduction. This means the three-year limitation period applies. You may also amend your return to revoke a Section 179 election you previously made. However, this new rule applies only to Section 179 property placed in service from January 1, 2003, through December 31, 2005. After that, the old rules come back into force. (IRS Reg. 1.179-5T.)

Rental Activity Start-Up Expenses

If you want to deduct your rental activity start-up expenses, you must file an election with the IRS on or before the date your first tax return for your rentals is due. For example, if your rental activity began in 2007, you must file the election with your 2007 tax return, due April 15, 2008 (or later, if you receive an extension). If you miss this deadline, you have one last chance to make your election: You may file an amended return making the election within six months after the date your original return was due (October 15 if you got an extension). If you fail to do this, you will lose your right to deduct your start-up expenses and you'll have to treat them as capital expenses. (See Chapter 8 for a detailed discussion of deducting rental activity startup expenses.)

Changes in Depreciation Deductions

When you buy a rental property, you have the option of depreciating the building, land improvements, and personal property in the building separately. This leads to larger depreciation deductions the first few years you own the property. Such segmented depreciation (also called cost segregation) is covered in Chapter 6.

If you failed to use segmented depreciation, can you amend your return in a later year to refigure your depreciation deduction using this method? Yes, but it can be difficult. The IRS issued a regulation in 2004 stating that amending a tax return to use segmented depreciation constitutes a change in accounting method which requires the IRS's prior consent. (IRS Reg. 1.446-1T(e)(2)(ii)(d)(2)(i).) This involves filing IRS Form 3115, Application for Change In Accounting Method, and providing detailed information about the change. You'll need an accountant to do this for you. However, the IRS says that its consent is not needed for property placed in service before January 1, 2004, the effective date of its regulation. (*IRS Cost Segregation Audit Techniques Guide* (April 30, 2004).)

Should You File Your Amendment as Late as Possible?

The IRS ordinarily has only three years after a return is filed to audit the return. Filing a Form 1040X does not extend this period. Thus, if you file your Form 1040X near the end of the three-year period, the IRS will have very little time to audit your return for the year involved. As a result, it might accept your claim without auditing your return. However, it might also refuse to accept your 1040X unless you agree to extend the time it has to audit your return for the year.

How to Amend Your Return

If you, like the majority of landlords, are a sole proprietor or co-owner of your rental property, you amend your income tax return by filing IRS Form 1040X, Amended U.S. Individual Income Tax Return. When you file Form 1040X to obtain a refund of taxes you've already paid, it is called a claim for refund.

Filing an amended tax return is not terribly difficult. You can usually do it yourself, with or without the aid of a computer tax preparation program. The heart of the form consists of three columns: A, B, and C. You record the relevant figures from your original tax return in Column A; the corrected information is listed in Column C; and the difference between the two is listed in Column B. You must also provide a brief explanation for the changes.

> **EXAMPLE:** Sam, the landlord mentioned at the beginning of this chapter who failed to take the home office deduction, could provide the following explanation: "Home office deduction was not taken in 2008 by mistake. I later discovered I qualified for the deduction because I own a rental property business and use one room in my home as an office to manage my properties and transact business with tenants, vendors, and other rental property business associates. I also use the office to perform administrative tasks, such as keeping records and doing budgets. This office is not used for personal purposes. It was used exclusively as my rental business office for all of 2008."

If you're amending your previous year's tax return and are entitled to an additional refund for that year, tax experts suggest that you wait until you receive your original refund check for that year. You can go ahead and cash the first refund check as soon as you receive it. Of course, you can file your amended return immediately if you were not entitled to a refund on your original return.

You must mail or hand deliver Form 1040X to the IRS. You can't file it electronically. If you mail it, send it by certified mail, with postal return receipt requested. This will let you know when the IRS received it. If you amend your returns for more than one year, mail each 1040X in a separate envelope. The 1040X instructions show where to mail the form.

You may also hand deliver the form to the IRS service center where you file your tax returns. If you do this, be sure to get a stamped copy as your filing receipt.

To obtain a refund due to an NOL (net operating loss), you may file either IRS Form 1045 alone, or with Form 1040X. You can often get your refund faster by using Form 1045 alone. The calculations required to figure out how much you can deduct from your income in prior years can be complicated. Tax preparation programs like *TurboTax* aren't designed to handle net operating losses, so it's a good idea to get some help from a tax professional. Refer to IRS Publication 536, *Net Operating Losses*, for more information.

> ⚠️ **Don't forget your state tax returns.** The IRS routinely shares information with states that impose income taxes (every state except Alaska, Florida, Nevada, South Dakota, Texas, Washington, and Wyoming). Thus, your state tax department will probably learn that you amended your federal tax return. For this reason, tax experts advise that you also amend your state tax returns for the years affected.

How the IRS Processes Refund Claims

The IRS doesn't like paying back money to taxpayers. When you file a Form 1040X, your tax return for that year will receive extra special attention. An IRS employee will pull your return and examine it and your 1040X to decide whether you're really entitled to a refund, and if so, how much. Your claim may be denied or accepted as filed, or the amended items may be audited. If a claim is audited, the procedures are almost the same as in the audit of a regular tax return. Moreover, the IRS has the option of extending the audit to your entire tax return, not just the amended items. Thus, *filing an amended tax return increases your chances of an audit.*

You should receive your refund, if you're entitled to one, in about 12 weeks. However, your refund may be reduced by amounts you owe for past-due child support, debts you owe to another federal agency, or past-due state income tax obligations. You will be notified if this happens.

If the IRS denies your claim, it must explain why—for example, because you filed it late. You have the right to appeal such a denial. For a detailed discussion of IRS appeals, refer to *Stand Up to the IRS*, by Frederick W. Daily (Nolo).

■

Chapter 20

Help Beyond This Book

There are many resources available to supplement and explain more fully the tax information covered in this book. Many of these resources are free; others are reasonably priced. The more expensive tax publications for professionals are often available at public libraries or law libraries. And, a lot of tax information is available on the Internet.

If you have a question about a specific tax deduction or any other tax-related matter, you can:

- consult a secondary tax source
- review the tax law, or
- see a tax professional.

You can do these suggested steps in any order you wish. For example, you can see a tax professional right away instead of doing any research yourself. This will save you time, but will cost you money.

Before you try to research tax law on your own, it's a good idea to learn how to do legal research. An excellent resource is *Legal Research: How to Find and Understand the Law*, by Stephen Elias and Susan Levinkind (Nolo), or you can go to Nolo's Legal Research Center at www.nolo.com.

Secondary Sources of Tax Information

Going straight to the tax code when you have a tax question is generally not the best approach. The tax code itself can be dry and difficult to decipher—particularly if you're trying to figure out how a particular law or rule applies to your situation. Instead of diving right into the code books, your best bet is to start with one of the many secondary sources that try to make the tax law more understandable. Unlike the primary sources listed below, these sources are not the law itself or the IRS's official pronouncements on the law. Instead, they are interpretations and explanations of the law intended to make it more understandable. Often, you'll be able to find the answer to your question in one or more of these sources. You can also learn about topics not covered in this book—for example, what constitutes income for tax purposes, how to complete your tax returns, or how to deal with an IRS audit.

Information From the IRS

The IRS has made a huge effort to inform the public about the tax law, creating hundreds of informative publications, an excellent website, and a telephone answering service. However, unlike the regulations and rulings issued by the IRS, these secondary sources of information are for informational purposes only. They are not official IRS pronouncements, and the IRS is not legally bound by them.

Reading IRS publications is a useful way to obtain information on IRS procedures and to get the agency's view of the tax law. But keep in mind that these publications only present the IRS's interpretation of the law, which may be very one-sided and even contrary to court rulings. That's why you shouldn't rely exclusively on IRS publications for information.

IRS Website

The IRS has one of the most useful Internet websites of any federal government agency. Among other things, almost every IRS form and informational publication can be downloaded from the site. The Internet address is www.irs.gov.

The IRS website has a special section for small businesses that contains much useful information for landlords. (www.irs.gov/businesses/small/index.html.) It includes:

- answers to basic tax questions and a calendar of tax deadlines
- online access to most IRS forms and information booklets
- tips to avoid common tax problems
- announcements of new IRS policies and procedures of particular interest to small businesses
- links to court opinions and to rulings and regulations on specific industries
- links to non-IRS sites for general tax information, and
- links to helpful small business resources.

IRS Booklets and CD-ROM

The IRS publishes over 350 free booklets explaining the tax code, called IRS Publications (Pubs, for short). Many of these publications are referenced in this book. Some are relatively easy to understand, others are incomprehensible or misleading. As with all IRS publications, they only present the IRS's interpretation of the tax laws—which may or may not be upheld by the federal courts. IRS publications of particular interest to landlords include:

- Publication 527, *Residential Rental Property*
- Publication 535, *Business Expenses*
- Publication 536, *Net Operating Losses (NOLs) for Individuals, Estates, and Trusts*

- Publication 551, *Basis of Assets*
- Publication 587, *Business Use of Your Home*
- Publication 925, *Passive Activity and At-Risk Rules,* and
- Publication 946, *How to Depreciate Property.*

You can download all of the booklets from the IRS website at www.irs.gov. You can also obtain free copies by calling 800-TAX-FORM (800-829-3676), or by contacting your local IRS office or sending an order form to the IRS.

IRS Telephone Information

The IRS offers a series of prerecorded tapes of information on various tax topics on a toll-free telephone service called TELETAX (800-829-4477). See IRS Publication 910 for a list of topics.

You can talk to an IRS representative on the telephone by calling 800-829-1040. (It is difficult to get through to someone from January through May.) Be sure to double check anything an IRS representative tells you over the phone—the IRS is notorious for giving misleading or outright wrong answers to taxpayers' questions, and the agency will not stand behind oral advice that turns out to be incorrect.

Other Online Tax Resources

In addition to the IRS website, there are hundreds of privately created websites on the Internet that provide tax information and advice. Some of this information is good; some is execrable. A comprehensive collection of Web links about all aspects of taxation can be found at www.taxsites.com. Other useful tax Web link pages can be found at:

- www.willyancey.com/tax_internet.htm
- www.abanet.org/taxes
- www.natptax.com/tax_links.html, and
- www.el.com/elinks/taxes.

Some useful tax-related websites include:

- www.accountantsworld.com
- www.unclefed.com
- www.smbiz.com/sbwday.html
- http://aol.smartmoney.com/tax/filing, and
- www.taxguru.net.

Nolo's Website

Nolo maintains a website that is useful for landlords. The site contains helpful articles, information about new legislation, book excerpts, and the Nolo catalog. The site also includes a legal encyclopedia with specific information for landlords, as well as a legal research center you can use to find state and federal statutes, including the Internal Revenue Code. The Internet address is www.nolo.com.

Tax Publications

If you're a person who likes to read books, you'll be happy to know that there are enough books about tax law to fill a library. Tax publications vary from the broadly focused to the highly detailed. You can find answers to most tax questions in one or more of these resources.

Publications for the Nonexpert

There are many books (like this one) that attempt to make the tax law comprehensible to the average person. The best known are the paperback tax preparation books published every year. These books emphasize individual taxes, but also have useful information for small landlords. Two of the best are:

- *The Ernst and Young Tax Guide*, and
- *J.K. Lasser's Your Income Tax* (both by John Wiley & Sons).

J.K. Lasser publishes other useful tax guides. You can find a list at: www. wiley.com/WileyCDA/Section/id-103210.html.

Nolo also publishes the following books that deal with tax issues of interest to landlords:

- *Stand Up to the IRS*, by Frederick W. Daily (Nolo), that explains how to handle an IRS audit, and
- *Working with Independent Contractors*, by Stephen Fishman (Nolo), that shows small businesses how to hire independent contractors without running afoul of the IRS or other government agencies.

A useful book focusing on real estate taxes for the nonexpert is *Aggressive Tax Avoidance for Real Estate Investors*, by John T. Reed. Reed self-publishes this book, and it is only available by ordering it from his website at www.johntreed.com.

Publications for Tax Professionals

Sometimes, you'll have a question you can't answer by looking at websites or tax publications for the layperson. In this event, you can consult one or more publications for tax professionals—accountants, CPAs, and attorneys. These are the most detailed and comprehensive secondary sources available.

There are six main publishing companies that publish reference materials for tax professionals:

- Business News Association (BNA), www.bna.com
- Commerce Clearing House (CCH), www.cch.com
- Klienrock Publishing, www.kleinrock.com
- Research Institute of America (RIA), www.riahome.com
- Tax Analysts, www.taxanalysts.com, and
- West Group, http://west.thomson.com.

These publishers produce an incredible volume of tax information, ranging from detailed analyses of the most arcane tax questions, to brief, one-volume guides to the entire federal tax law. Among their publications are:

Tax Services. These are highly detailed discussions of the tax law, organized by IRC section or topic and updated frequently—every week, or at least every month. The most authoritative is *The Law of Federal Income Taxation*, published by West Group (it's also called Mertens by tax professionals because it was originally edited by Jacob Mertens). Other tax services include the *United States Tax Reporter* (published by RIA) and *Standard Federal Tax Reporter* (published by CCH).

Tax Treatises. Tax treatises provide in-depth, book-length treatment of a particular tax topic. The two best one-volume treatises on real estate taxation are:

- *Federal Income Taxation of Real Estate*, by Gerald J. Robinson (Warren, Gorham & Lamont), and
- *Real Estate Taxation: A Practitioner's Guide*, by David E. Windish (CCH).

Other useful treatises are the Tax Management Portfolios, a series of paperback booklets published by BNA. If you're looking for information on a very precise tax issue, you might find what you need in a Portfolio.

Tax Citators. Tax citators summarize tax cases and compile and organize them by subject matter and IRC Section. By using a citator, you can find all the tax cases that have addressed a specific tax topic. Both CCH and RIA publish citators.

Tax Deskbooks. CCH publishes a well-known one-volume tax deskbook called the *Master Tax Guide* that provides an overview of the tax law. It's updated each year.

You can find a good discussion on how to use these tax materials in *West's Federal Tax Research* (South-Western College Publishing).

All of these publications are available in print form, on CD-ROMs, and on subscriber websites maintained by the publishers themselves or commercial databases (notably, Westlaw and Lexis, subscriber databases containing legal information). As you might expect, they are generally very expensive. You can also find them in a law library, some large public libraries, or a tax professional's office.

Tax Software

Today, millions of taxpayers use tax preparation software to complete their own income tax returns. The best-known programs are *Turbotax* and *TaxCut*. These programs contain most IRS tax forms, publications, and other tax guidance. Each has a helpful website at www.turbotax.com and www.taxcut.com, respectively.

The Tax Law

If you can't find an answer to your question in a secondary source, you might be able to find help in the tax law itself. Or, you may want to consult the tax law to verify (or clarify) what you've learned from secondary sources.

The tax law of the United States comes from several sources:

- the Internal Revenue Code
- IRS regulations
- court cases, and
- IRS rulings, interpretations, and tax advice.

Every branch of the federal government is involved in creating the tax law. The Internal Revenue Code is enacted by Congress (the legislative branch), IRS regulations and rulings are issued by the IRS (a department of the executive branch), and taxpayers may appeal the IRS's actions to the federal courts (the judicial branch).

The Tax Law Versus *War and Peace*	
	Number of pages
Internal Revenue Code	3,653
IRS Regulations	13,079
War and Peace by Leo Tolstoy	1,444

Internal Revenue Code

The Internal Revenue Code (IRC) is the supreme tax law of the land. The IRC (also called the code or the tax code) is written, and frequently rewritten, by Congress. The first tax code, adopted in 1913, contained 14 pages. Today, the tax code is more than 3,500 pages long.

The IRC is found in Title 26 of the United States Code (USC for short). The USC encompasses all of our federal laws. "Title" simply refers to the place within the massive USC where the IRC is found.

The entire tax code covers income taxes, social security taxes, excise taxes, estate and gift taxes, and tax procedure. It is organized by category and broken down into subtitles, chapters, subchapters, parts, subparts, sections, subsections, paragraphs, subparagraphs, and clauses. The income tax laws are in Chapter 1 of Subtitle A of the tax code. Most of the laws dealing with tax deductions are found in Parts VI and VII of Subchapter B of Chapter 1.

For our purposes, the most important thing to remember about the organization of the tax code is that each specific tax law is contained in a separate numbered section. For example, Section 469 covers the passive activity loss rules. For the sake of convenience, tax professionals will often refer to these numbered sections of the tax code.

> **EXAMPLE:** IRC § 469(c)(1)(A) means that this particular tax law is found in Title 26 of the USC (the Internal Revenue Code), Section 469, Subsection c, Paragraph 1, Subparagraph A.
>
> The tax code is published each year in a two-volume set (usually in paperback). You should be able to find it in the reference section of any public library. You can also purchase a set from various tax publishers, such as Commerce Clearing House and Research Institute of America. A complete set of the tax code costs over $80. You can also purchase a one-volume

abridged version for much less. This will likely contain all the tax code provisions you'll want to refer to. The entire United State Code (including the IRC) is also available on CD-ROM from the Government Printing Office for under $40.

Fortunately, the IRC is available for free on the Internet. You can get to the entire IRC from Nolo's Legal Research Center—go to www.nolo.com. Portions are also available on the IRS website (www.irs.gov) and several other websites.

⚠ **Make sure your tax code is current.** The IRC is amended every year; in recent years, these amendments have made major changes to the law. Make sure that any copy of the IRC you use in your research is current.

IRS Regulations

Even though the Internal Revenue Code contains over 3,600 pages, it does not provide adequate guidance for every situation that arises in real life. To supplement the IRC, the IRS issues regulations, called Treasury Regulations, Regulations, or Regs. Although written by the IRS, not Congress, these regulations have almost the same authoritative weight as the tax code itself.

While the tax code is usually written in broad and general terms, the regulations get down and dirty, providing details about how tax code provisions are intended to operate in the real world. Regulations are slightly easier to read than the tax code on which they are based and often include examples that can be helpful. The regulations cover many (but not all) of the tax code provisions.

To see if a particular IRC section is supplemented by a regulation, start with the number of the IRC section. If there is a corresponding regulation, it will bear the same number, usually preceded by the number "1."

EXAMPLE: Reg. 1.469 refers to a Treasury regulation interpreting IRC Section 469.

The regulations are published in a multivolume set by the Government Printing Office and tax publishers such as CCH and RIA. These are available in law libraries and may also be found in some large public libraries. Many regulations can be downloaded from the IRS website.

Court Cases

When a dispute arises between a taxpayer and the IRS, the taxpayer may take the matter to federal court. The courts are the final arbiters of tax disputes. A court may overrule the IRS if the court concludes that the IRS applied the tax code in a manner contrary to the United States Constitution or differently from what Congress intended.

Tax disputes are tried in three different courts: a special tax court that handles only tax disputes; the regular federal trial courts (called U.S. District Courts); and the Court of Federal Claims. If either the taxpayer or the IRS doesn't like the result reached at trial, it may appeal to the federal appellate courts (called the U.S. Court of Appeals), and even to the United States Supreme Court.

Decisions of these courts are published, along with explanations and discussions of the tax law. These court decisions provide valuable interpretations of the tax laws. Many, but not all, of these court interpretations are binding on the IRS. Thousands of court decisions dealing with tax law have been published, so chances are good that there is at least one decision on the issue that interests you.

To locate a published court decision, you must understand how to read a case citation. A citation provides the names of the people or companies involved on each side of the case, the volume of the legal publication (called a reporter) in which the case can be found, the page number on which it begins, and the year in which the case was decided. Here is an example of what a legal citation looks like: *Smith v. Jones*, 123 F.3d 456 (1995). Smith and Jones are the names of the people in the legal dispute. The case is reported in Volume 123 of the Federal Reporter, Third Series, beginning on page 456; the court issued the decision in 1995.

Opinions by the federal district courts are in a series of reporters called the Federal Supplement, or F.Supp. Any case decided by a federal court of appeals is found in a series of books called the Federal Reporter. Older cases are contained in the first series of the Federal Reporter, or F. More recent cases are contained in the second or third series of the Federal Reporter, F.2d or F.3d. Cases decided by the U.S. Supreme Court are found in three publications: United States Reports (identified as U.S.), the Supreme Court Reporter (identified as S.Ct.), and the Supreme Court Reports, Lawyer's Edition (identified as L.Ed.). Supreme Court case citations often refer to all three publications. Many, but not all, of these legal decisions are available free on the Internet. The website www.findlaw.com is a good place to start a search.

Tax court decisions from 1990 to date can be accessed at www.legalbitstream .com. More recent decisions can also be found at www.ustaxcourt.gov.

Virtually all legal decisions are available on the subscriber websites Lexis.com and Westlaw.com. You may be able to access these websites through a library or tax professional's office.

Hard copies of published decisions by the United States Tax Court can be found in the Tax Court Reports, or TC, published by the U.S. Government Printing Office. Tax court decisions can also be found in a reporter called Tax Court Memorandum Decisions, or TCM, published by Commerce Clearing House, Inc. Decisions from all federal courts involving taxation can be found in a reporter called U.S. Tax Cases, or USTC, published by Commerce Clearing House, Inc. These are available in law libraries.

For a detailed discussion of how to research court cases, see *Legal Research: How to Find and Understand the Law*, by Stephen Elias and Susan Levinkind (Nolo), or go to Nolo's Legal Research Center at www.nolo.com.

IRS Rulings, Interpretations, and Tax Advice

It might seem like the tax code, regulations, and court decisions would provide everything anyone ever wanted to know about tax law. But even more IRS guidance is available. The IRS publishes several types of statements (besides Regs) of its position on various tax matters. These pronouncements guide IRS personnel and taxpayers as to how the IRS will apply specific tax laws.

Unlike the tax code and regulations, these statements do not have the force of law. Rather, they are the IRS's own interpretation of the tax law, which is not necessarily binding on the courts (or on you, should you choose to challenge the IRS's interpretation in court). However, they give you a good idea of how the IRS would handle the situation involved.

Revenue Rulings

IRS Revenue Rulings (Rev. Rul.) are IRS announcements of how the tax law applies to a hypothetical set of facts. The IRS publishes over 100 of these rulings every year. These rulings represent the IRS's view of the tax law, and the IRS presumes that they are correct. If an auditor discovers that you have violated a revenue ruling, you will probably have to pay additional tax. On the other hand, if you can show an auditor that a revenue ruling supports your position, you probably won't have to pay more tax. If you have violated a revenue ruling, all is not necessarily lost. Revenue rulings are not binding on the courts, which can (and do) disregard them from time to time. Thus, it's possible you could win your case on appeal.

You can download free copies of all IRS Revenue Rulings from 1954 to date from www.taxlinks.com. Rulings from 1990 to date can be accessed at www. legalbitstream.com. Revenue rulings also appear in the weekly Internal Revenue *Cumulative Bulletin*, which is published by the U.S. Government Printing Office. Tax book publishers Prentice-Hall, Commerce Clearing House, and Research Institute of America also reprint IRS Revenue Rulings. They are indexed by IRC section and subject matter.

> **EXAMPLE:** Rev. Rul. 03-41 refers to IRS Revenue Ruling number 41, issued in 2003.

Revenue Procedures

Revenue procedures (Rev. Procs.) are IRS announcements dealing with procedural aspects of tax practice. Rev. Procs. are used primarily by tax return preparers. They often explain when and how to report tax items, such as how to claim a net operating loss on a tax form or return. Revenue procedures from 1990 to date can be accessed at www.legalbitstream.com. They are also contained in the weekly Internal Revenue *Cumulative Bulletin*, which you can find in larger public and law libraries, and that are reprinted by tax book publishers and on the IRS website. You can obtain free copies of many revenue procedures at www. legalbitstream.com.

> **EXAMPLE:** Rev. Proc. 99-15 refers to a published Revenue Procedure number 15, issued in 1999.

Letter Rulings

IRS letter rulings are IRS answers to specific written questions from taxpayers about complex tax situations. The only person who is entitled to rely on the ruling as legal authority is the taxpayer to whom the ruling is addressed; even if you find yourself in a similar position, the IRS is not legally required to follow the guidance it gave in the letter. However, letter rulings offer valuable insight into the IRS's position on tax treatment of complex transactions. Since 1976, letter rulings have been made available to the general public. Letter rulings to date can be accessed for free at www.legalbitstream.com. They are also published by tax publishers, and available at the subscription websites Lexis and Westlaw.

> **EXAMPLE:** Ltr. Ruling 9913043 (April 3, 1999) refers to a letter ruling issued on April 3, 1999. The first two numbers of the seven-digit identifier show the year it was issued, the next two indicate the week of the year, and the last three show the ruling for that week. Thus, this letter ruling was the 43rd issued during the 13th week of 1999.

IRS General Guidance

From time to time, the IRS gives general guidance and statements of policy in official announcements and notices similar to press releases. They appear in the weekly Internal Revenue *Cumulative Bulletin*. It doesn't usually pay to search IRS announcements or notices because they are too broad to answer specific questions.

Internal Revenue Manual

The *Internal Revenue Manual* (IRM) is a series of handbooks that serve as guides to IRS employees on tax law and procedure. The *IRM* tells IRS employees (usually auditors or collectors) how specific tax code provisions should be enforced. The *Manual* is for IRS internal use, but most of it is public and reprinted by private tax book publishers. It is available to the public in the Freedom of Information Act reading rooms of larger IRS offices, and in law libraries and some tax professionals' offices. Portions of the *IRM* are also available on the IRS website.

The *IRM* is revealing of IRS attitudes in certain areas—for example, Section 4.10.3 of the *Manual* describes the techniques IRS auditors are supposed to use when they examine depreciation deductions.

IRS Forms and Instructions

IRS forms are well known to us all, especially Form 1040, the annual personal income tax return. There are more than 650 other IRS forms, listed in Publication 676, *Catalog of Federal Tax Forms*. You can get them free at IRS offices or by calling 800-829-FORM or 800-829-1040. You can also download them from the IRS website at www.irs.gov. Many IRS forms come with instructions and explanations of the tax law.

Consulting a Tax Professional

You don't have to do your own tax research. There are hundreds of thousands of tax professionals (tax pros) in the United States ready and eager to help you—for a price. A tax pro can answer your questions, provide guidance to help you make key tax decisions, prepare your tax returns, and help you deal with the IRS if you get into tax trouble.

Types of Tax Pros

There are several different types of tax pros. They differ widely in training, experience, and cost.

- **Tax preparers.** As the name implies, tax preparers prepare tax returns. The largest tax preparation firm is H & R Block, but many mom-and-pop operations open for business in storefront offices during tax time. In most states, anybody can be a tax preparer; no licensing is required. Most tax preparers don't have the training or experience to handle taxes for landlords and, therefore, are probably not a wise choice.

- **Enrolled agents.** Enrolled agents (EAs) are tax advisors and preparers who are licensed by the IRS. They must have at least five years of experience or pass a difficult IRS test. They can represent taxpayers before the IRS, and in administrative proceedings, circuit court, and, possibly, tax court, if they pass the appropriate tests. Enrolled agents are the least expensive of the true tax pros but are reliable for tax return preparation and more routine tax matters. They can be quite adequate for many small landlords.

- **Certified Public Accountants.** Certified Public Accountants (CPAs) are licensed and regulated by each state. They undergo lengthy training and must pass a comprehensive exam. CPAs represent the high end of the tax pro spectrum. In addition to preparing tax returns, they perform sophisticated accounting and tax work. CPAs are found in large national firms or in small local outfits. The large national firms are used primarily by large businesses. Some states also license public accountants. These are competent, but are not as highly regarded as CPAs.

- **Tax attorneys.** Tax attorneys are lawyers who specialize in tax matters. The only time you'll ever need a tax attorney is if you get into serious trouble with the IRS or another tax agency and need legal representation before the IRS or in court. Some tax attorneys also give tax advice, but they are usually too expensive for small landlords. You're probably better off hiring a CPA if you need specialized tax help.

Finding a Tax Pro

The best way to find a tax pro is to obtain referrals from business associates, friends, or landlord associations such as your local apartment owners' association. If none of these sources can give you a suitable lead, try contacting the National Association of Enrolled Agents or one of its state affiliates. You can find a listing of affiliates at the NAEA website at www.naea.org. Local CPA societies can give you referrals to local CPAs. You can also find tax pros in the telephone book under "Accountants, Tax Return." Local bar associations can refer you to a tax attorney. Be aware that CPA societies and local bar associations refer from a list on a rotating basis, so you shouldn't construe a referral as a recommendation or certification of competence.

Your relationship with your tax pro will be one of your most important business relationships. Be picky about the person you choose. Talk with at least three tax pros before hiring one. You want a tax pro who takes the time to listen to you, answers your questions fully and in plain English, seems knowledgeable, and makes you feel comfortable. Make sure the tax pro works frequently with small landlords. A tax pro already familiar with the tax problems faced by landlords can often give you the best advice for the least money.

■

Index

Get the Latest in the Law

Nolo's Legal Updater
We'll send you an email whenever a new edition of your book is published!
Sign up at **www.nolo.com/legalupdater**.

Updates at Nolo.com
Check **www.nolo.com/update** to find recent changes in the law that
affect the current edition of your book.

Nolo Customer Service
To make sure that this edition of the book is the most recent one, call us at
800-728-3555 and ask one of our friendly customer service representatives
(7:00 am to 6:00 pm PST, weekdays only). Or find out at **www.nolo.com**.

Complete the Registration & Comment Card ...
... and we'll do the work for you! Just indicate your preferences below:

- -

Registration & Comment Card

NAME _____ DATE _____

ADDRESS _____

CITY _____ STATE _____ ZIP _____

PHONE _____ EMAIL _____

COMMENTS _____

WAS THIS BOOK EASY TO USE? (VERY EASY) 5 4 3 2 1 (VERY DIFFICULT)

☐ Yes, you can quote me in future Nolo promotional materials. *Please include phone number above.*

☐ Yes, send me **Nolo's Legal Updater** via email when a new edition of this book is available.

Yes, I want to sign up for the following email newsletters:

  ☐ **NoloBriefs** (monthly)
  ☐ **Nolo's Special Offer** (monthly)
  ☐ **Nolo's BizBriefs** (monthly)
  ☐ **Every Landlord's Quarterly** (four times a year)

☐ Yes, you can give my contact info to carefully selected
partners whose products may be of interest to me.

DELL4

NOLO

Nolo
950 Parker Street
Berkeley, CA 94710-9867
www.nolo.com

YOUR LEGAL COMPANION